OFFICIAL TOURIST BOARD GUIDE

Camping, Caravan
& Holiday Parks

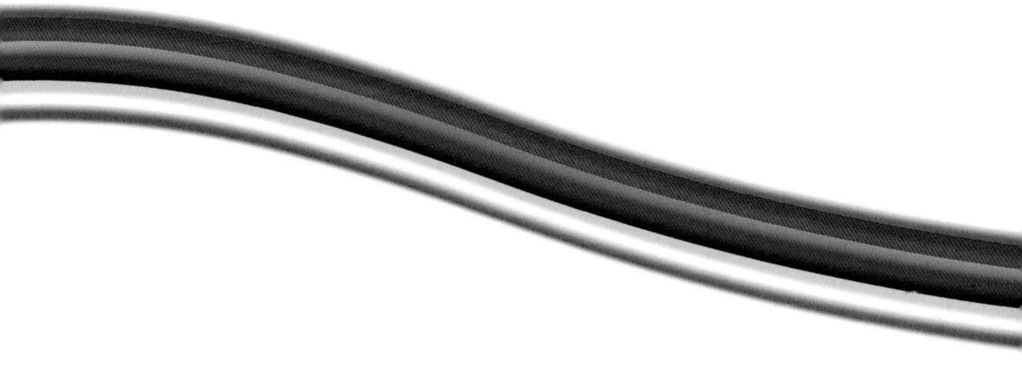

Contents

Further information

Useful indexes

VisitBritain

VisitBritain is the organisation created to market Britain to the rest of the world, and England to the British.

Formed by the merger of the British Tourist Authority and the English Tourism Council, its mission is to build the value of tourism by creating world-class destination brands and marketing campaigns.

It will also build partnerships with – and provide insights to – other organisations which have a stake in British and English tourism.

Botany Bay, Kent

How to use this guide

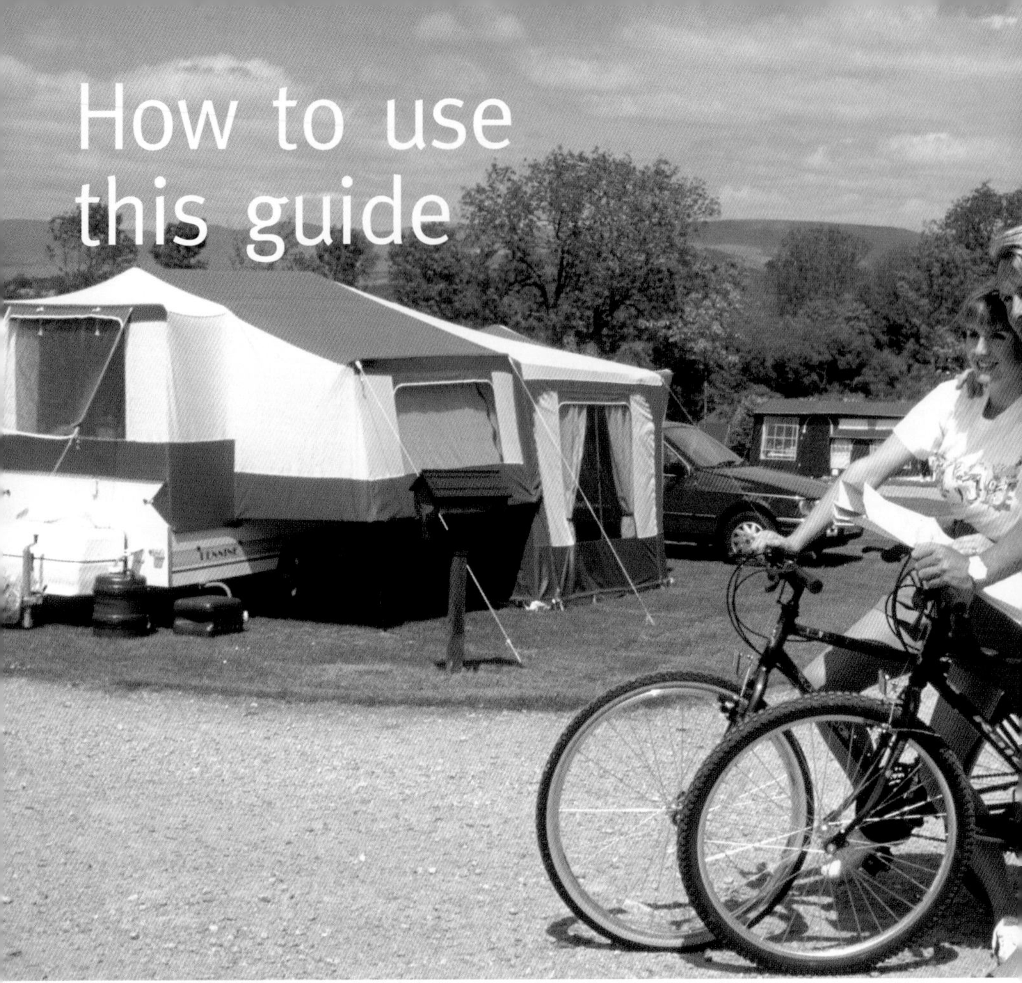

This official VisitBritain guide is packed with information from where to stay, to how to get there and what to see and do. In fact, everything you need to know to enjoy Britain.

Choose from a wide range of quality-assessed places to stay to suit all budgets and tastes. This guide contains a comprehensive listing of touring, camping and holiday parks, and holiday villages participating in the British Graded Holiday Parks Scheme.

Each park is visited annually by a professional assessor who applies nationally agreed standards so that you can book with confidence knowing your accommodation has been checked and rated for quality.

Check out the places to visit in each region, from towns and cities to spectacular coast and countryside, plus historic homes, castles and great family attractions! Regional maps show selected destinations as well as National Trails and sections of the National Cycle Network. For even more ideas go online at visitbritain.com.

Regional tourism contacts and tourist information centres are listed – contact them for further information. You'll also find **events, travel information, maps** and useful **indexes**.

Finding accommodation is easy...

1. REGIONAL SECTIONS

The guide is divided into regions (see page 3) and accommodation is listed alphabetically by place name within each region.

Start your search for accommodation in these sections. For an even wider choice in England, turn to the listings starting on page 258 where you will find ALL parks and holiday villages in England participating in the British Graded Holiday Parks Scheme, including those that have not taken a paid entry.

2. COLOUR MAPS

Use the colour maps, starting on page 32, to pinpoint the location of all parks featured in the regional sections.

Then refer to the place index at the back of the guide to find the page number. The index also includes tourism areas such as the New Forest and the Cotswolds.

3. INDEXES

The indexes, listed on page 295, make it easy to find accommodation that matches specific requirements; for example, parks suitable for guests with disabilities or those that welcome cyclists. And if you know the name of the park, use the property index.

Accommodation entries explained

Each entry contains detailed information to help you decide if it is right for you. This has been provided by proprietors and our aim is to ensure that it is as objective and factual as possible.

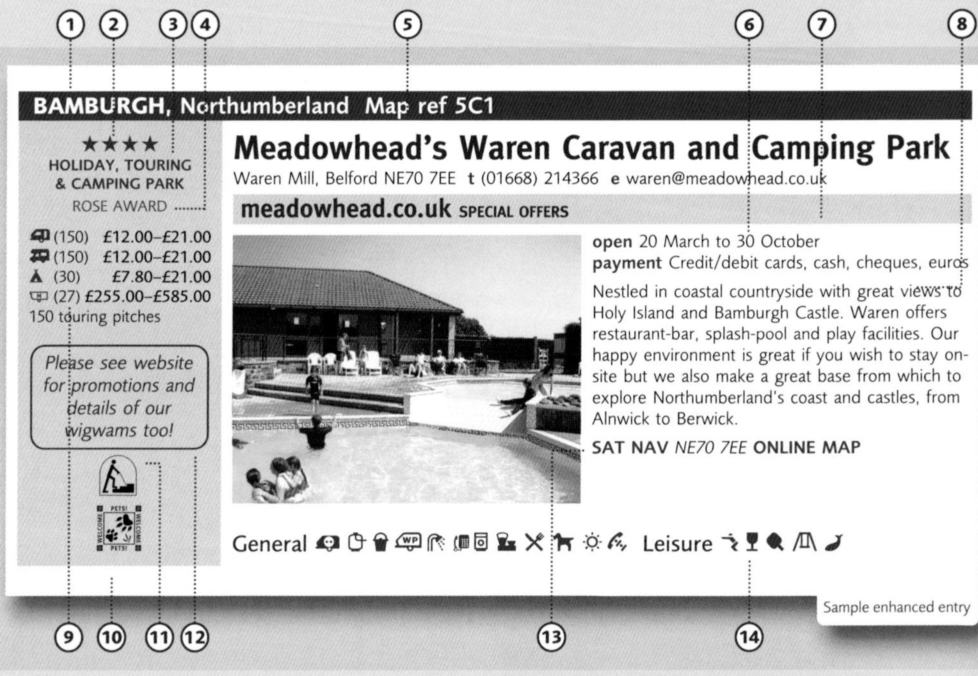

1 2 3 4 5 6 7 8
BAMBURGH, Northumberland Map ref 5C1
★★★★
HOLIDAY, TOURING & CAMPING PARK
ROSE AWARD
(150) £12.00–£21.00
(150) £12.00–£21.00
(30) £7.80–£21.00
(27) £255.00–£585.00
150 touring pitches
Please see website for promotions and details of our wigwams too!
Meadowhead's Waren Caravan and Camping Park
Waren Mill, Belford NE70 7EE t (01668) 214366 e waren@meadowhead.co.uk
meadowhead.co.uk SPECIAL OFFERS
open 20 March to 30 October
payment Credit/debit cards, cash, cheques, euros
Nestled in coastal countryside with great views to Holy Island and Bamburgh Castle. Waren offers restaurant-bar, splash-pool and play facilities. Our happy environment is great if you wish to stay on-site but we also make a great base from which to explore Northumberland's coast and castles, from Alnwick to Berwick.
SAT NAV NE70 7EE ONLINE MAP
General
Leisure
Sample enhanced entry
9 10 11 12 13 14

1 Listing under town or village with map reference

2 Star rating

3 Classification

4 Award (if applicable)

5 Site name, address, telephone number and email

6 Indicates when the site is open and payment accepted.

7 Website information (web addresses are shown without the prefix www.)

8 Description

9 Prices per pitch per night for touring pitches; per unit per week for static holiday units

10 Walkers, cyclists, pets and families welcome, where applicable

11 Accessible rating where applicable

12 Special promotions

13 Travel directions

14 At-a-glance facility symbols

Key to symbols

Information about many of the accommodation services and facilities is given in the form of symbols.

Pitches/Units

- Caravans (number of pitches and rates)
- Motor caravans (number of pitches and rates)
- Tents (number of pitches and rates)
- Caravan holiday homes (number of pitches and rates)
- Log cabins/lodges (number of units and rates)
- Chalets/villas (number of units and rates)

Leisure

- Swimming pool – indoor
- Swimming pool – outdoor
- Clubhouse with bar
- Regular evening entertainment
- Games room
- Outdoor play area
- Tennis court(s)
- Riding/pony-trekking nearby
- Fishing nearby
- Access to golf
- Cycle hire on site/nearby

General

- Overnight holding area
- Motor home pitches reserved for day trips off-site
- Electrical hook-up points
- Calor Gas/Camping Gaz purchase/exchange service
- Chemical toilet disposal point
- Motor home waste disposal point
- Showers
- Public telephone
- Laundry facilities
- Food shop on site
- Restaurant on site
- Pets welcome by arrangement
- Prior booking recommended in summer
- Wi-Fi
- Internet access

National Accessible Scheme

The National Accessible Scheme includes standards for hearing and visual impairment as well as mobility impairment – see pages 14-15 for further information.

Welcome schemes

Walkers, cyclists, families and pet owners are warmly welcomed where you see these signs – see page 12 for further information.

Ratings and awards at a glance

Reliable, rigorous, easy to use – look out for the following ratings and awards to help you choose with confidence.

Star ratings

Parks are awarded a rating of one to five stars following an assessment of the quality, cleanliness, maintenance and condition of the various facilities provided. It is not necessary to provide a wide range of facilities in order to achieve a high rating as the emphasis is on the quality of what is actually provided rather than a rating restricted by a lack of facilities.

Holiday Villages are assessed under a separate rating scheme and are awarded one to five stars based on both the quality of facilities **and** the range of services provided. The option to include breakfast and dinner is normally available. A variety of accommodation is offered, mostly in chalets.

For information on awards see overleaf

Ratings made easy

★
Simple, practical, no frills

★★
Well presented and well run

★★★
Very good level of quality and comfort

★★★★
Excellent standard throughout

★★★★★
Exceptional level of quality

Enjoy England Awards for Excellence

The prestigious and coveted Enjoy England Awards for Excellence showcase the very best in English tourism. Run by VisitBritain in association with England's regions, they include a Caravan Holiday Park of the Year category (see page 16).

National Accessible Scheme

Sites with a National Accessible Scheme rating have been thoroughly assessed to set criteria and provide access to facilities and services for guests with visual, hearing or mobility impairment (see page 14).

David Bellamy Conservation Award

This special award is a signpost to parks that are making real achievements in protecting our environment (see page 19).

Welcome schemes

VisitBritain runs four special Welcome schemes: Cyclists Welcome, Walkers Welcome, Welcome Pets! and Families Welcome. Scheme participants actively encourage these types of visitors and in many instances make special provision to ensure a welcoming, comfortable stay (see page 12).

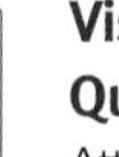

Visitor Attraction Quality Assurance

Attractions participating in this scheme are visited every year by a professional assessor and must achieve high standards in all aspects of the visitor experience. The assessment focuses on the nature of the welcome, hospitality, services and presentation as well as the standards of toilets, shop and café where provided.

What to expect

Star ratings

Parks are required to meet progressively higher standards of quality as they move up the scale from one to five stars:

ONE-STAR Acceptable ★

To achieve this grade, the park must be clean with good standards of maintenance and customer care.

TWO-STAR Good ★★

All the above points plus an improved level of landscaping, lighting, refuse disposal and maintenance. May be less expensive than more highly rated parks.

THREE-STAR Very Good ★★★

Most parks fall within this category; three stars represent the industry standard. The range of facilities provided may vary from park to park, but they will be of a very good standard and will be well maintained.

FOUR-STAR Excellent ★★★★

You can expect careful attention to detail in the provision of all services and facilities. Four star parks rank among the industry's best.

FIVE-STAR Exceptional ★★★★★

Highest levels of customer care will be provided. All facilities will be maintained in pristine condition in attractive surroundings.

Caravan Holiday Home Award Scheme

VisitBritain and VisitScotland run award schemes for individual holiday caravan homes on highly graded caravan parks. In addition to complying with standards for Holiday Parks, these exceptional caravans must have a shower or bath, toilet, mains electricity and water heating (at no extra charge) and a fridge (many also have a colour TV).

Award-winning parks listed in this guide show the relevant logo by their entry.

A special welcome

To help make your selection of accommodation easier VisitBritain has four special Welcome schemes which accommodation in England can be assessed to. Owners participating in these schemes go the extra mile to welcome walkers, cyclists, families or pet owners and provide additional facilities and services to make your stay even more comfortable.

Families Welcome

If you are searching for a great family break look out for the Families Welcome sign. The sign indicates that the proprietor offers additional facilities and services catering for a range of ages and family units. For families with young children, the accommodation will have special facilities such as cots and highchairs, storage for push-chairs and somewhere to heat baby food or milk. Where meals are provided, children's choices will be clearly indicated, with healthy options available.They'll also have information on local walks, attractions, activities or events suitable for children, as well as local child-friendly pubs and restaurants. Not all accommodation is able to cater for all ages or combinations of family units, so do check when you book.

Welcome Pets!

Want to travel with your faithful companion? Look out for accommodation displaying the Welcome Pets! sign. Participants in this scheme go out of their way to meet the needs of guests bringing dogs, cats and/or small birds. In addition to providing water and food bowls, torches or nightlights, spare leads and pet washing facilities, they'll buy in food on request, and offer toys, treats and bedding. They'll also have information on pet-friendly attractions, pubs, restaurants and recreation. Of course, not everyone is able to offer suitable facilities for every pet, so do check if there are any restrictions on the type, size and number of animals when you book.

Walkers Welcome

If walking is your passion seek out accommodation participating in the Walkers Welcome scheme. Facilities include a place for drying clothes and boots, maps and books for reference and a first-aid kit. Packed breakfasts and lunch are available on request in hotels and guesthouses, and you have the option to pre-order basic groceries in self-catering accommodation. A wide range of information is provided including public transport, weather, local restaurants and attractions, details of the nearest bank and all night chemists.

Cyclists Welcome

If you like to explore by bike seek out accommodation displaying the Cyclists Welcome symbol. Facilities include a lockable undercover area and a place to dry outdoor clothing and footwear, an evening meal if there are no eating facilities available within one mile, and a packed breakfast or lunch on request. Information is also provided on cycle hire and cycle repair shops, maps and books for reference, weather and details of the nearest bank and all night chemists and more.

For further information go online at enjoyengland.com/quality

Classifications explained

Parks vary greatly in style and in the facilities they offer. The following will help you decide which is right for you whether you are looking for an overnight caravan stop or an open-air family holiday with all the extras.

Camping Park

These sites only have pitches available for tents.

Touring Park

If you are planning to travel with your own caravan, motor home or tent, then look for a Touring Park.

Holiday Park

If you want to hire a caravan holiday home for a short break or longer holiday, or are looking to buy your own holiday home, a Holiday Park is the right choice. They range from small, rural sites to larger parks with all the added extras, such as a swimming pool.

Many parks will offer a combination of these classifications.

Holiday Village

Holiday villages usually comprise a variety of types of accommodation, with the majority in custom-built rooms, chalets for example. The option to book on a bed and breakfast, or dinner, bed and breakfast basis is normally available. A range of facilities, entertainment and activities are also provided which may, or may not, be included in the tariff.

Holiday Villages must meet a minimum entry requirement for both the provision and quality of facilities and services, including fixtures, fittings, furnishings, decor and any other extra facilities. Progressively higher levels of quality and customer care are provided at each star level.

Forest Holiday Village

A holiday village which is situated in a forest setting with conservation and sustainable tourism being a key feature. It will usually comprise a variety of accommodation, often purpose built; and with a range of entertainment, activities and facilities available on site free of charge or at extra cost.

National Accessible Scheme

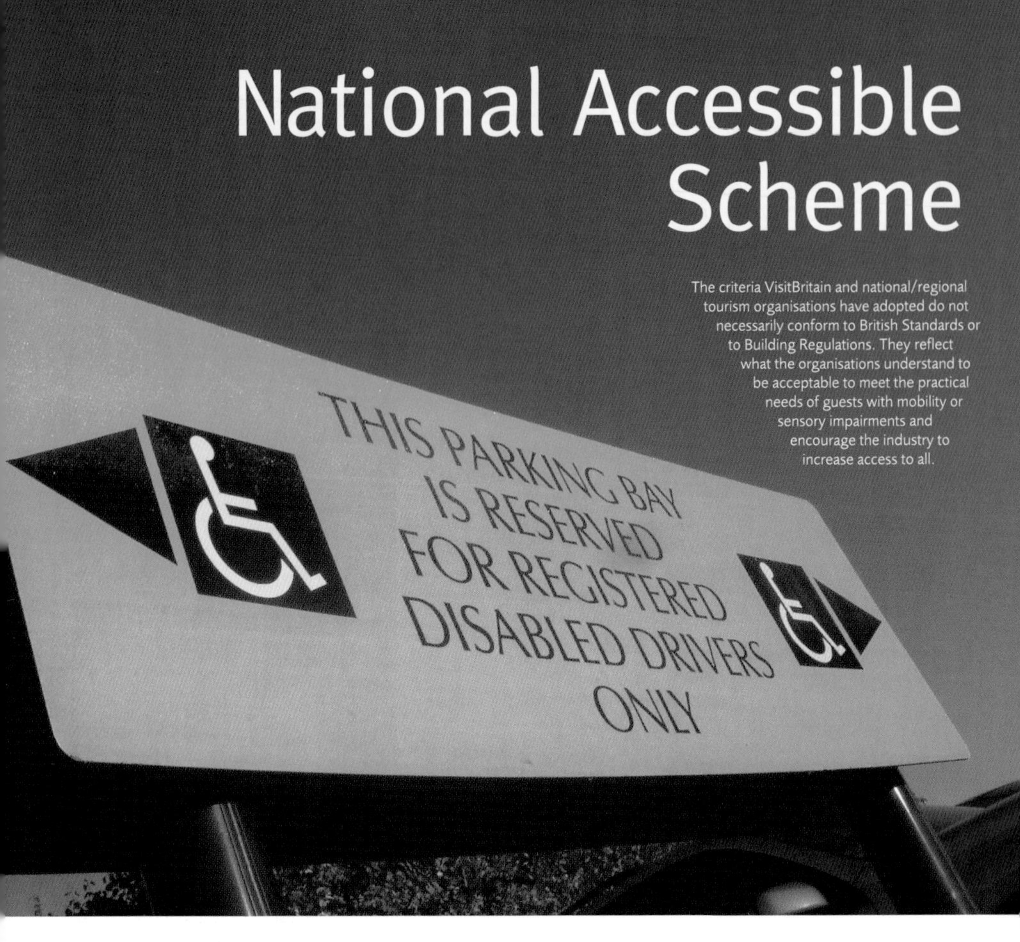

The criteria VisitBritain and national/regional tourism organisations have adopted do not necessarily conform to British Standards or to Building Regulations. They reflect what the organisations understand to be acceptable to meet the practical needs of guests with mobility or sensory impairments and encourage the industry to increase access to all.

Finding suitable accommodation is not always easy, especially if you have to seek out rooms with level entry or large print menus. Use the National Accessible Scheme to help you make your choice.

Proprietors of parks taking part in the National Accessible Scheme provide facilities and services to ensure a comfortable stay for guests with special hearing, visual or mobility needs. Look at the logos to find out the rating awarded to these exceptional places which provide specific items to make your stay easier and more comfortable, from handrails to tactile markings and level-access showers. Members of staff may have attended a disability awareness course and will know what assistance will really be appreciated.

Appropriate National Accessible Scheme symbols are included in the guide entries for English and Scottish sites (for differences, see opposite). If you have additional needs or special requirements we strongly recommend that you make sure these can be met by your chosen site before you confirm your reservation. The index at the back of the guide gives a list of sites that have received a National Accessible rating.

For a wider selection of accessible accommodation, order a copy of the *Easy Access Britain* guide featuring almost 500 places to stay. It is available from Tourism for All for £9.99 (plus P&P). Alternatively, visit tourismforall.org.uk for a directory of National Accessible Scheme and Tourism for All members.

The National Accessible Scheme forms part of the Tourism for All campaign that is being promoted by VisitBritain and national/regional tourism organisations. Additional help and guidance on finding suitable holiday accommodation can be obtained from:

Tourism for All
c/o Vitalise, Shap Road Industrial Estate, Kendal LA9 6NZ

information helpline 0845 124 9971
reservations 0845 124 9973
(lines open 9-5 Mon-Fri)

f (01539) 735567

e info@tourismforall.org.uk

w tourismforall.org.uk

Scotland

Category 1

Accessible to a wheelchair user travelling independently.

Category 2

Accessible to a wheelchair user travelling with assistance.

Category 3

Accessible to a wheelchair user able to walk a few paces and up a maximum of three steps.

Wales

Caravan holiday homes and parks in Wales should have an Access Statement available to visitors.

England

Mobility Impairment Symbols

Typically suitable for a person with sufficient mobility to climb a flight of steps but who would benefit from fixtures and fittings to aid balance.

Typically suitable for a person with restricted walking ability and for those who may need to use a wheelchair some of the time and can negotiate a maximum of three steps.

Typically suitable for a person who depends on the use of a wheelchair and transfers unaided to and from the wheelchair in a seated position. This person may be an independent traveller.

Typically suitable for a person who depends on the use of a wheelchair and needs assistance when transferring to and from the wheelchair in a seated position.

Access Exceptional is awarded to establishments that meet the requirements of independent wheelchair users or assisted wheelchair users shown above and also fulfil more demanding requirements with reference to the British Standards BS8300:2001.

Visual Impairment Symbols

Typically provides key additional services and facilities to meet the needs of visually impaired guests.

Typically provides a higher level of additional services and facilities to meet the needs of visually impaired guests.

Hearing Impairment Symbols

Typically provides key additional services and facilities to meet the needs of guests with hearing impairment.

Typically provides a higher level of additional services and facilities to meet the needs of guests with hearing impairment.

Enjoy England Awards for Excellence

Enjoy England Awards for Excellence are all about telling the world what a fantastic place England is to visit, whether it's for a day trip, a weekend break or a fortnight's holiday.

Organised by VisitBritain and sponsored by The Caravan Club, The Enjoy England Awards for Excellence are the annual accolades for English tourism, recognising the best places to stay and visit. Now in their 20th year, the Awards are known throughout the industry, promoting healthy competition and high standards. Competition is fierce, and entries are submitted to regional tourism organisations across England before being short-listed for the national finals, culminating in an Awards ceremony held in April each year.

There are fifteen categories, from visitor attractions and hotels to self-catering accommodation and caravan parks. Seek them out and experience them for yourself – you won't be disappointed.

The complete list of winners can be found online at enjoyengland.com.

Poston Mill Park – GOLD WINNER 2008

This five-star family-run holiday park is set in 33 acres of glorious countryside alongside the beautiful River Dore in Golden Valley, Hereford. Offering caravan holiday homes as well as pitches for touring caravans and tents, Poston Mill Park provides a fabulous location to escape and enjoy the natural English farmland. The site is secluded and excellently landscaped, and 'super pitches' are really spacious with private driveways. The owner's are commitment to conservation and the environment which is endorsed by the David Bellamy Conservation Gold Award that they hold.

There's something for all the family, including fishing, a 9-hole pitch and putt, croquet, badminton, pétanque, football pitch, a grass tennis court, and a small children's play area. And if you don't feel like cooking, the privately Mill Bar & Restaurant which adjoins the park is conveniently located for snacks, bar and à la carte meals.

You can also enjoy lovely walks by the river and around the park, including a large dog walking field. The Golden Valley is famous for its walks and cycle paths, and is close to the Offas Dyke Path – so don't forget to pack your boots or your bike.

There's so much to do in the area from visiting stunning stately homes and castles to playing golf. Hereford is just 9 miles away where you can visit the famous Cathedral and Mappa Mundi. Or take a trip to the book capital of the world – Hay on Wye. Enjoy a car-free day and catch the bus to Hereford or Hay on Wye from the park entrance.

t (01981) 550225
w bestparks.co.uk

Clockwise: Seafield Caravan Park; Sunset Park; Poston Mill Park

Caravan Holiday Park of the Year 2008

GOLD WINNER

Poston Mill Park, Peterchurch, Golden Valley, Herefordshire

★★★★★ *Holiday and Touring Park*

SILVER WINNERS

Seafield Caravan Park, Seahouses, Northumberland ★★★★★ *Holiday and Touring Park*

Sunset Park, Hambleton, near Blackpool, Lancashire ★★★★★ *Holiday Park*

David Bellamy Conservation Award

'These well-deserved awards are a signpost to parks which are making real achievements in protecting our environment. Go there and experience wrap-around nature...you could be amazed at what you find!' says Professor David Bellamy.

More than 600 gold, silver and bronze parks were named this year in the David Bellamy Conservation Awards, organised in conjunction with the British Holiday and Home Parks Association.

These parks are recognised for their commitment to conservation and the environment through their management of landscaping, recycling policies, waste management, the cultivation of flora and fauna and the creation of habitats designed to encourage a variety of wildlife onto the park. Links with the local community and the use of local materials are also important considerations.

Parks wishing to enter for a David Bellamy Conservation Award must complete a detailed questionnaire covering different aspects of their environmental policies, and describe what positive conservation steps they have taken. The park must also undergo an independent audit from a local wildlife or conservation body which is familiar with the area. Final assessments and the appropriate level of any award are then made personally by Professor Bellamy.

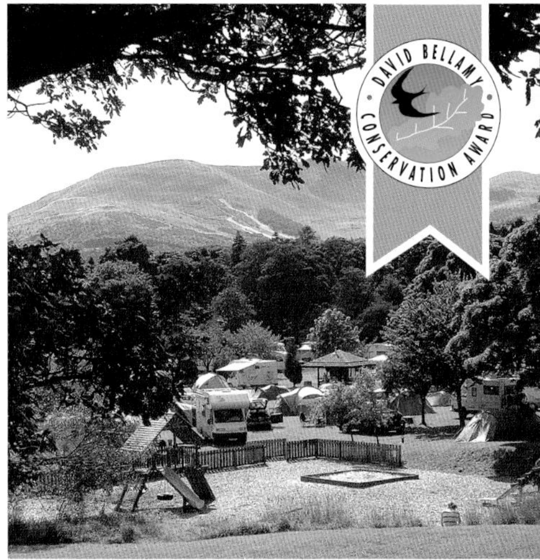

An index of award-winning parks featured in the regional pages of this guide can be found on page 314.

greatideas

Family fun

Kids and weather. They change mood from one moment to the next. Fortunately, that's also one of the most striking things about Britain's great outdoors and attractions: you just step across the threshold and its landscapes and entertainment venues offer all the varied play potential you need to fill holidays, sunny afternoons or rainy weekends.

So, there you are on the beach building sandcastles, paddling, eating ice cream and basking in the warm memory that you'll take home. You watch the teenagers hanging out with their surfboards, part of the family outing but doing their own thing. There's something for all ages and that's priceless in every sense of the word. Next time, maybe picnicking in woods, leaping through treetops on an aerial adventure, or getting your hands on heritage – whatever makes everyone happy.

Then it rains and you want to stay indoors. London's Science Museum is free, like a good number of England's top attractions, and that pleases Money Bags. Everyone immediately vanishes into one of the galleries: in Who Am I? you're morphing your face older and younger, in another you're discovering how to forecast weather, which could be useful for planning your next trip!

Anticipate the family's next mood. Animal magic at Chester Zoo, following Harry Potter to Alnwick Castle, or screaming your heads off at Drayton Manor Theme Park in Staffordshire? There's always another boredom-buster just around the corner.

For lots more great ideas visit visitbritain.com

Clockwise: Botany Bay, Kent; Blackpool Pleasure Beach, Lancashire; Wookey Hole Caves and Papermill, near Wells; Woburn Safari Park, Bedfordshire

Clockwise: Whinstone Lee Tor, Peak District, Derbyshire; Waterhead, Cumbria; Porlock Bay, Somerset; North York Moors

Rural escapes

Take one of hundreds of footpaths along the eastern end of Hope Valley in the Peak District and you'll find yourself at Stanage Edge. The wind whips around the gritstone outcrop, but all you can think about are the exhilarating panoramic views. Just a five-minute walk from the roadside car park, what a reward!

Ramble, cycle, relax over a picnic – in Britain's national parks you're quickly a world away from the day-to-day routine. Sea views across Porlock Bay, Exmoor, or purple waves of heather on the North York Moors work the yin and yang magic of nature. Wander with ponies on Dartmoor, enjoy the people-free hillsides of the Cheviots in Northumberland. What a sense of complete escape!

For a different experience follow the footpaths and cycleways to East Lancashire's Panopticons: gateway landmarks to magnificent countryside. Discover Burnley's huge Singing Ringing Tree crooning its low, mysterious song at Crown Point, or the striking steel Halo at Top o' Slate in Rossendale. They're fun, imaginative and easy to reach.

England boasts an astonishing diversity of natural wonders on the doorstep. From the flat waterscapes of the Norfolk Broads to the jutting peaks of the Lake District, from the ancient woodlands of the New Forest to Dorset's fossil-jewelled Jurassic Coast – there's scenery and breathing spaces to suit every activity and mood.

This is our natural heritage, shaped by primeval forces and just waiting to be explored. Step out and do so: you'll return with happily weary legs, a ravenous appetite and that wonderful tingling sensation on your face from a day in the fresh air.

For lots more great ideas visit visitbritain.com

greatideas

Food and drink

A quiet revolution has been simmering away in Britain. Fresh, locally-sourced and organic ingredients have become the order of the day. From bustling farmers' markets to family kitchens turning out hand-made puddings, jams and breads, dining in or out, you'll more than likely be presented with fresh wholesome food cooked with passion.

Start with the famous Ludlow Food Festival and follow the little-known Sausage Trail, an event in which the town's five independent butchers create new sausage varieties and vie for the crown of People's Choice. You'll find everything from organic rare breeds sausages to the Shropshire Sizzler – a rich blend of local pork, peaches and blue cheese. Take some back to base and spark up the barbie for a fantastic feast.

Fancy lunch while out exploring? Three cheers for the gastropub where high quality cooked-from-scratch bistro meals are served at bar room prices. As you tuck into a crisp salad and garlic mayo (made with free range eggs, of course) you begin to wonder if Chicken in a Basket wasn't just a bad dream.

At the charming Waffle House in St Alban's you can't help but admire the blend of inventiveness, quality produce and sheer dedication that goes into the cooking. Here you'll find waffles of every conceivable shape and size, served with freshly made toppings such as chilli con carne as well as an endless choice of sweet varieties.

The good news is, you'll find places like this all over Britain: it's a foodies' heaven.

For lots more great ideas visit visitbritain.com

Clockwise: Ludlow, Shropshire; Constantine Bay, Cornwall; Canterbury, Kent; tempting dessert

Clockwise: Joss Bay, Kent; Dunstanburgh, Northumberland; Curbar Edge, Peak District, Derbyshire; Watergate Bay, Cornwall

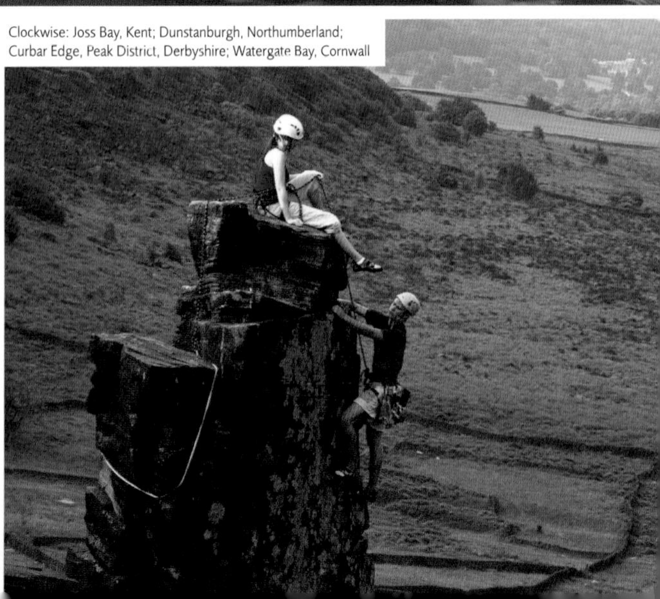

Sporting breaks

The kids first spot the kitesurfers and you stop to watch them skipping over waves like a shoal of exotic flying fish. Just 24 hours of pestering later and the whole family has signed up for a lesson. The rest of the day is a tumble of memories, pounding waves and breathless exhilaration.

Kitesurfing is one of the new breed of adrenalin sports to hit these shores – try it and maybe you'll be hooked. Windsurfing and sailing never go out of fashion, because Britain's coastline offers such superb waters. And there are plenty of stretches that are great for casting a line to hook a fish for supper.

If you've a head for heights, nerves of steel and stamina to match, the landlubber's life has plenty of challenges, too. Inch by inch, you climb your way up the vertical rock of Curbar Edge in the Peak District – then feel the flood of endorphins as you look out from the summit. It's worth every aching muscle!

But it doesn't all need to be sweat and grunt. Flying a kite on the Kent Downs can while away an absorbing hour. Nature trails and birdwatching at RSPB reserves awaken safari instincts. Share a cycling jaunt around Rutland Water or have a round of golf on a top links: concentrate now, think Tiger Woods and keep that hand-to-eye co-ordination. Or simply dust off the old bat and ball, hit the beach and show your pals just why you were captain of the school cricket team. Suddenly, you're watching the kitesurfers again and can't resist giving it another go.

For lots more great ideas visit visitbritain.com

Country ways

The Countryside Rights of Way Act gives people new rights to walk on areas of open countryside and registered common land.

To find out where you can go and what you can do, as well as information about taking your dog to the countryside, go online at countrysideaccess.gov.uk.

And when you're out and about...

Always follow the Country Code

- Be safe – plan ahead and follow any signs
- Leave gates and property as you find them
- Protect plants and animals, and take your litter home
- Keep dogs under close control
- Consider other people

Location Maps

Every place name featured in the regional accommodation sections of this guide has a map reference to help you locate it on the maps which follow. For example, to find Bournemouth, which has 'Map ref 2B3', turn to Map 2 and refer to grid square B3.

All place names appearing in the regional sections are shown with orange circles on the maps. This enables you to find other places in your chosen area which may have suitable accommodation – the place index (at the back of this guide) gives page numbers.

Key to regions: South West England

Orange circles indicate accommodation within the regional sections of this guide

Map 2

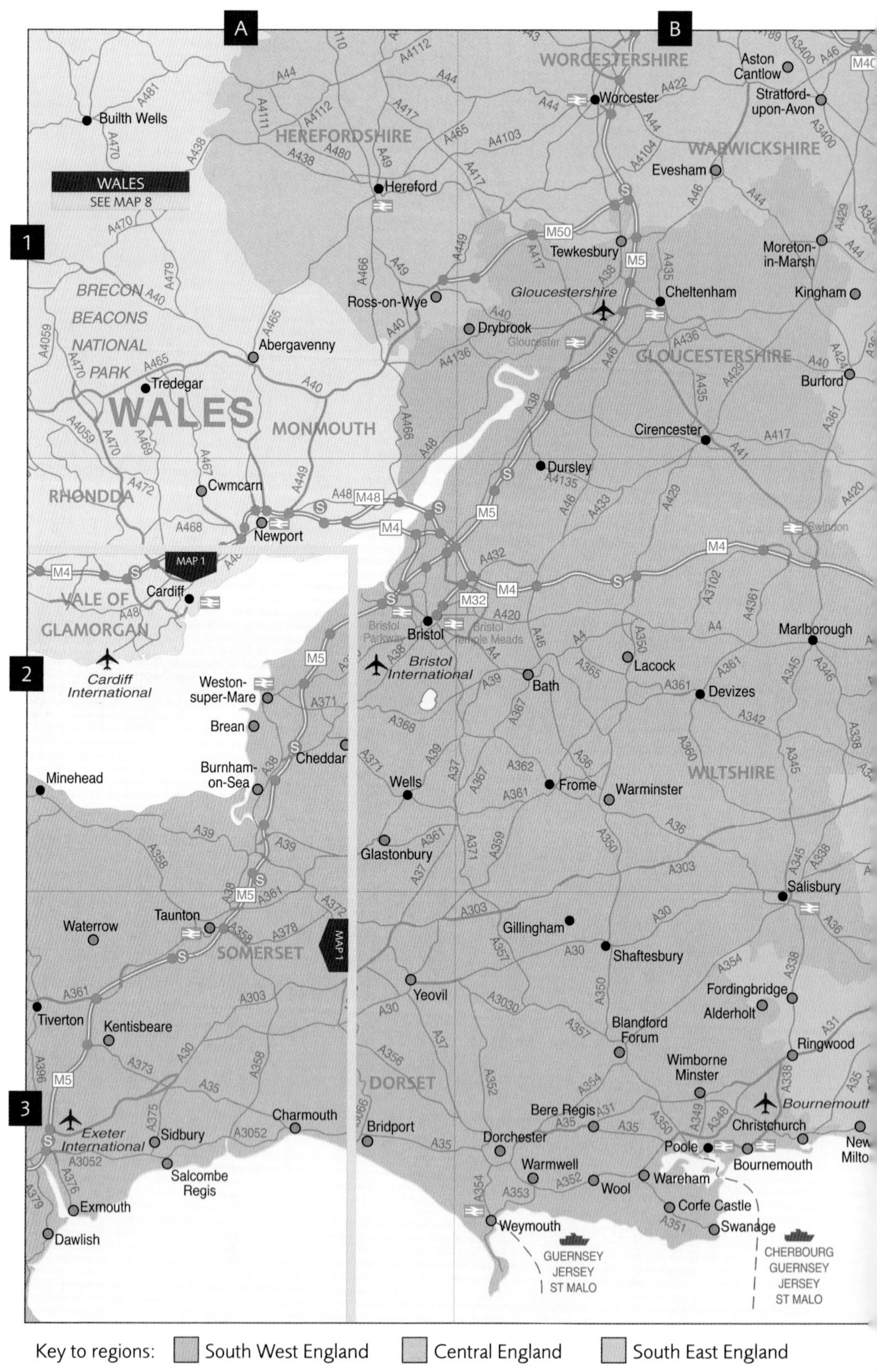

Key to regions: South West England Central England South East England

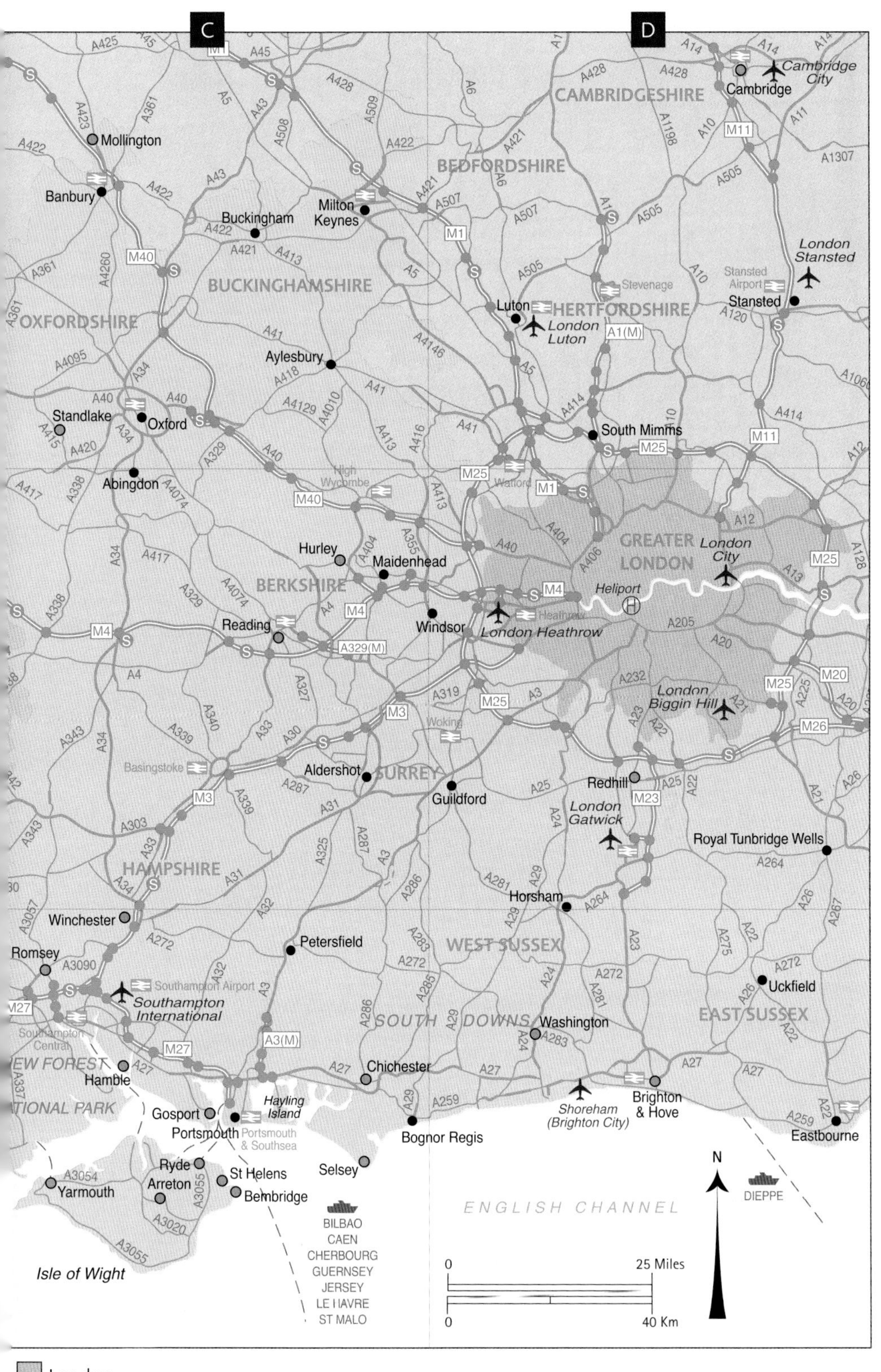

London

Orange circles indicate accommodation within the regional sections of this guide

Map 3

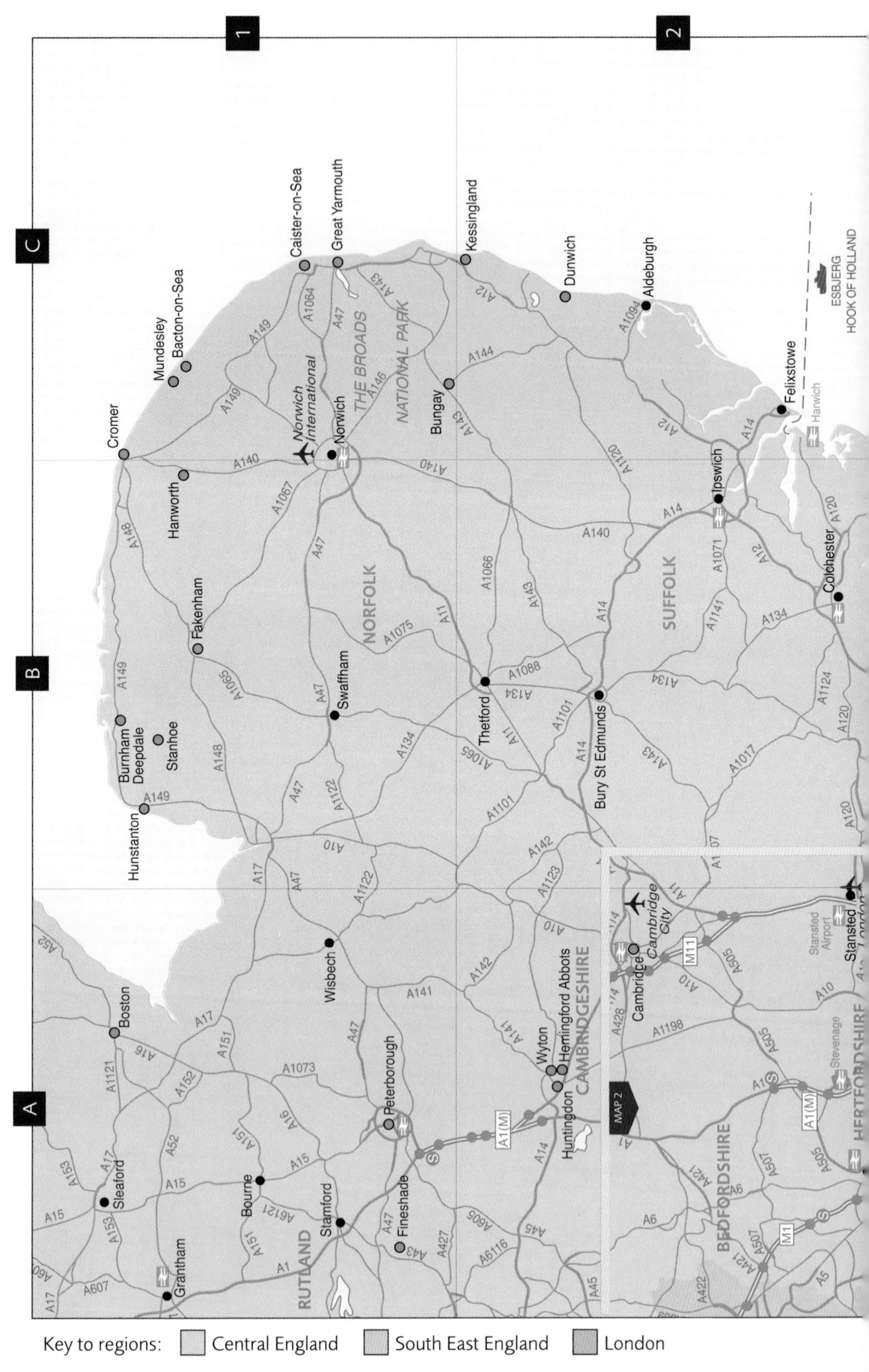

Key to regions: Central England South East England London

0
25 Miles
0
40 Km
N
3
4
OSTEND
BOULOGNE
CALAIS
DUNKIRK
Channel Tunnel
DIEPPE
ENGLISH CHANNEL
MAP 2
ESSEX
Mersea Island
Chelmsford
London Southend
Southend-on-Sea
London Luton
South Mimms
Watford
GREATER LONDON
London City
Heliport
Maidenhead
Windsor
London Heathrow
Heathrow
London Biggin Hill
Woking
SURREY
Guildford
Redhill
London Gatwick
Royal Tunbridge Wells
Horsham
WEST SUSSEX
SOUTH DOWNS
Washington
Uckfield
Brighton & Hove
Shoreham (Brighton City)
Bognor Regis
Eastbourne
Birchington
St Nicholas at Wade
Kent International
Ramsgate
Chatham
Faversham
Canterbury
Maidstone
NORTH SEA
KENT
Deal
Kingsdown
Marden
Ashford
Dover
Cranbrook
Folkestone
EAST SUSSEX
Battle
Lydd
Hastings
Bexhill-on-Sea
Pevensey Bay
M1
M2
M3
M4
M11
M20
M23
M25
M26
A2
A3
A5
A10
A12
A13
A20
A21
A22
A23
A24
A25
A26
A27
A28
A29
A40
A41
A127
A128
A130
A131
A205
A228
A229
A232
A249
A251
A252
A256
A257
A258
A259
A260
A262
A264
A265
A268
A269
A272
A274
A275
A281
A283
A286
A290
A299
A319
A355
A404
A406
A413
A414
A416
A1060
A2070
A4146

Map 4

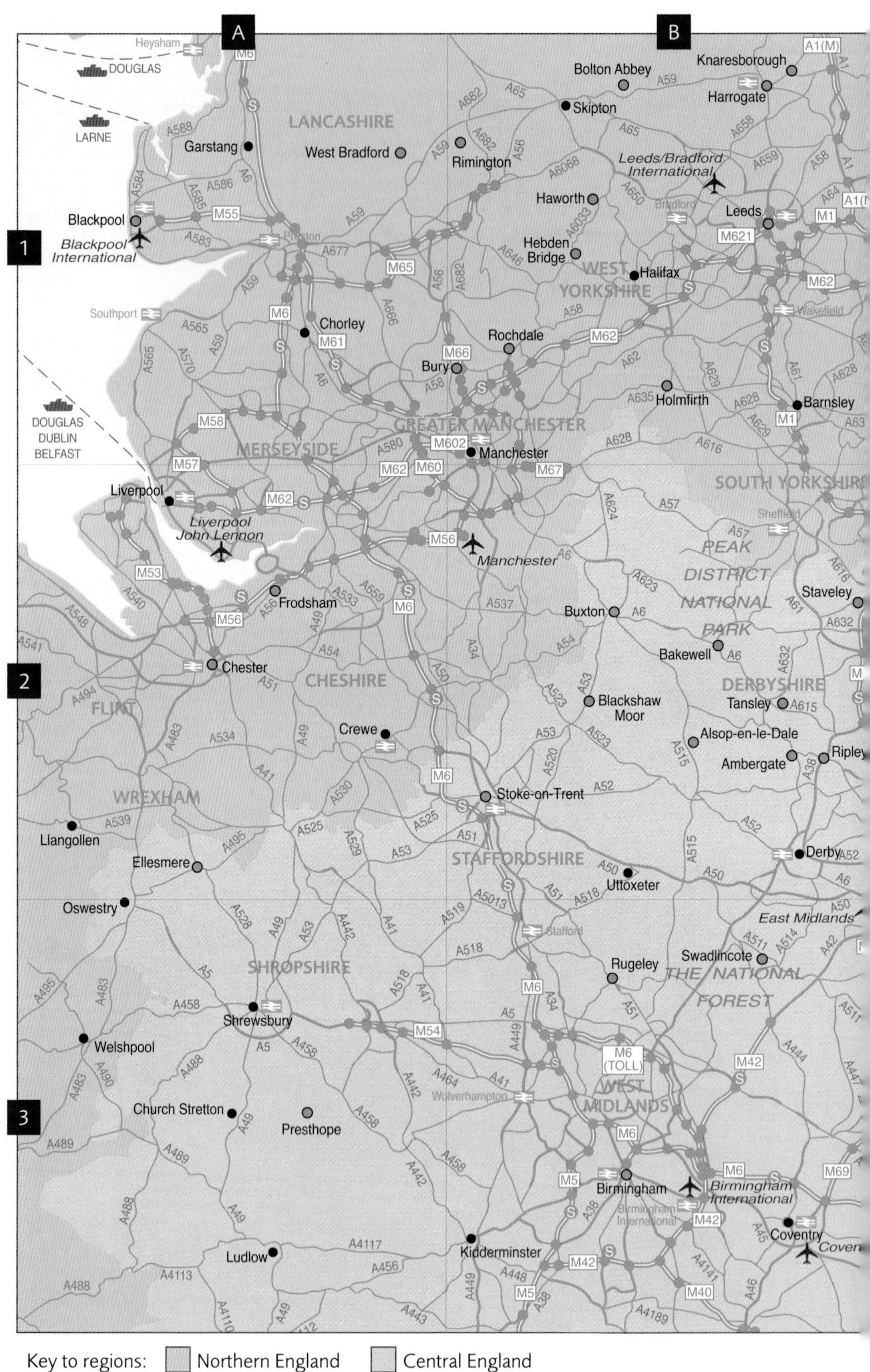

Key to regions: Northern England Central England

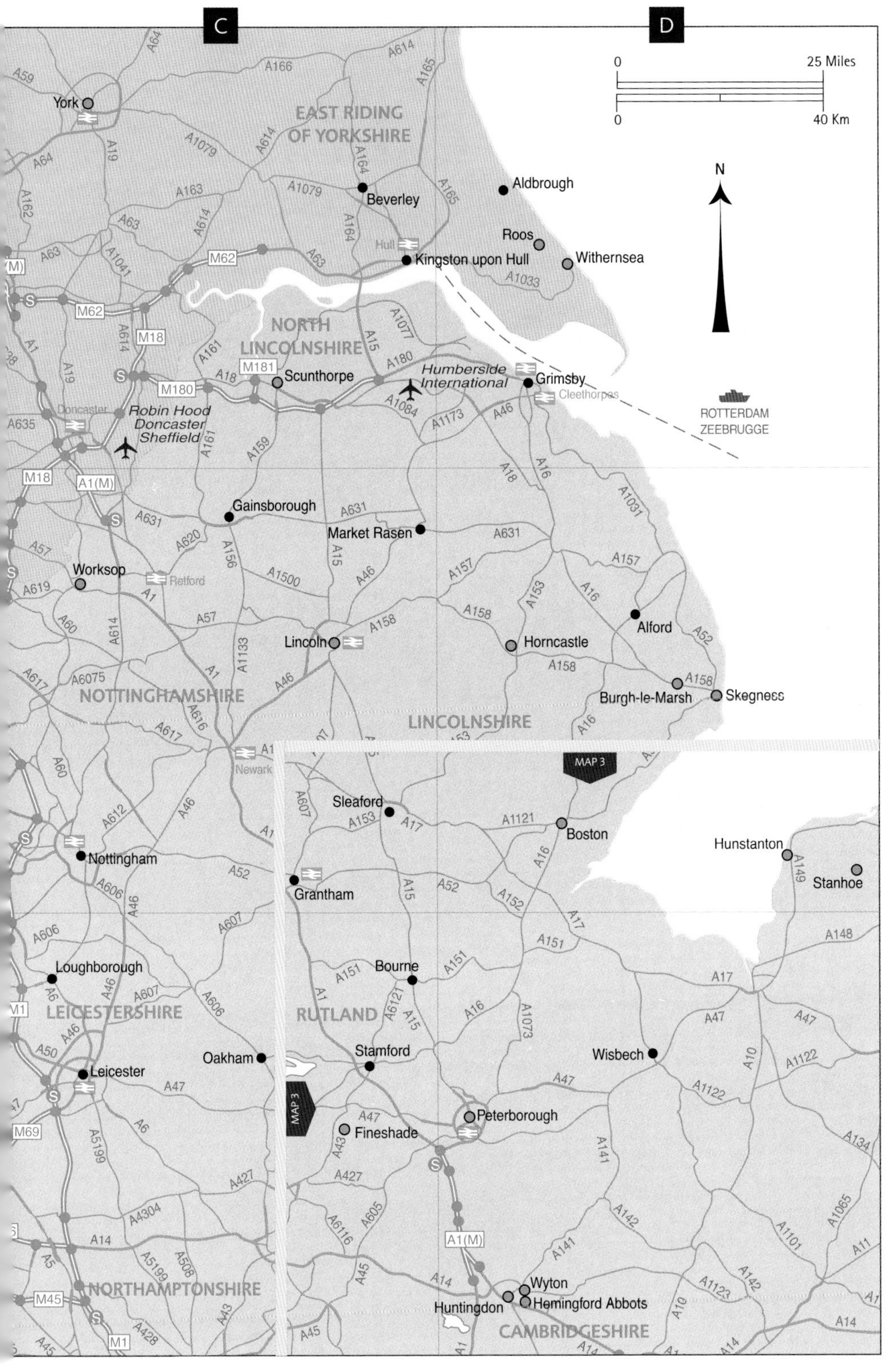

Orange circles indicate accommodation within the regional sections of this guide

Map 5

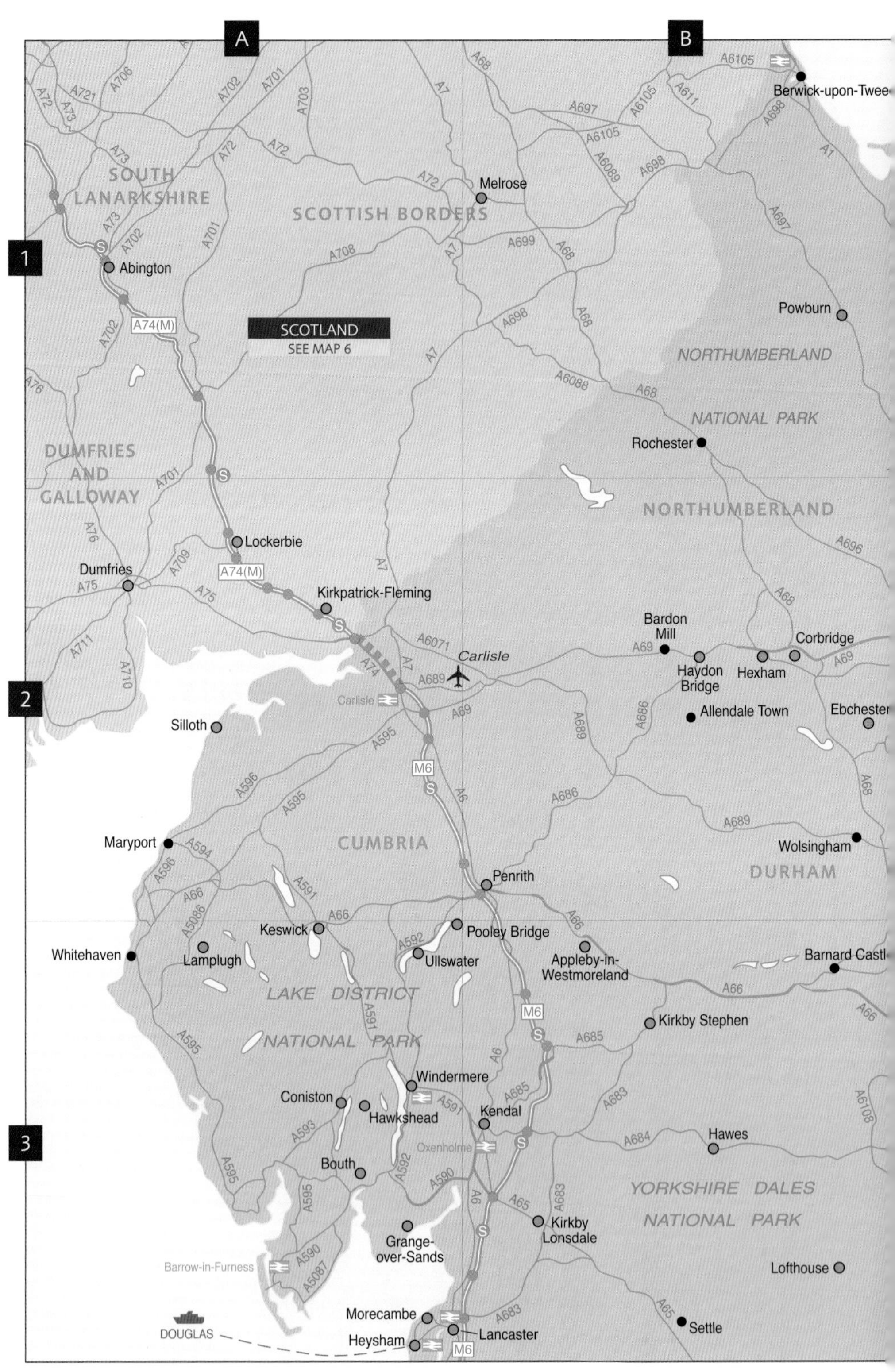

Key to regions: Northern England

Orange circles indicate accommodation within the regional sections of this guide

Map 6

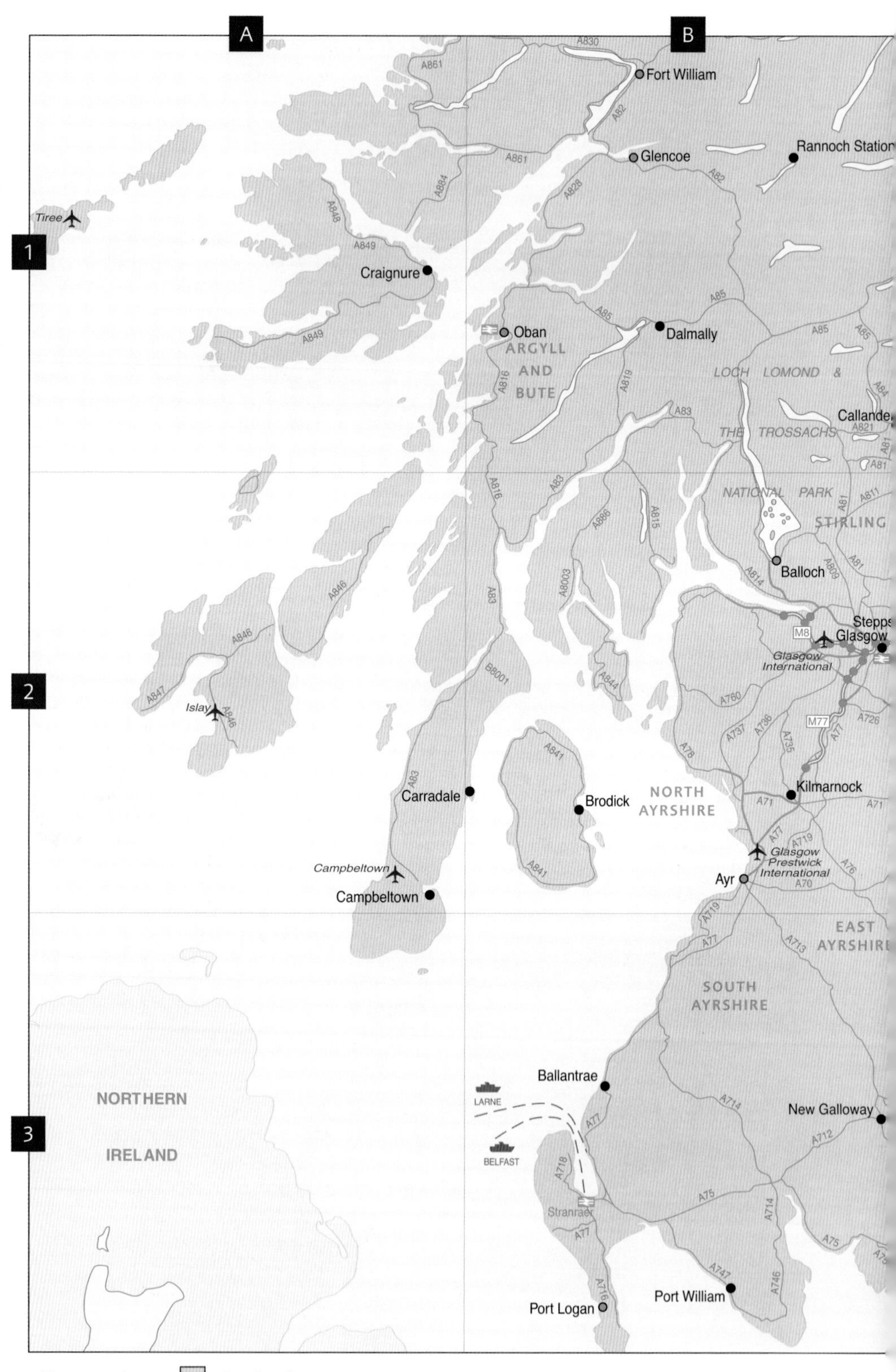

Key to regions: Scotland

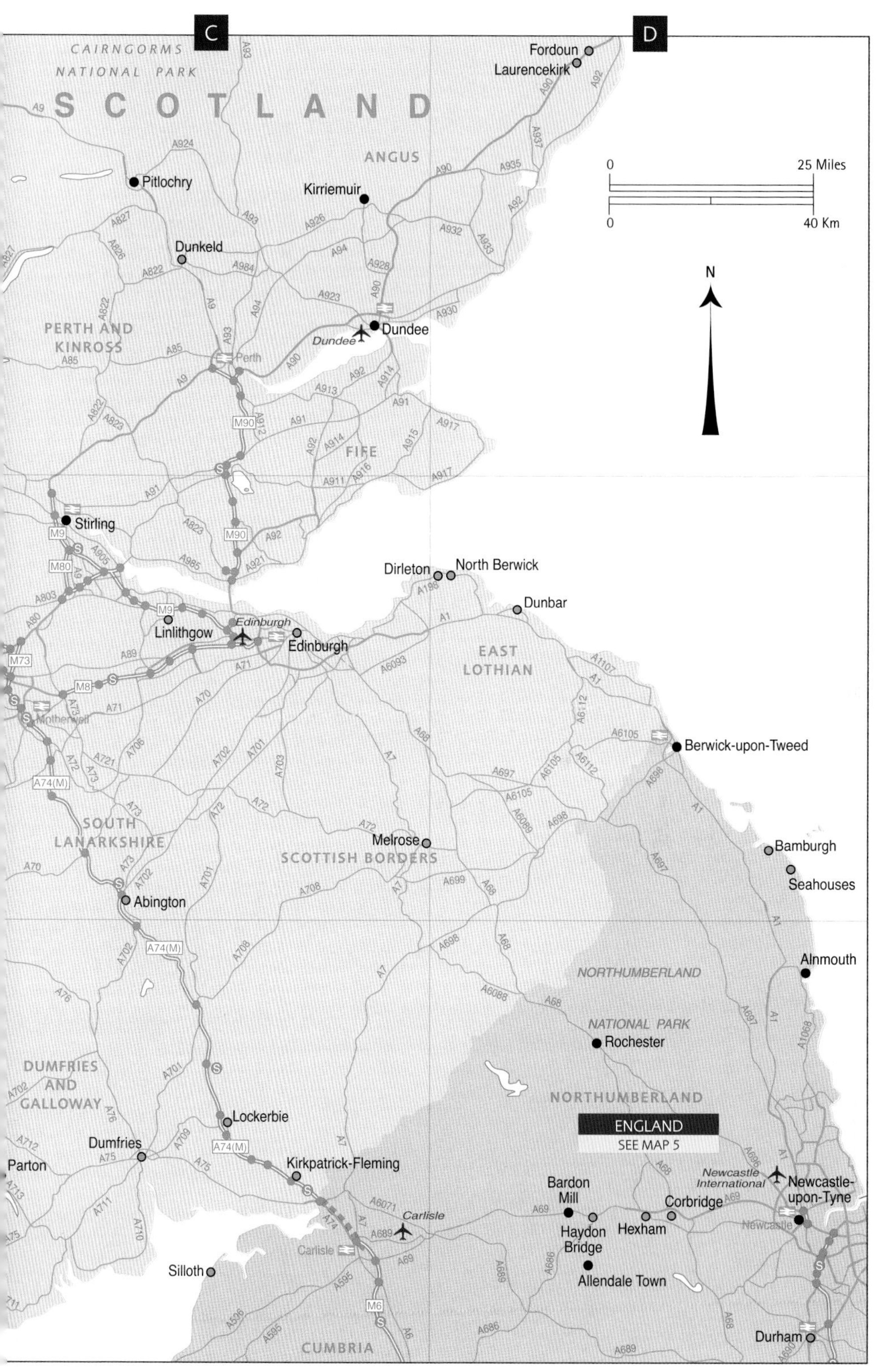

Orange circles indicate accommodation within the regional sections of this guide

Map 7

Key to regions: Scotland

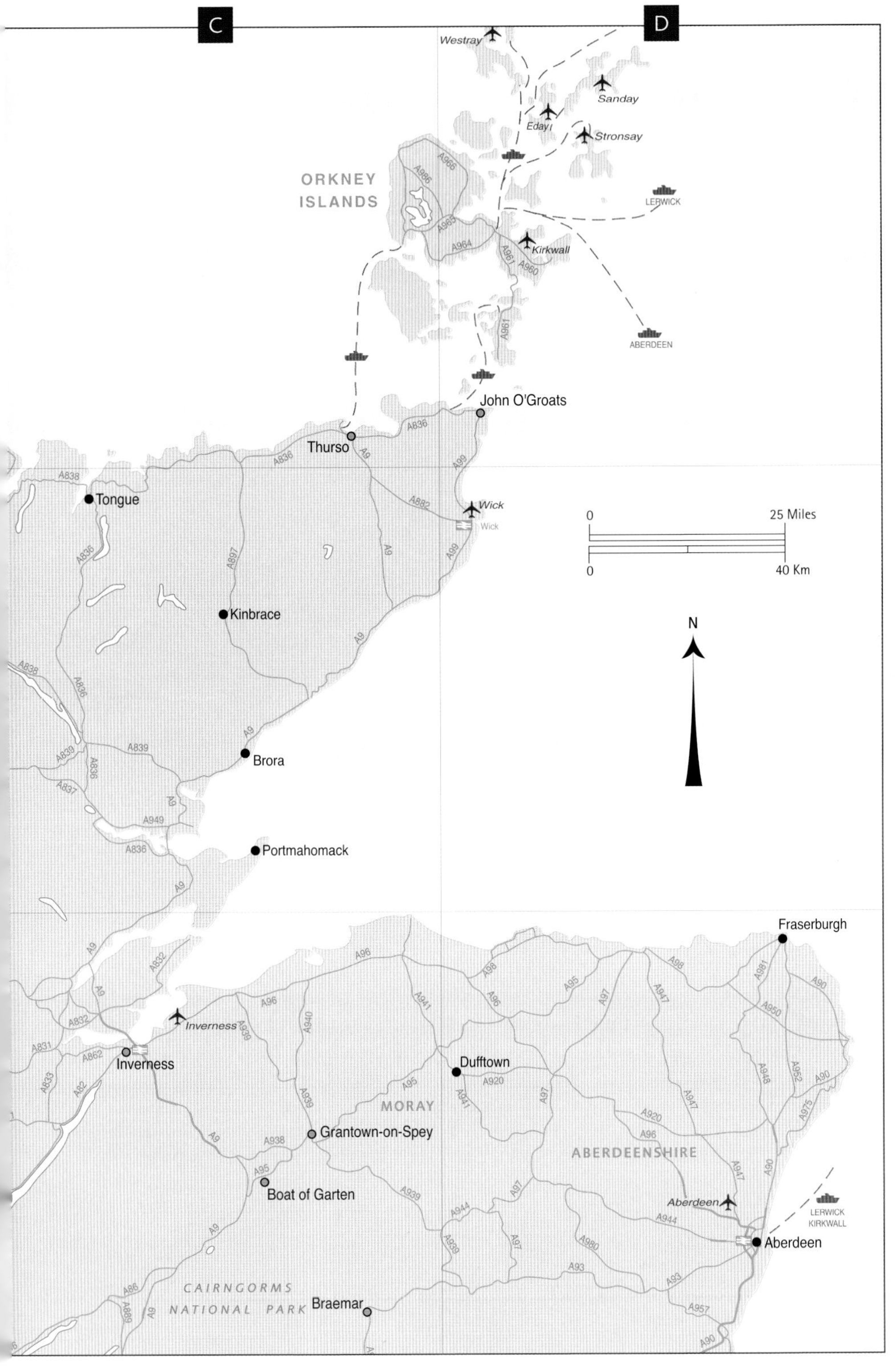

Orange circles indicate accommodation within the regional sections of this guide

Map 8

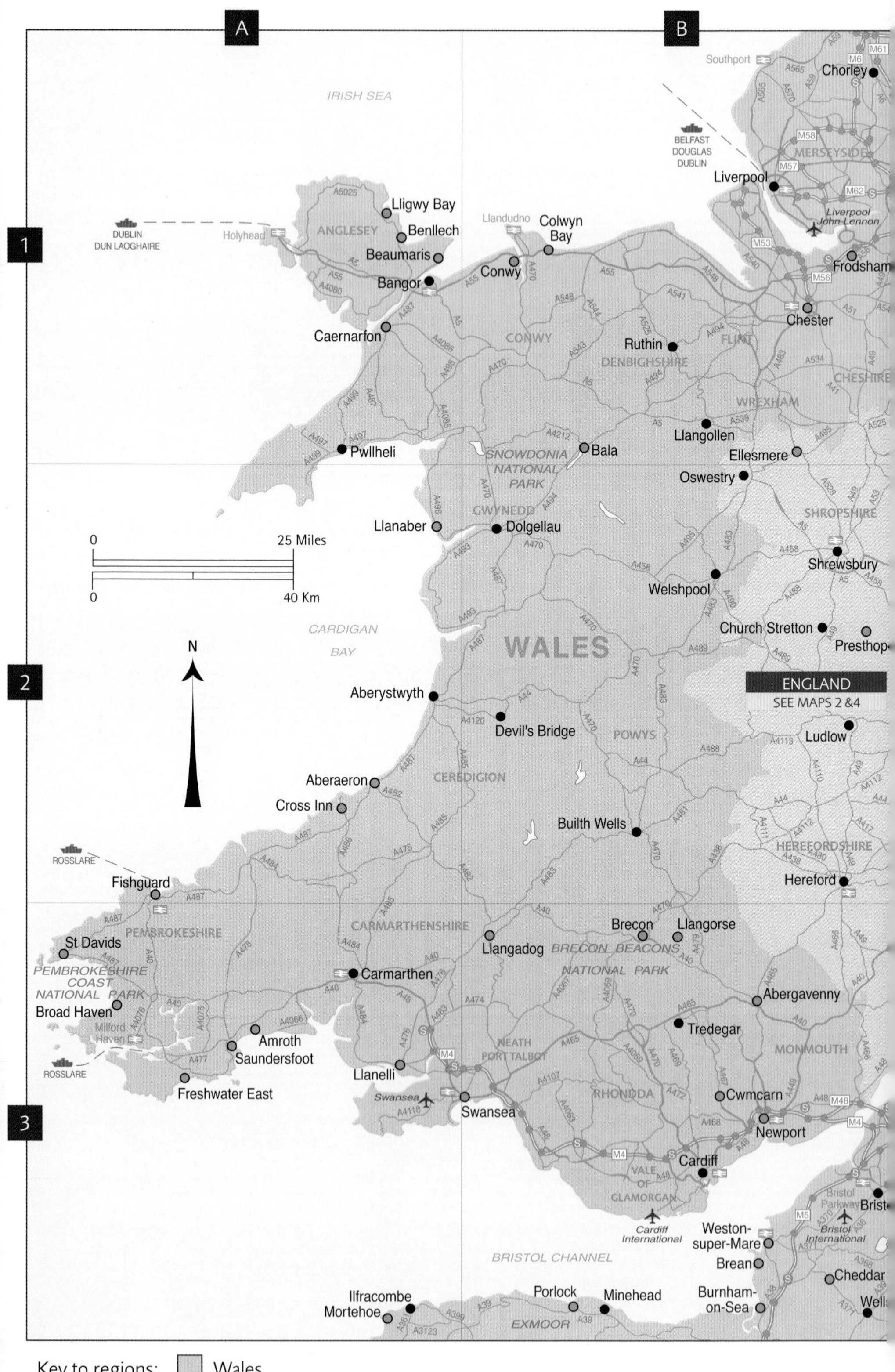

Key to regions: Wales

Orange circles indicate accommodation within the regional sections of this guide

Finding a park is easy

Britain's Camping, Caravan & Holiday Parks guide makes it quick and easy to find a place to stay. There are several ways to use this guide.

1

PARK INDEX

If you know the name of the site you wish to book, turn to the park index at the back where the relevant page number is shown.

2

PLACE INDEX

The place index at the back lists all locations with parks featured in the regional sections. A page number is shown where you can find full accommodation and contact details.

3

COLOUR MAPS

All the place names next to orange circles on the colour maps at the front have an entry in the regional sections. Refer to the place index for the page number where you will find one or more parks in your chosen town or village.

ALL ASSESSED ACCOMMODATION

Contact details for all British Graded Holiday Parks Scheme participants throughout England, together with their quality rating, are given in the back section of this guide. Parks with a full entry in the regional sections are shown in bold. Look in the park index for the page number where their full entry appears.

Northern England

Cheshire, Cumbria, Durham, Greater Manchester, Lancashire, Merseyside, Northumberland, Tees Valley, Tyne and Wear, Yorkshire

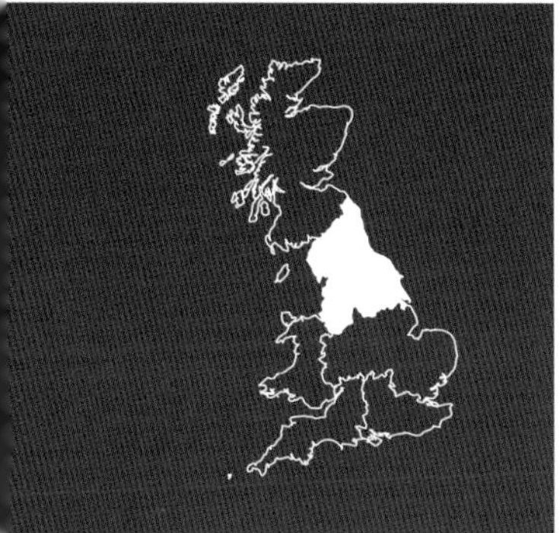

Clockwise: Bamburgh Castle, Northumberland; Liverpool; North Yorkshire Moors Railway

Great days out

Explore windswept moors and breathtaking coastlines. Admire mirrored-glass lakes and magnificent cathedrals. Discover pioneering industrial heritage and cutting-edge cities. Northern England is a proud fusion of history, dramatic landscapes and modern culture – not forgetting fun-filled seaside resorts!

Relive the revolution

Where did the Industrial Revolution gather pace? In Northern England, of course! Experience its legacy in so many ways. At **Beamish Museum**, a town, colliery village and farm have been recreated using authentic early 19th and 20thC buildings – get around by tramcar and chat to costumed interpreters. Children love living history this way. Hear vivid tales at the **National Coal Mining Museum for England** at Wakefield, put on hat, belt and battery and tour underground with an experienced miner. Clamber onto historic craft at **The National Waterways Museum**, Ellesmere Port. Or maybe trains are more your style? Go spotting at **Locomotion, The National Railway Museum** in Shildon, one of the oldest railway towns in the world. Steaming Days get dads as excited as the kids.

Natural highs

Wide-open spaces abound in the National Parks – Yorkshire alone has over 1,000 square miles to explore. Escape and hear your laughter in the breeze as you fly a kite from high on the **North York Moors**. You can always pick up tips from the professionals at Sunderland International Kite Festival. **The Lake District and Cumbria** have inspired poets, painters and climbers, and Wastwater was recently voted 'Britain's favourite view'. Enjoy it at ground level or hike up Scafell Pike, England's highest peak, for a stunning aerial picture. You'll also feel on top of the world cycling or walking to **East Lancashire's Panopticons**, a series of innovative structures pointing the way to panoramic countryside: Halo, illuminating the Rossendale night sky, is simply breathtaking.

For more firsts and highs, ramble the **North Pennines Area of Outstanding Natural Beauty**, Britain's first geopark. Weardale and Teesdale are renowned for dazzling waterfalls – aptly named **High Force** is England's highest. Build castles along rippled-sand beaches, such as Spittal and St Aidans, in the North East. Board a boat to **Holy Island** to learn the secrets of the Lindisfarne Gospels. And remember the binoculars on the **Farne Islands** – home to hundreds of thousands of puffins and dewy-eyed grey seals.

Wastwater, Cumbria

Join the Romans

Pace along **Hadrian's Wall** in the footsteps of soldiers nearly two millennia ago. Built in just six years, it runs for an amazing 73 miles. **Chesters** is Britain's best-preserved Roman cavalry fort and you can find out more about Romans in the region at **Tullie House**

Left to right: Alnwick Castle, Northumberland; York Minster

why not... cycle the shoreline of Coniston Water, perfect for easygoing family rides?

Museum and Art Gallery, Carlisle. In the walled city of Chester, Britain's best-preserved Roman town, visit the partially excavated amphitheatre or the **Dewa Roman Experience** where you can step aboard a Roman galley, stroll a reconstructed street and handle 'dig' discoveries.

Grand designs

Northern England has more than its fair share of remarkable buildings. Please the children with a visit to **Alnwick Castle**, aka Hogwarts in the first Harry Potter films. They'll be enthralled by one of the world's largest treehouses, too. **Tatton Park** in Cheshire is among the most complete historic estates, featuring a mansion, gardens, farm, Tudor Old Hall, deer park and speciality shops. And **Castle Howard**, near York, sets an impressive standard in home décor with its Canalettos, Holbeins and Gainsboroughs. Seek green-fingered inspiration at **Sheffield's Winter Garden**, which grows more than 2,500 plants from around the world in a huge temperate glasshouse the size of 5,000 domestic greenhouses!

Tiptoe beneath the towering vaulted ceilings of **York Minster**, the largest medieval Gothic cathedral in Northern Europe and home to glittering stained glass collections. Durham City's medieval cobbled streets are crowned by the magnificent towers of **Durham Castle and Cathedral** – 'the best cathedral on planet earth', according to travel writer Bill Bryson. And now's the time to discover the twin **Anglo-Saxon monasteries at Wearmouth and Jarrow**, the UK's nomination for World Heritage Status in 2009.

Young hearts and minds

Candyfloss and sticky rock, thrills and spills – **Blackpool** is your dream ticket for family fun. Book ringside seats at the **Tower Circus**, and gasp in amazement as international artists

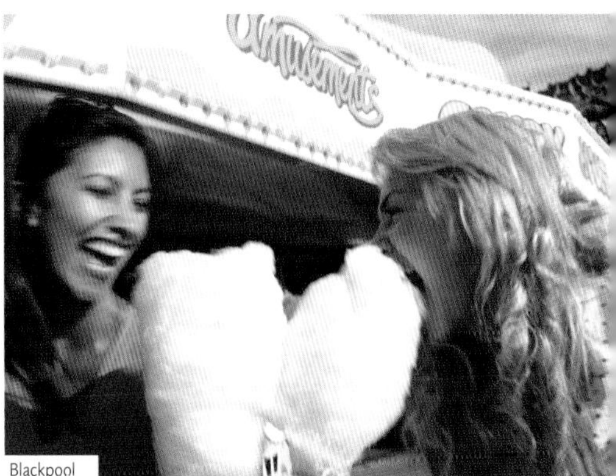

Blackpool

perform superhuman feats. Hop onto sock-popping rides at **Camelot Theme Park** near Chorley or **Go Ape!** in Grizedale Forest on rope bridges and Tarzan swings. Then stimulate the brain cells at **Rotherham's Magna** on an elemental interactive adventure through fire, earth, air and water. Or take the plunge at **The Deep** in Hull and come nose to nose with sharks in the submarium.

Modern city culture

There's also plenty to keep pulses racing in Northern England's dynamic cities where regeneration is the name of the game. Enjoy the renaissance of **NewcastleGateshead**, highlighted by the stunning architecture of the **Gateshead Millennium Bridge**. New artists at the **Baltic Centre for Contemporary Art** keep pushing the boundaries. Explore **Liverpool** and **Manchester**, both vibrant club scenes – of the soccer and night-time variety. Liverpool, revered birthplace of The Beatles, is still sparking from its European Capital of Culture 2008 status. Tour the revitalised **Albert Dock** along the World Heritage waterfront and sample the contemporary art of **Tate Liverpool**.

why not... join a ghost walk around York, claimed as Europe's most haunted city?

In **Manchester** head for **Salford Quays** and **The Lowry**, the inspirational waterfront centre for the visual arts and entertainment. The daring aluminium **Imperial War Museum North** designed by Daniel Libeskind is a showstopper, one of Manchester's many free museums. Next up: **Leeds** has a new must-see **City Museum** featuring an astounding Treasures Gallery. Middlesbrough, though not a city, also beckons with the recently opened **Middlesbrough Institute of Modern Art** housing works by Tracey Emin and other headline names.

Clockwise: NewcastleGateshead; The Deep, Hull; The Lowry, Manchester

Destinations

Berwick-upon-Tweed

England's northernmost town guards the mouth of the River Tweed. Marvel at some of the finest 16thC city walls in Europe, built by Elizabeth I to protect the town. Visit Bamburgh Castle and the beautiful gardens at Alnwick. Roam magnificent Heritage coastline and see Holy Island and the fairytale Lindisfarne Castle.

Bamburgh near Berwick-upon-Tweed

Blackpool

Britain's favourite holiday resort. Experience thrills and excitement at the Pleasure Beach, take tea in the magnificent Tower Ballroom, or stroll the seven miles of sandy beaches. Blackpool offers you world-class shows, cosmopolitan restaurants, vibrant nightlife, an active sports scene and breathtakingly beautiful scenery on the doorstep.

Chester

Experience one of Europe's top heritage cities. Walk the unique city walls, then visit the famous Rows, unique two-tiered galleries, to shop for everything from antiques to high fashion. Stroll along the banks of the beautiful River Dee, explore the Roman amphitheatre, and spend a day at Chester's famous Roodee Racecourse.

Cumbria – The Lake District

With breathtaking mountains and sparkling lakes, the unsurpassed scenery of Cumbria – The Lake District has inspired writers and poets across the ages. Explore the best walking and climbing routes that England has to offer, and see for yourself 'Britain's favourite view'. Take a lake cruise, visit wonderful homes and gardens or simply enjoy the views.

Durham

Described by Bill Bryson as 'a perfect little city.' Explore majestic Durham Cathedral, a World Heritage Site, and thought by many to be the finest Norman church architecture in England. Visit the tombs of St Cuthbert and the Venerable Bede. Take a coffee in the cobbled Market Place and enjoy the stunning floral displays, or walk down to the riverbank for magnificent views.

Hull

Enjoy the invigorating yet relaxing atmosphere that only a waterfront city can offer. Visit the Museum Quarter linking four of Hull's eight free museums. Don't miss 'The Deep', home to 40 sharks and one of the most spectacular sea-life attractions in the world. Marvel at the engineering of the Humber Bridge and, after dark, experience Hull's very own café bar culture.

Leeds

Rich local history, world-class sport, outstanding museums and galleries, and diverse year-round entertainment, that's Leeds. It's a shopaholic's dream, from the elegant Corn Exchange to the exquisite Victoria Quarter, not to mention the only Harvey Nichols outside London. See opera and dance at the Opera North and Northern Ballet and explore the Yorkshire Dales right on the doorstep.

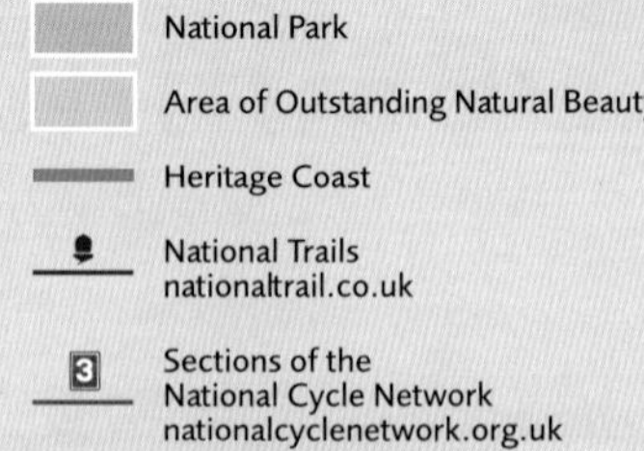

Northern England

National Park
Area of Outstanding Natural Beauty
Heritage Coast
National Trails
nationaltrail.co.uk
Sections of the
National Cycle Network
nationalcyclenetwork.org.uk
3
Berwick-upon-Tweed
Holy Island/
Lindisfarne
Bamburgh
Northumberland
Coast
Wooler
1
68
PENNINE
WAY
Alnwick
NORTHUMBERLAND
Kielder Water
and Forest Park
Druridge
Druridge
Bay
Bellingham
HADRIAN'S
WALL PATH
7
72
Tynemouth
South Shields
Solway
Coast
Carlisle
PENNINE
WAY
72
Newcastle
Gateshead
Sunderland
Silloth
7
7
Derwent
Reservoir
North
Pennines
Stanhope
14
Durham
14
Maryport
Penrith
Middleton-
in-Teesdale
1
Hartlepool
Workington
71
71
Keswick
Stockton-
on-Tees
Middlesbrough
Whitehaven
Kirkby
Stephen
Barnard
Castle
Darlington
Saltburn-by-the-Sea
Whitby
LAKE DISTRICT
Ambleside
Dalegarth
Windermere
NORTH YORK
MOORS
Ravenglass
68
PENNINE
WAY
71
CLEVELAND
WAY
Scarborough
Grange-
over-Sands
6
YORKSHIRE
DALES
Helmsley
Filey
Ulverston
Kirkby
Lonsdale
65
Arnside &
Silverdale
DALES WAY
Ripon
Howardian
Hills
Barrow-
in-Furness
Nidderdale
Bridlington
Lancaster
Forest of
Bowland
Harrogate
York
Skipton
YORKSHIRE
WOLDS WAY
Ilkley
1
Haworth
Leeds
Blackpool
65
Hull
Bradford
Preston
Blackburn
Wakefield
67
62
Withernsea
Southport
Halifax
Huddersfield
Chorley
Barnsley
PENNINE
BRIDLEWAY
62
Manchester
PEAK
DISTRICT
Doncaster
Liverpool
Rotherham
Sheffield
Neston
Ellesmere Port
Knutsford
Macclesfield
Chester
Nantwich
0
50 miles
0
75 kms

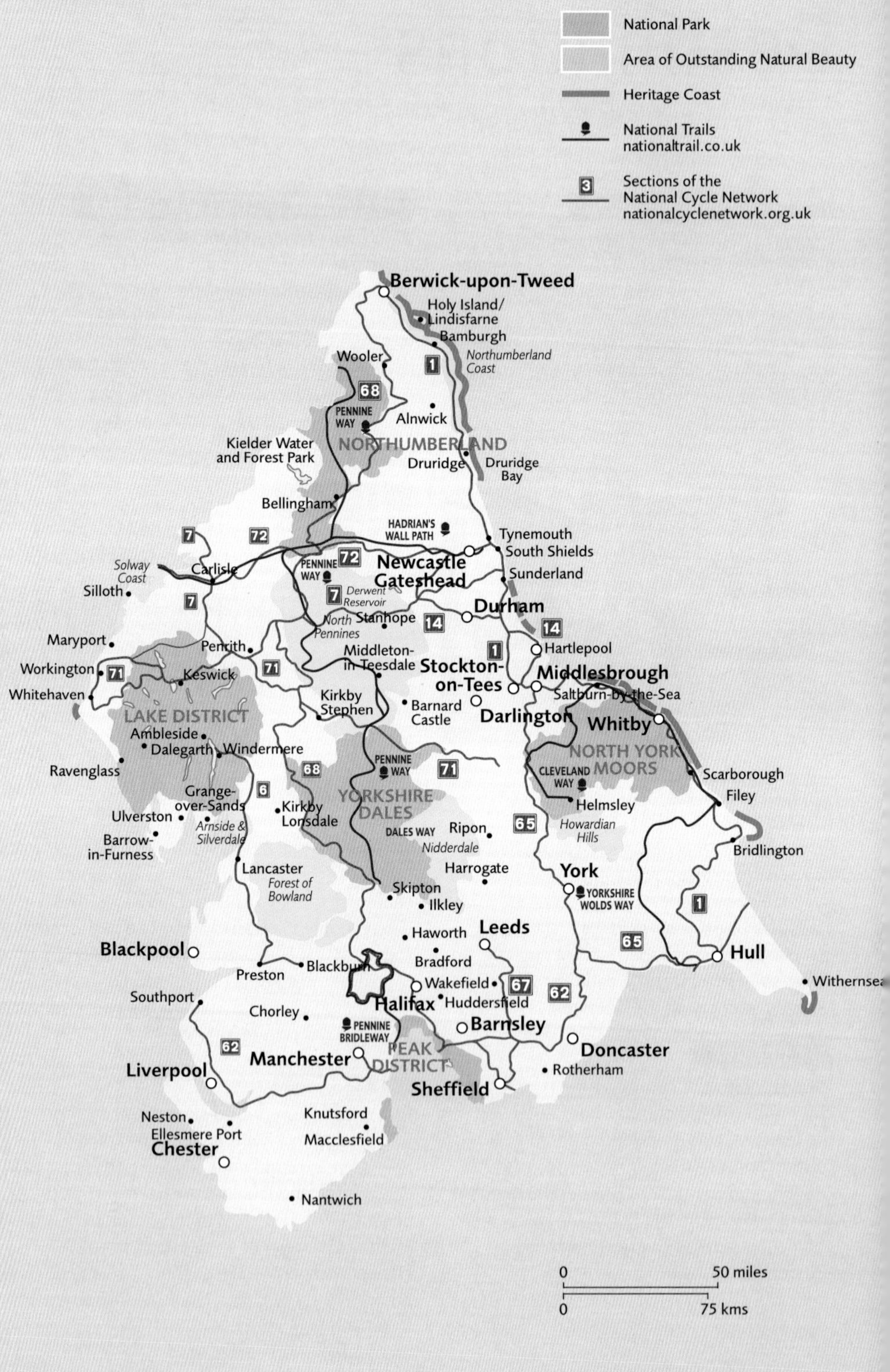

Durham

Liverpool

Experience the unique atmosphere of Liverpool. The birthplace of the Beatles and European Capital of Culture 2008 offers you more theatres, museums and galleries than any UK city outside London. Its history as one of the world's great ports has left a remarkable legacy of art and architecture to explore, not forgetting, the city's famous sporting pedigree. So if it's Strawberry Fields, Premiership football or Europe's finest culture you're looking for, it has to be Liverpool.

Manchester

Explore a city that has reinvented itself as a truly contemporary metropolis. You'll find modern landmark buildings, a wealth of art and culture, great bars and world-class hospitality. There's every experience imaginable, from fine dining and top-class theatre, to major sporting events and year-round festivals. It's a shopping destination in its own right, rivalling that of the capital, with top stores and chic boutiques.

Clockwise: Chester; Leeds; Martindale, Cumbria

NewcastleGateshead

Must-see attractions including the award-winning Gateshead Millennium Bridge, the Baltic Centre for Contemporary Art and the magnificent new Sage Gateshead, a stunning Sir Norman Foster building, with billowing curves of glass and steel catering for every genre of music. Rich in culture, architecture and history and with a great reputation for style, shopping and nightlife, the variety of life in NewcastleGateshead surprises even the most well travelled visitor.

Whitby

With its quaint cobbled streets and picturesque houses standing on the steep slopes of the River Esk, Whitby is dominated by its cliff top Abbey. Explore one of Britain's finest stretches of coastline. Climb the steps to the parish church of St Mary, whose churchyard inspired Bram Stocker's 'Dracula'. Then down to the historic quayside of this 1,000-year-old port and celebrate the town's seafaring tradition at the Captain Cook Festival, named in honour of Whitby's most famous son.

York

Visit award-winning attractions including the magnificent York Minster, and the world's biggest and best railway museum. Let 21stC technology transport you back to the Viking age at Jorvik, and wander through the terrifying York Dungeon. Pedestrianised streets make York an ideal city to explore on foot. Follow the city's specialist shopping trails '5 Routes to Shopping Heaven', or browse the specialist antique and book dealers.

For lots more great ideas visit enjoyEngland.com/destinations

Visitor attractions

Family and Fun

Aquarium of the Lakes
Lakeside, Cumbria
(015395) 30153
aquariumofthelakes.co.uk
Freshwater aquarium complete with underwater viewing tunnel.

Beamish, The North of England Open Air Museum

Beamish, Durham
(0191) 370 4000
beamish.org.uk
Award-winning open-air museum of working life.

Blackpool Tower & Circus
Blackpool, Lancashire
(01253) 622242
blackpooltower.co.uk
Entertainment for all ages, night and day.

Blue Planet Aquarium
Ellesmere Port, Cheshire
(0151) 357 8804
blueplanetaquarium.com
Underwater adventure in the UK's largest aquarium.

Chester Zoo
Chester, Cheshire
(01244) 380280
chesterzoo.org
Meet over 7,000 animals and 500 species.

Darlington Railway Centre and Museum
Darlington, Durham
(01325) 460532
drcm.org.uk
See, touch and feel living railway heritage.

The Deep

Hull, East Yorkshire
(01482) 381000
thedeep.co.uk
One of the world's most spectacular aquariums.

Hartlepool's Maritime Experience

Hartlepool, Durham
(01429) 860077
hartlepoolsmaritimeexperience.com
Authentic reconstruction of an 18thC seaport.

JORVIK Viking Centre
York, North Yorkshire
(01904) 543400
jorvik-viking-centre.co.uk
Meet the Vikings, face-to-face.

Killhope, The North of England Lead Mining Museum
Cowshill, Durham
(01388) 537505
durham.gov.uk/killhope
Award-winning underground experience.

Liverpool Football Club Museum and Stadium Tour
Liverpool
(0151) 260 6677
liverpoolfc.tv
Touch the famous 'This is Anfield' sign!

Locomotion: The National Railway Museum at Shildon
Shildon, Durham
(01388) 777999
locomotion.uk.com
Historic buildings and vehicles celebrate railway heritage.

Magna Science Adventure Centre
Rotherham, South Yorkshire
(01709) 720002
visitmagna.co.uk
An unforgettable, interactive science adventure.

Manchester United Museum & Tour
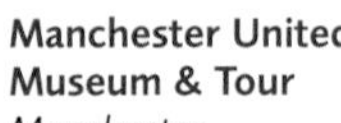
Manchester
0870 442 1994
manutd.com
Official tour of the 'Theatre of Dreams'.

Merseyside Maritime Museum
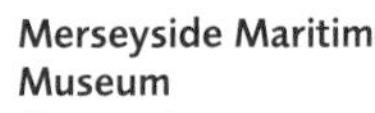
Liverpool
(0151) 478 4499
merseysidemaritimemuseum.org.uk
Liverpool's seafaring heritage brought to life.

MOSI (Museum of Science and Industry)

Manchester
(0161) 832 2244
mosi.org.uk
Five historic buildings packed with fascinating displays.

The National Waterways Museum

Ellesmere Port, Cheshire
(0151) 355 5017
nwm.org.uk
Britain's largest collection of inland waterway craft.

Nature's World

Middlesbrough
(01642) 594895
naturesworld.org.uk
Pioneering eco-garden of the future.

Saltburn Smugglers Heritage Centre

Saltburn-by-the-Sea, Tees Valley
(01287) 625252
redcar-cleveland.gov.uk/leisure
Meet costumed characters in ancient fishermens' cottages.

Seven Stories, The Centre for Children's Books
Newcastle upon Tyne, Tyne and Wear
0845 271 0777
sevenstories.org.uk
Britain's first centre dedicated to children's literature.

Yorkshire Waterways Museum
Goole, East Yorkshire
(01405) 768730
waterwaysmuseum.org.uk
Museum, adventure centre and nature trail.

Heritage

Alnwick Castle
Alnwick, Northumberland
(01665) 510777
alnwickcastle.com
Dazzling medieval castle with glorious state rooms.

Arley Hall & Gardens
Northwich, Cheshire
(01565) 777353
arleyhallandgardens.com
Charming stately home and award-winning gardens.

Bamburgh Castle
Bamburgh, Northumberland
(01668) 214515
bamburghcastle.com
Imposing castle in dramatic coastal setting.

Beeston Castle
Beeston, Cheshire
(01829) 260464
english-heritage.org.uk
13thC castle with views over eight counties.

Belsay Hall, Castle and Gardens
Newcastle upon Tyne, Tyne and Wear
(01661) 881636
english-heritage.org.uk
Medieval castle, 17thC manor and gardens.

Brodsworth Hall and Gardens
Doncaster, South Yorkshire
(01302) 724969
english-heritage.org.uk
Italianate house with marvellous labyrinthine gardens.

Castle Howard
York, North Yorkshire
(01653) 648444
castlehoward.co.uk
Magnificent 18thC house in stunning parkland.

Chester Cathedral
Chester, Cheshire
(01244) 324756
chestercathedral.com
Medieval cathedral with spectacular carved choir stalls.

Durham Castle
Durham
(0191) 334 3800
durhamcastle.com
Superb Norman castle in World Heritage Site.

Fountains Abbey and Studley Royal Water Garden
Ripon, North Yorkshire
(01765) 608888
fountainsabbey.org.uk
12thC monastic ruin with captivating landscaped gardens.

Harewood House
Harewood, West Yorkshire
(0113) 218 1010
harewood.org
Stunning architecture and exquisite Adam interiors.

Holker Hall and Gardens
Cark in Cartmel, Cumbria
(015395) 58328
holker-hall.co.uk
Magnificent Neo-Elizabethan mansion and award-winning gardens.

Levens Hall & Gardens
Levens, Cumbria
(015395) 60321
levenshall.co.uk
Elizabethan mansion and world-famous topiary gardens.

Lyme Park
Disley, Cheshire
(01663) 766492
nationaltrust.org.uk
Tudor house transformed into an Italianate palace.

National Coal Mining Museum for England
Wakefield, West Yorkshire
(01924) 848806
ncm.org.uk
Award-winning museum of the English coalfields.

Newby Hall & Gardens
Ripon, North Yorkshire
0845 450 4068
newbyhall.com
One of England's renowned Adam houses.

North Yorkshire Moors Railway
Pickering, North Yorkshire
(01751) 472508
nymr.co.uk
Nostalgic steam excursions through spectacular landscapes.

Ripley Castle
Ripley, North Yorkshire
(01423) 770152
ripleycastle.co.uk
Medieval castle set in a delightful estate.

Sewerby Hall and Gardens
Sewerby, East Yorkshire
(01262) 673769
sewerby-hall.co.uk
Country house and gardens in cliff-top location.

Speke Hall, Garden and Estate
Speke, Merseyside
(0151) 427 7231
nationaltrust.org.uk
Wonderful, rambling Tudor mansion with Victorian interiors.

Indoors

1853 Gallery
Shipley, West Yorkshire
(01274) 531163
saltsmill.org.uk
Works by Hockney in historic mill buildings.

BALTIC Centre for Contemporary Art
Gateshead, Tyne and Wear
(0191) 478 1810
balticmill.com
Dynamic international art.

The Bowes Museum
Barnard Castle, Durham
(01833) 690606
thebowesmuseum.org.uk
Outstanding European fine and decorative arts.

Captain Cook Birthplace Museum
Middlesbrough
(01642) 311211
captcook-ne.co.uk
Learn about Cook's life.

Discovery Museum
Newcastle upon Tyne, Tyne and Wear
(0191) 232 6789
twmuseums.org.uk/discovery
The history of Tyneside brought to life.

Imperial War Museum North
Manchester
(0161) 836 4000
iwm.org.uk
Dynamic displays reflecting the impact of war.

Jodrell Bank Visitor Centre
Holmes Chapel, Cheshire
(01477) 571339
jb.man.ac.uk/scicen
Home of the world-famous Lovell Telescope.

Leeds City Art Gallery
Leeds, West Yorkshire
(0113) 247 8256
leeds.gov.uk/artgallery
Remarkable collection of 20thC British art.

The Lowry
Salford, Manchester
(0161) 876 2000
thelowry.com
World-renowned art gallery, exhibitions and theatre.

Millennium Galleries
Sheffield, South Yorkshire
(0114) 278 2600
sheffieldgalleries.org.uk
Vibrant galleries of arts, craft and design.

mima, Middlesbrough Institute of Modern Art
Middlesbrough
(01642) 726720
visitmima.com
Inspiring modern and contemporary art.

National Glass Centre
Sunderland, Tyne and Wear
(0191) 515 5555
nationalglasscentre.com
Stunning displays and live glass-blowing.

National Media Museum
Bradford, West Yorkshire
0870 701 0200
nationalmediamuseum.org.uk
Seven-floor gallery featuring giant IMAX screen.

Royal Armouries Museum
Leeds, West Yorkshire
(0113) 220 1916
royalarmouries.org
Thrilling entertainment and world-famous arms collection.

Tullie House Museum and Art Gallery
Large Visitor Attraction of the Year - Silver
Carlisle, Cumbria
(01228) 618718
tulliehouse.co.uk
Jacobean house, Pre-Raphaelite art and interactive fun.

South Shields Museum and Art Gallery
South Shields, Tyne and Wear
(0191) 456 8740
twmuseums.org.uk/southshields
Explore the history of South Tyneside.

Sunderland Museum and Winter Gardens
Sunderland, Tyne and Wear
(0191) 553 2323
twmuseums.org.uk/sunderland
Stunning winter gardens and imaginative galleries.

Tate Liverpool
Liverpool
(0151) 702 7400
tate.org.uk/liverpool
Housing the National Collection of Modern Art.

Thackray Museum
Leeds, West Yorkshire
(0113) 244 4343
thackraymuseum.org
Experience Victorian slums, explore the human body.

The Whitworth Art Gallery
Manchester
(0161) 275 7450
whitworth.man.ac.uk
Internationally famous collection of British watercolours.

World Museum Liverpool
Liverpool
(0151) 478 4393
liverpoolmuseums.org.uk
Featuring the award-winning Natural History Centre.

The World of Glass
St Helens, Merseyside
(01744) 22766
worldofglass.com
Live glass-blowing and multi-media shows.

Outdoors

Chesters Roman Fort (Hadrian's Wall)
Chollerford, Northumberland
(01434) 681379
english-heritage.org.uk
The best-preserved Roman cavalry fort in Britain.

Go Ape! High Wire Forest Adventure – Grizedale
Grizedale, Cumbria
0845 643 9215
goape.co.uk
High-adrenaline adventure in the trees.

Go Ape! High Wire Forest Adventure – Dalby
Low Dalby, North Yorkshire
0845 643 9215
goape.co.uk
Exhilarating course of bridges, swings and slides.

Hadrian's Wall Path National Trail
Hexham, Northumberland
(01434) 322002
nationaltrail.co.uk/hadrianswall
84-mile trail stretching from coast to coast.

Kielder Castle Forest Park Centre
Kielder, Northumberland
(01434) 250209
forestry.gov.uk
Visitor centre for England's largest forest.

National Wildflower Centre
Liverpool
(0151) 738 1913
nwc.org.uk
A peaceful haven with seasonal wildflower displays.

RHS Garden Harlow Carr
Harrogate, North Yorkshire
(01423) 565418
rhs.org.uk/harlowcarr
Spectacular 58-acre garden with year-round interest.

RSPB Blacktoft Sands Nature Reserve

Whitgift, East Yorkshire
(01405) 704665
rspb.org.uk
Spot avocets, bitterns and marsh harriers.

Windermere Lake Cruises
Lakeside, Cumbria
(015394) 43360
windermere-lakecruises.co.uk
Sail the Lakes on launches and steamers.

WWT Washington Wetland Centre
Washington, Tyne and Wear
(0191) 416 5454
wwt.org.uk
100-acre conservation site with diverse wildlife.

Yorkshire Sculpture Park
Wakefield, West Yorkshire
(01924) 832631
ysp.co.uk
Browse art alfresco on beautiful 18thC parkland.

ASSURANCE OF A GREAT DAY OUT
Attractions with this sign participate in the Visitor Attraction Quality Assurance Scheme which recognises high standards in all aspects of the visitor experience.

Events 2009

Bradford International Film Festival
Bradford
bradfordfilmfestival.org.uk
Feb - Mar

Jorvik Viking Festival
York
jorvik-viking-centre.co.uk
18 - 22 Feb

John Smith's Grand National
Liverpool
aintree.co.uk
2 - 4 Apr

Chester Food and Drink Festival 2009
Chester
chesterfoodanddrink.com
10 - 13 Apr

Arley Horse Trials and Country Fair 2009
Northwich
arleyhallandgardens.com
16 - 17 May

Great Yorkshire Show
Harrogate
greatyorkshireshow.co.uk
Jul

Sunderland International Air Show
Sunderland
sunderland-airshow.com
25 - 26 Jul

Stockton International Riverside Festival
Stockton
sirf.co.uk
29 Jul - 2 Aug

St Leger Festival
Doncaster
doncaster-racecourse.co.uk
Sep

Regional contacts and information

For more information on accommodation, attractions, activities, events and holidays in Northern England, contact one of the following regional or local tourism organisations. Their websites have a wealth of information and many produce free publications to help you get the most out of your visit.

England's Northwest

There are various publications and guides about England's Northwest available from the following Tourist Boards or by logging on to **visitenglandsnorthwest.com** or calling **0845 600 6040**:

Visit Chester and Cheshire
Chester Railway Station, 1st Floor, West Wing Offices, Station Road, Chester CH1 3NT
t (01244) 405600
t 0845 073 1324 (accommodation booking)
e info@visitchesterandcheshire.co.uk
w visitchester.com or visitcheshire.com

Cumbria Tourism
Windermere Road, Staveley, Kendal LA8 9PL
t (015398) 22222
e info@cumbriatourism.org
w golakes.co.uk

The Lancashire and Blackpool Tourist Board
St George's House, St George's Street
Chorley PR7 2AA
t (01257) 226600 (Brochure request)
e info@visitlancashire.com
w visitlancashire.com

Visit Manchester – The Tourist Board For Greater Manchester
Carver's Warehouse, 77 Dale Street
Manchester M2 2HG
t 0161 237 1010
t 0871 222 8223 (information and brochure request)
e touristinformation@visitmanchester.com
w visitmanchester.com

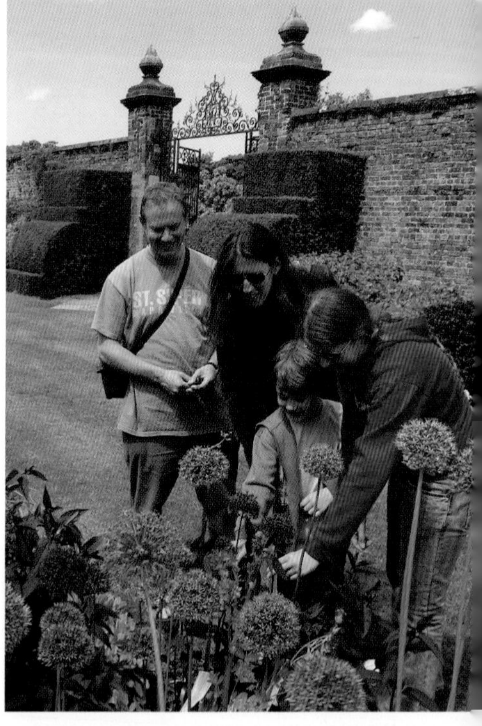

The Mersey Partnership – The Tourist Board for the Liverpool City Region
12 Princes Parade, Liverpool L3 1BG
t (0151) 233 2008 (information enquiries)
t 0844 870 0123 (accommodation booking)
e info@visitliverpool.com (accommodation enquiries)
e 08place@liverpool.gov.uk (information enquiries)
w visitliverpool.com

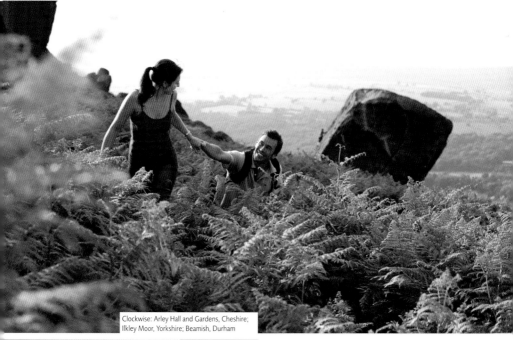

Clockwise: Arley Hall and Gardens, Cheshire; Ilkley Moor, Yorkshire; Beamish, Durham

Yorkshire

The following publications are available from the Yorkshire Tourist Board by logging on to **yorkshire.com** or calling **0844 888 5123**:

- **Yorkshire Accommodation Guide 2009**
  Information on Yorkshire, including hotels, self catering, camping and caravan parks.

- **Make Yorkshire Yours Magazine**
  This entertaining magazine is full of articles and features about what's happening in Yorkshire, including where to go and what to do.

North East

Log on to the North East England website at **visitnortheastengland.com** for further information on accommodation, attractions, events and special offers throughout the region. A range of free guides are available for you to order online or by calling **0870 160 1781**:

- **Holiday and Short Breaks Guide**
  Information on North East England, including hotels, bed and breakfast, self-catering, caravan and camping parks and accessible accommodation as well as events and attractions throughout the region.

- **Cycling Guide**
  A guide to day rides, traffic-free trails and challenging cycling routes.

- **Gardens Guide**
  A guide to the region's most inspirational gardens.

- **Walking Guide**
  Circular trails and long distance routes through breathtaking countryside.

Tourist Information Centres

When you arrive at your destination, visit an Official Partner Tourist Information Centre for quality assured help with accommodation and information about local attractions and events, or email your request before you go. To search for attractions and Tourist Information Centres on the move just text INFO to 62233, and a web link will be sent to your mobile phone. To find a Tourist Information Centre by region visit enjoyEngland.com/find-tic.

Accrington	Town Hall, Blackburn Rd	(01254) 872595	tourism@hyndburnbc.gov.uk
Alnwick	2 The Shambles	(01665) 511333	alnwicktic@alnwick.gov.uk
Altrincham	20 Stamford New Road	(0161) 912 5931	tourist.information@trafford.gov.uk
Ashton-under-Lyne	Wellington Road	(0161) 343 4343	tourist.information@tameside.gov.uk
Aysgarth Falls	Aysgarth Falls National Park Centre	(01969) 662910	aysgarth@ytbtic.co.uk
Barnard Castle	Flatts Road	(01833) 690909	tourism@teesdale.gov.uk
Barnoldswick	Fernlea Avenue	(01282) 666704	tourist.info@pendle.gov.uk
Barrow-in-Furness	Duke Street	(01229) 876505	touristinfo@barrowbc.gov.uk
Batley	Bradford Road	(01924) 426670	batley@ytbtic.co.uk
Beverley	34 Butcher Row	(01482) 391672	beverley.tic@eastriding .gov.uk
Blackburn	50-54 Church Street	(01254) 53277	visit@blackburn.gov.uk
Blackpool	1 Clifton Street	(01253) 478222	tic@blackpool.gov.uk
Bolton	Le Mans Crescent	(01204) 334321	tourist.info@bolton.gov.uk
Bowness	Glebe Road	(015394) 42895	bownesstic@lake-district.gov.uk
Bradford	Centenary Square	(01274) 433678	tourist.information@bradford.gov.uk
Bridlington	25 Prince Street	(01262) 673474	bridlington.tic@eastriding.gov.uk
Brigg	Market Place	(01652) 657053	brigg.tic@northlincs.gov.uk
Burnley	Croft Street	(01282) 664421	tic@burnley.gov.uk
Bury	Market Street	(0161) 253 5111	touristinformation@bury.gov.uk
Carlisle	Greenmarket	(01228) 625600	tourism@carlisle-city.gov.uk
Chester (Town Hall)	Northgate Street	(01244) 402111	tis@chester.gov.uk
Cleethorpes	42-43 Alexandra Road	(01472) 323111	cleetic@nelincs.gov.uk
Cleveleys	Victoria Square	(01253) 853378	cleveleystic@wyrebc.gov.uk
Clitheroe	12-14 Market Place	(01200) 425566	tourism@ribblevalley.gov.uk
Congleton	High Street	(01260) 271095	tourism@congleton.gov.uk
Coniston	Ruskin Avenue	(015394) 41533	mail@conistontic.org
Danby	Lodge Lane	(01439) 772737	moorscentre@northyorkmoors-npa.gov.uk
Darlington	13 Horsemarket	(01325) 388666	tic@darlington.gov.uk
Doncaster	38-40 High Street	(01302) 734309	tourist.information@doncaster.gov.uk

Durham	2 Millennium Place	(0191) 384 3720	touristinfo@durhamcity.gov.uk
Ellesmere Port	Kinsey Road	(0151) 356 7879	cheshireoaks.cc@visitor-centre.net
Filey*	The Evron Centre, John Street	(01723) 383637	fileytic@scarborough.gov.uk
Fleetwood	The Esplanade	(01253) 773953	fleetwoodtic@wyrebc.gov.uk
Garstang	High Street	(01995) 602125	garstangtic@wyrebc.gov.uk
Grassington	Colvend, Hebden Road	(01756) 751690	grassington@ytbtic.co.uk
Guisborough	Church Street	(01287) 633801	guisborough_tic@redcar-cleveland.gov.uk
Halifax	Piece Hall	(01422) 368725	halifax@ytbtic.co.uk
Harrogate	Crescent Road	(01423) 537300	tic@harrogate.gov.uk
Hartlepool	Church Square	(01429) 869706	hpooltic@hartlepool.gov.uk
Hawes	Station Yard	(01969) 666210	hawes@ytbtic.co.uk
Haworth	2/4 West Lane	(01535) 642329	haworth@ytbtic.co.uk
Hebden Bridge	New Road	(01422) 843831	hebdenbridge@ytbtic.co.uk
Helmsley	Helmsley Castle	(01439) 770173	helmsley@ytbtic.co.uk
Hexham	Wentworth Car Park	(01434) 652220	hexham.tic@tynedale.gov.uk
Holmfirth	49-51 Huddersfield Road	(01484) 222444	holmfirth.tic@kirklees.gov.uk
Hornsea*	120 Newbegin	(01964) 536404	hornsea.tic@eastriding.gov.uk
Huddersfield	3 Albion Street	(01484) 223200	huddersfield.tic@kirklees.gov.uk
Hull	1 Paragon Street	(01482) 223559	tourist.information@hullcc.gov.uk
Humber Bridge	Ferriby Road	(01482) 640852	humberbridge.tic@eastriding.gov.uk
Ilkley	Station Rd	(01943) 602319	ilkley@ytbtic.co.uk
Kendal	Highgate	(01539 725758	kendaltic@southlakeland.gov.uk
Keswick	Market Square	(017687) 72645	keswicktic@lake-district.gov.uk
Knaresborough	9 Castle Courtyard	0845 389 0177	kntic@harrogate.gov.uk
Knutsford	Toft Road	(01565) 632611	ktic@macclesfield.gov.uk
Lancaster	29 Castle Hill	(01524) 32878	lancastertic@lancaster.gov.uk
Leeds	The Arcade, City Station	(0113) 242 5242	tourinfo@leeds.gov.uk
Leeming Bar	The Yorkshire Maid, The Great North Road	(01677 424262	leeming@ytbtic.co.uk

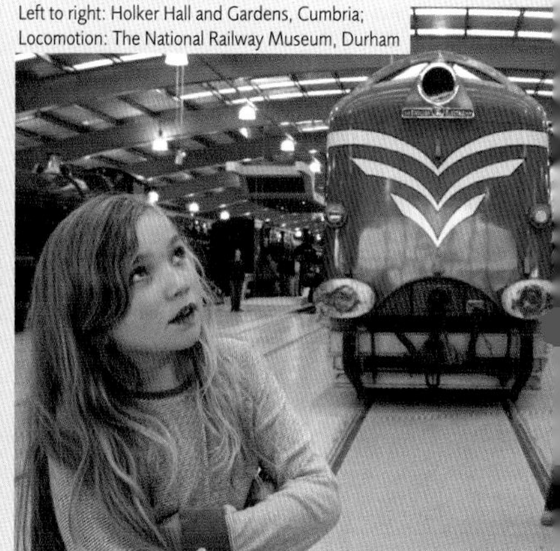

Left to right: Holker Hall and Gardens, Cumbria; Locomotion: The National Railway Museum, Durham

Leyburn	Railway Street	(01969) 623069	leyburn@ytbtic.co.uk
Liverpool 08 Place	Whitechapel	(0151) 233 2459	contact@liverpool.08.com
Liverpool John Lennon Airport	Speke Hall Avenue	0906 680 6886**	info@visitliverpool.com
Lytham St Annes	67 St Annes Road West	(01253) 725610	touristinformation@fylde.gov.uk
Macclesfield	Town Hall	(01625) 504114	informationcentre@macclesfield.gov.uk
Malham	National Park Centre	(01969) 652380	malham@ytbtic.co.uk
Malton	58 Market Place	(01653) 600048	maltontic@btconnect.com
Manchester Visitor Information Centre	Lloyd St	0871 222 8223	touristinformation@marketing-manchester.co.uk
Morecambe	Marine Road Central	(01524) 582808	morecambetic@lancaster.gov.uk
Morpeth	Bridge Street	(01670) 500700	tourism@castlemorpeth.gov.uk
Nantwich	Market Street	(01270) 537359	touristi@crewe-nantwich.gov.uk
Newcastle-upon-Tyne	8-9 Central Arcade	(0191) 277 8000	tourist.info@newcastle.gov.uk
Northwich	1 The Arcade	(01606) 353534	tourism@valeroyal.gov.uk
Oldham	12 Albion Street	(0161) 627 1024	ecs.tourist@oldham.gov.uk
Otley	Nelson Street	(01943) 462485	otleytic@leedslearning.net
Pateley Bridge*	18 High Street	0845 389 0177	pbtic@harrogate.gov.uk
Pendle Heritage Centre	Park Hill	(01282) 661701	heritage.centre@pendle.gov.uk
Penrith	Middlegate	(01768) 867466	pen.tic@eden.gov.uk
Pickering	The Ropery	(01751) 473791	pickering@ytbtic.co.uk
Preston	Lancaster Road	(01772) 253731	tourism@preston.gov.uk
Redcar	Esplanade	(01642) 471921	redcar_tic@redcar-cleveland.gov.uk
Reeth	Hudson House, The Green	(01748) 884059	reeth@ytbtic.co.uk
Richmond	Victoria Road	(01748) 828742	richmond@ytbtic.co.uk
Ripon	Minster Road	(01765) 604625	ripontic@harrogate.gov.uk
Rochdale	The Esplanade	(01706) 924928	tic@link4life.org
Rotherham	40 Bridgegate	(01709) 835904	tic@rotherham.gov.uk
St Helens	The World of Glass	(01744) 755150	info@sthelenstic.com
Salford	The Lowry, Pier 8	(0161) 848 8601	tic@salford.gov.uk
Saltburn-by-the-Sea	3 Station Buildings	(01287) 622422	saltburn_tic@redcar-cleveland.gov.uk
Scarborough	Brunswick Shopping Centre	(01723) 383636	tourismbureau@scarborough.gov.uk
Scarborough (Harbourside)	Sandside	(01723) 383636	harboursidetic@scarborough.gov.uk
Settle	Cheapside	(01729) 825192	settle@ytbtic.co.uk
Sheffield	14 Norfolk Row	(0114) 2211900	visitor@sheffield.gov.uk
Skipton	35 Coach Street	(01756) 792809	skipton@ytbtic.co.uk
Stockport	30 Market Place	(0161) 474 4444	tourist.information@stockport.gov.uk
Sunderland	50 Fawcett Street	(0191) 553 2000	tourist.info@sunderland.gov.uk
Sutton Bank	Sutton Bank Visitor Centre	(01845) 597426	suttonbank@ytbtic.co.uk

Thirsk	49 Market Place	(01845) 522755	thirsktic@hambleton.gov.uk
Todmorden	15 Burnley Road	(01706) 818181	todmorden@ytbtic.co.uk
Wakefield	9 The Bull Ring	0845 601 8353	tic@wakefield.gov.uk
Warrington	Academy Way	(01925) 428585	informationcentre@warrington.gov.uk
Wetherby	17 Westgate	(01937) 582151	wetherbytic@leedslearning.net
Whitby	Langborne Road	(01723) 383637	whitbytic@scarborough.gov.uk
Whitehaven	Market Place	(01946) 598914	tic@copelandbc.gov.uk
Wigan	62 Wallgate	(01942) 825677	tic@wlct.org
Wilmslow	Rectory Fields	(01625) 522275	i.hillaby@macclesfield.gov.uk
Windermere	Victoria Street	(015394) 46499	windermeretic@southlakeland.gov.uk
Withernsea*	131 Queen Street	(01964) 615683	withernsea.tic@eastriding.gov.uk
York (De Grey Rooms)	Exhibition Square	(01904) 550099	info@visityork.org
York (Railway Station)	Station Road	(01904) 550099	info@visityork.org

*seasonal opening

**calls to this number are charged at premium rate

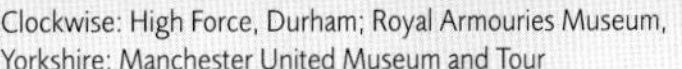

Clockwise: High Force, Durham; Royal Armouries Museum, Yorkshire; Manchester United Museum and Tour

Country ways

The Countryside Rights of Way Act gives people new rights to walk on areas of open countryside and registered common land.

To find out where you can go and what you can do, as well as information about taking your dog to the countryside, go online at countrysideaccess.gov.uk.

And when you're out and about...

Always follow the Country Code

- Be safe – plan ahead and follow any signs
- Leave gates and property as you find them
- Protect plants and animals, and take your litter home
- Keep dogs under close control
- Consider other people

where to stay in

Northern England

All place names in the blue bands are shown on the maps at the front of this guide.

A complete listing of all VisitBritain assessed parks in England appears at the back.

Accommodation symbols

Symbols give useful information about services and facilities. On page 7 you can find a key to these symbols.

APPLEBY-IN-WESTMORLAND, Cumbria Map ref 5B3

★★★★★
HOLIDAY, TOURING & CAMPING PARK

(226) £17.00–£31.50
(157) £17.00–£31.50
(65) £17.00–£31.50
226 touring pitches

Wild Rose Park

Ormside, Appleby-in-Westmorland CA16 6EJ **t** (017683) 51077

Friendly, family park in the lovely, unspoilt Eden Valley with mountain views. Within easy reach of the Lakes and the Dales. Spotless, super loos and private wash cubicles.

open All year
payment Credit/debit cards, cash, cheques

General Leisure

BAMBURGH, Northumberland Map ref 5C1

★★★
HOLIDAY & TOURING PARK

(34) £17.00–£18.00
(34) £17.00–£18.00
34 touring pitches

Glororum Caravan Park

Glororum, Bamburgh NE69 7AW **t** (01668) 214457 **e** info@glororum-caravanpark.co.uk

glororum-caravanpark.co.uk

Situated one mile from Bamburgh in peaceful surroundings within easy reach of many historic castles including Alnwick with its magnificent gardens. Endless walks on award-winning beaches only a mile away. No tents.

open April to October
payment Credit/debit cards, cash, cheques

General Leisure

BAMBURGH, Northumberland Map ref 5C1

★★★★
HOLIDAY, TOURING & CAMPING PARK
ROSE AWARD

(150) £12.00–£21.00
(150) £12.00–£21.00
(30) £7.80–£21.00
(27) £255.00–£585.00
150 touring pitches

Please see website for promotions and details of our wigwams too!

Meadowhead's Waren Caravan and Camping Park

Waren Mill, Belford NE70 7EE **t** (01668) 214366 **e** waren@meadowhead.co.uk

meadowhead.co.uk SPECIAL OFFERS

open 20 March to 30 October
payment Credit/debit cards, cash, cheques, euros

Nestled in coastal countryside with great views to Holy Island and Bamburgh Castle. Waren offers restaurant-bar, splash-pool and play facilities. Our happy environment is great if you wish to stay on-site but we also make a great base from which to explore Northumberland's coast and castles, from Alnwick to Berwick.

SAT NAV *NE70 7EE* **ONLINE MAP**

General Leisure

BEDALE, North Yorkshire Map ref 5C3

★★★★
TOURING & CAMPING PARK

(25) £9.00–£11.00
(25) £9.00–£11.00
(25) £6.00–£8.00
(3) £90.00–£180.00
25 touring pitches

Pembroke Caravan Park

19 Low Street, Leeming Bar, Northallerton DL7 9BW **t** (01677) 422652

Small, sheltered site catering for touring vans, including motor caravans and tents. Excellent A1 night halt.

open March to October
payment Cash, cheques

General Leisure

BLACKPOOL, Lancashire Map ref 4A1

★★★★
HOLIDAY PARK

(18) £155.00–£535.00

Newton Hall Holiday Park

Staining Road, Blackpool FY3 0AX **t** (01253) 882512 **e** reception@newtonhall.net

partingtons.com

open 1 March to 15 November
payment Credit/debit cards, cash, cheques

Family park ideally situated in open country, 2.5 miles from Blackpool town centre. Caravans and flats for hire. New leisure complex. Regular live entertainment. No pets. Loads to do.

SAT NAV *FY3 0AX*

General Leisure

BLACKPOOL, Lancashire Map ref 4A1

★★★
HOLIDAY, TOURING & CAMPING PARK

£14.50–£22.00
£14.50–£22.00
(6) £155.00–£535.00
122 touring pitches

Windy Harbour Holiday Centre

Windy Harbour Road, Singleton FY6 8NB **t** (01253) 883064 **e** info@windyharbour.net

windyharbour.net

open 1 March to 15 November
payment Credit/debit cards, cash, cheques

Situated on banks of River Wyre in the beautiful Fylde countryside. Family-run park with many facilities including club with family room, newly refurbished swimming pool, extensive outdoor play area, amusement arcade and shop. Very easy access from M55 motorway.

SAT NAV *FY6 8NB*

General Leisure

BOLTON ABBEY, North Yorkshire Map ref 4B1

★★★★★
TOURING PARK

(57) £14.00–£26.60
(57) £14.00–£26.60
57 touring pitches

Strid Wood Caravan Club Site

Skipton BD23 6AN **t** (01756) 710433

caravanclub.co.uk

One of the prettiest sites on our network and part of the Bolton Abbey Estate in open glades surrounded by woodland and the glorious Yorkshire Dales. Within the boundaries of the estate are some 75 miles of footpaths through moors, woods and farmland.

open March 2009 to January 2010
payment Credit/debit cards, cash, cheques

General

BOUTH, Cumbria Map ref 5A3

★★★★★
HOLIDAY & TOURING PARK
ROSE AWARD

(26) £12.50–£21.00
(4) £12.50–£21.00
(3) £200.00–£515.00
30 touring pitches

Black Beck Caravan Park

Bouth, Ulverston LA12 8JN **t** (01229) 861274 **e** reception@blackbeck.com

open 1 March to 15 November
payment Credit/debit cards, cash, cheques

Black Beck is situated within the Lake District National Park, nestled in the beautiful Rusland Valley between the southern tips of Lake Windermere and Coniston. Surrounded by spectacular woodland scenery. Jacuzzi and sauna.

SAT NAV *LA12 8JN*

General Leisure

BURY, Greater Manchester Map ref 4B1

★★★★★
TOURING PARK

(85) £14.00–£26.60
(85) £14.00–£26.60
85 touring pitches

Burrs Country Park Caravan Club Site

Woodhill Road, Bury BL8 1BN **t** (0161) 761 0489

caravanclub.co.uk

open All year
payment Credit/debit cards, cash, cheques

On a historic mill site, Burrs has much to offer, including relaxing river and countryside walks as well as easy access into Manchester.

SAT NAV *BL8 1BN*

Special member rates mean you can save your membership subscription in less than a week. Visit our website to find out more.

General

CHESTER, Cheshire Map ref 4A2

★★★★★
TOURING & CAMPING PARK

(100) £14.90–£28.30
(100) £14.90–£28.30
on application
100 touring pitches

THE CARAVAN CLUB

Chester Fairoaks Caravan Club Site

Rake Lane, Little Stanney, Chester CH2 4HS **t** (0151) 355 1600

caravanclub.co.uk

A tranquil site only six miles from the walled city of Chester with its famous zoo, historic sites, top-class entertainment and excellent shopping. Take an open-top bus or walk around the walls to absorb the colourful atmosphere.

open All year
payment Credit/debit cards, cash, cheques

General Leisure

CHESTER, Cheshire Map ref 4A2

★★★★★
HOLIDAY, TOURING & CAMPING PARK

(45) £12.00–£19.00
(15) £12.00–£19.00
(15) £12.00–£19.00
(6) £250.00–£450.00
45 touring pitches

Manor Wood Country Caravan Park

Manor Wood, Coddington, Chester CH3 9EN **t** (01829) 782990 & 07762 817827
e info@manorwoodcaravans.co.uk

cheshire-caravan-sites.co.uk

Touring caravan park for 45 units in the Cheshire countryside. Enjoying spectacular views, fishing, swimming, play area and a tennis court on site. Accessible to all.

open All year
payment Credit/debit cards, cash, cheques

General Leisure

For **key to symbols** see page 7

CONISTON, Cumbria Map ref 5A3

★★★★★
HOLIDAY PARK
ROSE AWARD

(6) Min £17.00
(15) £205.00–£560.00

Crake Valley Holiday Park

Lake Bank, Water Yeat, Ulverston LA12 8DL **t** (01229) 885203 **e** crakevalley@coniston1.fslife.co.uk

crakevalley.co.uk

Small, top-graded holiday park. Caravans and lodges for hire in secluded setting opposite Coniston Water. Ideal base for touring the Lakes.

open March to October
payment Cash, cheques

General

CONISTON, Cumbria Map ref 5A3

★★★★
TOURING & CAMPING PARK

(280) £12.20–£25.10
(280) £12.20–£25.10
on application
280 touring pitches

THE CARAVAN CLUB

Park Coppice Caravan Club Site

Park Gate, Coniston LA21 8LA **t** (015394) 41555

caravanclub.co.uk

open March to November
payment Credit/debit cards, cash, cheques

Landscaped site set in 63 acres of National Trust woodland. Lake for watersports, on-site play areas, orienteering courses and Red Squirrel Nature Trail.

SAT NAV *LA21 8LA*

Special member rates mean you can save your membership subscription in less than a week. Visit our website to find out more.

General Leisure

CORBRIDGE, Northumberland Map ref 5B2

★★★
TOURING & CAMPING PARK

(40) £11.00–£14.00
(40) £11.00–£14.00
(40) £4.00–£10.00
40 touring pitches

Well House Farm – Corbridge

Newton, Stocksfield NE43 7UY **t** (01661) 842193 **e** info@wellhousefarm.co.uk

wellhousefarm.co.uk

Peaceful family-run site on a farm near Corbridge one mile south of Hadrian's Wall. Ideal for exploring Northumberland and surrounding areas.

open March to October
payment Cash, cheques

General Leisure

DURHAM Map ref 5C2

★★★★
TOURING PARK

(20) Max £16.00
(20) Max £16.00
(2)
50 touring pitches

Finchale Abbey Caravan Park

Finchale Abbey Farm, Finchale Abbey, Durham DH1 5SH **t** (0191) 386 6528 & 07989 854704
e godricawatson@hotmail.com

finchaleabbey.co.uk GUEST REVIEWS

open All year
payment Credit/debit cards, cash, cheques

Finchdale Abbey (Priory) touring park is set in beautiful countryside overlooking the ruins, surrounded by the River Wear. Fishing, golf, riverside walks and the local bar are a short distance away. Durham is 2.75 miles away by bike along scenic bridle paths. New, fully serviced supersites £20 per night.

SAT NAV *DH1 5SH* **ONLINE MAP**

General Leisure

DURHAM Map ref 5C2

★★★★★ TOURING & CAMPING PARK

(77) £14.00–£26.60
(77) £14.00–£26.60
on application
77 touring pitches

Grange Caravan Club Site

Meadow Lane, Durham DH1 1TL **t** (0191) 384 4778

caravanclub.co.uk

open All year
payment Credit/debit cards, cash, cheques

An open, level site, this is a lovely location for a short break and an ideal stopover en route to or from Scotland.

SAT NAV *DH1 1TL*

Special member rates mean you can save your membership subscription in less than a week. Visit our website to find out more.

General Leisure

DURHAM Map ref 5C2

★★★★ HOLIDAY, TOURING & CAMPING PARK

ROSE AWARD

(35) £13.50–£16.50
(35) £13.50–£16.50
(10) £13.50–£16.50
(3) £295.00–£350.00
45 touring pitches

Strawberry Hill Farm Camping & Caravanning Park

Running Waters, Old Cassop, Durham DH6 4QA **t** (0191) 372 3457 **e** info@strawberryhf.co.uk

strawberry-hill-farm.co.uk

Situated in open countryside with magnificent, panoramic views. Ideally situated to explore the World Heritage site of the castle and cathedral. For further details please see website.

open March to December
payment Credit/debit cards, cash, cheques, euros

General Leisure

EBCHESTER, Durham Map ref 5B2

★★★★ TOURING & CAMPING PARK

(31) £9.50–£10.50
(6) £9.50–£10.50
(6) £8.00–£12.00
31 touring pitches

Byreside Caravan Site

Hamsterley Colliery, Newcastle upon Tyne NE17 7RT **t** (01207) 560280

byresidecaravansite.co.uk

Quiet and secluded site on family-run farm, adjacent to Derwent Walk Country Park and cycle track. Easy access to both Durham and Northumberland countryside.

open All year
payment Credit/debit cards, cash, cheques

General

FILEY, North Yorkshire Map ref 5D3

★★★★★ HOLIDAY PARK

£12.00–£20.00
£12.00–£20.00
(25) £12.00–£20.00
60 touring pitches

Orchard Farm Holiday Village

Stonegate, Hunmanby, Filey YO14 0PU **t** (01723) 891582

Family park in edge-of-village location with easy access to resorts of Filey, Scarborough and Bridlington. Amenities include children's play area, fishing lake and entertainment during peak season.

open March to October
payment Cash, cheques

General Leisure

What shall we do today?

For ideas on places to visit, see the beginning of this regional section or go online at visitbritain.com.

FRODSHAM, Cheshire Map ref 4A2

★★★★
HOLIDAY PARK
(10) £214.00–£577.00

Ridgeway Country Holiday Park

The Ridgeway, Frodsham WA6 6XQ **t** (01928) 734981 **e** sue@ridgewaypark.com

ridgewaypark.com

open 1 March to 2 January
payment Credit/debit cards, cash, cheques

An ideal base for exploring the scenic Cheshire countryside, yet within close proximity to Liverpool and Chester. Prices weekly for the lodges and caravans. Short-break prices available.

SAT NAV *WA6 6XQ* **ONLINE MAP**

General Leisure

GRANGE-OVER-SANDS, Cumbria Map ref 5A3

★★★★
HOLIDAY & TOURING PARK
ROSE AWARD

(3) £11.00–£15.00
(3) £11.00–£15.00
(5) £10.00–£13.00
(2) £250.00–£375.00
8 touring pitches

Greaves Farm Caravan Park

Field Broughton, Grange-over-Sands LA11 6HR **t** (015395) 36329 & (015395) 36587

Small, quiet site two miles north of Cartmel. A convenient base for Lake District touring, and under personal supervision of the owner. Directions given with booking confirmation.

open March to October
payment Cash, cheques

General

GRANGE-OVER-SANDS, Cumbria Map ref 5A3

★★★★★
TOURING PARK
(131) £14.00–£26.60
(131) £14.00–£26.60
131 touring pitches

Meathop Fell Caravan Club Site

Meathop, Grange-over-Sands LA11 6RB **t** (015395) 32912

caravanclub.co.uk

open All year
payment Credit/debit cards, cash, cheques

Peaceful site, ideal for exploring the southern Lake District. Kendal, famous for its mint cake, is within easy reach; Grange-over-Sands and Ulverston are close by.

SAT NAV *LA11 6RB*

Special member rates mean you can save your membership subscription in less than a week. Visit our website to find out more.

General Leisure

HARROGATE, North Yorkshire Map ref 4B1

★★★★★
HOLIDAY & TOURING PARK
(200) £16.00–£18.00
(57) £16.00–£18.00
200 touring pitches

High Moor Farm Park

Skipton Road, Felliscliffe, Harrogate HG3 2LT **t** (01423) 563637 **e** highmoorfarmpark@btconnect.com

Secluded site surrounded by trees on the edge of the Yorkshire Dales.

open April to October
payment Credit/debit cards, cash, cheques

General Leisure

HARROGATE, North Yorkshire Map ref 4B1

★★★★★
HOLIDAY, TOURING & CAMPING PARK
ROSE AWARD

- £16.00–£32.00
- £16.00–£32.00
- £16.00–£32.00

141 touring pitches

Peak season: 7 nights for the price of 6. Off-peak season: 4 nights for the price of 3.

Rudding Holiday Park

Follifoot, Harrogate HG3 1JH **t** (01423) 870439 **e** holiday-park@ruddingpark.com

ruddingpark.com SPECIAL OFFERS

payment Credit/debit cards, cash, cheques, euros

Award-winning campsite just three miles south of Harrogate, in peaceful setting, offering Deer House pub, swimming pool, golf course, six-hole short course, driving range and shop. Closed February. Self-catering timber lodges also available.

SAT NAV *HG3 1JH* **ONLINE MAP**

General Leisure

HAWES, North Yorkshire Map ref 5B3

★★★

HOLIDAY, TOURING & CAMPING PARK

- (25) Min £11.50
- (5) Min £11.00
- (40) Min £11.00
- (2) £170.00–£215.00

70 touring pitches

Bainbridge Ings Caravan and Camping Site

Hawes DL8 3NU **t** (01969) 667354 **e** janet@bainbridge-ings.co.uk

bainbridge-ings.co.uk

Quiet, clean, well-organised, family-run site. Pitches situated around the edge of open fields with magnificent views. Ten-minute walk into Hawes. Excellent centre for walking and touring the Dales.

payment Cash, cheques

General Leisure

HAWKSHEAD, Cumbria Map ref 5A3

★★★★
HOLIDAY, TOURING & CAMPING PARK

- (25) £17.50–£21.50
- £15.00–£17.75
- (75) £15.00–£17.75
- (20) £264.00–£520.00

100 touring pitches

The Croft Caravan and Camp Site

North Lonsdale Road, Hawkshead, Ambleside LA22 0NX **t** (015394) 36374
e enquiries@hawkshead-croft.com

hawkshead-croft.com

Quiet family site at Hawkshead village, close to shops and pubs. Flat, grassy and well-sheltered holiday homes for hire.

open Mid-March to 19 January
payment Credit/debit cards, cash, cheques

General Leisure

HAWORTH, West Yorkshire Map ref 4B1

★★★★
HOLIDAY, TOURING & CAMPING PARK

- £11.00–£19.50
- (2) Min £10.00
- (15) Min £9.50
- (2) £100.00–£295.00

60 touring pitches

Upwood Holiday Park

Blackmoor Road, Oxenhope, Haworth, Keighley BD22 9SS **t** (01535) 644242
e info@upwoodpark.co.uk

upwoodpark.co.uk SPECIAL OFFERS

payment Credit/debit cards, cash, cheques

A family-owned park pleasantly situated close to the Yorkshire Dales National Park – an ideal base from which to explore the area by car or on foot. Large, modern toilet facilities, comfortable lounge bar serving snacks, games room with pool and table tennis, small shop for essential items.

SAT NAV *BD22 9SS* **ONLINE MAP**

General Leisure

For **key to symbols** see page 7

HAYDON BRIDGE, Northumberland Map ref 5B2

★★★★
HOLIDAY, TOURING & CAMPING PARK

(8) £14.00
(8) £14.00
(3) £8.00–£14.00

Poplars Riverside Caravan Park

East Lands Ends, Haydon Bridge, Hexham NE47 6BY **t** (01434) 684427

A secluded riverside site at Haydon Bridge with 550yds to fishing. Near to shops and convenient for Hadrian's Wall.

open March to October
payment Cash, cheques

General Leisure

HEBDEN BRIDGE, West Yorkshire Map ref 4B1

★★★★★
TOURING PARK

(45) £9.30–£20.70
(45) £9.30–£20.70
45 touring pitches

THE CARAVAN CLUB

Lower Clough Foot Caravan Club Site

Cragg Vale, Hebden Bridge HX7 5RU **t** (01422) 882531

caravanclub.co.uk

open March to November
payment Credit/debit cards, cash, cheques

Pretty site, set in a grassy enclave, well screened by mature trees and bordered by a stream. Good for walkers.

SAT NAV *HX7 5RU*

Special member rates mean you can save your membership subscription in less than a week. Visit our website to find out more.

General Leisure

HEXHAM, Northumberland Map ref 5B2

★★★★
TOURING & CAMPING PARK

(32) £13.50–£14.50
(6) £13.50–£14.50
(10) £9.50–£12.00
42 touring pitches

Fallowfield Dene Caravan and Camping Park

Acomb, Hexham NE46 4RP **t** (01434) 603553 **e** den@fallowfielddene.co.uk

fallowfielddene.co.uk

In unspoilt countryside, 1.5 miles from the village of Acomb. The site is within easy reach of Hadrian's Wall and many places of interest.

open March to November
payment Credit/debit cards, cash, cheques

General Leisure

HEXHAM, Northumberland Map ref 5B2

★★★
TOURING & CAMPING PARK

(40) £12.00–£15.00
(30) £12.00–£15.00
(16) Min £8.00
40 touring pitches

Hexham Racecourse Caravan Site

Yarridge Road, High Yarridge, Hexham NE46 2JP **t** (01434) 606847 **e** hexrace@aol.com

hexham-racecourse.co.uk

Set in beautiful open countryside with panoramic views. Close to Hadrian's Wall, and within travelling distance of Northumberland, County Durham, Cumbria and Tyneside.

open May to September
payment Cash, cheques

General Leisure

Do you have access needs?

Look for the National Accessible Scheme symbols if you have special hearing, visual or mobility needs. An index of parks participating in the scheme can be found at the back of this guide.

HEYSHAM, Lancashire Map ref 5A3

★★★
HOLIDAY, TOURING & CAMPING PARK

£15.00–£19.00
£15.00–£19.00
(11) £10.00–£14.50
(26) £149.00–£497.00
87 touring pitches

Ocean Edge Leisure Park

Moneyclose Lane, Morecambe LA3 2XA **t** 0870 774 4024 **e** enquiries@southlakelandparks.co.uk

southlakelandparks.co.uk SPECIAL OFFERS · REAL-TIME BOOKING

A scenic park situated on the shores of Morecambe Bay. The park facilities are unrivalled including indoor heated swimming pool, family cabaret lounge with themed weekends, children's indoor play area and amusement arcade.

open 1 March to 15 November
payment Credit/debit cards, cash, cheques

General
Leisure

HOLMFIRTH, West Yorkshire Map ref 4B1

★★★★
TOURING & CAMPING PARK

(62) £11.00–£12.00
(62) £9.50–£11.00
(62) £9.50–£11.00
62 touring pitches

Fourth night free for every 3 nights booked from 7 Jun-9 Jul 09 upon producing this advertisement when paying at reception.

Holme Valley Camping and Caravan Park

Thongsbridge, Holmfirth HD9 7TD **t** (01484) 665819 **e** enquiries@holmevalleycamping.com

holmevalleycamping.com

open All year
payment Credit/debit cards, cash, cheques, euros

Picturesque, peaceful park in central 'Summer Wine' country. Grass, concrete and gravel pitches. Optional 16-amp hook-ups. Well-stocked food shop with off-licence. Fishing in small lake and river. Small children's play area. Five minutes' walk from village with pub food, post office, buses and trains. David Bellamy Gold Conservation Award.

SAT NAV *HD9 7TD*

General Leisure

KENDAL, Cumbria Map ref 5B3

★★★★
HOLIDAY, TOURING & CAMPING PARK

(26) £12.50–£22.00
(26) £12.50–£22.00
(5) £8.00–£22.00
26 touring pitches

Waters Edge Caravan Park

Crooklands, Milnthorpe LA7 7NN **t** (015395) 67708

watersedgecaravanpark.co.uk

open 1 March to 14 November
payment Credit/debit cards, cash, cheques

Small, friendly site set in open countryside close to M6. Lake District, Morecambe, Yorkshire Dales within easy reach. All hardstanding pitches. Reception area with small shop. Lounge, bar, pool room, patio area. Modern shower block with laundry and washing-up facilities. Local pub/restaurant within 300yds.

SAT NAV *LA7 7NN*

General Leisure

Check the maps for park locations

Colour maps at the front pinpoint all the places where parks are featured within the regional sections of this guide. Pick your location and then refer to the place index at the back to find the page number.

For **key to symbols** see page 7

KESWICK, Cumbria Map ref 5A3

★★★★
TOURING & CAMPING PARK

£10.00–£15.50
(3) £10.00–£15.50
(80) £9.00–£11.50
13 touring pitches

Castlerigg Farm Camping and Caravan Site

Castlerigg, Keswick CA12 4TE **t** (017687) 72479 **e** info@castleriggfarm.com

castleriggfarm.com GUEST REVIEWS • SPECIAL OFFERS • REAL-TIME BOOKING

A quiet, family-run site with exceptional panoramic views. Ideal base for walking. Approximately 25 minutes' walk to Keswick. Site located on left of lane.

open March to November
payment Cash, cheques

General Leisure

KESWICK, Cumbria Map ref 5A3

★★★★
HOLIDAY, TOURING & CAMPING PARK

(53) £15.00–£21.00
(53) £14.00–£21.00
(120) £13.00–£16.00
(7) £220.00–£470.00

10% discount on your stay for all ANWB, ACSI, ADAC cardholders.

Castlerigg Hall Caravan & Camping Park

Castlerigg Hall, Keswick CA12 4TE **t** (017687) 74499 **e** info@castlerigg.co.uk

castlerigg.co.uk SPECIAL OFFERS

open 20 March to 9 November
payment Credit/debit cards, cash, cheques

Situated 1.5 miles south east of the pretty market town of Keswick, our elevated position commands wonderful panoramic views of Derwentwater and the surrounding fells. Formerly a Lakeland hill farm, Castlerigg Hall has been sympathetically developed into a quality touring park. Many scenic walks are available directly from the park.

SAT NAV *CA12 4TE*

General Leisure

KIRKBY LONSDALE, Cumbria Map ref 5B3

★★★★★
HOLIDAY, TOURING & CAMPING PARK

(17) £11.00–£24.00
(17) £11.00–£24.00
(12) £11.00–£17.00
17 touring pitches

Woodclose Caravan Park

Kirkby Lonsdale LA6 2SE **t** (01524) 271597 **e** info@woodclosepark.com

woodclosepark.com

open March to November
payment Credit/debit cards, cash, cheques

A quiet, picturesque, exclusive site situated between the Lakes and the Dales, a short walk from Kirkby Lonsdale. All pitches are supplied with electric and TV hook-up points. The camping field is sheltered and secluded. Children's play area and shop. David Bellamy Gold Conservation Award.

SAT NAV *LA6 2SE*

General Leisure

KIRKBY STEPHEN, Cumbria Map ref 5B3

★★★★★
TOURING & CAMPING PARK

(43) £15.20–£17.00
(43)
(15)
58 touring pitches

Pennine View Caravan Park

Station Road, Kirkby Stephen CA17 4SZ **t** (017683) 71717

Family-run caravan park on edge of small market town of Kirkby Stephen, just off A685. Easy reach of Lake District and Yorkshire Dales.

open March to October
payment Credit/debit cards, cash, cheques

General Leisure

KNARESBOROUGH, North Yorkshire Map ref 4B1

★★★★★
TOURING PARK
(70) £14.00–£26.60
(70) £14.00–£26.60
on application
70 touring pitches

THE CARAVAN CLUB

Knaresborough Caravan Club Site

New Road, Scotton, Knaresborough HG5 9HH **t** (01342) 336732

caravanclub.co.uk

open March 2009 to January 2010
payment Credit/debit cards, cash, cheques

Popular family destination located in Lower Nidderdale, gateway to the Yorkshire Dales. Knaresborough and the city of Harrogate are within easy reach.

SAT NAV *HG5 9HH*

Special member rates mean you can save your membership subscription in less than a week. Visit our website to find out more.

General Leisure

LAMPLUGH, Cumbria Map ref 5A3

★★★★
TOURING PARK
(53) £9.30–£20.70
(53) £9.30–£20.70
53 touring pitches

Dockray Meadow Caravan Club Site

Lamplugh CA14 4SH **t** (01946) 861357

caravanclub.co.uk

open March to November
payment Credit/debit cards, cash, cheques

Site close to lesser-known lake beauties including Cogra Moss and Ennerdale. Within easy reach of Keswick.

SAT NAV *CA14 4SH*

Special member rates mean you can save your membership subscription in less than a week. Visit our website to find out more.

General Leisure

LANCASTER, Lancashire Map ref 5A3

★★★
TOURING & CAMPING PARK
(30) £11.00–£14.00
(5) £11.00–£14.00
(5) £7.00–£10.00
40 touring pitches

New Parkside Farm Caravan Park

Denny Beck, Caton Road LA2 9HH **t** (01524) 770723

Peaceful, friendly grassy park on a working farm with extensive views of Lune Valley and Ingleborough. Excellent base for exploring Morecambe Bay, the Lake District and Yorkshire Dales.

open March to October
payment Cash, cheques

General Leisure

LEEDS, West Yorkshire Map ref 4B1

★★★★
HOLIDAY, TOURING & CAMPING PARK
(30) £12.50–£15.00
(15) £12.50–£15.00
(15) £10.00–£15.00
60 touring pitches

St Helena's Caravan Site

Otley Old Road, Leeds LS18 5HZ **t** (0113) 284 1142

Secluded site with showers, WCs and washing facilities. Local amenities include golf, fishing, walking. Ten minutes' drive to Otley and the Yorkshire Dales. Note: over 18s only.

open April to October
payment Cash, cheques

General Leisure

LEEDS BRADFORD INTERNATIONAL AIRPORT

See under Leeds

LOFTHOUSE, North Yorkshire Map ref 5B3

★★★★
TOURING & CAMPING PARK
£12.00–£27.00
£12.00–£27.00
£12.00–£27.00
40 touring pitches

Studfold Farm Caravan and Camping Park

Studfold Farm, Lofthouse, Pateley Bridge HG3 5SG **t** (01423) 755084
e ianwalker@studfold.fsnet.co.uk

studfoldfarm.co.uk GUEST REVIEWS · SPECIAL OFFERS

Studfold Farm Caravan and Camping Park is superbly situated at the heart of Nidderdale in North Yorkshire, seven miles north of Pateley Bridge, in beautiful hill country close to How Stean Gorge.

open Easter to October
payment Cash, cheques

General Leisure

MARKINGTON, North Yorkshire Map ref 5C3

★★★★
HOLIDAY, TOURING & CAMPING PARK
(12) £16.00–£20.00
(2) £16.00–£20.00
(6) £16.00–£20.00
(5) £280.00–£375.00
12 touring pitches

Yorkshire Hussar Inn & Caravan Park

J S Brayshaw Caravans Ltd, High Street, Markington, Nr Harrogate HG3 3NR **t** (01765) 677327
e yorkshirehussar@yahoo.co.uk

yorkshire-hussar-inn.co.uk

Yorkshire Hussar Inn Holiday Caravan Park is a secluded family park behind a village pub, with five luxury holiday caravans for hire. Close to Fountains Abbey and the Dales.

open Easter to October
payment Cash, cheques

General Leisure

MORECAMBE, Lancashire Map ref 5A3

★★★★
HOLIDAY PARK
(14) £178.00–£552.00

Regent Leisure Park

Westgate, Morecambe LA3 3DF **t** 0870 774 4024 **e** enquiries@southlakelandparks.co.uk

southlakelandparks.co.uk SPECIAL OFFERS · REAL-TIME BOOKING

Regent's excellent facilities include family cabaret lounge, indoor children's play area, an indoor leisure centre with heated pool and an outdoor weather pitch. Caravans fully equipped with two and three bedrooms available.

open 1 March to 15 January
payment Credit/debit cards, cash, cheques

General Leisure

PENRITH, Cumbria Map ref 5B2

★★★★★
HOLIDAY & TOURING PARK
(45) £18.00–£21.00
(7) £18.00–£21.00
52 touring pitches

Luxury pine holiday lodges for sale. See website for details.

Flusco Wood Caravan Park

Flusco, Penrith CA11 0JB **t** (017684) 80020 **e** admin@fluscowood.co.uk

fluscowood.co.uk

open Easter to October
payment Cash, cheques

A very high-standard and quiet woodland touring caravan park with fully serviced pitches and centrally heated amenity building. Short drive to many attractions and places of interest in the Lake District.

SAT NAV *CA11 0JB*

General Leisure

PICKERING, North Yorkshire Map ref 5D3

★★★★
HOLIDAY, TOURING & CAMPING PARK
(41) £16.00
(41) £16.00
41 touring pitches

Wayside Caravan Park

Pickering YO18 8PG **t** (01751) 472608 **e** waysideparks@freenet.co.uk

waysideparks.co.uk

Sheltered, quiet, south-facing holiday home, touring park, delightfully located with lovely country views. A walker's paradise. Steam railway. Castle Howard nearby. Whitby, Scarborough and York within a 45-minute drive. Holiday homes for sale.

open March to October
payment Credit/debit cards, cash, cheques

General Leisure

POOLEY BRIDGE, Cumbria Map ref 5A3

★★★★
CAMPING PARK
£12.00–£22.00
(90) £12.00–£22.00

Waterside House Campsite

Waterside House, Howtown, Penrith CA10 2NA **t** (017684) 86332
e enquire@watersidefarm-campsite.co.uk

watersidefarm-campsite.co.uk

Beautiful lakeside location on working farm with excellent toilet, shower and laundry facilities. Mountain bike, Canadian canoe and boat hire. Boat storage available.

open March to October
payment Cash, cheques

General Leisure

POWBURN, Northumberland Map ref 5B1

★★★★★
TOURING & CAMPING PARK
(76) £10.60–£23.20
(76) £10.60–£23.20
on application
76 touring pitches

Special member rates mean you can save your membership subscription in less than a week. Visit our website to find out more.

THE CARAVAN CLUB

River Breamish Caravan Club Site

Powburn, Alnwick NE66 4HY **t** (01665) 578320

caravanclub.co.uk

open March to November
payment Credit/debit cards, cash, cheques

This site is set amid the Cheviot Hills, with excellent walking and cycling in the immediate area. A footbridge in Branton takes you over the river to the delightful Breamish Valley.

SAT NAV *NE66 4HY*

General

RIBBLE VALLEY

See under Rimington

RIMINGTON, Lancashire Map ref 4B1

★★★★★
HOLIDAY & TOURING PARK
(4) £16.00
(4) £16.00
39 touring pitches

Rimington Caravan Park

Hardacre Lane, Gisburn, Nr Clitheroe BB7 4EE **t** (01200) 445355
e rimingtoncaravanpark@btinternet.com

rimingtoncaravanpark.co.uk

Quiet, family-run site with clean, modern facilities. Set in picturesque countryside, just off the beaten track.

open March to October
payment Cash, cheques

General Leisure

RIPON, North Yorkshire Map ref 5C3

★★★★★
TOURING & CAMPING PARK

(30) £9.00–£18.00
(10) £9.00–£18.00
(60) £9.00–£18.00
100 touring pitches

Special rates Tue-Thu at certain times during season.

Sleningford Watermill Caravan & Camping Park

North Stainley, Ripon HG4 3HQ **t** (01765) 635201 **e** sleningford@hotmail.co.uk

sleningfordwatermill.co.uk

open April to October
payment Credit/debit cards, cash, cheques

A beautiful, tranquil and friendly riverside park set in semi-wooded parkland, between Ripon and Masham. On-site fly-fishing and white-water canoeing available. Ideal for families, bird watchers and nature lovers. (Access available for canoeing all year.)

SAT NAV *HG4 3HQ*

General Leisure

ROCHDALE, Greater Manchester Map ref 4B1

★★★★★
TOURING & CAMPING PARK

Max £15.00
(6) Max £15.00
(4)
24 touring pitches

Gelder Wood Country Park

Oak Leigh Cottage, Ashworth Road, Rochdale OL11 5UP **t** (01706) 364858 **e** gelderwood@aol.com

The country park comprises ten acres of well-maintained grounds and 15 acres of mature woodland. Within walking distance of several restaurants to suit all tastes.

open All year except Christmas and New Year
payment Cash, cheques

General Leisure

ROCHDALE, Greater Manchester Map ref 4B1

★★★
HOLIDAY, TOURING & CAMPING PARK

(30) £10.00–£14.00
(10) £10.00–£14.00
(10) £8.00–£14.00
50 touring pitches

Hollingworth Lake Caravan Park

Roundhouse Farm, Hollingworth Lake, Littleborough OL15 0AT **t** (01706) 378661

open All year
payment Cash, cheques

A popular, five-acre park adjacent to Hollingworth Lake, at the foot of the Pennines, within easy reach of many local attractions. Backpackers walking the Pennine Way are welcome at this family-run park. Hardstanding and grass area. Excellent train service into Manchester Victoria. 20 minutes from Littleborough/Smithybridge.

SAT NAV *OL15 0AT*

General Leisure

ROOS, East Riding of Yorkshire Map ref 4D1

★★★★
HOLIDAY & TOURING PARK
ROSE AWARD

(16) £10.00–£16.00
(2) £10.00–£16.00
(26) £94.00–£358.00
18 touring pitches

Sand-le-Mere Caravan & Leisure Park

Seaside Lane, Tunstall HU12 0JQ **t** (01964) 670403 **e** info@sand-le-mere.co.uk

sand-le-mere.co.uk

A great place to stay, with its natural park and mere leading to a gentle slope to the beach. No cliffs to climb.

open 1 March to 1 January
payment Credit/debit cards, cash, cheques, euros

General Leisure

SCARBOROUGH, North Yorkshire Map ref 5D3

★★★★★
TOURING & CAMPING PARK

£11.50–£25.00
£11.50–£25.00
£9.00–£20.00
200 touring pitches

Cayton Village Caravan Park

Mill Lane, Cayton Bay, Scarborough YO11 3NN **t** (01723) 583171 **e** info@caytontouring.co.uk

caytontouring.co.uk

The very best of coast and country. Luxurious facilities, adventure playground, site shop. Beach half a mile, Scarborough three miles, Filey four miles. Adjoining village with shops, pubs and bus service.

open March to October.
payment Credit/debit cards, cash, cheques

General Leisure

SCARBOROUGH, North Yorkshire Map ref 5D3

★★★★
HOLIDAY PARK
ROSE AWARD

(50) £14.00–£22.00
(50) £10.00–£22.00
(100) £10.00–£18.00
(40) £120.00–£475.00
150 touring pitches

Crows Nest Caravan Park

Gristhorpe, Filey YO14 9PS **t** (01723) 582206 **e** enquiries@crowsnestcaravanpark.com

crowsnestcaravanpark.com SPECIAL OFFERS · REAL-TIME BOOKING

This family-owned, rose-award-winning park is situated between the attractions of Scarborough and the tranquillity of Filey. Full facilities. Holidays and short breaks for families and couples.

payment Credit/debit cards, cash, cheques

General Leisure

SCARBOROUGH, North Yorkshire Map ref 5D3

★★★★★
HOLIDAY, TOURING & CAMPING PARK
ROSE AWARD

(220) £18.00–£28.50
(30) £22.50–£28.50
(50) £14.00–£19.00
(20) £230.00–£595.00
300 touring pitches

Early-booking discount: £25 off full week's hire. 10% discount off full week's pitch fees, booked by post in advance.

Flower of May Holiday Parks Ltd

Lebberston, Scarborough YO11 3NU **t** (01723) 584311 **e** info@flowerofmay.com

flowerofmay.com

open Easter to October
payment Credit/debit cards, cash, cheques

Excellent facilities on family-run park. Luxury indoor pool, adventure playground, golf course. Ideal for coast and country. Prices based per pitch, per night, for four people with car. Luxury hire caravans. Serviced seasonal touring pitches.

SAT NAV *YO11 3NU*

General Leisure

SCARBOROUGH, North Yorkshire Map ref 5D3

★★★★★
HOLIDAY, TOURING & CAMPING PARK

(74) £15.00–£22.00
(74) £15.00–£22.00
(20) £15.00–£22.00
(1) £220.00–£370.00
94 touring pitches

Jasmine Park

Cross Lane, Snainton, Scarborough YO13 9BE **t** (01723) 859240 **e** enquiries@jasminepark.co.uk

jasminepark.co.uk SPECIAL OFFERS · REAL-TIME BOOKING

payment Credit/debit cards, cash, cheques

Family-owned, tranquil park in picturesque countryside setting between Scarborough (eight miles) and Pickering. Superbly maintained facilities. Yorkshire Caravan Park of the Year 2002/2004. National Silver Award 2005. Tents and tourers welcome. Seasonal pitches and storage available. Luxury caravan for hire.

SAT NAV *YO13 9BE* **ONLINE MAP**

General Leisure

For **key to symbols** see page 7

SCARBOROUGH, North Yorkshire Map ref 5D3

★★★★★
TOURING PARK
(125) £13.50–£21.00
(40) £13.50–£21.00
125 touring pitches

Lebberston Touring Park

Lebberston, Scarborough YO11 3PE **t** (01723) 585723 **e** info@lebberstontouring.co.uk

lebberstontouring.co.uk

open March to October
payment Credit/debit cards, cash, cheques

Quiet country location. Well-spaced pitches. Extensive south-facing views. Ideal park for a peaceful, relaxing break. Fully modernised amenity blocks. Dogs on lead.

SAT NAV *YO11 3PE*

General

SEAHOUSES, Northumberland Map ref 5C1

★★★★★
HOLIDAY & TOURING PARK
ROSE AWARD
(18) £22.00–£42.00
(18) £22.00–£42.00
(37) £315.00–£675.00
18 touring pitches

Seasonal discounts available on 3-, 4- and 7-day breaks.

Seafield Caravan Park

Seafield Road, Seahouses NE68 7SP **t** (01665) 720628 **e** info@seafieldpark.co.uk

seafieldpark.co.uk SPECIAL OFFERS

payment Credit/debit cards, cash, cheques

Luxurious holiday homes for hire on Northumberland's premier park. Fully appointed caravans. Superior, fully serviced touring pitches. Prices include full use of Ocean Club facilities (www.ocean-club.co.uk). Gold Award Winner Enjoy England Awards for Excellence 2006.

SAT NAV *NE68 7SP*

General Leisure

SILLOTH, Cumbria Map ref 5A2

★★★★
HOLIDAY & TOURING PARK
(16) £15.00
(16) £15.00
16 touring pitches

Seacote Caravan Park

Skinburness Road, Silloth CA7 4QJ **t** (01697) 331121 **e** seacote@bfcltd.co.uk

seacotecaravanpark.co.uk

open 1 March to 15 November
payment Credit/debit cards, cash, cheques

Peaceful, carefree and tranquil. Well-sheltered level holiday park with 70 holiday homes, 16 touring pitches. All pitches have hardstanding and electric hook-up. The park is fully illuminated, less than two minutes' walk from the sea and 1.5 miles from the centre of Silloth.

SAT NAV *CA7 4QJ* **ONLINE MAP**

General Leisure

What do the star ratings mean?

Detailed information about star ratings can be found at the back of this guide.

SILLOTH, Cumbria Map ref 5A2

★★★
HOLIDAY, TOURING & CAMPING PARK

£15.00
£15.00
(10) £15.00
(10) £230.00–£390.00
21 touring pitches

Tanglewood Caravan Park

Causewayhead, Silloth CA7 4PE **t** (01697) 331253 **e** tanglewoodcaravanpark@hotmail.com

tanglewoodcaravanpark.co.uk

Tanglewood is a friendly, family-run park on the edge of the beautiful, relaxing Lake District National Park. We pride ourselves on our quality of service. Pet-friendly.

open All year except February
payment Credit/debit cards, cash, cheques

General Leisure

SLINGSBY, North Yorkshire Map ref 5C3

★★★★★
HOLIDAY, TOURING & CAMPING PARK
ROSE AWARD

(32) £10.00–£18.00
(32) £10.00–£18.00
(32) £10.00–£18.00
(20) £140.00–£455.00
32 touring pitches

FAMILIES WELCOME

Robin Hood Caravan & Camping Park

Green Dyke Lane, Slingsby, York YO62 4AP **t** (01653) 628391 **e** info@robinhoodcaravanpark.co.uk

robinhoodcaravanpark.co.uk SPECIAL OFFERS · REAL-TIME BOOKING

A privately owned park set in the heart of picturesque Ryedale. Peaceful and tranquil, but within easy reach of York, North Yorkshire Moors, Flamingo Land and the coast.

payment Credit/debit cards, cash, cheques

General Leisure

STOCKTON-ON-TEES, Tees Valley Map ref 5C3

★★★★★
TOURING & CAMPING PARK

(115) £10.60–£23.20
(115) £10.60–£23.20
on application
115 touring pitches

THE CARAVAN CLUB

White Water Caravan Club Park

Tees Barrage, Stockton-on-Tees TS18 2QW **t** (01642) 634880

caravanclub.co.uk

open All year
payment Credit/debit cards, cash, cheques

Pleasantly landscaped site, part of the largest white-water canoeing and rafting course built to an international standard in Britain. Nearby Teesside Park for shopping, restaurants etc.

SAT NAV *TS18 2QW*

Special member rates mean you can save your membership subscription in less than a week. Visit our website to find out more.

General Leisure

ULLSWATER, Cumbria Map ref 5A3

★★★★★
HOLIDAY & TOURING PARK

£16.00–£23.00
(34) £16.00–£23.00
34 touring pitches

Waterfoot Caravan Park

Pooley Bridge, Penrith CA11 0JF **t** (017684) 86302 **e** enquiries@waterfootpark.co.uk

waterfootpark.co.uk

open 1 March to 14 November
payment Credit/debit cards, cash, cheques

Situated in the grounds of a Georgian mansion overlooking Ullswater. The park has an excellent touring area with a mix of hardstanding and lawned areas. The reception and shop are open daily. Licensed bar and games room with pool table. Children's play area. David Bellamy Conservation Gold Award.

SAT NAV *CA11 0JF*

General Leisure

For **key to symbols** see page 7

WEST BRADFORD, Lancashire Map ref 4A1

★★★
HOLIDAY, TOURING & CAMPING PARK

(80) £19.00–£22.00
£19.00–£22.00
(20) £15.00–£25.00
(10) £220.00–£440.00
100 touring pitches

Three Rivers Woodland Park

Eaves Hall Lane, West Bradford, Clitheroe BB7 3JG **t** (01200) 423523

threeriverspark.co.uk

open All year
payment Credit/debit cards, cash, cheques

A family park set in 45 acres. An ideal base for visiting the Trough of Bowland and Yorkshire Dales, yet only two miles from Clitheroe. Luxury holiday hire caravans with central heating and double-glazing.

SAT NAV *BB7 3JG*

General Leisure

WHITBY, North Yorkshire Map ref 5D3

★★★★
HOLIDAY PARK
ROSE AWARD

(10) £220.00–£420.00

Flask Holiday Home Park

Robin Hood's Bay, Fylingdales, Whitby YO22 4QH **t** (01947) 880592 **e** info@flaskinn.com

flaskinn.com

open From Easter to October.
payment Credit/debit cards, cash, cheques

Small, family-run site between Whitby and Scarborough, in the North York Moors. All super-luxury caravans have central heating and double glazing. Also Freeview TV, DVD, fridge/freezer and microwave. Outside decking and seating.

SAT NAV *YO22 4QH* **ONLINE MAP**

General Leisure

WHITBY, North Yorkshire Map ref 5D3

★★★★★
TOURING & CAMPING PARK

£15.00–£18.00
(6) £15.00–£18.00
100 touring pitches

5% discount off 7-night stays.

Ladycross Plantation Caravan Park

Whitby YO21 1UA **t** (01947) 895502 **e** enquiries@ladycrossplantation.co.uk

ladycrossplantation.co.uk

open March to October
payment Credit/debit cards, cash, cheques

Peaceful site in 30 acres of woodland within North York Moors National Park. Ideal for exploring historic Whitby, north east coast, Heartbeat Country, North York Moors Steam Railway and beautiful local villages. Stately homes, adventure experiences and theme parks for the young at heart within easy reach. David Bellamy Gold Conservation Award. Welcome Host.

SAT NAV *YO21 1UA*

General

Using map references

Map references refer to the colour maps at the front of this guide.

WHITBY, North Yorkshire Map ref 5D3

★★★★★
HOLIDAY, TOURING & CAMPING PARK
ROSE AWARD

(20) £12.50–£20.00
(20) £12.50–£20.00
(80) £8.00–£20.00
(30) £150.00–£595.00
100 touring pitches

Middlewood Farm Holiday Park

Middlewood Lane, Fylingthorpe, Robin Hood's Bay, Whitby YO22 4UF **t** (01947) 880414
e info@middlewoodfarm.com

middlewoodfarm.com

open 1 March to 4 January
payment Credit/debit cards, cash, cheques

Peaceful, award-winning family park. A walker's paradise with magnificent, panoramic coastal and moorland views! Level, sheltered hardstandings, luxury heated facilities, private bathroom, children's play area. Ten-minute walk to pub/shops/beach and Robin Hood's Bay. Superb caravans for hire. A friendly welcome awaits!

SAT NAV *YO22 4UF* **ONLINE MAP**

General Leisure

WINDERMERE, Cumbria Map ref 5A3

★★★★★
HOLIDAY & TOURING PARK
ROSE AWARD

£18.50–£27.00
£18.50–£27.00
(50) £214.00–£698.00
38 touring pitches

Fallbarrow Park

Rayrigg Road, Bowness-on-Windermere, Windermere LA23 3DL **t** (015395) 69835

southlakelandparks.co.uk SPECIAL OFFERS

open 1 March to 14 January
payment Credit/debit cards, cash, cheques

In the heart of the Lake District, Fallbarrow Park extends a warm welcome to tourers, motorhomes and those looking to hire a static caravan or lodge. The park boasts an unrivalled setting in a natural environment covering 32 acres of wooded parkland.

SAT NAV *LA23 3DL*

General Leisure

WINDERMERE, Cumbria Map ref 5A3

★★★★★
HOLIDAY & TOURING PARK

(43) £11.00–£27.00
£11.00–£27.00
43 touring pitches

Hill of Oaks and Blakeholme Caravans

Newby Bridge, Nr Ulverston LA12 8NR **t** (015395) 31578 **e** enquiries@hillofoaks.co.uk

hillofoaks.co.uk GUEST REVIEWS • SPECIAL OFFERS

open March to November
payment Credit/debit cards, cash, cheques

Award-winning caravan park situated on the shores of Windermere. Very much family orientated, the park has a play area and nature walks through the woodland. The site has six jetties, boat launching and access to watersport activities. Shop and disabled facilities. Children's play area. David Bellamy Gold Conservation Award.

SAT NAV *LA12 8NR* **ONLINE MAP**

General Leisure

Has every park been assessed?

All parks in this guide has been rated for quality, or is awaiting assessment, by a professional national tourist board assessor.

WINDERMERE, Cumbria Map ref 5A3

★★★★★
HOLIDAY, TOURING & CAMPING PARK
ROSE AWARD

(12) £16.50–£23.00
(12) £18.50–£27.00
(11) £18.50–£27.00
(7) £428.00–£931.00
38 touring pitches

Limefitt Park

Patterdale Road, Windermere LA23 1PA **t** (015395) 69835 **e** enquiries@southlakelandparks.co.uk

southlakelandparks.co.uk SPECIAL OFFERS • REAL-TIME BOOKING

open 1 March to 14 January
payment Credit/debit cards, cash, cheques

Spectacularly situated in one of Lakeland's most beautiful valleys capturing the very essence of the Lake District National Park. Limefitt offers unrivalled facilities.

SAT NAV *LA23 1PA*

General Leisure

WINDERMERE, Cumbria Map ref 5A3

★★★★★
HOLIDAY & TOURING PARK

(23) £16.50–£23.00
(8) £16.50–£23.00
(142) £230.00–£640.00
18 touring pitches

White Cross Bay Holiday Park and Marina

Ambleside Road, Troutbeck Bridge, Windermere LA23 1LF **t** (015395) 69835
e enquiries@southlakelandparks.co.uk

southlakelandparks.co.uk SPECIAL OFFERS • REAL-TIME BOOKING

open 1 March to 14 November
payment Credit/debit cards, cash, cheques

Framed by woodland and inspiring fells, the park nestles on the shores of Lake Windermere. A superb centre in one of the Lake District's most exclusive locations.

SAT NAV *LA23 1LF* **ONLINE MAP**

General
Leisure

WITHERNSEA, East Riding of Yorkshire Map ref 4D1

★★★★
HOLIDAY, TOURING & CAMPING PARK

(20) £15.00–£17.00
(10) £15.00–£17.00
(1) £160.00–£360.00
30 touring pitches

Willows Holiday Park

Hollym Road, Withernsea HU19 2PN **t** (01964) 612233 **e** info@highfield-caravans.co.uk

highfield-caravans.co.uk

Set in attractive countryside, within easy reach of sea and town centre. Licensed club with family room, fishing lake, play area, mini-golf, laundry. Supermarket nearby, beach ten minutes. Tourers until 31 October.

open March to December
payment Cash, cheques

General Leisure

Where can I get help and advice?

Tourist Information Centres offer friendly help with accommodation and holiday ideas as well as suggestions of places to visit and things to do. You'll find contact details at the beginning of each regional section.

WOMBLETON, North Yorkshire Map ref 5C3

★★★★★
TOURING & CAMPING PARK

(100) £15.00–£19.00
(8) £15.00–£19.00
(10) £8.00–£17.00
118 touring pitches

Wombleton Caravan Park

Moorfield Lane, York YO62 7RY **t** (01751) 431684 **e** info@wombletoncaravanpark.co.uk

wombletoncaravanpark.co.uk

Halfway between Helmsley and Kirkbymoorside, a flat level site with electric hook-ups. A small shop for general enquiries, touring and seasonal pitches, tents welcome.

open March to October
payment Cash, cheques

General Leisure

YORK, North Yorkshire Map ref 4C1

★★★★★
TOURING & CAMPING PARK

£16.00–£17.50
£16.00–£17.50
£15.00
87 touring pitches

Alders Caravan Park

Home Farm, Monk Green, Alne, York YO61 1RY **t** (01347) 838722 **e** enquiries@homefarmalne.co.uk

alderscaravanpark.co.uk

open March to October
payment Credit/debit cards, cash, cheques

On a working farm in historic parkland where visitors may enjoy peace and tranquillity. York (on bus route), moors, dales and coast nearby. Level, dry site, tastefully landscaped, adjoins village cricket ground. Woodland walk. Close to A19 and A1. Luxury toilet and shower facilities.

SAT NAV *YO61 1RY*

General Leisure

YORK, North Yorkshire Map ref 4C1

★★★★
HOLIDAY, TOURING & CAMPING PARK
ROSE AWARD

(20) £12.00–£14.00
(20) £12.00–£14.00
(20) £12.00–£14.00
(5) £210.00–£640.00
20 touring pitches

Allerton Park Caravan Park

Allerton Park, Knaresborough HG5 0SE **t** (01423) 330569 **e** enquiries@yorkshireholidayparks.co.uk

yorkshireholidayparks.co.uk

A peaceful camping and caravan park 0.5 miles east of the A1 leading from the A59 York to Harrogate road. An ideal touring base for the York area. Timber lodges to hire/buy.

open February to December
payment Credit/debit cards, cash, cheques

General Leisure

YORK, North Yorkshire Map ref 4C1

★★★★★
TOURING PARK
(115) £14.00–£26.60
(115) £14.00–£26.60
115 touring pitches

Beechwood Grange Caravan Club Site

Malton Road, York YO32 9TH **t** (01904) 424637

caravanclub.co.uk

open March 2009 to January 2010
payment Credit/debit cards, cash, cheques

Situated just outside York in countryside. Plenty of space for children to play. Ideal for families. Within close range of historic York and Yorkshire's varied attractions.

SAT NAV *YO32 9TH*

Special member rates mean you can save your membership subscription in less than a week. Visit our website to find out more.

THE CARAVAN CLUB

General Leisure

YORK, North Yorkshire Map ref 4C1

★★★★★
TOURING & CAMPING PARK
(102) £14.90–£28.30
(102) £14.90–£28.30
on application
102 touring pitches

Rowntree Park Caravan Club Site

Terry Avenue, York YO23 1JQ **t** (01904) 658997

caravanclub.co.uk

open All year
payment Credit/debit cards, cash, cheques

On the banks of the river Ouse in the heart of York, this popular site is just a few minutes' walk from the city centre. York is a feast, there's so much to see and do – visit the lovely Minster with its dazzling stained glass windows and walk the city walls.

SAT NAV *YO23 1JQ*

Special member rates mean you can save your membership subscription in less than a week. Visit our website to find out more.

General Leisure

YORK, North Yorkshire Map ref 4C1

★★★★
HOLIDAY & TOURING PARK
ROSE AWARD
(20) £12.00–£14.00
(20) £12.00–£14.00
(10) £12.00–£14.00
(6) £225.00–£410.00
20 touring pitches

Weir Caravan Park

Buttercrambe Road, Stamford Bridge, York YO41 1AN **t** (01759) 371377
e enquiries@yorkshireholidayparks.co.uk

yorkshireholidayparks.co.uk

On level grassland seven miles east of York on the A166. Near the river where fishing is available. Village, pubs, restaurants etc are within a five-minute walk.

open March to October
payment Credit/debit cards, cash, cheques

General Leisure

It's all quality-assessed accommodation

Our commitment to quality involves wide-ranging accommodation assessment. Ratings and awards were correct at the time of going to press but may change following a new assessment. Please check at time of booking.

YORK, North Yorkshire Map ref 4C1

★★★★★
TOURING PARK

(20)	£14.00–£19.00
(20)	£14.00–£19.00
(20)	£14.00–£19.00

20 touring pitches

YCP York Caravan Park and Storage

Stockton Lane, York YO32 9UB **t** (01904) 424222 **e** mail@yorkcaravanpark.com

yorkcaravanpark.com GUEST REVIEWS · SPECIAL OFFERS

A beautiful caravan park two miles from York, surrounded by countryside. All pitches have electricity, water, TV and drains, and are much larger than average. Hardstanding available. Bus stop outside.

open 15 March to 6 November
payment Credit/debit cards, cash, cheques, euros

General Leisure

YORK, North Yorkshire Map ref 4C1

★★★★
TOURING & CAMPING PARK

(20)	£10.00–£18.50
(20)	£10.00–£18.50
(10)	£10.00–£18.50

40 touring pitches

Book 7 nights in advance and only pay for 6 (excl Bank Holidays).

York Touring Caravan Site

Towthorpe Lane, Towthorpe, York YO32 9ST **t** (01904) 499275 **e** info@yorkcaravansite.co.uk

yorkcaravansite.co.uk

open All year
payment Credit/debit cards, cash, cheques

Small, family-run, secluded park in an idyllic countryside setting, only five miles from York centre. Spacious pitches and superior facilities. Modern, free showers and toilets. On-site state-of-the-art golf driving range and nine-hole pay and play course.

SAT NAV *YO32 9ST*

General Leisure

Welcome Pets!

Want to travel with your faithful companion? Look out for quality-assessed accommodation displaying the Welcome Pets! sign.

Participants in this scheme go out of their way to meet the needs of guests bringing dogs, cats and/or small birds. In addition to providing water and food bowls, torches or nightlights, spare leads and pet washing facilities, they'll buy in food on request, and offer toys, treats and bedding. They'll also have information on pet-friendly attractions, pubs, restaurants and recreation.

Of course, not everyone is able to offer suitable facilities for every pet, so do check if there are any restrictions on the type, size and number of animals when you book.

Wherever you and your pet are travelling in England, the Welcome Pets! scheme will help you find the perfect break.

Central England

Bedfordshire, Cambridgeshire, Derbyshire, Essex, Herefordshire, Hertfordshire, Leicestershire, Lincolnshire, Norfolk, Northamptonshire, Nottinghamshire, Rutland, Shropshire, Staffordshire, Suffolk, Warwickshire, West Midlands, Worcestershire

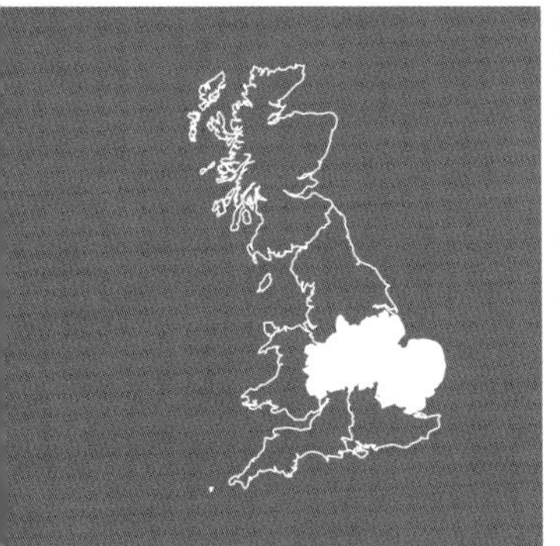

Clockwise: Holkham Hall, Norfolk; Royal Worcester, Worcestershire; Lincoln Cathedral, Lincolnshire

Great days out

Active pursuits, lazy days and family fun – find them all in Central England. Pull on your walking boots and challenge the Pennines, drift along the canals that criss-cross the region, follow the trail to the Major Oak in Sherwood Forest. And do come for the world-class – sometimes uniquely quirky – culture.

It's child's play

Game for anything? Then plunge in – there's such a wide choice of fun family days out. Start with a Thrill Hopper ticket giving great value access to four hair-raising theme park attractions: **Alton Towers** (try the exciting new Battle Galleons interactive water ride), **Drayton Manor Theme Park** (now with Europe's first Thomas Land for engine fiends), Tamworth **SnowDome** and **Waterworld**.

Bewilderwood, Norfolk

Next up, how about the **National Space Centre**, Leicester, where you can see if you cut it as an astronaut. Check your pulse and hit the assault course at **Conkers**, Swadlincote, in the heart of the National Forest, or tackle the zip wires and crocklebogs of **Bewilderwood**, Wroxham. Encounter lions, tigers and elephants at **Woburn Safari Park**, and get to **Dudley Zoological Gardens** for feeding time.

Good sport!

Discover natural sporting arenas to suit every pace and purpose. Walking, cycling, climbing, potholing: it's all here. Saunter along **Offa's Dyke Path**, stride part of the **Heart of England Way**, or dip into stretches of the **Pennine Way**. In the west of the region, the vistas that embrace the **Malverns** are superb. Cyclists of all ages love the flat terrain in the East of England, and you can hire bikes to explore the woodland trails at **Clumber Park**, Worksop. Mountain bikers (especially keen youngsters) can enjoy a challenge on traffic-free circular rides in **Bacton Woods**, Norfolk.

Then up the ante because action and adventure are bywords for the **Peak District and Derbyshire**. Climbers of all abilities come to grapple with limestone and gritstone crags. Potholers relish some of the most challenging caves in Britain. And if you're really more of a spectator, book your place trackside for sensational, high-octane Formula 1 racing at **Silverstone**, or have a flutter at **Newmarket**, the historical home of British horseracing.

Take the waters

Pack buckets, spades and binoculars then head for mile upon mile of sandy and shingle beaches from Essex to Lincolnshire. Hunker down in a hide along the coast at **RSPB Minsmere** to spy wading birds and waterfowl. Share the bustling delights of seaside resorts like Felixstowe, Southend-on-Sea and Great Yarmouth. For something quieter, seek out the havens of Frinton-on-Sea, Covehithe and Anderby Creek plus numerous quaint fishing villages.

Left to right: The Roaches, Staffordshire; RSPB Minsmere Nature Reserve, Suffolk

did you know... Derbyshire's Dovedale was formed from ancient coral reefs? Enjoy the ultimate ramble!

Inland, explore rivers and dykes in the **Fens**, a magical water world extending over Cambridgeshire, Lincolnshire, Norfolk and Rutland. At **Fenscape** interactive discovery centre in Spalding, learn all about the unique landscape and heritage. For lazy days with friends and family, what could be more calming than the reed-fringed waterways of the **Norfolk Broads**? When energy levels rise again, cast off for some sailing at **Rutland Water & Nature Reserve** and exhilarating watersports at **Carsington Water**.

Creative culture

With such a rich mix of history and raw natural beauty it's not surprising Central England inspires creativity. Visit the haunts of famous local lads: the **Stour Valley** of John Constable immortalised in *The Hay Wain* and **Stratford-upon-Avon** where young William Shakespeare lived – look around his birthplace then catch a performance by the **Royal Shakespeare Company**, there's nothing like Shakespeare enacted in his home town. Tour Gothic **Newstead Abbey**, full of Lord Byron's possessions and manuscripts, and gain insights into the life and music of Sir Edward Elgar at **The Elgar Birthplace Museum**, Lower Broadheath.

Today the region thrives with festivals and events ranging from classical to contemporary culture. On a musical note, Benjamin Britten's **Aldeburgh Festival** at Snape Maltings, Suffolk, is the place for classical concerts in a rural setting.

Royal Shakespeare Company, Warwickshire

The annual **DH Lawrence Festival** helps to attract thousands to the author's home town of Eastwood. Unique and quirky happenings are also to the fore, at **Whittlesea Straw Bear Festival** and **Shrewsbury's Cartoon Festival**.

Historic highlights

Linger in **Shrewsbury** to savour the historic atmosphere, or browse the streets of **Worcester** – places noted for their charming Tudor half-timbered architecture. Reach for your camera as you pass through **Much Wenlock**, one of the beautiful black and white villages of Shropshire. Castles and grand homes dot the landscape – **Warwick Castle, Hatfield House** and **Chatsworth** are favourites. For Elizabethan architecture at its most impressive, **Hardwick Hall** is hard to beat. Gothic **Lincoln Cathedral** on its lofty hill and **Lincoln Castle**, where one of only four surviving copies of Magna Carta is held, are must-visit heritage showpieces.

did you know... Lincoln Cathedral doubled as Westminster Abbey in The Da Vinci Code film?

Also step back into the area's proud industrial past, at the **Ironbridge Gorge Museums** – kids soon switch on their imaginations to design and technology at **Enginuity**. Have a chat with working craftsmen at **The Black Country Living Museum**. Trace the history of fighter planes at the **Imperial War Museum Duxford**, Europe's premier aviation museum. At the **Wedgwood Visitor Centre**, Stoke-on-Trent, you can tour the factory and throw a pot or two under the helpful eye of an expert.

Plumbread, pies and shopping

Central England serves up a mouthwatering range of distinctive foods: succulent Melton Mowbray pork pies, Red Leicester and Stilton, Lincolnshire plumbread and Bakewell pudding – often imitated, never matched. Head for Britain's food capital, pretty **Ludlow** on the Welsh borders, to discover what lures so many top chefs to the **Ludlow Marches Food and Drink Festival**. And then there's retail therapy at its most irresistible. Remember the **Bullring** in **Birmingham**? A space the size of more than 26 football pitches – all dedicated to shopping and entertainment. Soak up the colourful atmosphere of multicultural **Leicester** and try on a sari or two.

Clockwise: Imperial War Museum Duxford, Cambridgeshire; Wedgwood Visitor Centre, Staffordshire; Henry Moore Foundation, Hertfordshire

Destinations

Birmingham

A dynamic city combining a fascinating history with a world-class cultural scene. Lose yourself in shopping heaven in the stunningly remodelled Bullring, wander through the historic Jewellery Quarter then sit back and enjoy the Symphony Orchestra in the magnificent Symphony Hall. Indulge your sweet tooth at Cadbury World, or take in a major event at the NEC or NIA. You'll also find yourself at the heart of a region full of history and heritage, beautiful quaint villages and access to lush rolling countryside – Birmingham really is a gateway to the heart of England!

Cambridge

Cambridge

The name Cambridge instantly summons breathtaking images – the Backs carpeted with spring flowers, King's College Chapel, punting on the river Cam and, of course, the calm of the historic college buildings. Cambridge still has the atmosphere of a bustling market town, notwithstanding its international reputation. Explore its winding streets and splendid architecture, and choose from a range of attractions, museums, hotels, restaurants and pubs. Situated in the heart of East Anglia but less than an hour from London by high speed rail link.

Colchester

Find internationally important treasures located in award-winning museums or visit cutting-edge contemporary galleries. It's a shopper's heaven with specialist shops and big name stores, and the range of cuisine makes Colchester a magnet for food lovers – don't miss the annual Colchester Oyster Feast.

Great Yarmouth

One of the UK's most popular seaside resorts, with an enviable mix of sandy beaches, attractions, entertainment and heritage. Beyond the seaside fun is a charming town that is steeped in history. Visit the medieval town walls, stroll the historic South Quay and discover Nelson's 'other' column. When the sun goes down colourful illuminations light up the night sky.

Hereford

In this ancient city on the banks of the River Wye, you'll find historic buildings housing modern shops and modern buildings holding historic treasures. Don't miss Hereford Cathedral with its priceless Mappa Mundi and Chained Library. Wander through the spacious High Town and the new Left Bank Village. Visit the Cider Museum to learn about Hereford's claim to be 'The Apple of England's Eye'.

Lincoln

Possessing magnificent architectural heritage, centred on its world famous Cathedral and Castle, Lincoln is a vivacious City – mixing 2,000 years of heritage with excellent shopping and lively arts and events. The Brayford Waterfront quarter is home to some of the newest places to eat and drink. Events include the famous Christmas Market and the Brayford Waterfront Festival.

Left to right: Chatsworth, Derbyshire; Alton Towers, Staffordshire

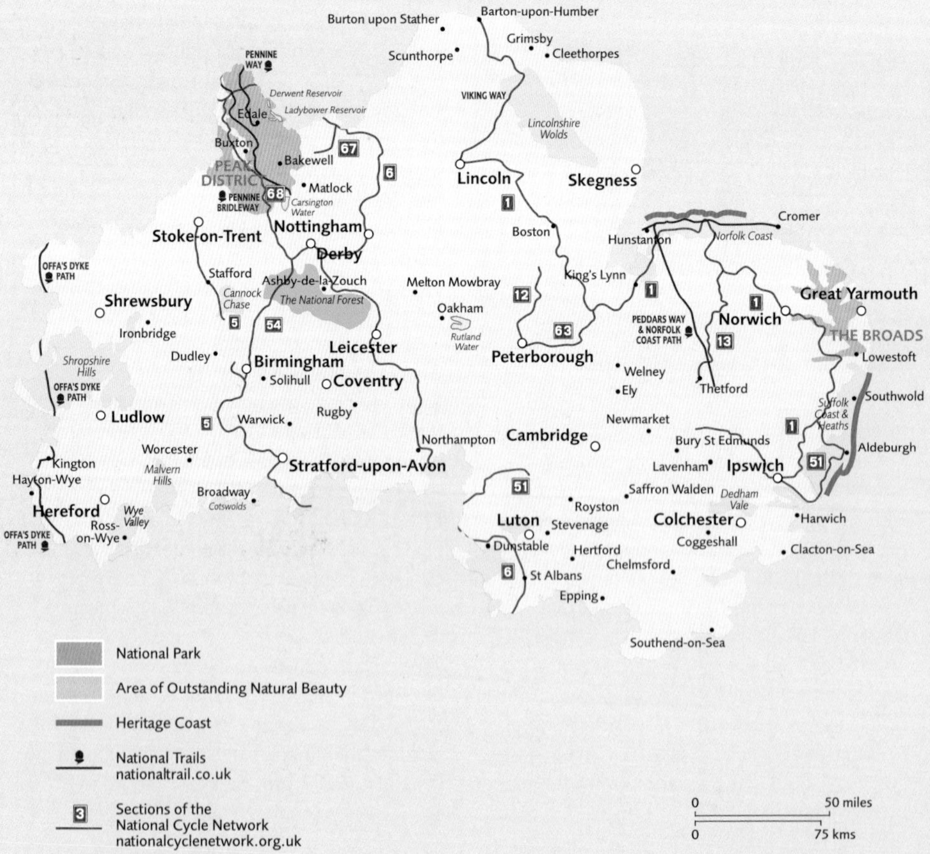

Burton upon Stather
Barton-upon-Humber
Grimsby
Scunthorpe
Cleethorpes
PENNINE WAY
Derwent Reservoir
Ladybower Reservoir
Edale
VIKING WAY
Lincolnshire Wolds
Buxton
67
Bakewell
PEAK DISTRICT
6
Matlock
Lincoln
Skegness
PENNINE BRIDLEWAY
68
Carsington Water
1
Stoke-on-Trent
Nottingham
Boston
Hunstanton
Cromer
Norfolk Coast
Derby
OFFA'S DYKE PATH
Stafford
Ashby-de-la-Zouch
Melton Mowbray
King's Lynn
Cannock Chase
The National Forest
12
1
Shrewsbury
Oakham
Great Yarmouth
5
54
Rutland Water
63
PEDDARS WAY & NORFOLK COAST PATH
Norwich
Ironbridge
13
THE BROADS
Leicester
Peterborough
Shropshire Hills
Dudley
Birmingham
Lowestoft
Welney
OFFA'S DYKE PATH
Solihull
Coventry
Ely
Thetford
Southwold
Ludlow
Rugby
Suffolk Coast & Heaths
5
Warwick
Newmarket
1
Worcester
Northampton
Cambridge
Bury St Edmunds
Aldeburgh
Kington
Malvern Hills
Stratford-upon-Avon
Lavenham
Ipswich
51
Hay-on-Wye
Broadway
51
Saffron Walden
Dedham Vale
Hereford
Cotswolds
Royston
Wye Valley
Luton
Stevenage
Colchester
Harwich
Ross-on-Wye
OFFA'S DYKE PATH
Dunstable
Hertford
Coggeshall
Clacton-on-Sea
Chelmsford
6
St Albans
Epping
Southend-on-Sea

National Park
Area of Outstanding Natural Beauty
Heritage Coast
National Trails nationaltrail.co.uk
3 Sections of the National Cycle Network nationalcyclenetwork.org.uk

0 50 miles
0 75 kms

Ludlow

Ludlow

Discover the place Betjemen described as 'the loveliest town in England.' Britain's first 'slow' town is also a gastronomic capital and host to the renowned Ludlow Marches Food & Drink Festival. You'll find a host of speciality food shops, and more restaurants and inns than you can shake a cocktail stick at. To walk off lunch, stroll in the enchanting Angel Gardens, or take in a performance at the open-air theatre in the stunning medieval ruin of Ludlow Castle.

Norwich

Norwich, county town of Norfolk, is an enchanting cathedral city and a thriving modern metropolis. See some of the finest medieval architecture in Britain in the cathedral and castle, and wander an intricate network of winding streets. The city's newest centrepiece, The Forum, represents contemporary architecture at its best. You'll find excellent shopping as well as a vibrant mix of theatres, cinemas, arts festivals, exhibitions, museums, and a vast array of restaurants.

Clockwise: Brayford Waterfront, Lincoln; Colchester Castle; Birmingham

Nottingham

Nottingham is the undisputed capital of the East Midlands, boasting a sophisticated urban environment with an enviable reputation for clubs, theatres, cinemas and galleries, not to mention a deserved reputation as one of the top retail centres in the country. History is never far away, though, with reminders of Nottingham's legendary hero Robin Hood and his adversary the Sheriff of Nottingham. Explore the Castle Museum and Art Gallery, and Wollaton Hall, one of the most ornate Tudor buildings in Britain, complete with 500-acre deer park.

Peak District

The Peak District is Britain's first and most popular National Park. Roam on open moorland to the north and take in the magnificent views over the Derwent Dams. Further south, stroll alongside sparkling rivers in wildlife-rich valleys far from the hustle and bustle of town. The Peak Park Rangers lead regular guided walks – choose from long hikes to village tours. Take in the grandeur of Chatsworth House or Haddon Hall, and sample the local oatcakes with Hartington Stilton, followed by a delicious Bakewell pudding.

Stratford-upon-Avon

Unearth a magical blend of heritage and drama in and around Shakespeare's home town. Explore five houses with Shakespeare connections including Anne Hathaway's Cottage and Shakespeare's Birthplace. Visit one of England's most beautiful parish churches at Holy Trinity to see Shakespeare's grave and enjoy some of his great works performed by the world's largest classical theatre company, the RSC. Take a boat out on the River Avon, wander the boutiques, specialist stores and gift shops, and discover some of Britain's finest historic houses and gardens.

For lots more great ideas visit enjoyEngland.com/destinations

Visitor attractions

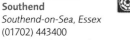

Family and Fun

Adventure Island Southend

Southend-on-Sea, Essex
(01702) 443400
adventureisland.co.uk
Great rides and attractions for all ages.

Alton Towers Theme Park
Alton, Staffordshire
0870 520 4060
altontowers.com
High-adrenalin adventure and family fun.

Banham Zoo
Banham, Norfolk
(01953) 887771
banhamzoo.co.uk
Wildlife spectacular featuring rare and endangered animals.

Bewilderwood
Wroxham, Norfolk
(01603) 783900
bewilderwood.co.uk
Treehouses, zip wires and jungle bridges.

Black Country Living Museum

Dudley, West Midlands
(0121) 557 9643
bclm.co.uk
Twenty-six acres of fascinating living history.

Cadbury World
Birmingham
0845 450 3599
cadburyworld.co.uk
Chocolate-making demonstrations and free samples.

Colchester Zoo
Stanway, Essex
(01206) 331292
colchester-zoo.com
Featuring superb cat and primate collections.

Conkers
Swadlincote, Leicestershire
(01283) 216633
visitconkers.com
Interactive adventure in the National Forest.

Coventry Transport Museum
Coventry, West Midlands
(024) 7623 4270
transport-museum.com
World-renowned exhibition of British road transport.

Drayton Manor Theme Park
Tamworth, Staffordshire
0844 472 1950
draytonmanor.co.uk
The biggest, wettest and scariest rides around.

Dudley Zoological Gardens

Dudley, West Midlands
(01384) 215313
dudleyzoo.org.uk
Lions and tigers, snakes and spiders!

Imperial War Museum Duxford
Large Visitor Attraction of the Year – Gold
near Cambridge
(01223) 835000
duxford.iwm.org.uk
The sights, sounds and power of aircraft.

Ironbridge Gorge Museums
Ironbridge, Shropshire
(01952) 884391
ironbridge.org.uk
World Heritage Site featuring ten superb museums.

National Sea Life Centre
Birmingham
(0121) 643 6777
sealifeeurope.com
Marvel at over 3,000 sea creatures.

National Space Centre
Leicester
0870 607 7223
spacecentre.co.uk
Test your abilities as an astronaut.

Nene Valley Railway
Peterborough, Cambridgeshire
(01780) 784444
nvr.org.uk
The golden age of steam comes alive.

The Poppy Line – North Norfolk Railway
Sheringham, Norfolk
(01263) 820800
nnr.co.uk
5.5 mile heritage railway through delightful countryside.

Pleasurewood Hills Leisure Park
Lowestoft, Suffolk
(01502) 586000
pleasurewoodhills.co.uk
Adrenaline-fuelled thrills and spills.

Severn Valley Railway
Bewdley, Worcestershire
(01299) 403816
svr.co.uk

Journey through 16 miles of beautiful countryside.

Twycross Zoo
Twycross, Leicestershire
(01827) 880250
twycrosszoo.com
Meet the famous gorillas, orang-utans and chimpanzees.

Warwick Castle
Warwick, Warwickshire
(01926) 406611
warwick-castle.co.uk
Enthralling medieval castle in 60-acre grounds.

Woburn Safari Park

Woburn, Bedfordshire
(01525) 290407
woburnsafari.co.uk
Wild animals just a windscreen's width away.

Heritage

Alford Manor House
Alford, Lincolnshire
(01507) 463073
alfordmanorhouse.co.uk
Britain's largest thatched manor house.

Althorp
Althorp, Northamptonshire
(01604) 770107
althorp.com
Historic Spencer family seat containing Diana exhibition.

Belton House, Park and Gardens
Belton, Lincolnshire
(01476) 566116
nationaltrust.org.uk
Fine example of Restoration country-house architecture.

Belvoir Castle
Belvoir, Leicestershire
(01476) 871002
belvoircastle.com
Fine stately home in stunning setting.

Burghley House
Stamford, Lincolnshire
(01780) 752451
burghley.co.uk
The grandest house of the Elizabethan age.

Canons Ashby House
Canons Ashby, Northamptonshire
(01327) 861900
nationaltrust.org.uk
Tranquil Elizabethan home of the Dryden family.

Chatsworth House
Bakewell, Derbyshire
(01246) 565300
chatsworth.org
One of Britain's truly great historic houses.

Doddington Hall & Gardens
Lincoln
(01522) 694308
doddingtonhall.com
Superb Elizabethan mansion set in romantic gardens.

Ely Cathedral
Ely, Cambridgeshire
(01353) 667735
cathedral.ely.anglican.org
Tour one of England's finest cathedrals.

Gainsborough Old Hall
Gainsborough, Lincolnshire
(01427) 612669
lincolnshire.gov.uk
Medieval manor house with original interiors.

Haddon Hall
Bakewell, Derbyshire
(01629) 812855
haddonhall.co.uk
Medieval and Tudor manor house with gardens.

Hardwick Hall
Chesterfield, Derbyshire
(01246) 850430
nationaltrust.org.uk
Elizabethan country house, gardens and parkland.

Hatfield House
Hatfield, Hertfordshire
(01707) 287010
hatfield-house.co.uk
Magnificent childhood home of Elizabeth I.

Hedingham Castle
Castle Hedingham, Essex
(01787) 460261
hedinghamcastle.co.uk
The finest Norman keep in England.

Hereford Cathedral
Hereford, Herefordshire
(01432) 374200
herefordcathedral.org
Magnificent cathedral housing the precious Mappa Mundi.

Holkham Hall
Wells-next-the-Sea, Norfolk
(01328) 713103
holkham.co.uk
Classic 18thC Palladian-style mansion.

Kirby Hall
Corby, Northamptonshire
(01536) 203230
Elizabethan house with superb carved decoration.

Knebworth House
Knebworth, Hertfordshire
(01438) 812661
knebworthhouse.com
Re-fashioned Tudor house in 250-acre grounds.

Lincoln Cathedral

Lincoln
(01522) 561600
lincolncathedral.com
One of Europe's finest gothic buildings.

Newstead Abbey

near Nottingham
(01623) 455900
newsteadabbey.org.uk
The ancestral home of Lord Byron.

Norwich Cathedral
Norwich, Norfolk
(01603) 218300
cathedral.org.uk
Majestic Norman cathedral with 14thC roof bosses.

Nottingham Castle
Nottingham
(0115) 915 3700
nottinghamcity.gov.uk/museums
17thC mansion on a medieval-castle site.

Rockingham Castle Small Visitor Attraction of the Year – Silver
Rockingham, Northamptonshire
(01536) 770240
rockinghamcastle.com
Elizabethan house with splendid artworks and gardens.

Sandringham
Sandringham, Norfolk
(01553) 612908
sandringham-estate.co.uk
The country retreat of HM The Queen.

Shugborough – The Complete Working Historic Estate
Shugborough, Staffordshire
(01889) 881388
shugborough.org.uk
Fine mansion set in rare, surviving estate.

Sulgrave Manor
Sulgrave, Northamptonshire
(01295) 760205
sulgravemanor.org.uk
The home of George Washington's ancestors.

Weston Park
near Shifnal, Shropshire
(01952) 852100
weston-park.com
Charming stately home with beautiful gardens.

Woburn Abbey
Woburn, Bedfordshire
(01525) 290333
woburnabbey.co.uk
Palladian mansion set in 3,000-acre deer park.

Indoors

78 Derngate
Northampton
(01604) 603407
78derngate.org.uk
Terraced house transformed by Charles Rennie Mackintosh.

Birmingham Museum & Art Gallery
Birmingham
(0121) 303 2834
bmag.org.uk
Fine and applied arts featuring Pre-Raphaelites.

Compton Verney
Compton Verney, Warwickshire
(01926) 645500
comptonverney.org.uk
Art gallery housed in Robert Adam mansion.

The Elgar Birthplace Museum
Lower Broadheath, Worcestershire
(01905) 333224
elgarmuseum.org
Fascinating insight into the great composer's life.

Fitzwilliam Museum
Cambridge
(01223) 332900
fitzmuseum.cam.ac.uk
Internationally renowned collection of antiques and art.

Newark Castle
Newark, Nottinghamshire
(01636) 655765
newark-sherwooddc.gov.uk
Discover an exciting Civil War history.

Red House Glass Cone
Stourbridge, West Midlands
(01384) 812750
dudley.gov.uk/redhousecone
Live glassmaking, craft studios, tunnels and furnaces.

Royal Air Force Museum, Cosford
Cosford, Shropshire
(01902) 376200
rafmuseum.org
Warplanes, missiles, aero-engines and flight simulator.

Royal Shakespeare Company
Stratford-upon-Avon, Warwickshire
(01789) 403444
rsc.org.uk
Year-round performances of the great works.

Shakespeare's Birthplace
Stratford-upon-Avon, Warwickshire
(01789) 204016
shakespeare.org.uk
Acclaimed exhibition housed in Shakespeare's childhood home.

Shuttleworth Collection
Biggleswade, Bedfordshire
(01767) 627927
shuttleworth.org
Unique collection of historic aircraft.

Time and Tide – Museum of Great Yarmouth Life
Great Yarmouth, Norfolk
(01493) 743930
museums.norfolk.gov.uk
Discover a rich maritime and fishing heritage.

The Wedgwood Visitor Centre
Stoke-on-Trent, Staffordshire
(01782) 282986
thewedgwoodvisitorcentre.com
Famous pottery set in glorious Staffordshire countryside.

Outdoors

Castle Ashby Gardens
Castle Ashby, Northamptonshire
(01604) 696187
castleashby.co.uk
Capability Brown landscaped gardens and parkland.

Foxton Locks
Foxton, Leicestershire
(01908) 302500
foxtonlocks.com
Fascinating ten-lock 'staircase' climbing a 75ft hill.

Go Ape! High Wire Forest Adventure – Sherwood
Mansfield, Nottinghamshire
0845 643 9215
goape.co.uk
Rope bridges, swings and zip slides.

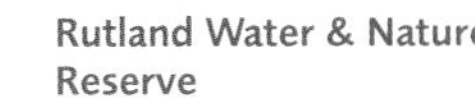

Peveril Castle
Castleton, Derbyshire
(01433) 620613
english-heritage.org.uk
Ruined Norman castle with impressive curtain wall.

RHS Garden Hyde Hall
Chelmsford, Essex
(01245) 400256
rhs.org.uk
28-acre hill-top garden with year-round interest.

RSPB Minsmere Nature Reserve
Saxmundham, Suffolk
(01728) 648281
rspb.org.uk
One of the RSPB's finest reserves.

Rutland Water & Nature Reserve
Oakham, Rutland
(01572) 770651
rutlandwater.org.uk
Important wildfowl sanctuary with leisure centre.

Sherwood Forest Country Park
Edwinstowe, Nottinghamshire
(01623) 823202
sherwoodforest.org.uk
Native woodland packed with adventure.

Silverstone Circuit
Silverstone, Northamptonshire
0870 4588 200
silverstone.co.uk
The home of British motor racing.

Sutton Hoo Burial Site
Woodbridge, Suffolk
(01394) 389700
nationaltrust.org.uk
Anglo-Saxon royal burial site.

The Trentham Estate
Stoke-on-Trent, Staffordshire
(01782) 646646
trentham.co.uk
One of Britain's most important historic gardens.

Welney Wetland Centre
Welney, Norfolk
(01353) 860711
wwt.org.uk
1,000-acre wetland reserve attracting wild swans.

Wrest Park
Silsoe, Bedfordshire
(01525) 860152
english-heritage.org.uk
Magnificent 18thC formal gardens with orangery.

ASSURANCE OF A GREAT DAY OUT
Attractions with this sign participate in the Visitor Attraction Quality Assurance Scheme which recognises high standards in all aspects of the visitor experience.

Events 2009

Crufts
Birmingham
the-kennel-club.org.uk
5 - 8 Mar

St George's Day Festival, Wrest Park Gardens
Silsoe
english-heritage.org.uk
Apr

Luton Carnival
Luton
luton.gov.uk
May

Southend Airshow
Southend-on-Sea
southendairshow.com
May

University of the Great Outdoors - Activity event
Ledbury
visitherefordshire.co.uk
3 - 4 May

Aldeburgh Festival of Music and the Arts
Snape
aldeburgh.co.uk
Jun

Althorp Literary Festival
Northampton
althorp.com
Jun

Stamford Shakespeare Festival
Rutland
stamfordshakespeare.co.uk
Jun - Aug

Robin Hood Festival
Nottingham
nottinghamshire.gov.uk/robinhoodfestival
Jul - Aug

Flavours of Herefordshire Food Festival
Holmer
visitherefordshire.co.uk
24 - 25 Oct

Lincoln Christmas Market
Lincoln
Dec

Regional contacts and information

For more information on accommodation, attractions, activities, events and holidays in Central England, contact one of the following regional or local tourism organisations. Their websites have a wealth of information and many produce free publications to help you get the most out of your visit.

Heart of England

Further information is available from the following organisations:

Marketing Birmingham
t (0121) 202 5115
w visitbirmingham.com

Black Country Tourism
w blackcountrytourism.co.uk

Visit Coventry & Warwickshire
t (024) 7622 7264
w visitcoventryandwarwickshire.co.uk

Visit Herefordshire
t (01432) 260621
w visitherefordshire.co.uk

Shakespeare Country
t 0870 160 7930
w shakespeare-country.co.uk

Shropshire Tourism
t (01743) 462462
w shropshiretourism.info

Destination Staffordshire
t 0870 500 4444
w enjoystaffordshire.com

Stoke-on-Trent
t (01782) 236000
w visitstoke.co.uk

Destination Worcestershire
t (01905) 728787
w visitworcestershire.org

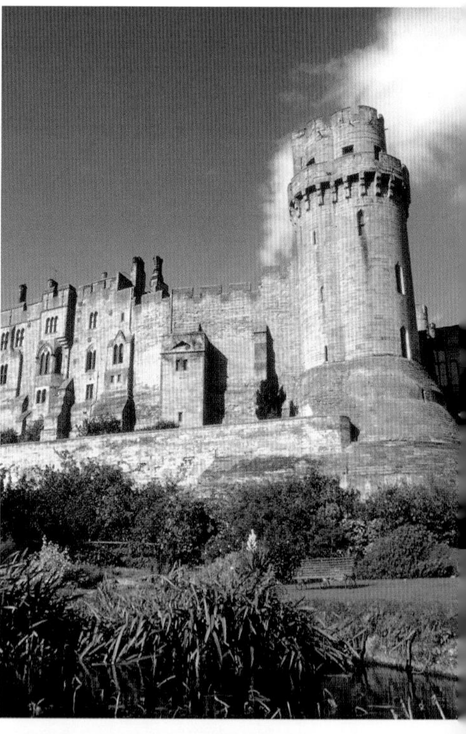

Help before you go

To search for attractions and Tourist Information Centres on the move just text INFO to 62233, and a web link will be sent to your mobile phone.

Clockwise: Warwick Castle, Warwickshire; Rutland Water, Rutland; The Broads, Norfolk

East of England

East of England Tourism
t (01284) 727470
e info@eet.org.uk
w visiteastofengland.com

The comprehensive website is updated daily. Online brochures and information sheets can be downloaded including What's New; Major Events; Lights, Camera, Action! (film and television locations); Stars and Stripes (connections with the USA) and a range of Discovery Tours around the region.

East Midlands

The publications listed are available from the following organisations:

East Midlands Tourism
w discovereastmidlands.com
- **Discover East Midlands**

Experience Nottinghamshire
t 0844 477 5678
w visitnotts.com
- **Nottinghamshire Essential Guide, Where to Stay Guide, Stay Somewhere Different, City Breaks, Family Days Out**
- **Robin Hood Breaks**
- **Pilgrim Fathers**

Peak District and Derbyshire
t 0870 444 7275
w visitpeakdistrict.com
- **Peak District and Derbyshire Visitor Guide**
- **Peak District and Derbyshire Short Break Ideas**
- **Camping and Caravanning Guide**
- **Bess of Hardwick 400th Anniversary**

Lincolnshire
t (01522) 873800
w visitlincolnshire.com
- **Visit Lincolnshire – Destination Guide, Great days out, Gardens & Nurseries, Aviation Heritage, Good Taste**
- **Keep up with the flow**

Explore Northamptonshire
t (01604) 838800
w explorenorthamptonshire.co.uk
- **Explore Northamptonshire Visitor Guide, County Map**

Leicestershire
t 0844 888 5181
w goleicestershire.com
- **Inspiring short breaks and holidays in Leicestershire**
- **Stay, Play, Explore**
- **Great Days Out in Leicestershire**

Discover Rutland
t (01572) 653026
w discover-rutland.co.uk
- **Discover Rutland**

Tourist Information Centres

When you arrive at your destination, visit an Official Partner Tourist Information Centre for quality assured help with accommodation and information about local attractions and events, or email your request before you go. To search for attractions and Tourist Information Centres on the move just text INFO to 62233, and a web link will be sent to your mobile phone. To find a Tourist Information Centre by region visit enjoyEngland.com/find-tic.

Aldeburgh	152 High Street	(01728) 453637	atic@suffolkcoastal.gov.uk
Ashbourne	13 Market Place	(01335) 343666	ashbourneinfo@derbyshiredales.gov.uk
Ashby-de-la-Zouch	North Street	(01530) 411767	ashby.tic@nwleices.gov.uk
Bakewell	Bridge Street	(01629) 813227	bakewell@peakdistrict-npa.gov.uk
Bewdley	Load Street	(01299) 404740	bewdleytic@wyreforestdc.gov.uk
Birmingham Rotunda	150 New Street	0844 888 3883	callcentre@marketingbirmingham.com
Bishop's Stortford	The Old Monastery	(01279) 655831	tic@bishopsstortford.org
Brackley	2 Bridge Street	(01280) 700111	tic@southnorthants.gov.uk
Braintree	Market Square	(01376) 550066	tic@braintree.gov.uk
Bridgnorth	Listley Street	(01746) 763257	bridgnorth.tourism@shropshire.gov.uk
Burton upon Trent	Horninglow Street	(01283) 508111	tic@eaststaffsbc.gov.uk
Bury St Edmunds	6 Angel Hill	(01284) 764667	tic@stedsbc.gov.uk
Buxton	The Crescent	(01298) 25106	tourism@highpeak.gov.uk
Castleton	Buxton Road	(01433) 620679	castleton@peakdistrict-npa.gov.uk
Chesterfield	Rykneld Square	(01246) 345777	tourism@chesterfield.gov.uk
Church Stretton	Church Street	(01694) 723133	churchstretton.scf@shropshire.gov.uk
Colchester	Trinity Street	(01206) 282920	vic@colchester.gov.uk
Coventry Cathedral	Cathedral Ruins, 1 Hill Top	(024) 7623 4297	tic@cvone.co.uk
Coventry Ricoh	Phoenix Way	0844 873 6397	richoh@cvone.co.uk
Coventry Transport Museum	Hales Street	(024) 7622 7264	tic@cvone.co.uk
Derby	Market Place	(01332) 255802	tourism@derby.gov.uk
Felixstowe	91 Undercliff Road West	(01394) 276770	ftic@suffolkcoastal.gov.uk
Flatford	Flatford Lane	(01206) 299460	flatfordvic@babergh.gov.uk
Harwich	Iconfield Park	(01255) 506139	harwichtic@btconnect.com
Hereford	1 King Street	(01432) 268430	tic-hereford@herefordshire.gov.uk
Hunstanton	The Green	(01485) 532610	hunstanton.tic@west-norfolk.gov.uk
Ipswich	St Stephens Lane	(01473) 258070	tourist@ipswich.gov.uk
Ironbridge	Coalbrookdale	(01952) 884391	tic@ironbridge.org.uk

King's Lynn	Purfleet Quay	(01553) 763044	kings-lynn.tic@west-norfolk.gov.uk
Lavenham	Lady Street	(01787) 248207	lavenhamtic@babergh.gov.uk
Leamington Spa	The Parade	(01926) 742762	leamington@shakespeare-country.co.uk
Leek	Stockwell Street	(01538) 483741	tourism.services@staffsmoorlands.gov.uk
Leicester	7/9 Every Street	0906 294 1113**	info@goleicestershire.com
Lichfield	Castle Dyke	(01543) 412112	info@visitlichfield.com
Lincoln	9 Castle Hill	(01522) 873213	tourism@lincoln.gov.uk
Lowestoft	Royal Plain	(01502) 533600	touristinfo@waveney.gov.uk
Ludlow	Castle Street	(01584) 875053	ludlow.tourism@shropshire.gov.uk
Maldon	Coach Lane	(01621) 856503	tic@maldon.gov.uk
Malvern	21 Church Street	(01684) 892289	malvern.tic@malvernhills.gov.uk
Matlock	Crown Square	(01629) 583388	matlockinfo@derbyshiredales.gov.uk
Matlock Bath	The Pavillion	(01629) 55082	matlockbathinfo@derbyshiredales.gov.uk
Newmarket	Palace Street	(01638) 667200	tic.newmarket@forest-heath.gov.uk
Northampton	The Royal & Dernage Theatre	(01604) 838800	northampton.tic@northamptonshire enterprise.ltd.uk
Oswestry	Mile End	(01691) 662488	tic@oswestry-bc.gov.uk
Oundle	14 West Street	(01832) 274333	oundletic@east-northamptonshire.gov.uk
Peterborough	3-5 Minster Precincts	(01733) 452336	tic@peterborough.gov.uk
Ripley	Market Place	(01773) 841488	touristinformation@ambervalley.gov.uk
Ross-on-Wye	Edde Cross Street	(01989) 562768	tic-ross@herefordshire.gov.uk
Rugby	Rugby Art Gallery Museum & Library	(01788) 533217	visitor.centre@rugby.gov.uk
Saffron Walden	Market Square	(01799) 510444	tourism@uttleford.gov.uk
Shrewsbury	The Square	(01743) 281200	visitorinfo@shrewsbury.gov.uk
Sleaford	Carre Street	(01529) 414294	tic@n-kesteven.gov.uk
Solihull	Homer Road	(0121) 704 6130	artscomplex@solihull.gov.uk
Southwold	69 High Street	(01502) 724729	southwold.tic@waveney.gov.uk
Stafford	Market Street	(01785) 619619	tic@staffordbc.gov.uk
Stoke-on-Trent	Victoria Hall, Bagnall Street	(01782) 236000	stoke.tic@stoke.gov.uk
Stowmarket	The Museum of East Anglian Life	(01449) 676800	tic@midsuffolk.gov.uk
Stratford-upon-Avon	Bridgefoot	0870 160 7930	stratfordtic@shakespeare-country.co.uk
Sudbury	Market Hill	(01787) 881320	sudburytic@babergh.gov.uk
Swadlincote	West Street	(01283) 222848	Jo@sharpespotterymuseum.org.uk
Tamworth	29 Market Street	(01827) 709581	tic@tamworth.gov.uk
Warwick	Jury Street	(01926) 492212	touristinfo@warwick-uk.co.uk
Witham	61 Newland Street	(01376) 502674	ticwitham@braintree.gov.uk
Woodbridge	Station Buildings	(01394) 382240	wtic@suffolkcoastal.gov.uk
Worcester	High Street	(01905) 728787	touristinfo@cityofworcester.gov.uk

*seasonal opening

**calls to this number are charged at premium rate

Ratings you can trust

When you're looking for a place to stay, you need a rating system you can trust. The British Graded Holiday Parks Scheme, operated jointly by VisitBritain, VisitScotland and Visit Wales, gives you a clear guide as to what to expect.

Based on the internationally recognised rating of one to five stars, the system puts great emphasis on quality and reflects customer expectations.

Parks are visited annually by professional assessors who award a rating based on cleanliness, environment and the quality of services and facilities provided.

Cymru Wales
Parc Teithio
Touring Park
★★★

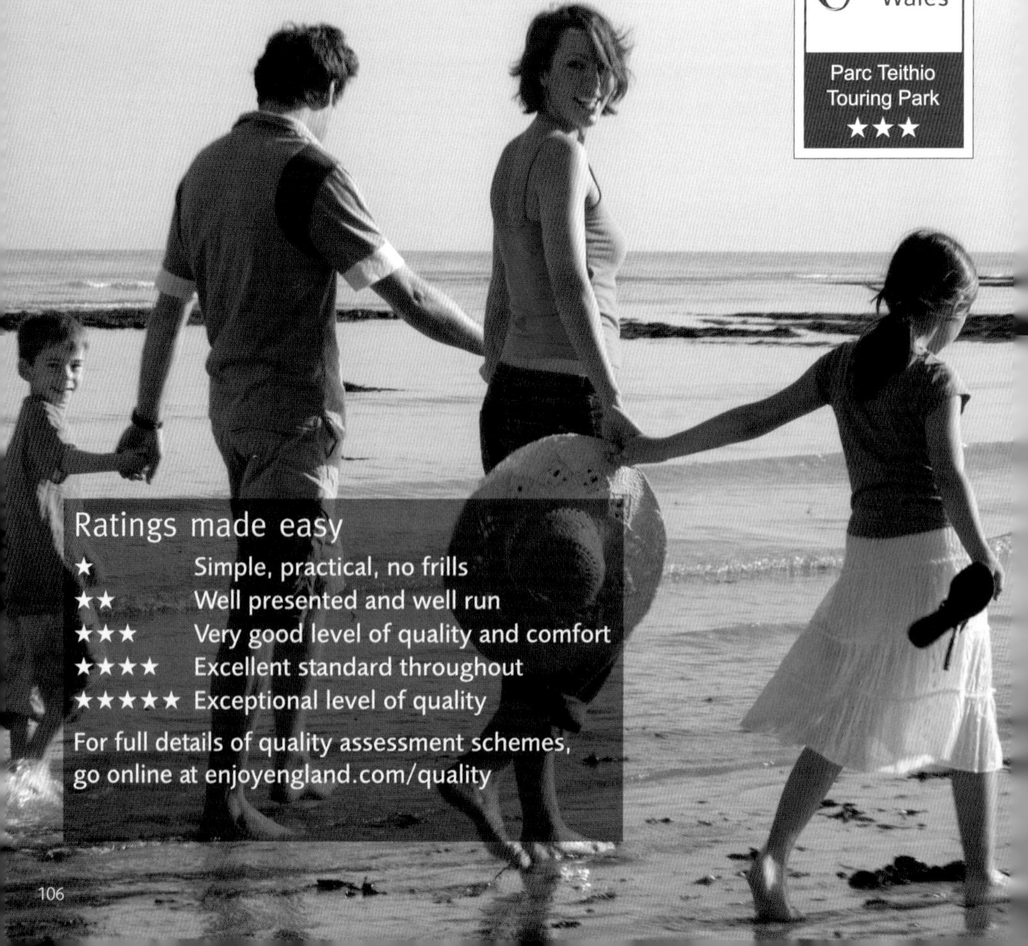

Ratings made easy

★	Simple, practical, no frills
★★	Well presented and well run
★★★	Very good level of quality and comfort
★★★★	Excellent standard throughout
★★★★★	Exceptional level of quality

For full details of quality assessment schemes, go online at enjoyengland.com/quality

where to stay in

Central England

All place names in the blue bands are shown on the maps at the front of this guide.

A complete listing of all VisitBritain assessed parks in England appears at the back.

Accommodation symbols

Symbols give useful information about services and facilities. On page 7 you can find a key to these symbols.

ALSOP-EN-LE-DALE, Derbyshire Map ref 4B2

★★★★
HOLIDAY, TOURING & CAMPING PARK

(81) £10.50–£21.70
(81) £10.50–£21.70
(30) £10.50–£21.70
111 touring pitches

Receive £15 discount for every 7-night stay (includes multiples of 7-night stays).

Rivendale Caravan and Leisure Park

Buxton Road, Alsop-en-le-Dale, Ashbourne DE6 1QU **t** (01335) 310311
e enqs@rivendalecaravanpark.co.uk

rivendalecaravanpark.co.uk

payment Credit/debit cards, cash, cheques

Surrounded by spectacular Peak District scenery, convenient for Alton Towers, Chatsworth, Dove Dale and Carsington Water. Ideal for cyclists and ramblers with a network of footpaths and trails accessible directly from site. Choice of all-grass, hardstanding or 50/50 pitches. Closed 7 January to 1 February.

SAT NAV *DE6 1QU*

General Leisure

AMBERGATE, Derbyshire Map ref 4B2

Rating Applied For
TOURING & CAMPING PARK

(82) £14.00–£26.00
(82) £14.00–£26.00
on application
82 touring pitches

Special member rates mean you can save your membership subscription in less than a week. Visit our website to find out more.

The Firs Caravan Club Site

Crich Lane, Belper DE56 2JH **t** (01773) 852913

caravanclub.co.uk

open March to November
payment Credit/debit cards, cash, cheques

The Firs is set within a special landscape area situated on a hilltop in the heart of the Derbyshire countryside. Peaceful and well presented, there are breathtaking views to the west over the edge of the Derwent Valley Mills World Heritage Site. It is a popular touring base for the Peak District and Derbyshire Dales.

SAT NAV *DE56 2JH*

General Leisure

ASTON CANTLOW, Warwickshire Map ref 2B1

★★★
HOLIDAY, TOURING & CAMPING PARK
(24) £16.50
(24) £16.50
(10) £12.50
(5) £315.00–£415.00
24 touring pitches

Island Meadow Caravan Park

The Mill House, Aston Cantlow B95 6JP **t** (01789) 488273
e holiday@islandmeadowcaravanpark.co.uk

islandmeadowcaravanpark.co.uk GUEST REVIEWS

A quiet, peaceful riverside park just outside the historic village of Aston Cantlow and within six miles of Stratford. An ideal centre for Warwick, Evesham, Birmingham and the Cotswolds. Gold David Bellamy Conservation Award.

open March to October
payment Cash, cheques, euros

General Leisure

BACTON-ON-SEA, Norfolk Map ref 3C1

★★★★★
HOLIDAY PARK
ROSE AWARD
(25) £116.00–£525.00

10% discount on selected weeks for 2 persons or 2 persons and a baby under 2 years.

Cable Gap Holiday Park

Coast Road, Bacton, Norwich NR12 0EW **t** (01692) 650667 **e** holiday@cablegap.co.uk

cablegap.co.uk

open February to November
payment Credit/debit cards, cash, cheques

Cable Gap Holiday Park is a friendly family-run park. You will receive a warm welcome from both us and our staff. Our caravans are of a high standard with most double-glazed and centrally heated. We also have a brick built chalet suitable for the disabled.

SAT NAV *NR12 0EW*

General

BAKEWELL, Derbyshire Map ref 4B2

★★★★★
TOURING PARK
(120) £14.90–£30.00
(120) £14.90–£30.00
120 touring pitches

THE CARAVAN CLUB

Chatsworth Park Caravan Club Site

Chatsworth, Bakewell DE45 1PN **t** (01246) 582226

caravanclub.co.uk

open All year
payment Credit/debit cards, cash, cheques

Breathtaking setting in walled garden on the Estate. Farmyard and adventure playground for children. The Peak District National Park's towns are nearby.

SAT NAV *DE45 1PN*

Special member rates mean you can save your membership subscription in less than a week. Visit our website to find out more.

General Leisure

Remember to check when booking

Please remember that all information in this guide has been supplied by the proprietors well in advance of publication. Since changes do sometimes occur it's a good idea to check details at the time of booking.

BIRMINGHAM, West Midlands Map ref 4B3

★★★★★
TOURING PARK
(99) £14.00–£26.60
(99) £14.00–£26.60
99 touring pitches

Chapel Lane Caravan Club Site

Chapel Lane, Wythall, Birmingham B47 6JX **t** (01564) 826483

caravanclub.co.uk

open All year
payment Credit/debit cards, cash, cheques

Wythall is a quiet, rural area yet convenient for Birmingham (nine miles) and the NEC (13 miles). Visit Cadbury's World or explore the surrounding countryside and local canals.

SAT NAV *B47 6JX*

Special member rates mean you can save your membership subscription in less than a week. Visit our website to find out more.

THE CARAVAN CLUB

General Leisure

BIRMINGHAM INTERNATIONAL AIRPORT

See under Birmingham

BLACKSHAW MOOR, Staffordshire Map ref 4B2

★★★★★
TOURING PARK
(89) £12.20–£25.10
(89) £12.20–£25.10
89 touring pitches

Blackshaw Moor Caravan Club Site

Blackshaw Moor, Leek ST13 8TW **t** (01538) 300203

caravanclub.co.uk

open March 2009 to January 2010
payment Credit/debit cards, cash, cheques

A most attractive level and terraced site with spacious pitches on the quieter, southern edge of the Peak District with some of the best views and walks in the region.

SAT NAV *ST13 8TW*

THE CARAVAN CLUB

General Leisure

BOSTON, Lincolnshire Map ref 3A1

★★★
HOLIDAY, TOURING & CAMPING PARK
£15.00
£15.00
£7.50–£15.00
(4) £230.00–£250.00
87 touring pitches

Orchard Park

Frampton Lane, Hubberts Bridge, Boston PE20 3QU **t** (01205) 290368
e davidmay@orchardholidaypark.fsnet.co.uk

orchardpark.co.uk

open All year except Christmas
payment Cash, cheques

Just a five-minute riverside walk takes you to the village, station and pub serving meals all day. Coarse fishing available. Situated between the Forty Foot River and the B1192. No children.

SAT NAV *PE20 3QU*

General Leisure

BUNGAY, Suffolk Map ref 3C1

★★★
TOURING & CAMPING PARK

(45) £12.00–£16.00
(45) £12.00–£16.00
(45) £12.00–£16.00
45 touring pitches

Outney Meadow Caravan Park

Outney Meadow, Bungay NR35 1HG **t** (01986) 892338 **e** c.r.hancy@ukgateway.net

outneymeadow.co.uk

Within easy walking distance of the market town of Bungay. Situated between the River Waveney and the golf course. Ideal base for exploring the beautiful countryside. Fishing, bikes and canoes available.

open March to October
payment Cash, cheques

General Leisure

BURGH-LE-MARSH, Lincolnshire Map ref 4D2

★★★
HOLIDAY, TOURING & CAMPING PARK

£11.00–£17.00
£11.00–£17.00
£11.00–£17.00
(8) £175.00–£340.00
17 touring pitches

Sycamore Farm Park

Chalk Lane, Skegness PE24 5HN **t** (01754) 810833 **e** lloyd@sycamorefarm.net

sycamorefarm.net

Small touring park in a tranquil, picturesque location with a fishing lake and outstanding holiday accommodation on site. Plenty to see and do nearby, please see our website for more details.

open March to October
payment Cash, cheques

General Leisure

BURGH-LE-MARSH, Lincolnshire Map ref 4D2

★★★★
TOURING & CAMPING PARK

£15.00–£17.00
£15.00–£17.00
£12.00–£15.00
(9) £355.00–£435.00
54 touring pitches

Sycamore Lakes Touring Site

Skegness Road, Burgh le Marsh PE24 5LN **t** (01754) 811411

sycamorelakes.co.uk

open March to November
payment Cash, cheques

Set in 30 acres of landscaped grounds with four fishing lakes (well stocked with carp, tench, rudd, roach and perch). Spacious, level pitches (hard standing and grass) with hook-ups. Superb amenity block. Lakeside cafeteria, Sunday lunch, carvery/steak evenings. Tackle shop, dog walk and footpaths. Plenty of space to relax and unwind. Nine lakeside cottages and cabins.

SAT NAV *PE24 5LN* **ONLINE MAP**

General Leisure

BURNHAM DEEPDALE, Norfolk Map ref 3B1

★★★★
CAMPING PARK

(78) Min £9.00
(78) Min £9.00

See website for list of events and activities run throughout the year, including conservation weekends, environmental courses and special breaks.

Deepdale Camping

Deepdale Farm, Burnham Deepdale PE31 8DD **t** (01485) 210256 **e** info@deepdalefarm.co.uk

deepdalefarm.co.uk GUEST REVIEWS • SPECIAL OFFERS

open All year
payment Credit/debit cards, cash, cheques

Quiet, eco-friendly campsite for tents and small camper vans in the heart of Burnham Deepdale on the beautiful Norfolk coast Area of Outstanding Natural Beauty. Tipis, sleeping up to six people, also available. Perfect for walking, birdwatching, cycling, watersports, kiting or just as a place to relax.

SAT NAV *PE31 8DD* **ONLINE MAP**

General Leisure

BUXTON, Derbyshire Map ref 4B2

★★★
TOURING & CAMPING PARK

(30) £12.00–£15.00
(30) £12.00–£15.00
(30) £10.00–£12.00
30 touring pitches

Cottage Farm Caravan Park

Beech Croft, Blackwell, Buxton SK17 9TQ **t** (01298) 85330 **e** mail@cottagefarmsite.co.uk

cottagefarmsite.co.uk

We are a family-run site, southerly facing with easy access from the A6. We can boast a beautiful walk along the River Wye at nearby Cheedale. Limited facilities Nov-Mar.

open All year
payment Cash, cheques

General

BUXTON, Derbyshire Map ref 4B2

★★★★★
TOURING & CAMPING PARK

(117) £12.20–£25.10
(117) £12.20–£25.10
on application
117 touring pitches

Grin Low Caravan Club Site

Grin Low Road, Ladmanlow, Buxton SK17 6UJ **t** (01298) 77735

caravanclub.co.uk

open March to November
payment Credit/debit cards, cash, cheques

Attractively landscaped site ideally situated for Buxton, at the centre of the Peak District National Park, and for visiting Chatsworth and Haddon Hall.

SAT NAV *SK17 6UJ*

Special member rates mean you can save your membership subscription in less than a week. Visit our website to find out more.

General Leisure

BUXTON, Derbyshire Map ref 4B2

★★★★
HOLIDAY, TOURING & CAMPING PARK
ROSE AWARD

(65) £14.00–£24.00
(15) £14.00–£24.00
(70) £14.00–£24.00
(12) £150.00–£487.00
65 touring pitches

Lime Tree Park

Dukes Drive, Buxton SK17 9RP **t** (01298) 22988 **e** info@limetreeparkbuxton.co.uk

limetreeparkbuxton.co.uk

A convenient site in a gently sloping valley on the southern outskirts of Buxton. Facilities for touring and camping. From the town centre, travel south for 0.75 miles on A515, then turn left after Buxton hospital.

open February to December
payment Credit/debit cards, cash, cheques

General Leisure

BUXTON, Derbyshire Map ref 4B2

★★★
HOLIDAY, TOURING & CAMPING PARK

(95) £11.25–£15.50
(14) £11.25–£15.50
(30) £11.25–£15.50
125 touring pitches

Newhaven Caravan and Camping Park

Newhaven, Nr Buxton SK17 0DT **t** (01298) 84300 **e** bobmacara@ntlworld.com

newhavencaravanpark.co.uk

Halfway between Ashbourne and Buxton in the Peak District National Park. Well-established park with modern facilities, close to the Tessington and High Peak trails, historic houses and Derbyshire Dales. Static caravans for sale.

open March to October
payment Credit/debit cards, cash, cheques

General Leisure

Look at the maps for park locations

Colour maps at the front pinpoint the location of all parks found in the regional sections.

CAISTER-ON-SEA, Norfolk Map ref 3C1

★★★★
HOLIDAY PARK
(30) £99.00–£495.00

Elm Beach Caravan Park

Manor Road, Caister-on-Sea, Great Yarmouth NR30 5HG **t** (01493) 721630
e enquiries@elmbeachcaravanpark.com

elmbeachcaravanpark.com

Quiet caravan park situated on clean, sandy beach. Open from March through to the New Year. All caravans heated and fully equipped.

payment Credit/debit cards, cash, cheques

General Leisure

CAMBRIDGE, Cambridgeshire Map ref 2D1

★★★★★
TOURING & CAMPING PARK
(60) £12.20–£25.10
(60) £12.20–£25.10
on application
60 touring pitches

Cherry Hinton Caravan Club Site

Lime Kiln Road, Cherry Hinton, Cambridge CB1 8NQ **t** (01223) 244088

caravanclub.co.uk

open All year
payment Credit/debit cards, cash, cheques

Imaginatively landscaped site set in old quarry workings, bordered by a nature trail. Cambridge 0.5 miles (Park & Ride bus), Newmarket 14 miles.

SAT NAV *CB1 8NQ*

Special member rates mean you can save your membership subscription in less than a week. Visit our website to find out more.

THE CARAVAN CLUB

General Leisure

CAMBRIDGE, Cambridgeshire Map ref 2D1

★★★★★
TOURING & CAMPING PARK
(60) £12.50–£15.00
(60) £12.50–£15.00
(60) £9.75–£15.00
120 touring pitches

Low-season rate for Senior Citizens – 10% discount for stay of 3 nights or longer.

Highfield Farm Touring Park

Long Road, Comberton, Cambridge CB23 7DG **t** (01223) 262308
e enquiries@highfieldfarmtouringpark.co.uk

highfieldfarmtouringpark.co.uk

open April to October
payment Cash, cheques, euros

A popular, family-run park with excellent facilities close to the university city of Cambridge and Imperial War Museum, Duxford. Ideally situated for touring East Anglia. Please view our website for further information.

SAT NAV *CB23 7DG*

General Leisure

CROMER, Norfolk Map ref 3C1

★★★★
TOURING & CAMPING PARK
(101) £14.90–£28.30
(101) £14.90–£28.30
101 touring pitches

THE CARAVAN CLUB

Seacroft Caravan Club Site

Runton Road, Cromer NR27 9NH **t** (01263) 514938

caravanclub.co.uk

An ideal site for a family holiday. Within walking distance of the beach. Heated swimming pool, communal barbecue, bar, restaurant, takeaway and a separate field for recreational use.

open May 2009 to January 2010
payment Credit/debit cards, cash, cheques

General Leisure

DUNWICH, Suffolk Map ref 3C2

★★★★
HOLIDAY PARK
(30) £15.00–£26.00
(20) £15.00–£26.00
(20) £15.00–£26.00
110 touring pitches

Cliff House Holiday Park

Minsmere Road, Dunwich, Saxmundham IP17 3DQ **t** (01728) 648282
e info@cliffhouseholidays.co.uk

cliffhouseholidays.co.uk

Secluded woodland park offering privacy with access to the beach. Last year's winner of East of England Holiday Park of the Year. Gold David Bellamy Conservation Award.

open All year except Christmas and New Year
payment Credit/debit cards, cash, cheques

General Leisure

ELLESMERE, Shropshire Map ref 4A2

★★★★★
HOLIDAY & TOURING PARK
£18.00–£23.00
£18.00–£23.00
(1) £295.00–£435.00
60 touring pitches

Fernwood Caravan Park

Lyneal, Ellesmere SY12 0QF **t** (01948) 710221 **e** enquiries@fernwoodpark.co.uk

fernwoodpark.co.uk

Picturesque, 25-acre country park for static holiday homes, tourers and motor homes. Forty acres' adjacent woodland and lake for coarse fishing. Shop and launderette. Pets welcome.

payment Credit/debit cards, cash, cheques

General Leisure

EVESHAM, Worcestershire Map ref 2B1

★★★★★
HOLIDAY & TOURING PARK
£19.00–£24.00
£19.00–£24.00
(4) £300.00–£440.00
120 touring pitches

The Ranch Caravan Park

Station Road, Honeybourne, Evesham WR11 7PR **t** (01386) 830744 **e** enquiries@ranch.co.uk

ranch.co.uk

An established family-run holiday park located in Honeybourne, six miles from Evesham. Level pitches in a landscaped setting. Well situated for visiting the Cotswolds and Shakespeare Country.

open March to November
payment Credit/debit cards, cash, cheques

General Leisure

FAKENHAM, Norfolk Map ref 3B1

★★★
TOURING PARK
(120) £12.00–£25.00
(30) £12.00–£25.00
(30) £7.00–£25.00
120 touring pitches

Open to all but with discounts for Caravan Club members. Special rates for rally groups. Check website for events.

Fakenham Racecourse

The Racecourse, Fakenham NR21 7NY **t** (01328) 862388 **e** caravan@fakenhamracecourse.co.uk

fakenhamracecourse.co.uk REAL-TIME BOOKING

open All year
payment Credit/debit cards, cash, cheques

Fakenham Racecourse is the ideal base for caravanning and camping holidays in Norfolk. Just ten miles from a magnificent coastline and on the edge of the market town of Fakenham, the site is set in beautiful countryside and sheltered by conifers. The grounds and modern facilities are excellently maintained.

SAT NAV *NR21 7NY* **ONLINE MAP**

General Leisure

CYCLISTS WELCOME WELCOME CYCLISTS

Fancy a cycling holiday?

For a fabulous freewheeling break, seek out accommodation participating in our Cyclists Welcome scheme. Look out for the symbol and plan your route online at nationalcyclenetwork.org.

FINESHADE, Northamptonshire Map ref 3A1

★★★★
TOURING PARK
(83) £9.30–£20.70
(83) £9.30–£20.70
83 touring pitches

Top Lodge Caravan Club Site

Fineshade, Duddington, Corby NN17 3BB **t** (01780) 444617

caravanclub.co.uk

open March to November
payment Credit/debit cards, cash, cheques

Tranquil, open meadowland site surrounded by woodland where you can walk freely, watch birds and deer and enjoy a profusion of wild flowers. Own sanitation required.

SAT NAV *NN17 3BB*

Special member rates mean you can save your membership subscription in less than a week. Visit our website to find out more.

THE CARAVAN CLUB

General Leisure

GREAT YARMOUTH, Norfolk Map ref 3C1

★★★★
HOLIDAY PARK
£8.00–£14.00
£8.00–£14.00
£7.00–£14.00
70 touring pitches

The Grange Touring Park

Yarmouth Road, Ormesby St Margaret, Great Yarmouth NR29 3QG **t** (01493) 730306
e info@grangetouring.co.uk

grangetouring.co.uk GUEST REVIEWS · SPECIAL OFFERS

Level grassy park with lighting, made-up roadways and first-class facilities. Three miles north of Great Yarmouth, at the junction of A149 and B1159. One mile from the Broads.

open End of March to September
payment Credit/debit cards, cash, cheques, euros

General Leisure

GREAT YARMOUTH, Norfolk Map ref 3C1

★★★
TOURING PARK
(40) £11.00–£15.00
(6) £11.00–£15.00
(10) £100.00–£350.00
46 touring pitches

Grasmere Caravan Park

Bultitudes Loke, Yarmouth Road, Caister-on-Sea, Great Yarmouth NR30 5DH **t** (01493) 720382

grasmere-wentworth.co.uk

Small family park with no on-site entertainment. Approach Caister on A149, then follow brown tourist signs.

open April to October
payment Credit/debit cards, cash, cheques

General

GREAT YARMOUTH, Norfolk Map ref 3C1

★★★★
HOLIDAY PARK
(115) £12.20–£25.10
(115) £12.20–£25.10
115 touring pitches

Great Yarmouth Caravan Club Site

Great Yarmouth Racecourse, Jellicoe Road, Great Yarmouth NR30 4AU **t** (01493) 855223

caravanclub.co.uk

open March to November
payment Credit/debit cards, cash, cheques

Spacious, level site in a very popular family resort offering wide, sandy beaches, countless seaside attractions and fishing, golf, sailboarding, ballroom dancing and bowls.

SAT NAV *NR30 4AU*

Special member rates mean you can save your membership subscription in less than a week. Visit our website to find out more.

THE CARAVAN CLUB

General Leisure

HANWORTH, Norfolk Map ref 3B1

★★★★★
TOURING & CAMPING PARK

(100) £10.00–£15.00
(100) £10.00–£15.00
(125) £10.00–£15.00
125 touring pitches

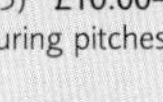

Deer's Glade Caravan & Camping Park

White Post Road, Hanworth, Norwich NR11 7HN **t** (01263) 768633 **e** info@deersglade.co.uk

deersglade.co.uk GUEST REVIEWS

A quiet, rural, family-run park in a lovely woodland clearing, in north Norfolk. Ideal for walking, fishing, cycling, spotting wildlife and visiting the north Norfolk coast and Norfolk Broads.

open All year
payment Credit/debit cards, cash, cheques

General Leisure

HEMINGFORD ABBOTS, Cambridgeshire Map ref 3A2

★★★★
HOLIDAY, TOURING & CAMPING PARK

(20) £12.50–£16.00
(20) £12.50–£16.00
(20) £12.50–£16.00
(9) £245.00–£370.00
20 touring pitches

Quiet Waters Caravan Park

Hemingford Abbots, Huntingdon PE28 9AJ **t** (01480) 463405 **e** quietwaters.park@btopenworld.com

quietwaterscaravanpark.co.uk

A quiet riverside park situated in centre of picturesque village. Many local walks and cycle routes. Ideal for fishing from own banks. Family run.

open March to October
payment Credit/debit cards, cash, cheques

General Leisure

HORNCASTLE, Lincolnshire Map ref 4D2

★★★★
HOLIDAY, TOURING & CAMPING PARK

(90) £12.00–£21.00
(10) £12.00–£21.00
(10) £12.00–£16.00
110 touring pitches

Ashby Park

Horncastle, West Ashby LN9 5PP **t** (01507) 527966 **e** ashbypark@btconnect.com

ukparks.co.uk/ashby

open 1 March to 6 January
payment Credit/debit cards, cash, cheques

David Bellamy Gold Conservation Award park offering a friendly and informal atmosphere, peace and tranquillity, good walks, seven fishing lakes and a diversity of wildlife. Set in 70 acres of unspoilt countryside. Open for statics 1 March to 6 January, touring 1 March to 1 December. Practical Caravan Top 100 Parks 2007.

SAT NAV *LN9 5PP*

General Leisure

HUNSTANTON, Norfolk Map ref 3B1

★★★★★
HOLIDAY, TOURING & CAMPING PARK
ROSE AWARD

(157) £13.00–£41.00
(50) £13.00–£41.00
(125) £12.00–£39.00
(156) £250.00–£1,350.00
332 touring pitches

Superb themed breaks every autumn. Beauty breaks, music weekends, Turkey and Tinsel breaks. Please check website for more details.

Searles Leisure Resort

South Beach Road, Hunstanton PE36 5BB **t** (01485) 534211 **e** bookings@searles.co.uk

searles.co.uk SPECIAL OFFERS

open All year except Christmas
payment Credit/debit cards, cash, cheques

The quality family holiday resort. Family-run, and established for fifty years, Searles has something for everyone: excellent pitches and hook-ups, superb accommodation, bars, restaurants, entertainment, swimming pools, nine-hole golf-course, fishing lake and more – all 200yds from a sandy beach. The ideal base for exploring the Norfolk coast.

SAT NAV *PE36 5BB* **ONLINE MAP**

General
Leisure

For **key to symbols** see page 7

HUNTINGDON, Cambridgeshire Map ref 3A2

★★★★
HOLIDAY & TOURING PARK
(76) £14.00–£26.60
(76) £14.00–£26.60
76 touring pitches

Special member rates mean you can save your membership subscription in less than a week. Visit our website to find out more.

Grafham Water Caravan Club Site

Church Road, Grafham, Huntingdon PE28 0BB **t** (01480) 810264

caravanclub.co.uk

open All year
payment Credit/debit cards, cash, cheques

This is an attractive site situated half a mile west of picturesque Grafham village and a similar distance north of Grafham Water. Remarkably peaceful, surrounded by arable land and a narrow tree belt. Heated outdoor swimming pool and children's play area.

SAT NAV *PE28 0BB*

General Leisure

KESSINGLAND, Suffolk Map ref 3C2

★★★★★
HOLIDAY, TOURING & CAMPING PARK
ROSE AWARD
£23.00–£27.00
£23.00–£27.00
£10.00–£27.00
(6) £285.00–£560.00
63 touring pitches

Heathland Beach Caravan Park

London Road, Lowestoft NR33 7PJ **t** (01502) 740337 **e** heathlandbeach@btinternet.com

heathlandbeach.co.uk GUEST REVIEWS · REAL-TIME BOOKING

Heathland Beach is a spacious, award-winning, family-owned holiday park situated on a picturesque cliff overlooking the secluded beach at Kessingland. Heathland Beach abounds with excellent facilities.

open Easter to October
payment Credit/debit cards, cash, cheques

General Leisure

LINCOLN, Lincolnshire Map ref 4C2

★★★
TOURING PARK
£10.50–£18.50
£10.50–£18.50
(14) £6.50–£15.00
26 touring pitches

Hartsholme Country Park

Skellingthorpe Road, Lincoln LN6 0EY **t** (01522) 873578 **e** hartsholmecp@lincoln.gov.uk

lincoln.gov.uk

Flat, level grassy site set in mature wooded park. Ideal for a relaxing family holiday or when visiting friends and relatives. Easy access to city centre and tourist sites. Also open some weekends in November.

open March to October
payment Credit/debit cards, cash, cheques

General Leisure

MERSEA ISLAND, Essex Map ref 3B3

★★★★
HOLIDAY, TOURING & CAMPING PARK
(60) £12.00–£25.00
(60) £12.00–£25.00
(60) £12.00–£25.00
(25) £220.00–£450.00
60 touring pitches

Waldegraves Holiday Park

Waldegraves Lane, Mersea Island, Colchester CO5 8SE **t** (01206) 382898
e holidays@waldegraves.co.uk

waldegraves.co.uk SPECIAL OFFERS · REAL-TIME BOOKING

Ideal family park, grassland sheltered with trees and four fishing lakes, undercover golf driving range, pitch and putt, heated swimming pool, private beach, two play areas. Licensed bar and restaurant. .

open March to November
payment Credit/debit cards, cash, cheques

General Leisure

What if I need to cancel?

It's advisable to check the proprietor's cancellation policy at the time of booking in case you have to change your plans.

MUNDESLEY, Norfolk Map ref 3C1

★★★
HOLIDAY & TOURING PARK

(40) £8.00–£20.00
(40) £8.00–£20.00
(2) £200.00–£395.00
40 touring pitches

New holiday caravans for sale and hire.

Sandy Gulls Cliff Top Touring Park

Cromer Road, Mundesley, Norwich NR11 8DF **t** (01263) 720513

payment Cash, cheques

The area's only cliff-top touring park. Located just south of Cromer. All pitches have panoramic sea views, electric/TV hook-ups. Free access to superb shower facilities. Miles of clean, sandy beaches and rural footpaths. Managed by the owning family for forty years. We don't cater for children or teenagers. Gold David Bellamy Conservation Award.

SAT NAV *NR11 8DF*

General Leisure

NORFOLK BROADS

See under Bungay, Caister-on-Sea, Great Yarmouth

PEAK DISTRICT

See under Alsop-en-le-Dale, Bakewell, Buxton

PETERBOROUGH, Cambridgeshire Map ref 3A1

★★★★★
HOLIDAY PARK

(252) £12.20–£25.10
(252) £12.20–£25.10
252 touring pitches

THE CARAVAN CLUB

Ferry Meadows Caravan Club Site

Ham Lane, Peterborough PE2 5UU **t** (01733) 233526

caravanclub.co.uk

open All year
payment Credit/debit cards, cash, cheques

Set in 500-acre Nene Country Park. Plenty of activities including canoeing, windsurfing and sailing. Also nature trails, two golf courses, pitch and putt and bird sanctuary.

SAT NAV *PE2 5UU*

Special member rates mean you can save your membership subscription in less than a week. Visit our website to find out more.

PRESTHOPE, Shropshire Map ref 4A3

★★★
TOURING PARK

(71) £7.00–£14.00
(71) £7.00–£14.00
71 touring pitches

Presthope Caravan Club Site

Stretton Road, Much Wenlock TF13 6DQ **t** (01746) 785234

caravanclub.co.uk

open March to September
payment Credit/debit cards, cash, cheques

Peaceful site on the southern slope of Wenlock Edge. Winner of the 2004 Sites in Bloom Award. An interesting site for the naturalist with abundant wildlife. Beautiful countryside surrounds the site.

SAT NAV *TF13 6DQ*

Simply Six: all-inclusive fee for a standard pitch, including electricity, will be £6 per night. A supplement for non-members applies.

General Leisure

RIPLEY, Derbyshire Map ref 4B2

★★★★
TOURING & CAMPING PARK

£20.00–£25.00
£20.00–£25.00
£15.00–£20.00
24 touring pitches

Golden Valley Caravan & Camping

The Tanyard, Coach Road, Golden Valley, Ripley DE55 4ES **t** (01773) 513881
e enquiries@goldenvalleycaravanpark.co.uk

goldenvalleycaravanpark.co.uk

open All year
payment Credit/debit cards, cash, cheques

Secluded woodland hideaway. All-weather children's play facilities. Electric hook-ups on individual landscaped sites. Jacuzzi, gymnasium, pool table, bar, cafe and takeaway. Fishing on site. Next to Butterley Railway. Function room. New Fort Adventure facility. Gold David Bellamy Conservation Award.

SAT NAV *DE55 4ES*

General Leisure

ROSS-ON-WYE, Herefordshire Map ref 2A1

★★★★★
TOURING & CAMPING PARK

(150) £17.60–£23.00
(150) £17.60–£23.00
(150) £17.60–£23.00
150 touring pitches

Broadmeadow Caravan Park

Broadmeadows, Ross-on-Wye HR9 7BW **t** (01989) 768076 **e** broadm4811@aol.com

150 pitches available with luxurious facilities, on the edge of Ross-on-Wye.

open April to September
payment Credit/debit cards, cash

General

RUGELEY, Staffordshire Map ref 4B3

★★★★
HOLIDAY PARK
ROSE AWARD

(9) £119.00–£490.00

Silver Trees Holiday Park

Stafford Brook Road, Penkridge Bank, Rugeley WS15 2TX **t** (01889) 582185
e info@silvertreesholidaypark.co.uk

silvertreesholidaypark.co.uk

Rose Award holiday homes to hire in quiet woodland park, suitable for couples and families enjoying wildlife, walks and cycling on Cannock Chase. Area of Outstanding Natural Beauty. View deer from your caravan!

open March to January
payment Credit/debit cards, cash, cheques

General Leisure

SCUNTHORPE, Lincolnshire Map ref 4C1

★★★★★
TOURING PARK

(15) £14.00
(15) £14.00
(5) £10.00
35 touring pitches

Brookside Caravan Park

Stather Road, Burton upon Stather, Scunthorpe DN15 9DH **t** (01724) 721369
e brooksidecp@aol.com

brooksidecaravanpark.co.uk GUEST REVIEWS

Quiet, family-run park that will meet all your requirements, with views over the River Trent and woodland.

open All year
payment Cash, cheques

General Leisure

SHERWOOD FOREST

See under Worksop

SKEGNESS, Lincolnshire Map ref 4D2

★★★
HOLIDAY & TOURING PARK

(67) £15.00–£21.00
(67) £15.00–£21.00
(120) £190.00–£480.00
67 touring pitches

Richmond Holiday Centre

Richmond Drive, Skegness PE25 3TQ **t** (01754) 762097 **e** sales@richmondholidays.com

richmondholidays.com

The ideal holiday base, a gentle stroll from the bustling resort of Skegness with its funfairs, sandy beaches and donkey rides. Nightly entertainment during the peak weeks.

open March to October
payment Credit/debit cards, cash, cheques

General Leisure

SKEGNESS, Lincolnshire Map ref 4D2

★★★
HOLIDAY, TOURING & CAMPING PARK

£14.00
£18.00
£14.00
250 touring pitches

Skegness Water Leisure Park

Walls Lane, Ingoldmells, Skegness PE25 1JF **t** (01754) 899400
e enquiries@skegnesswaterleisurepark.co.uk

skegnesswaterleisurepark.co.uk

Family-orientated caravan and camping site 'where the coast meets the countryside'. Ten-minute walk to award-winning beaches with scenic, rural views.

open March to November
payment Credit/debit cards, cash, cheques

General Leisure

STANHOE, Norfolk Map ref 3B1

★★★★
TOURING PARK

£9.00–£11.00
£9.00–£11.00
£9.00–£11.00
30 touring pitches

The Rickels Caravan and Camping Park

Bircham Road, Stanhoe, King's Lynn PE31 8PU **t** (01485) 518671

The Rickels is a quiet, friendly, high-quality family-run park which offers a peaceful, relaxed atmosphere in which you can enjoy a pleasant and restful holiday. Adults only. Set in three acres of grassland.

open April to October
payment Cash, cheques

General Leisure

STAVELEY, Derbyshire Map ref 4B2

Rating Applied For
HOLIDAY, TOURING & CAMPING PARK

(86) £14.00–£26.60
(86) £14.00–£26.60
86 touring pitches

Special member rates mean you can save your membership subscription in less than a week. Visit our website to find out more.

THE CARAVAN CLUB

Poolsbrook Country Park Caravan Club Site

Staveley, Chesterfield S43 3LS **t** (01246) 470659

caravanclub.co.uk

open March to November
payment Credit/debit cards, cash, cheques

This site incorporates a number of sustainable resource and energy features and is set within the 165-acre Pools Brook Country Park. Once the site of a colliery, the land has been transformed into this tremendous country park with amenities including visitor centre, cafe and children's adventure play area. With lakes for fishing, extensive trails for cyclists and walkers to explore, an added bonus is that the country park also adjoins the Trans-Pennine Trail.

SAT NAV *S43 3LS*

General Leisure

Do you like walking?

Walkers feel at home in accommodation participating in our Walkers Welcome scheme. Look out for the symbol. Consider walking all or part of a long-distance route – go online at nationaltrail.co.uk.

STOKE-ON-TRENT, Staffordshire Map ref 4B2

★★★★★
HOLIDAY, TOURING & CAMPING PARK
ROSE AWARD

(60) £15.00–£18.00
(10) £10.00–£20.00
(50) £10.00–£12.00
(7) £270.00–£420.00
120 touring pitches

Early-season discounts on caravan holiday homes. Free 2nd-day admission to Alton Towers for 2 persons (ring for information).

Star Caravan & Camping Park

Star Road, Cotton, Alton Towers Area ST10 3BZ **t** (01538) 702219

starcaravanpark.co.uk GUEST REVIEWS

open All year except Christmas and New Year
payment Credit/debit cards, cash, cheques

The closest touring park to Alton Towers. Strict 11pm-all-quiet rule on site. No single-sex groups allowed. Families and mixed couples always welcomed. Set in stunning countryside surrounded by mature trees and hedgerows. Ten miles from four market towns, and only four miles from the Peak District National Park.

SAT NAV *ST10 3BZ* **ONLINE MAP**

General Leisure

STRATFORD-UPON-AVON, Warwickshire Map ref 2B1

★★★
TOURING & CAMPING PARK

(50) £15.00–£18.00
(50) £15.00–£18.00
(50) £14.00–£17.00
50 touring pitches

Dodwell Park

Evesham Rd, Stratford-upon-Avon CV37 9SR **t** (01789) 204957 **e** enquiries@dodwellpark.co.uk

dodwellpark.co.uk

Small, family-run touring park two miles south west of Stratford-upon-Avon on the B439. Country walks to River Avon and Luddington village. Ideal for visiting Warwick Castle, Shakespeare's birthplace and the Cotswolds.

open All year
payment Credit/debit cards, cash, cheques

General Leisure

SWADLINCOTE, Derbyshire Map ref 4B3

★★★
TOURING & CAMPING PARK

(25) £14.00–£17.00
(5) £14.00–£17.00
(60) £10.00–£20.00
30 touring pitches

Beehive Farm Woodland Lakes

Rosliston, Swadlincote DE12 8HZ **t** (01283) 763981 **e** info@beehivefarm-woodlandlakes.co.uk

beehivefarm-woodlandlakes.co.uk

In the heart of the National Forest and within easy reach of the Derbyshire Dales and many great local attractions, Beehive Farm Woodland Lakes is a great place to stay over.

open All year except Christmas and New Year
payment Credit/debit cards, cash, cheques

General Leisure

TANSLEY, Derbyshire Map ref 4B2

★★★★
TOURING PARK

(100) £16.00–£23.00
(100) £16.00–£23.00
100 touring pitches

Lickpenny Caravan Park

Lickpenny Lane, Tansley, Matlock DE4 5GF **t** (01629) 583040 **e** lickpenny@btinternet.com

lickpennycaravanpark.co.uk

Peaceful location within easy reach of Matlock Bath, Bakewell and Chatsworth. All pitches hardstanding with 16-amp electric hook-up. Each pitch is separated by own boundary, with ample room for caravan, car and awning.

open All year
payment Credit/debit cards, cash, cheques

General Leisure

What shall we do today?

For ideas on places to visit, see the beginning of this regional section or go online at visitbritain.com.

WORKSOP, Nottinghamshire Map ref 4C2

★★★★★
TOURING PARK
(183) £14.90–£28.30
(183) £14.90–£28.30
183 touring pitches

THE CARAVAN CLUB

Clumber Park Caravan Club Site

Lime Tree Avenue, Clumber Park, Worksop S80 3AE **t** (01909) 484758

caravanclub.co.uk

open All year
payment Credit/debit cards, cash, cheques

There's a great feeling of spaciousness here, for the site is on 20 acres within 4,000 acres of parkland. Set in the heart of Sherwood Forest and redeveloped to a high standard in 2002. Visit Nottingham Castle and the watersports centre at Holme Pierrepont.

SAT NAV *S80 3AE*

Midweek discount: pitch fee for standard pitches for stays on any Tue, Wed or Thu night outside peak season dates will be reduced by 50%.

General Leisure

WYE VALLEY

See under Ross-on-Wye

WYTON, Cambridgeshire Map ref 3A2

★★★★
HOLIDAY PARK
(40) Min £14.50
(10) Min £14.50
(10) Min £11.00
40 touring pitches

10% discount on all bookings 7 nights or over paid in full on arrival. 7 days' fishing for the price of 6.

Wyton Lakes Holiday Park

Banks End, Wyton, Huntingdon PE28 2AA **t** (01480) 412715 **e** loupeter@supanet.com

wytonlakes.com

open April to October
payment Cash, cheques

Adults-only park. Some pitches beside the on-site carp and coarse-fishing lakes. River frontage. Close to local amenities.

SAT NAV *PE28 2AA* **ONLINE MAP**

General Leisure

South East England

Berkshire, Buckinghamshire, East Sussex, Hampshire, Isle of Wight, Kent, Oxfordshire, Surrey, West Sussex

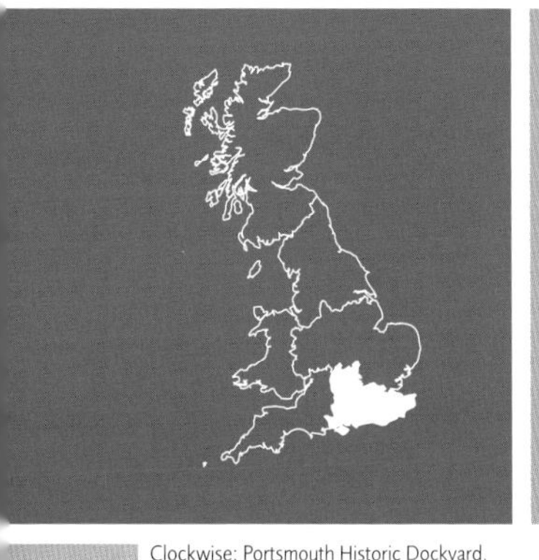

Clockwise: Portsmouth Historic Dockyard, Hampshire; Deal, Kent; Oxford

Great days out

The South East is your quintessential slice of England. Explore iconic chalk cliffs and 400 miles of glorious coastline, fairytale castles, colourful gardens and historic cities. Whilst singles and couples will find plenty to enjoy, this region is bursting with great family days out that the kids will treasure forever.

Enjoy the ride!

Get set, **Go Ape!** on a high-wire forest adventure course, now at Bedgebury Pinetum and Wendover Woods as well as other exciting locations across the South East. White-knuckle rides like **Thorpe Park's** Inferno and Slammer keep the thrills coming and there's always something new to try: take a dizzying spin on **Legoland Windsor's** Longboat Invader, twirl and tilt on the amazing

Paultons Park, Hampshire

Sky Swinger at **Paultons Park**, or hop aboard the spooky ghost train Horror Hotel at **Brighton Pier**. At Winchester's **Intech Science Centre and Planetarium** you can even fly through the solar system and visit a black hole. Enjoy the rides of your life!

Who killed Harold?

Explore a region that has witnessed some of the most momentous events in British history, from the Battle of Hastings in 1066 to the air raids of the Second World War. At **Battle Abbey** stand on the exact spot where tradition says King Harold fell and take the interactive audio tour of the battlefield to find out what really happened on that fateful day. Clamber aboard the world-famous HMS Victory at **Portsmouth Historic Dockyard**, then experience the challenges of the modern Navy in Action Stations.

Formidable **Dover Castle** on the Kent coast puts you right on the frontline of history: tour the **Secret Wartime Tunnels** deep beneath the gleaming White Cliffs, where the evacuation of Dunkirk was masterminded. Another of the country's dazzling landmarks, **Canterbury Cathedral**, opens the door on the infamous murder of Thomas Becket. And just for fun, why not follow in the footsteps of Morse and Lewis beneath the dreaming spires of **Oxford** to solve a fictional mystery or two?

Shore pleasures

South coast beaches keep alive all the best traditions of the seaside, with a zesty twist of watersport action. **Eastbourne**, **Bournemouth**, **Brighton** and **Margate** were popular playgrounds for the Victorians – Queen Victoria loved to escape to her Isle of Wight home, **Osborne House**. Save your small change for the slot machines on the pier where it's hot doughnuts or fish and chips all round. If you're looking for something a bit more peaceful, there are still many gems to uncover. Scamper about the sand dunes at **West Wittering**, just down the Sussex coast from **Bognor Regis**, and watch the zigzagging kitesurfers at **Pevensey Bay**. Get your own adrenalin fix at the **Calshot Activities Centre** where you can try all sorts of watersports, including sailing on the Solent.

Left to right: Hever Castle, Kent; Royal Pavilion, Brighton, East Sussex

did you know... you're walking on 80 million years of geological history along the White Cliffs of Dover?

Castles, castles everywhere

Become king, queen, lord or lady for a day visiting the South East's magnificent castles. **Bodiam** is a picture-perfect medieval moated fortress and **Arundel** is full of priceless collections. Dreamy **Leeds** in Kent was restored by Henry VIII for his first queen, Catherine of Aragon. It might have been the ultimate romantic gesture, except that he abandoned her for his second wife, Anne Boleyn – visit Anne's beautiful childhood home, **Hever Castle**, too. **Windsor Castle** has been a royal residence for nine centuries and reflects changing royal tastes through the ages. But nothing quite prepares you for the **Royal Pavilion** at Brighton, George IV's eccentric Indian-style palace!

Follow nature's way

Kent is rightly famed as the Garden of England, so sample some real horticultural treats like **Sissinghurst Castle Garden**, lovingly created by Vita Sackville-West. Discover Kew's country garden and the Millennium Seed Bank at **Wakehurst Place**, near Haywards Heath. Follow the ancient tracks of the **South Downs Way** for an exhilarating breath of fresh air, or hop over to the **Isle of Wight** where you can cycle Round the Island in eight hours. Phew! Play hide and seek along the paths and bridleways of the **New Forest** and watch out for wild ponies as they gently graze. You'll encounter elephants and other exotic creatures at **Howletts Wild Animal Park**.

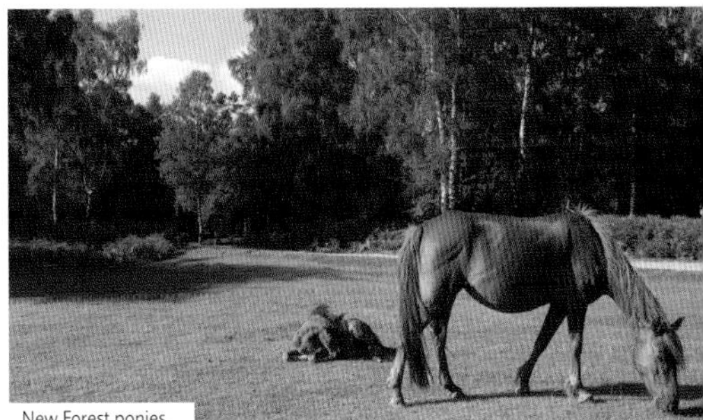

New Forest ponies

Have a Dickens of a time

Catch the buzz of a festival or event, whatever the time of year. From rock 'n' pop to hops, from rowing to sailing, from Dickens to dancing round a maypole – the rich tapestry of life. **The Brighton Festival** comes to the funky seaside town every May and is an exuberant celebration of world-class art and entertainment. If you're looking for the epitome of elegance, dress up for **Glyndebourne's** season of opera, **Royal Ascot**, **Henley Royal Regatta** or **Cowes Week** – four internationally famous spectacles.

Or join Mr Pickwick and other jolly characters in Victorian costume on the streets of Broadstairs during the **Dickens Festival**. The town was the author's favourite 'English watering place'. There's rock, pop and hip hop mixed with liberal helpings of mud at August's **Reading Festival**. And kids can always find something fantabulous to fill the school holidays at **The Roald Dahl Museum and Story Centre**, Great Missenden: from whizzpopping, hands-on science workshops to delumptious cookery classes.

Time to indulge

Had your fill of sightseeing? Then it's time to indulge! Shopaholics: head for the charming world of The Lanes, **Brighton**, to hunt out stylish gifts and antiques. Browse for hours in the country's largest second-hand bookshop, Baggins at **Rochester**. Pop into **Oxford Castle** where boutique stalls, outdoor music performances, wining and dining are set against an unusual prison backdrop. If you need to boost your energy levels, you're in just the right region, too: embark on an epicurean journey through lots of orchards, breweries and vineyards, including England's largest vineyard at **Denbies Wine Estate**. Then savour more of the genuine flavours of South East England in the oyster houses and fine restaurants.

why not... visit the world's oldest and largest occupied castle – Windsor Castle?

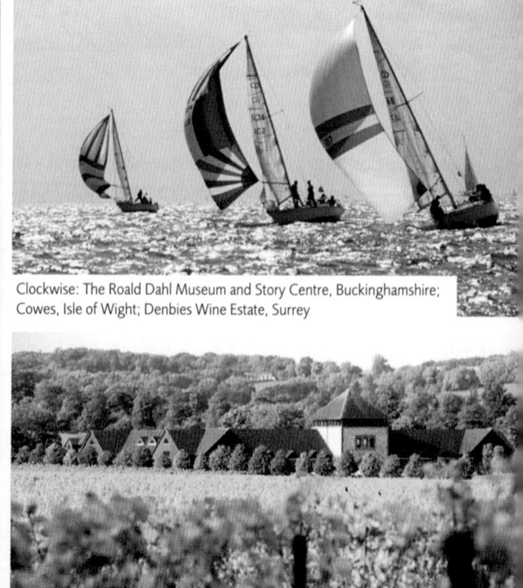

Clockwise: The Roald Dahl Museum and Story Centre, Buckinghamshire; Cowes, Isle of Wight; Denbies Wine Estate, Surrey

Destinations

Brighton

England's favourite seaside city, Brighton is historic, elegant and offbeat. Wander a beachfront packed with cafés and bars, then step into town for fine antiques and designer boutiques. Don't miss the Royal Pavilion, surely the most extravagant royal palace in Europe, and come in springtime for an arts festival second to none. Find the world's cuisine in over 400 restaurants, and then relax with dance, comedy or music in the thriving pub and club culture. Brighton has it all – and just 50 minutes by train from central London.

Brighton

Canterbury

Marvel with fellow 'pilgrims' from the four corners of the world as Canterbury Cathedral dominates your approach to this World Heritage Site. Let Canterbury Tales 'Medieval Misadventures' take you on a journey back to Chaucer's England. Wander traffic-free daytime streets to enjoy historic buildings and modern attractions, and then head further afield to explore the valleys, woods and coastline of this beautiful region of Kent.

Dover

Discover the rich history of Dover – 'the lock and key of England'. Tour Dover Castle and relive the epic sieges of 1216-17. Delve into the secrets contained in the Wartime Tunnels, nerve centre for the evacuation of Dunkirk. Enjoy the pier and stroll the stylish marina before heading out of town to tour the scenic beaches of White Cliffs Country.

Isle of Wight

Sixty miles of spectacular coastline, picturesque coves and safe bathing in bays of golden sand. Explore the maritime history of Cowes, the beautiful and historic town of Newport and take the family to the welcoming resorts of Shanklin and Ventnor. Follow the trail of dinosaurs, ancient tribes, Romans and monarchs.

New Forest

Roam a landscape little changed since William the Conqueror gave it his special protection over 900 years ago. Discover wild heath and dappled woodland, roaming ponies, thatched hamlets, bustling market towns, and tiny streams meandering to the sparkling expanse of the Solent. Explore great attractions too, from Buckler's Hard to the National Motor Museum Beaulieu.

Oxford

This ancient university city is both timeless and modern. Wander among its 'dreaming spires' and tranquil college quadrangles. Find national and international treasures displayed in a family of museums. Hire a punt and spend the afternoon drifting along the River Cherwell or seek out bustling shops and fashionable restaurants. Experience candlelit evensong in college chapels or Shakespeare in the park, and after dark enjoy the cosmopolitan buzz.

Left to right: Great Dixter, East Sussex; Thorpe Park, Surrey

National Park

South Downs National Park (designated but not yet confirmed)

Area of Outstanding Natural Beauty

Heritage Coast

National Trails nationaltrail.co.uk

Sections of the National Cycle Network nationalcyclenetwork.org.uk

Ferry routes

0 — 50 miles

0 — 75 kms

Royal Tunbridge Wells

Portsmouth

At the heart of the city is Portsmouth Historic Dockyard where there is so much naval heritage to explore. Climb the new striking Spinnaker Tower or take a harbour tour to see naval ships. If you're after retail therapy, head for Gunwharf Quays. Portsmouth also has its own resort area, Southsea, with four miles of beach and promenade.

Royal Tunbridge Wells

Ever since the discovery of the Chalybeate Spring 400 years ago, visitors have been coming here. The health-giving waters still flow and the Pantiles, the famous colonnaded walkway, is now home to a wonderful selection of boutiques, antiques shops, bars and cafés. The village atmosphere of the old high street and Chapel Place, adds to the town's reputation as one of the most desirable destinations in the South East. Surrounded by beautiful countryside, and a wealth of castles, stately homes and gardens, there's so much to explore.

Clockwise: Portsmouth; Windsor Castle; Dover Castle

Winchester

Winchester is best known for its 11thC cathedral and the Great Hall, which for over 600 years has housed the mysterious Arthurian round table. Wander through the city's popular shopping streets, admire the architecture and enjoy quirky open air events. Home of good food, birthplace of cricket, resting place of author Jane Austen and inspiration to the many craft-makers and artists who live here, Winchester is a destination for all seasons.

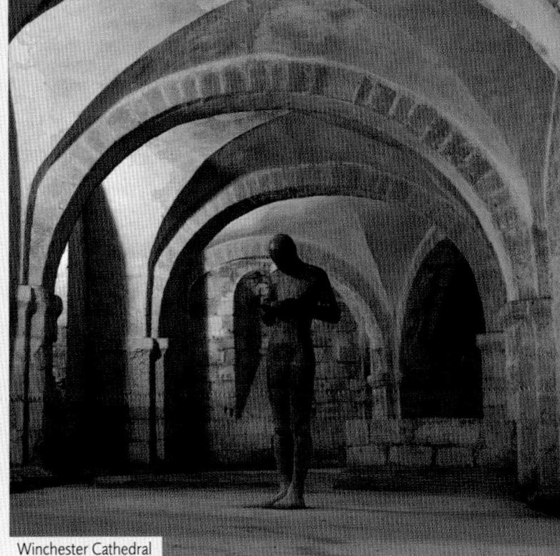
Winchester Cathedral

Windsor

Explore Windsor and the Royal Borough to the west of London. Gaze at the priceless treasures in the Royal Collection at Windsor Castle, royal home and fortress for over 900 years. Henry VI founded Eton College in 1440. Lose yourself in the history of the cloisters and the chapel. Sail the rapids at Legoland's incredible Vikings' River Splash, and find peace and quiet in the rural landscape of Royal Berkshire, traversed by the timeless flow of the Thames.

For lots more great ideas visit enjoyEngland.com/destinations

Visitor attractions

Family and Fun

Blue Reef Aquarium
Hastings, East Sussex
(01424) 718776
discoverhastings.co.uk
Meet tropical sharks and giant crabs.

The Canterbury Tales
Canterbury, Kent
(01227) 479227
canterburytales.org.uk
Audiovisual recreation of life in medieval England.

Didcot Railway Centre
Didcot, Oxfordshire
(01235) 817200
didcotrailwaycentre.org.uk
Living museum of the Great Western Railway.

Dinosaur Isle
Sandown, Isle of Wight
(01983) 404344
dinosaurisle.com
Britain's first purpose-built dinosaur attraction.

Farming World
Boughton, Kent
(01227) 751144
farming-world.com
Working farm packed with family fun.

Guildford Spectrum
Guildford, Surrey
(01483) 443322
guildfordspectrum.co.uk
Olympic-sized ice rink and tenpin bowling.

Gulliver's Land
Milton Keynes, Buckinghamshire
(01925) 444888
gulliversfun.co.uk
Family magic for children aged 2-13 years.

Harbour Park
Littlehampton, West Sussex
(01903) 721200
harbourpark.com
All-weather theme park with dodgems.

The Historic Dockyard Chatham
Chatham, Kent
(01634) 823800
chdt.org.uk
Maritime heritage site with stunning architecture.

The Hop Farm Country Park
Paddock Wood, Kent
(01622) 872068
thehopfarm.co.uk
Once-working hop farm in 400 unspoilt acres.

Howletts Wild Animal Park
Canterbury, Kent
(01227) 721286
totallywild.net
Gorillas and tigers in 90-acre parkland.

Isle of Wight Zoo
Sandown, Isle of Wight
(01983) 403883
isleofwightzoo.com
Zoo specialising in big cats and primates.

LEGOLAND Windsor
Windsor, Berkshire
0870 504 0404
legoland.co.uk
More Lego bricks than you dreamed possible.

The Look Out Discovery Centre
Bracknell, Berkshire
(01344) 354400
bracknell-forest.gov.uk/lookout
Interactive science park with over 70 exhibits.

Marwell Zoological Park
Winchester, Hampshire
(01962) 777407
marwell.org.uk
Relaxing and fascinating zoological park.

Mid-Hants Railway Watercress Line
Alresford, Hampshire
(01962) 733810
watercressline.co.uk
Ten-mile steam railway through beautiful countryside.

National Motor Museum Beaulieu
Beaulieu, Hampshire
(01590) 612345
beaulieu.co.uk
Vintage cars in glorious New Forest setting.

Paultons Park

Romsey, Hampshire
(023) 8081 4442
paultonspark.co.uk
Over 50 rides for all the family.

Port Lympne Wild Animal Park, Mansion and Gardens
Lympne, Kent
(01303) 264647
totallywild.net
Rare and endangered species in 600-acre park.

Portsmouth Historic Dockyard
Portsmouth, Hampshire
(023) 9283 9766
historicdockyard.co.uk
Home to the Mary Rose and HMS Victory.

River & Rowing Museum
Henley-on-Thames, Oxfordshire
(01491) 415600
rrm.co.uk
Award-wining museum with year-round exhibitions.

The Roald Dahl Museum and Story Centre
Small Visitor Attraction of the Year - Gold
Great Missenden, Buckinghamshire
(01494) 892192
roalddahlmuseum.org
The life behind so many well-loved books.

Romney, Hythe and Dymchurch Railway
Littlestone-on-Sea, Kent
(01797) 362353
rhdr.org.uk
The world's only main line in miniature.

Thorpe Park
Chertsey, Surrey
0870 444 4466
thorpepark.com
Thrills and spills for all the family.

Weald & Downland Open Air Museum
Chichester, West Sussex
(01243) 811348
wealddown.co.uk
Rescued historic buildings in beautiful 50-acre setting.

Heritage

1066 Battle Abbey and Battlefield
Battle, East Sussex
(01424) 775705
english-heritage.org.uk
William the Conqueror's abbey commemorates the fallen.

Arundel Castle
Arundel, West Sussex
(01903) 883136
arundelcastle.org
Castle and stately home with priceless collections.

Bateman's
Burwash, East Sussex
(01435) 882302
nationaltrust.org.uk
Jacobean house, the home of Rudyard Kipling.

Blenheim Palace
Woodstock, Oxfordshire
(01993) 811091
blenheimpalace.com
Baroque palace and beautiful Capability Brown parkland.

Bodiam Castle
Bodiam, East Sussex
(01580) 830196
nationaltrust.org.uk
Magical late-medieval moated castle.

Canterbury Cathedral
Canterbury, Kent
(01227) 762862
canterbury-cathedral.org
Seat of the Archbishop of Canterbury.

Chichester Cathedral
Chichester, West Sussex
(01243) 782595
chichestercathedral.org.uk
Splendid medieval cathedral with art treasures.

Dapdune Wharf
Guildford, Surrey
(01483) 561389
nationaltrust.org.uk
Interactive exhibitions and a restored Wey barge.

Dover Castle and Secret Wartime Tunnels
Dover, Kent
(01304) 211067
english-heritage.org.uk
Historic nerve centre for Battle of Britain.

Farnham Castle
Farnham, Surrey
(01252) 721194
farnhamcastle.com
Historic home of the Bishops of Winchester.

Fishbourne Roman Palace

Chichester, West Sussex
(01243) 785859
sussexpast.co.uk/fishbourne
Remains of Roman residence with beautiful mosaics.

Goodwood House
Chichester, West Sussex
(01243) 755048
goodwood.co.uk
Stately home with superb art and furniture.

Guildford Castle
Guildford, Surrey
(01483) 444750
guildford.gov.uk
Imposing ruins and restored 12thC stone keep.

Hever Castle and Gardens

near Edenbridge, Kent
(01732) 865224
hevercastle.co.uk
Moated castle, the childhood home of Anne Boleyn.

Leeds Castle and Gardens
near Maidstone, Kent
(01622) 765400
leeds-castle.com
Medieval castle set on two islands.

Mottisfont Abbey Garden, House and Estate
Mottisfont, Hampshire
(01794) 340757
nationaltrust.org.uk
Glorious grounds of 13thC former priory.

Osborne House

East Cowes, Isle of Wight
(01983) 200022
english-heritage.org.uk
Queen Victoria's opulent seaside retreat.

Penshurst Place and Gardens

Penshurst, Kent
(01892) 870307
penshurstplace.com
Medieval manor house with Tudor gardens.

Petworth House & Park

Petworth, West Sussex
(01798) 342207
nationaltrust.org.uk
Magnificent house and internationally important art collection.

Polesden Lacey
near Dorking, Surrey
(01372) 452048
nationaltrust.org.uk
Opulent Edwardian interiors in downland setting.

Royal Pavilion
Brighton, East Sussex
(01273) 290900
royalpavilion.org.uk
King George IV's extravagant seaside palace.

Waverley Abbey
Farnham, Surrey
(01483) 252000
english-heritage.org.uk
Ruins of England's first Cistercian abbey.

Winchester Cathedral
Winchester, Hampshire
(01962) 857200
winchester-cathedral.org.uk
Magnificent medieval cathedral with soaring Gothic nave.

Windsor Castle
Windsor, Berkshire
(020) 7766 7304
royalcollection.org.uk
Official residence of HM The Queen.

Indoors

Ashford Designer Outlet
Ashford, Kent
(01233) 895900
ashforddesigneroutlet.com
One of Europe's most spectacular shopping destinations.

Bletchley Park
Bletchley, Buckinghamshire
(01908) 640404
bletchleypark.org.uk
Wartime code-breaking with the famous Enigma machines.

De La Warr Pavilion
Bexhill-on-Sea, East Sussex
(01424) 229111
dlwp.com
Superb Modernist pavilion housing theatre and gallery.

Denbies Wine Estate

Dorking, Surrey
(01306) 876616
denbiesvineyard.co.uk
Englands largest vineyard, set in 265 acres.

Dickens World
Chatham, Kent
(01634) 890421
dickensworld.co.uk
Fascinating journey through Dickens' life and times.

Gunwharf Quays
Portsmouth, Hampshire
(023) 9283 6700
gunwharf-quays.com
Innovative retail, restaurant and leisure destination.

Mercedes-Benz World
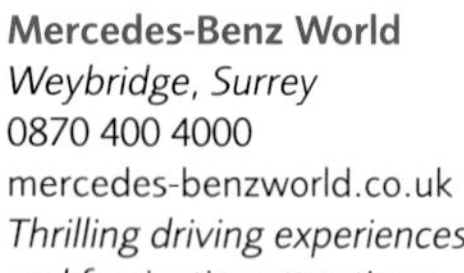
Weybridge, Surrey
0870 400 4000
mercedes-benzworld.co.uk
Thrilling driving experiences and fascinating attractions.

Pallant House Gallery
Chichester, West Sussex
(01243) 774557
pallant.org.uk
Queen Anne house holding renowned art collection.

Outdoors

Ascot Racecourse
Ascot, Berkshire
0870 727 1234
ascot.co.uk
Flat and jump racing throughout the year.

Bedgebury National Pinetum

Goudhurst, Kent
(01580) 879820
forestry.gov.uk/bedgebury
The world's finest collection of conifers.

Borde Hill Garden
Haywards Heath, West Sussex
(01444) 450326
bordehill.co.uk
Beautiful and botanically rich heritage garden.

Claremont Landscape Garden
Esher, Surrey
(01372) 467806
nationaltrust.org.uk
One of the finest English landscape gardens.

Exbury Gardens and Steam Railway

Exbury, Hampshire
(023) 8089 1203
exbury.co.uk
Vast woodland garden with circular railway.

Gardens and Grounds of Herstmonceux Castle
Herstmonceux, East Sussex
(01323) 833816
herstmonceux-castle.com
Magnificent moated castle with Elizabethan gardens.

Go Ape!
Choose from three South East locations

Bracknell, Berkshire

Leeds Castle, near Maidstone, Kent

Wendover Woods, Buckinghamshire

0845 643 9215
goape.co.uk
Rope bridges, swings and zip slides.

High Beeches Gardens
Handcross, West Sussex
(01444) 400589
highbeeches.com
Peaceful, landscaped woodland and water gardens.

Leonardslee Lakes and Gardens

Lower Beeding, West Sussex
(01403) 891212
leonardslee.com
Glorious rhododendrons and azaleas in 240-acre valley.

Loseley Park
Guildford, Surrey
(01483) 304440
loseley-park.com
Beautiful Elizabethan mansion and gardens.

Nymans Garden
Handcross, West Sussex
(01444) 405250
nationaltrust.org.uk
Romantic garden with outstanding rare tree collection.

Painshill Park
Cobham, Surrey
(01932) 868113
painshill.co.uk
Beatifully restored and renovated park with follies.

RHS Garden Wisley

Woking, Surrey
(01483) 224234
rhs.org.uk
A working encyclopedia of British gardening.

Sissinghurst Castle Garden
Sissinghurst, Kent
(01580) 710700
nationaltrust.org.uk
Celebrated gardens of enclosed compartments around mansion.

Spinnaker Tower

Portsmouth, Hampshire
(023) 9285 7520
spinnakertower.co.uk
Breathtaking views from 170m landmark.

Wakehurst Place Gardens
near Haywards Heath, West Sussex
(01444) 894066
kew.org
Kew's beautiful country garden.

ASSURANCE OF A GREAT DAY OUT
Attractions with this sign participate in the Visitor Attraction Quality Assurance Scheme which recognises high standards in all aspects of the visitor experience.

Events 2009

Sea your history
Portsmouth
seayourhistory.org.uk
Until Apr 2009

A Study in Sherlock
Portsmouth
portsmouthmuseums.co.uk
All year

New Year Steam Day
Didcot
didcotrailwaycentre.org.uk
1 Jan

Sandown Park's Golden Cup Final
Esher
sandown.co.uk
Apr

Brighton Festival
Brighton
brightonfestival.org
2 - 24 May

Derby Day at Epsom Downs Racecourse
Epsom
epsomderby.co.uk
Jun

Royal Ascot
Ascot
royalascot.co.uk
16 - 20 Jun

Henley Royal Regatta
Henley-on-Thames
hrr.co.uk
1 Jul - 5 Jul

Skandia Cowes Week
Cowes
skandiacowesweek.co.uk
1 - 8 Aug

Ringwood Carnival at Market Place and The Bickerley
Ringwood
ringwoodcarnival.org
19 Sep*

** provisional date at time of going to press*

Regional contacts and information

For more information on accommodation, attractions, activities, events and holidays in South East England, contact the regional tourism organisation below. The website has a wealth of information and you can order or download publications.

South East England

The following publications are available from Tourism South East by logging on to **visitsoutheastengland.com** or calling **(023) 8062 5400**:

Publications

- **Escape into the Countryside**
- **Distinctive Country Inns**
- **We Know Just the Place**

E-Brochures

- **Family Fun**
- **Timeless Treasures**
- **Just the Two of Us**

Clockwise: Freshwater Bay, Isle of Wight; Savill Garden, Surrey; Bewl Water, Kent; Canterbury Cathedral, Kent

Tourist Information Centres

When you arrive at your destination, visit an Official Partner Tourist Information Centre for quality assured help with accommodation and information about local attractions and events, or email your request before you go. To search for attractions and Tourist Information Centres on the move just text INFO to 62233, and a web link will be sent to your mobile phone. To find a Tourist Information Centre by region visit enjoyEngland.com/find-tic.

Bicester	Unit 86a, Bicester Village	(01869) 369055	bicester.vc@cherwell-dc.gov.uk
Brighton	Pavilion Buildings	0906 711 2255**	brighton-tourism@brighton-hove.gov.uk
Canterbury	12/13 Sun Street	(01227) 378100	canterburyinformation@canterbury.gov.uk
Chichester	29a South Street	(01243) 775888	chitic@chichester.gov.uk
Cowes	9 The Arcade	(01983) 813818	info@islandbreaks.co.uk
Dover	The Old Town Gaol	(01304) 205108	tic@doveruk.com
Hastings	Queens Square	(01424) 781111	hic@hastings.gov.uk
Newport	High Street	(01983) 813818	info@islandbreaks.co.uk
Oxford	15/16 Broad Street	(01865) 726871	tic@oxford.gov.uk
Portsmouth	Clarence Esplanade	(023) 9282 6722	vis@portsmouthcc.gov.uk
Portsmouth	The Hard	(023) 9282 6722	vis@portsmouthcc.gov.uk
Rochester	95 High Street	(01634) 843666	visitor.centre@medway.gov.uk
Royal Tunbridge Wells	The Pantiles	(01892) 515675	touristinformationcentre @tunbridgewells.gov.uk
Ryde	81-83 Union Street	(01983) 813818	info@islandbreaks.co.uk
Sandown	8 High Street	(01983) 813818	info@islandbreaks.co.uk
Shanklin	67 High Street	(01983) 813818	info@islandbreaks.co.uk
Southampton	9 Civic Centre Road	(023) 8083 3333	tourist.information@southampton.gov.uk
Winchester	High Street	(01962 840500	tourism@winchester.gov.uk
Windsor	Royal Windsor Central Station	(01753) 743900	windsor.tic@rbwm.gov.uk
Yarmouth	The Quay	(01983) 813818	info@islandbreaks.co.uk

**calls to this number are charged at premium rate

Never has a rose meant so much

Everyone has a trusted friend, someone who tells it straight. Well, that's what the Enjoy England Quality Rose does: reassures you before you check into your holiday accommodation that it will be just what you want, because it's been checked out by independent assessors. Which means you can book with confidence and get on with the real business of having a fantastic break.

enjoy**England**.com

★★★
HOLIDAY PARK

The **Quality Rose** is the mark of England's *official*, nationwide quality assessment scheme and covers just about every place you might want to stay, using a clear star rating system: from caravan parks to stylish boutique hotels, farmhouse B&Bs to country house retreats, self-catering cottages by the sea to comfy narrowboats perfect for getting away from it all. Think of the Quality Rose as your personal guarantee that your expectations will be met.

Our ratings made easy

★	Simple, practical, no frills
★★	Well presented and well run
★★★	Very good level of quality and comfort
★★★★	Excellent standard throughout
★★★★★	Exceptional level of quality

Look no further. Just look out for the Quality Rose.
Find out more at enjoy**England**.com/quality

where to stay in

South East England

All place names in the blue bands are shown on the maps at the front of this guide.

A complete listing of all VisitBritain assessed parks in England appears at the back.

Accommodation symbols

Symbols give useful information about services and facilities. On page 7 you can find a key to these symbols.

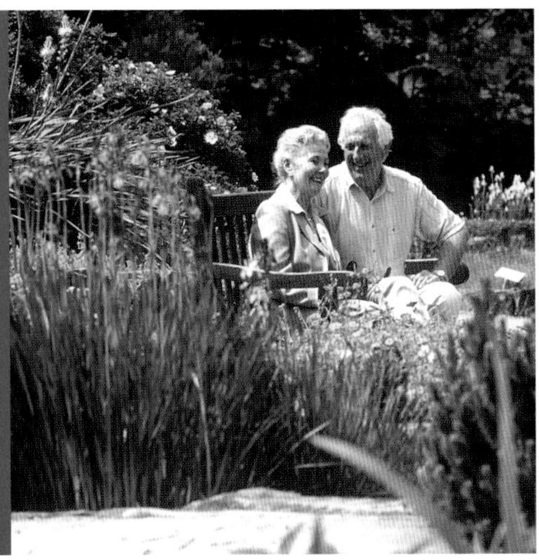

ARRETON, Isle of Wight Map ref 2C3

★★
HOLIDAY PARK
(10) £8.00–£9.00
(5) £8.00–£9.00
(5)
10 touring pitches

Perreton Farm

East Lane, Arreton, Newport PO30 3DL **t** (01983) 865218 **e** roger.perreton@virgin.net

islandbreaks.co.uk

Farm with countryside views, quiet location. Ideal for walkers and cyclists with plenty of footpaths. Cycle track nearby with hire facilities on farm. Dogs welcome. Good pubs in village.

open April to October
payment Cash, cheques

General Leisure

ASHFORD, Kent Map ref 3B4

★★★★★
HOLIDAY, TOURING & CAMPING PARK
£14.00–£21.00
£14.00–£21.00
£12.00–£18.00
(5) £220.00–£450.00
70 touring pitches

Broadhembury Holiday Park

Steeds Lane, Kingsnorth, Ashford TN26 1NQ **t** (01233) 620859 **e** holidaypark@broadhembury.co.uk

broadhembury.co.uk GUEST REVIEWS • SPECIAL OFFERS • REAL-TIME BOOKING

For walking, cycling, visiting castles and gardens or just relaxing, Broadhembury, in quiet Kentish countryside, is a park for all seasons. Convenient for Channel crossings and Canterbury.

open All year
payment Credit/debit cards, cash, cheques, euros

General Leisure

BATTLE, East Sussex Map ref 3B4

★★★★★
HOLIDAY PARK
ROSE AWARD
(54) £192.00–£995.00

Christmas and New Year holidays available.

Crowhurst Park

Telham Lane, Battle TN33 0SL **t** (01424) 773344 **e** enquiries@crowhurstpark.co.uk

crowhurstpark.co.uk

open 4 March to 4 January
payment Credit/debit cards, cash, cheques

Quality development of luxury Scandinavian-style pine lodges within the grounds of a 17thC country estate. Facilities include leisure club with indoor swimming pool, bar, restaurant and children's playground. David Bellamy Gold Conservation Award.

SAT NAV *TN33 0SL*

General Leisure

BEMBRIDGE, Isle of Wight Map ref 2C3

★★★
HOLIDAY PARK

(400) £12.00–£28.50
(400) £12.00–£28.50
(400) £12.00–£28.50
(230) £88.00–£848.00
400 touring pitches

Special offers are available from time to time – please visit our website for full details.

Whitecliff Bay Holiday Park

Hillway Road, Bembridge PO35 5PL **t** (01983) 872671 **e** holiday@whitecliff-bay.com

whitecliff-bay.com SPECIAL OFFERS • REAL-TIME BOOKING

open March to October
payment Credit/debit cards, cash, cheques, euros

Situated in an Area of Outstanding Natural Beauty, the park offers great-value family holidays. There are facilities on site for all ages. Pets welcome in low season.

SAT NAV *PO35 5PL*

General Leisure

BEXHILL-ON-SEA, East Sussex Map ref 3B4

★★★★
HOLIDAY, TOURING & CAMPING PARK

(55) £9.50–£10.50
(55) £8.20–£9.20
(55) £9.20–£10.20
(2) £135.00–£340.00
55 touring pitches

Cobbs Hill Farm Caravan & Camping Park

Watermill Lane, Sidley, Bexhill-on-Sea TN39 5JA **t** (01424) 213460 **e** cobbshillfarmuk@hotmail.com

cobbshillfarm.co.uk

Quiet site in countryside with selection of farm animals. Touring and hire vans, level pitches, tent and rally fields. Near Hastings, Battle and Eastbourne.

payment Credit/debit cards, cash, cheques

General Leisure

BIRCHINGTON, Kent Map ref 3C3

★★★★★
HOLIDAY, TOURING & CAMPING PARK

(100) £13.50–£22.50
(100) £13.50–£22.50
(100) £13.50–£22.50
300 touring pitches

Two Chimneys Holiday Park

Shottendane Road, Birchington CT7 0HD **t** (01843) 841068 **e** info@twochimneys.co.uk

twochimneys.co.uk

open Easter to October
payment Credit/debit cards, cash, cheques

A friendly, family-run country site near sandy beaches. Spacious, level pitches. Modern wc/shower and laundry facilities including disabled. Children's play and ball-games areas.

SAT NAV *CT7 0HD*

General Leisure

Don't forget www.

Web addresses throughout this guide are shown without the prefix www. Please include www. in the address line of your browser. If a web address does not follow this style it is shown in full.

BRIGHTON & HOVE, East Sussex Map ref 2D3

★★★★★
TOURING & CAMPING PARK
(169) £14.90–£28.30
(169) £14.90–£28.30
on application
169 touring pitches

THE CARAVAN CLUB

Sheepcote Valley Caravan Club Site

East Brighton Park, Brighton BN2 5TS **t** (01273) 626546

caravanclub.co.uk

open All year
payment Credit/debit cards, cash, cheques

Located on the South Downs, just two miles from Brighton. Visit the Marina, with its shops, pubs, restaurants and cinema, and take a tour of the exotic Royal Pavilion.

SAT NAV *BN2 5TS*

Special member rates mean you can save your membership subscription in less than a week. Visit our website to find out more.

General Leisure

BURFORD, Oxfordshire Map ref 2B1

★★★★★
TOURING PARK
(120) £12.20–£25.10
(120) £12.20–£25.10
120 touring pitches

THE CARAVAN CLUB

Burford Caravan Club Site

Bradwell Grove, Burford OX18 4JJ **t** (01993) 823080

caravanclub.co.uk

open March to November
payment Credit/debit cards, cash, cheques

Attractive, spacious site opposite Cotswold Wildlife Park. Burford has superb Tudor houses, a museum and historic inns. A great base from which to explore the Cotswolds.

SAT NAV *OX18 4JJ*

Special member rates mean you can save your membership subscription in less than a week. Visit our website to find out more.

General Leisure

CANTERBURY, Kent Map ref 3B3

★★★★
HOLIDAY, TOURING & CAMPING PARK
(15) £14.00–£20.00
(5) £14.00–£20.00
(25) £13.00–£18.50
(7) £190.00–£420.00
45 touring pitches

Yew Tree Park

Stone Street, Petham, Canterbury CT4 5PL **t** (01227) 700306 **e** info@yewtreepark.com

yewtreepark.com SPECIAL OFFERS

payment Credit/debit cards, cash, cheques

Picturesque country park close to Canterbury, centrally located for exploring Kent. Naturally landscaped touring and camping facilities. Holiday units. Heated pool.

SAT NAV *CT4 5PL*

General Leisure

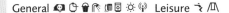

Do you have access needs?

Look for the National Accessible Scheme symbols if you have special hearing, visual or mobility needs.

CHICHESTER, West Sussex Map ref 2C3

★★
HOLIDAY, TOURING & CAMPING PARK

(15) £14.00
(15) £14.00

Bell Caravan Park

Bell Lane, Birdham, Chichester PO20 7HY **t** (01243) 512264

Quiet, sheltered park convenient for Chichester and the coast. At village of Birdham, turn left into Bell Lane. Park is a few hundred yards on the left.

open March to October
payment Cash, cheques

General Leisure

COTSWOLDS

See under Burford, Kingham, Standlake
See also Cotswolds in South West England section

EASTBOURNE, East Sussex Map ref 3B4

★★★
TOURING & CAMPING PARK

(60) £12.00–£19.00
(60) £12.00–£19.00
(60) £12.00–£19.00
60 touring pitches

Special low season midweek offer: 3 nights for the price of 2. Contact us for more details.

Fairfields Farm Caravan & Camping Park

Eastbourne Road, Westham, Pevensey BN24 5NG **t** (01323) 763165 **e** enquiries@fairfieldsfarm.com

fairfieldsfarm.com GUEST REVIEWS

open April to October
payment Credit/debit cards, cash, cheques

A quiet country touring site on a working farm. Clean facilities, lakeside walk with farm pets and free fishing for campers. Close to the beautiful seaside resort of Eastbourne, and a good base from which to explore the diverse scenery and attractions of south east England.

SAT NAV *BN24 5NG*

General Leisure

FOLKESTONE, Kent Map ref 3B4

★★★★★
TOURING & CAMPING PARK

(140) £12.20–£25.10
(140) £12.20–£25.10
140 touring pitches

Black Horse Farm Caravan Club Site

385 Canterbury Road, Densole, Folkestone CT18 7BG **t** (01303) 892665

caravanclub.co.uk

open All year
payment Credit/debit cards, cash, cheques

Set in the heart of farming country in the Kentish village of Densole on the Downs. This is a quiet and relaxed country site, ideally suited for families wishing to visit the many interesting local attractions including the historic city of Canterbury. For nature lovers there are many walks.

SAT NAV *CT18 7BG*

Special member rates mean you can save your membership subscription in less than a week. Visit our website to find out more.

General Leisure

PETS! WELCOME WELCOME PETS!

Where is my pet welcome?

Want to take your cherished companion with you on holiday? Proprietors participating in our Welcome Pets! scheme go out of their way to make special provision for you and your pet. Look out for the symbol.

FORDINGBRIDGE, Hampshire Map ref 2B3

★★★★★
HOLIDAY PARK
ROSE AWARD
(131) £199.00–£1,255.00
233 touring pitches

Sandy Balls Holiday Centre

Godshill, Fordingbridge SP6 2JZ **t** 0845 270 2248 **e** post@sandy-balls.co.uk

sandy-balls.co.uk SPECIAL OFFERS • REAL-TIME BOOKING

open All year
payment Credit/debit cards, cash, cheques

Nestled in 120 acres of woods and parkland in the New Forest National Park, Sandy Balls has something for everyone. Guests can enjoy dinner at The Bistro, a woodland walk, a dip in one of the swimming pools, or get active at the Leisure Club and Cycle Centre!

SAT NAV *SP6 2JZ*

General Leisure

GATWICK AIRPORT

See under Redhill

GOSPORT, Hampshire Map ref 2C3

★★★
HOLIDAY, TOURING & CAMPING PARK
(120) £16.00–£25.00
(120) £16.00–£25.00
(120) £11.00–£25.00
(30) £220.00–£480.00
120 touring pitches

Kingfisher Caravan Park

Browndown Road, Stokes Road, Gosport PO13 9BG **t** (023) 9250 2611
e info@kingfisher-caravan-park.co.uk

kingfisher-caravan-park.co.uk

Family-run park, five minutes' walk to the beach. On-site clubhouse, restaurant, shop, launderette, children's room. Caravans to hire or buy.

open All year
payment Credit/debit cards, cash, cheques

General Leisure

HAMBLE, Hampshire Map ref 2C3

★★★
HOLIDAY, TOURING & CAMPING PARK
(77) £14.00–£30.00
(77) £14.00–£30.00
(77) £12.00–£25.00
(18) £261.00–£810.00
77 touring pitches

Riverside Holidays

Satchell Lane, Hamble SO31 4HR **t** (023) 8045 3220 **e** enquiries@riversideholidays.co.uk

riversideholidays.co.uk

Quiet park overlooking marina and River Hamble, on edge of picturesque sailing village with many pubs and restaurants. Caravan holiday homes and pine lodges for hire, plus camping and touring facilities.

open All year
payment Credit/debit cards, cash, cheques

General Leisure

HASTINGS, East Sussex Map ref 3B4

★★★★
HOLIDAY, TOURING & CAMPING PARK
£18.00–£20.00
£18.00–£20.00
(240) £16.00–£18.00
132 touring pitches

Hastings Touring Park

Barley Lane, Hastings TN35 5DX **t** (01424) 423583

Touring park on the south coast, on the outskirts of historic Hastings close to beaches. Just off the main London Road, A21 and A259, close to main town centre.

open Easter to first week of September
payment Credit/debit cards, cash, cheques

General Leisure

HOVE

See under Brighton & Hove

What do the star ratings mean?

Detailed information about star ratings can be found at the back of this guide.

HURLEY, Berkshire Map ref 2C2

★★★★
HOLIDAY PARK
(138) £11.00–£18.00
(138) £11.00–£18.00
(62) £9.00–£16.00
(10) £260.00–£460.00
200 touring pitches

Hurley Riverside Park

Hurley, Maidenhead SL6 5NE **t** (01628) 824493 **e** info@hurleyriversidepark.co.uk

hurleyriversidepark.co.uk

open March to October
payment Credit/debit cards, cash, cheques

Our family-run park is situated in the picturesque Thames Valley, surrounded by farmland. Access to the Thames Path. Ideal location for visiting Windsor, Legoland, Oxford and London. Gold David Bellamy Conservation Award.

SAT NAV *SL6 5NE* **ONLINE MAP**

General Leisure

ISLE OF WIGHT

See under Bembridge, Ryde, St Helens, Yarmouth

KINGHAM, Oxfordshire Map ref 2B1

★★★★★
HOLIDAY PARK
ROSE AWARD
(30) £420.00–£1,125.00

Prices from £61 per night.

Bluewood Park

Kingham, Chipping Norton OX7 6UJ **t** (01608) 659946 **e** rachel@bluewoodpark.com

bluewoodpark.com GUEST REVIEWS • SPECIAL OFFERS • REAL-TIME BOOKING

open All year
payment Credit/debit cards, cash, cheques

Escape to Bluewood Park. Nestled in a bluebell wood in an Area of Outstanding Natural Beauty, the park is a superb base for exploring the Cotswolds. This exclusive development of luxury and contemporary accommodation, each with its own hot tub, is the perfect place to relax and unwind.

SAT NAV *OX7 6UJ*

General Leisure

KINGSDOWN, Kent Map ref 3C4

★★★★★
HOLIDAY PARK
(50) £219.00–£677.00

Kingsdown Park Holiday Village

Upper Street, Kingsdown, Deal CT14 8AU **t** (01304) 361205 **e** info@kingsdownpark.net

kingsdownpark.net SPECIAL OFFERS

This picturesque park provides the perfect base for exploring Kent. Comfortable lodges and excellent leisure facilities ensure you are not disappointed.

open March to October and 20 December to 3 January
payment Credit/debit cards, cash, cheques

General Leisure

Looking for an ideal family break?

For accommodation offering additional facilities and services for a range of ages and family units, look out for the Families Welcome symbol. Owners of these properties will go out of their way to welcome families.

MAIDSTONE, Kent Map ref 3B3

Rating Applied For
TOURING & CAMPING PARK
(65) £12.20–£25.10
(65) £12.20–£25.10
65 touring pitches

Special member rates mean you can save your membership subscription in less than a week. Visit our website to find out more.

THE CARAVAN CLUB

Bearsted Caravan Club Site

Ashford Road, Hollingbourne, Maidstone ME17 1XH **t** (01622) 730018

caravanclub.co.uk

open All year
payment Credit/debit cards, cash, cheques

The site gently slopes towards the open perimeter grounds of Leeds Castle. Surrounded by fields, one of which is a horse paddock and slightly set back from the main road, this site offers an ideal, peaceful stop-off point en route to the ferry ports.

SAT NAV *ME17 1XH*

General Leisure

MARDEN, Kent Map ref 3B4

★★★★★
TOURING & CAMPING PARK
(100) £13.00–£19.00
(33) £13.00–£19.00
(20) £13.00–£18.00
100 touring pitches

Tanner Farm Touring Caravan & Camping Park

Goudhurst Road, Tonbridge TN12 9ND **t** (01622) 832399 **e** enquiries@tannerfarmpark.co.uk

tannerfarmpark.co.uk

open All year
payment Credit/debit cards, cash, cheques

Immaculate, secluded park surrounded by beautiful countryside on family farm. Ideal touring base for the area. Gold David Bellamy Conservation Award. Bed and breakfast also available. Green Tourism Business Scheme silver. Caravan Club AS.

SAT NAV *TN12 9ND*

General Leisure

MOLLINGTON, Oxfordshire Map ref 2C1

★★★★
TOURING & CAMPING PARK
£12.50–£13.50
£12.50–£13.50
(15) £6.00–£10.00
36 touring pitches

Anita's Touring Caravan Park

Church Farm, Mollington, Banbury OX17 1AZ **t** (01295) 750731 **e** anitagail@btopenworld.com

caravancampingsites.co.uk

Family-run site on working farm. Quality toilet/shower facility. Central to many places of interest, the Cotswolds, National Trust properties, Blenheim, Oxford, Stratford. Rallies welcome. Three superb self-catering cottages for hire.

open All year
payment Cash, cheques

General Leisure

NEW FOREST

See under Fordingbridge, New Milton, Ringwood

Using map references

The map references refer to the colour maps at the front of this guide. The first figure is the map number, the letter and figure that follow indicate the grid reference on the map.

NEW MILTON, Hampshire Map ref 2B3

★★★★
HOLIDAY PARK
(19) £170.00–£555.00

Glen Orchard Holiday Park

Walkford Lane, New Milton BH25 5NH **t** (01425) 616463 **e** enquiries@glenorchard.co.uk

glenorchard.co.uk

Small family park in secluded, landscaped setting close to beaches, forest, riding, golf and fishing. Convenient for Bournemouth, Christchurch, Lymington, Southampton and Isle of Wight.

open March to October
payment Credit/debit cards, cash, cheques

General Leisure

PEVENSEY BAY, East Sussex Map ref 3B4

★★★
HOLIDAY, TOURING & CAMPING PARK
(40) £14.50–£19.50
(4) £14.50–£19.50
(50) £14.50–£19.50
(8) £180.00–£595.00
94 touring pitches

Bay View Park

Old Martello Road, Pevensey Bay BN24 6DX **t** (01323) 768688 **e** holidays@bay-view.co.uk

bay-view.co.uk

Family site on a private road next to the beach. Play area. New showers and laundry. Small, well-stocked shop. Ideal touring base.

open March to October
payment Credit/debit cards, cash, cheques

General Leisure

READING, Berkshire Map ref 2C2

★★★★
TOURING & CAMPING PARK
(58) £15.00–£22.00
(58) £15.00–£22.00
(14) £13.00–£18.00
58 touring pitches

Wellington Country Park

Odiham Road, Riseley, Reading RG7 1SP **t** (0118) 932 6444 **e** info@wellington-country-park.co.uk

wellington-country-park.co.uk REAL-TIME BOOKING

A wealth of enjoyment. Nature trails, children's play areas, miniature railway, crazy golf. Special events throughout the season.

open February to November
payment Credit/debit cards

General Leisure

REDHILL, Surrey Map ref 2D2

★★★★
TOURING PARK
(150) £12.20–£25.10
(150) £12.20–£25.10
150 touring pitches

THE CARAVAN CLUB

Alderstead Heath Caravan Club Site

Dean Lane, Redhill RH1 3AH **t** (01737) 644629

caravanclub.co.uk

open All year
payment Credit/debit cards, cash, cheques

Quiet site with views over rolling, wooded North Downs. Denbies Wine Estate nearby. For day trips try Chessington and Thorpe Park and the lively city of Brighton. Non-members welcome.

SAT NAV *RH1 3AH*

Special member rates mean you can save your membership subscription in less than a week. Visit our website to find out more.

What if I need to cancel?

It is advisable to check the proprietor's cancellation policy in case you have to change your plans at a later date.

RINGWOOD, Hampshire Map ref 2B3

★★★★ TOURING & CAMPING PARK

(150) £16.50–£27.00
(150) £16.50–£27.00
(150) £16.50–£27.00
150 touring pitches

Shamba Holidays

230 Ringwood Road, St Leonards, Ringwood BH24 2SB **t** (01202) 873302
e enquiries@shambaholidays.co.uk

shambaholidays.co.uk

Family-run touring and camping park close to the New Forest and Bournemouth with its fine beaches. Modern toilet/shower facilities, heated indoor/outdoor pool, licensed clubhouse, games room, takeaway, shop.

open March to October
payment Credit/debit cards, cash, cheques

General Leisure

ROMSEY, Hampshire Map ref 2C3

★★★★ HOLIDAY, TOURING & CAMPING PARK

(70) £16.00–£24.00
(70) £16.00–£24.00
(40) £14.00–£24.00
(6) £280.00–£500.00
70 touring pitches

Hill Farm Caravan Park

Branches Lane, Sherfield English, Romsey SO51 6FH **t** (01794) 340402 **e** gib@hillfarmpark.com

hillfarmpark.com

Set in 11 acres of beautiful countryside on the edge of the New Forest, our family-run site provides an ideal base from which to visit the area. Touring pitches from March to October, holiday homes from February to January.

payment Cash, cheques

General Leisure

RYDE, Isle of Wight Map ref 2C3

★★ TOURING & CAMPING PARK

(6) Min £4.50
(6) Min £4.50
(20) Min £4.50
32 touring pitches

Roebeck Camping and Caravan Park

Gatehouse Road, Upton Cross PO33 4BP **t** (01983) 611475 **e** andrew.cross@roebeck-farm.co.uk

roebeck-farm.co.uk REAL-TIME BOOKING

A small campsite set in 10 acres of farmland on the outskirts of Ryde, with toilet, shower and laundry facilities. Also tipi hire available.

open May to October
payment Credit/debit cards, cash, cheques, euros

General Leisure

RYDE, Isle of Wight Map ref 2C3

★★★★ TOURING & CAMPING PARK

£11.00–£16.50
£11.00–£16.50
£11.00–£16.50
100 touring pitches

Whitefield Forest Touring Park

Brading Road PO33 1QL **t** (01983) 617069 **e** pat&louise@whitefieldforest.co.uk

whitefieldforest.co.uk

New family-run touring park located in the tranquil setting of Whitefield Forest. All pitches are level and spacious, with new amenities block including baby, family and disabled facilities.

open 30 March to 5 October
payment Credit/debit cards, cash, cheques

General Leisure

ST HELENS, Isle of Wight Map ref 2C3

★★★ TOURING & CAMPING PARK

(70) £10.00
(70) £10.00
(70) £10.00
70 touring pitches

Carpenters Farm Campsite

Carpenters Road, St Helens, Ryde PO33 1YL **t** (01983) 874557 **e** info@carpentersfarm.co.uk

carpentersfarm.co.uk

Farm campsite with beautiful views in picturesque rural setting, adjacent to RSPB Reserve and SSSI. Close to beaches and attractions. Relaxed atmosphere on site. Families, groups and pets very welcome.

open All year
payment Cash, cheques

General Leisure

For **key to symbols** see page 7

ST NICHOLAS AT WADE, Kent Map ref 3C3

★★
TOURING & CAMPING PARK

(15) £12.00–£16.00
(5) £12.00–£14.00
(55) £9.00–£13.00
75 touring pitches

St Nicholas Camping Site

Court Road, St Nicholas at Wade, Birchington CT7 0NH **t** (01843) 847245

The site – flat, grassy and well-sheltered – is on the outskirts of the village, close to the village shop. The resort of Thanet is within easy reach. The site is signposted from the A299 and A28.

payment Cash, cheques

General Leisure

SELSEY, West Sussex Map ref 2C3

★★★★★
TOURING PARK

(250) £18.50–£32.00
(250) £18.50–£32.00
(50) £16.50–£30.00
250 touring pitches

Warner Farm Touring Park

Warner Lane, Selsey, Chichester PO20 9EL **t** (01243) 604499 & (01243) 606080
e touring@bunnleisure.co.uk

warnerfarm.co.uk GUEST REVIEWS · SPECIAL OFFERS

open March to October
payment Credit/debit cards, cash, cheques

A top-quality camping and touring holiday park. With a choice of well-maintained standard, electric or service pitches and excellent wash facilities, you can have a relaxing and carefree holiday here. Bunn Leisure's fantastic entertainment and children's activities are also available to use. A friendly atmosphere and welcome awaits you! Please see website for current prices.

SAT NAV *PO20 9EL* **ONLINE MAP**

General Leisure

SELSEY, West Sussex Map ref 2C3

★★★★
HOLIDAY PARK
ROSE AWARD

(250) £125.00–£1,500.00

See website for special promotions.

West Sands Holiday Park

Mill Lane, Selsey, Chichester PO20 9BH **t** (01243) 606080 **e** holidays@bunnleisure.co.uk

bunnleisure.co.uk SPECIAL OFFERS

open March to October
payment Credit/debit cards, cash, cheques

Situated on the beachfront overlooking beautiful coastline, West Sands is our liveliest holiday park. With everything you could want for a fun-filled family holiday...let your children play at the fun-fair and kids' clubs; enjoy fantastic entertainment; relax at the superb Oasis pool complex...we can't wait to see you!

SAT NAV *PO20 9BH* **ONLINE MAP**

General Leisure

STANDLAKE, Oxfordshire Map ref 2C1

★★★
HOLIDAY, TOURING & CAMPING PARK

(214) £16.50–£18.50
(214) £16.50–£18.50
(214) £14.00–£16.00
(7) £240.00–£500.00
214 touring pitches

Hardwick Parks

The Downs, Standlake, Witney OX29 7PZ **t** (01865) 300501 **e** info@hardwickparks.co.uk

hardwickparks.co.uk

Rural park near Witney, large level touring fields, lakes and river on site. Tents, caravans, trailer tents and motorhomes welcome. Static holiday caravans for hire and for sale.

open April to October
payment Credit/debit cards, cash, cheques

General Leisure

STANDLAKE, Oxfordshire Map ref 2C1

★★★★★
TOURING & CAMPING PARK
(37) £15.90–£25.90
(37) £15.90–£25.90
(16) £14.90–£21.90
90 touring pitches

Lincoln Farm Park

High Street, Standlake OX29 7RH **t** (01865) 300239 **e** info@lincolnfarm.co.uk

lincolnfarmpark.co.uk GUEST REVIEWS · REAL-TIME BOOKING

open All year except Christmas and New Year
payment Credit/debit cards, cash, cheques, euros

Award-winning park situated in the village of Standlake with two village pubs, each serving food. Our immaculate facilities comprise two indoor heated pools, spas, saunas, steam room, children's pool, launderette, campers' kitchen, family bathroom, central heating. A bus stops at the park entrance for those wishing to visit historic Oxford.

SAT NAV *OX29 7RH* **ONLINE MAP**

General Leisure

WASHINGTON, West Sussex Map ref 2D3

★★★★
TOURING & CAMPING PARK
(21) Max £19.00
(5) Max £19.00
(80) Max £19.00
21 touring pitches

Washington Caravan & Camping Park

London Road, Washington RH20 4AJ **t** (01903) 892869 **e** washcamp@amserve.com

washcamp.com

The park is set in beautifully landscaped grounds beneath the South Downs affording the right atmosphere for an enjoyable stay. Well situated for visiting places of interest.

open All year
payment Credit/debit cards, cash, cheques

General Leisure

WINCHESTER, Hampshire Map ref 2C3

★★★
TOURING & CAMPING PARK
(120) £10.60–£23.20
(120) £10.60–£23.20
on application
120 touring pitches

THE CARAVAN CLUB

Morn Hill Caravan Club Site

Morn Hill, Winchester SO21 2PH **t** (01962) 869877

caravanclub.co.uk

open March to November
payment Credit/debit cards, cash, cheques

Large, split-level site from which to explore Winchester. Oxford, Chichester, the New Forest, Salisbury and Stonehenge are all within an hour's drive.

SAT NAV *SO21 2PH*

Midweek discount: pitch fee for standard pitches for stays on any Tue, Wed or Thu night outside peak season dates will be reduced by 50%.

General Leisure

YARMOUTH, Isle of Wight Map ref 2C3

★★★★★
HOLIDAY & TOURING PARK
ROSE AWARD
£15.00–£25.00
£15.00–£25.00
£15.00–£25.00
(65)
175 touring pitches

The Orchards Holiday Caravan & Camping Park

Main Road PO41 0TS **t** (01983) 531331 **e** info@orchards-holiday-park.co.uk

orchards-holiday-park.co.uk GUEST REVIEWS · SPECIAL OFFERS

Situated in beautiful countryside with wonderful downland views. 65 superb luxury holiday caravans and 175 touring pitches. Indoor and outdoor pools, shop, takeaway, pool-side cafe, play areas and dog-walking area. Excellent walking and cycling from the park.

open Mid February to December
payment Cash, cheques

General Leisure

For **key to symbols** see page 7

London

Clockwise: Buckingham Palace; Shakespeare's Globe; Tower Bridge

Great days out

So you think you know London? Take another look because there's always another secret to discover or something new to try, as well as inspirational itineraries to follow for weekends and days out. Just remember to leave yourself with enough time for everything (a year or more should do).

Culture vulture

Does Turner turn you on? The Impressionists impress? Then London is your place. With some 70 large museums and over 30 major art galleries, it's a top culture capital. The **Museum of London** is a good start for insights into local life. Experience the Great Fire of London 1666 through the eyes of survivors – what really happened? New galleries opening 2010 include the city's 21stC story.

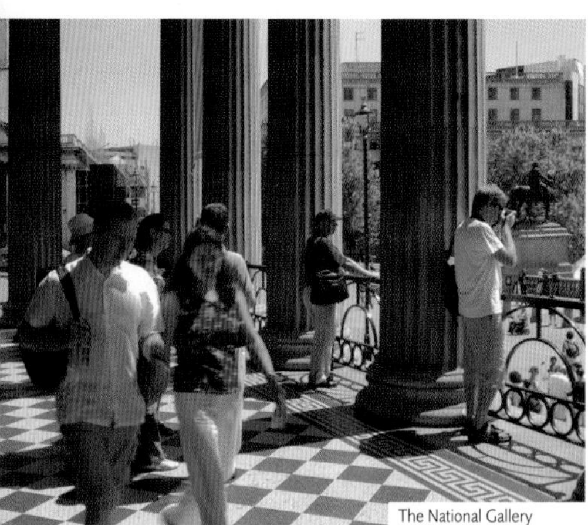

The National Gallery

At the **National Gallery** see famous works of art by Van Gogh, Monet and da Vinci amongst an outstanding collection of Western European paintings. Nearby, **Somerset House** is bursting with Old Master and Impressionist paintings, decorative arts and treasures from the Hermitage Museum, St Petersburg. Its Admiralty Restaurant serves delicious lunches, too. And **Tate Britain**, just along the Thames, explores over 500 years of British art.

Take a boat trip to **Greenwich** for an adventure through Britain's seafaring history at the **National Maritime Museum**. And do leave time for lesser-known gems like the **Ben Uri Gallery, The London Jewish Museum of Art**. Or the **Royal London Hospital Archives and Museum** telling the fascinating story of the hospital and featuring people like the unfortunate 'Elephant Man'.

Greenfingered London

Fabulous **Chelsea Flower Show** in May is a horticultural highspot of everyone's year. But at any time there are plenty of green (and every other floral colour) delights to dig into. **Kew Gardens** are the ultimate destination: over 300 acres growing more than 30,000 types of plants.

For an unusual surprise, take the train from Victoria Station to **Eltham Palace**, where 19-acre gardens combine medieval and 20thC elements. The trip to Charles Darwin's **Down House**, Orpington, also gets creative juices flowing: follow the path he paced in the beautiful gardens as he contemplated his revolutionary theories. And if you want a fragrant souvenir to take home, browse **Columbia Road Flower Market** on Sunday mornings, an absolute blaze of colour.

why not... climb the Monument (311 steps) in the City for superb views?

Left to right: South Bank; Westminster

did you know... dozens of museums and galleries are free to visit, including Tate Britain?

Ladies who lunch

London does shopping, eating and pampering so well! And, ladies, you deserve a girls' outing. Check what's chic in **Knightsbridge** and the top designer stores on the **Kings Road**. Or perfect the quirky and vintage look shopping around **Notting Hill** and **Portobello Road**. Then enjoy a leisurely lunch with **Bateaux London Restaurant Cruisers**, watching the sights drift by, or tea at **The Ritz** or **Browns**. Dinner at **The Ivy** or **Le Caprice** sounds tempting, too.

Sports galore

There's plenty of sport, too. London's great venues like **Wimbledon** – the **Lawn Tennis Museum** gives great insights into the world-famous championship. There's no need to wait for match days to enjoy a trip to **Chelsea Football Club**, the **Emirates Stadium** or **Lord's**. Behind-the-scenes tours bring to life soccer and cricket dreams. Take the kids, they love sport in the capital as well.

Luvvies London

Nearly 150 theatres raise the curtain on drama, opera, dance and more. Kick off in style with a **West End** show – ask about good deals at the tkts booth in **Leicester Square**, London's official reduced theatre ticket operation. Sip pre-performance drinks at the luvvie-friendly **French House**, **Toucan** or **Dog & Duck** pub, and digest the night's entertainment at **Joe Allen**, where you might spot a thesp or two. Next day, join a back-stage tour – the **Theatre Royal**, Drury Lane is just one venue that opens its doors. And stroll along the **South Bank**, the heart of cultural cool, to see what's on at the **Southbank Centre**. Round off with a tour of the magnificent **Shakespeare's Globe**.

Tea at Harrods

Big kids

For some family-friendly fun hop aboard the **London Eye**, rising slowly to view 55 famous landmarks across the city. Keep spirits high with a visit to the **Tower of London**, possibly the country's most haunted building – was that the scream of a ghostly nobleman being led to the executioner's block? **Hampton Court Palace** also has a host of spooks, including Henry VIII's fifth wife Catherine Howard. Who ever said history was dull?

Don't get lost in the palace's famous maze. Explore all nine decks of **HMS Belfast**, from the Captain's Bridge to the boiler and engine rooms, well below the ship's waterline. See the sick bay and operations room and imagine life on board during World War II. Who would guess you could be in a vast landscape of lagoons, lakes and ponds within 25 minutes of central London? The **London Wetland Centre** in Barnes is Europe's best urban site for watching wildlife, including hundreds of bird species. Come nose to nose with sharks and deadly stone fish at the **London Aquarium**. If you've energy to spare, let off steam in one of London's many parks. Picnic and play footie in **St James's Park** or go boating on the Serpentine in **Hyde Park**.

why not... explore Regent's Canal from Little Venice to the Docklands?

The main event

London living can be pretty high octane, no more so than for event-goers. From **Chinese New Year** Celebrations to **The Proms** to lights-on for Christmas, the calendar is packed. Gather beside the Thames for spring's **Oxford and Cambridge Boat Race**, everyone likes tradition. And a summer's evening at **Kenwood House**, Hampstead, passes perfectly at a picnic concert. Hit the streets around Ladbroke Grove for the steelbands and exuberant costumes that make **Notting Hill Carnival** swing. Admire the Golden State Coach at the **Lord Mayor's Show**, processing to the Royal Courts of Justice. And there are always those impromptu smile-breakers, like street performers around **Covent Garden**. Samuel Pepys watched a Punch and Judy show here in 1662 and open-air entertainment has flourished ever since.

Left to right: Covent Garden; Hampton Court Palace

Destinations

Covent Garden

Designer shops such as Paul Smith and Nicole Farhi, mid range shops like Karen Millen, Monsoon and Oasis and the downright quirky such as Lush, the cosmetic maker, all have a presence here. Sample the impressive array of organic cheeses at Neal's Yard or grab a table at Carluccio's Delicatessen. Settle down for some entertainment in the Piazza: music, comedy, pavement artists and jugglers. If it's culture your after, step into the magnificently refurbished Royal Opera House for a performance or a backstage tour.

Covent Garden

Greenwich

Stand with one foot in the East and one foot in the West astride the Greenwich Meridian, and set your watch by the red 'Time Ball' that drops each day at 1300hrs precisely and has done so for 170 years. There's a laid-back feel to Greenwich. Take time to browse the market stalls – crafts, antiques, records, bric-a-brac and, most famously, vintage clothing. Then pop into a riverside pub for lunch and some mellow jazz.

Kew

Stroll the finest botanic gardens in the country – 400 acres and 40,000 plant varieties. The Palm House hosts a tropical jungle of plants including bananas, pawpaws and mangoes. Marvel at the giant Amazonian water lily, aloe vera and several carnivorous plants in the Princess of Wales Conservatory where ten climatic zones are recreated. You'll find activities for children and a full calendar of special events.

Notting Hill

A colourful district filled with clubs, bars and dance venues, and now trendier than ever. Wander the celebrated Portobello Road market where over 1,500 traders compete for your custom at the Saturday antiques market. Find jewellery, silverware, paintings and more. Summertime is carnival time and the Caribbean influence has ensured the phenomenal growth of the world-famous, multi-cultural Notting Hill Carnival. Join the throng of millions – exotic costume recommended. On a quieter day, visit beautiful Holland Park, a haven of greenery with its own theatre.

Richmond

The River Thames runs through the heart of the beautiful borough of Richmond. Arrive by summer riverboat from Westminster Pier and explore the delightful village with its riverside pubs, specialist boutiques, galleries and museums. Glimpse herds of deer in the Royal parks and step into history in Henry VIII's magnificent Hampton Court Palace, the oldest Tudor palace in England. Round off your visit with a world-class rugby match at Twickenham Stadium.

Clockwise: Kenwood House; Hyde Park; Chinese New Year

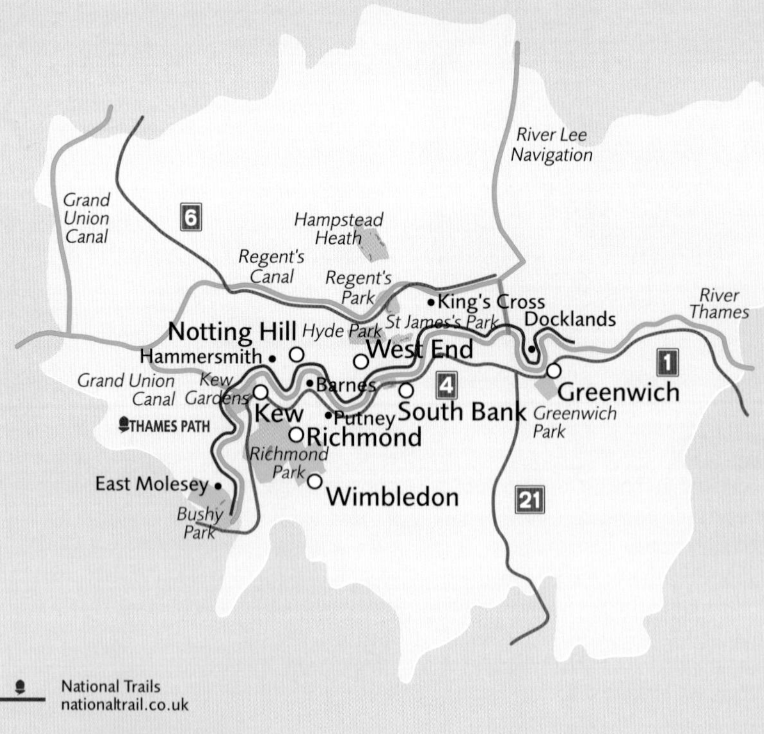

National Trails
nationaltrail.co.uk

3 Sections of the National Cycle Network
nationalcyclenetwork.org.uk

Kew Gardens

The West End

Shop in the best department stores and international designer boutiques in Oxford Street, Regent Street and Bond Street. Take lunch in a stylish eatery, and then see a major exhibition at the Royal Academy of Arts. At the heart of the West End are the landmarks of Trafalgar Square and Piccadilly Circus, and just a few minutes' stroll will take you into legendary Soho, the entertainment heart of the city, crammed with bars, pubs, clubs and restaurants.

South Bank

One of London's coolest quarters, the South Bank positively teems with must-see attractions and cultural highlights. Tate Modern has gained a reputation as one of the greatest modern art galleries in the world boasting works by Moore, Picasso, Dali, Warhol and Hepworth. Take in a play at the National Theatre or Shakespeare's magnificently restored Globe, and hit the heights on British Airways London Eye, the world's highest observation wheel.

Wimbledon

Wimbledon village is only ten miles from the centre of London but you could be in the heart of the countryside. Enjoy the open spaces of Wimbledon Common then wander along the charming high street with its unique medieval buildings, boutiques and pavement cafés. Visit the legendary All England Club where the Lawn Tennis Museum is a must-see for fans of the sport, not to mention the chance to tour the legendary Centre Court.

For lots more great ideas visit enjoyEngland.com/destinations

Clockwise: Greenwich; Notting Hill; Richmond Park

Visitor attractions

Family and Fun

Chelsea Football Club Stadium Tours
Fulham, SW6
0871 984 1955
chelseafc.com
Get behind the scenes at Stamford Bridge.

Emirates Stadium Tour and Museum
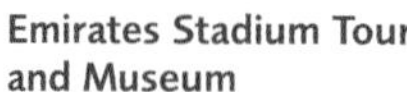
Highbury, N5
(020) 7704 4504
arsenal.com
Get to know Arsenal's stunning stadium.

HMS Belfast
Southwark, SE1
(020) 7940 6300
iwm.org.uk
A fascinating piece of British naval history.

London Aquarium
South Bank, SE1
(020) 7967 8000
londonaquarium.co.uk
Come face-to-face with two-metre long sharks.

The London Dungeon
Southwark, SE1
(020) 7403 7221
thedungeons.com
So much fun it's frightening!

London Eye
South Bank, SE1
0870 5000 600
ba-londoneye.com
The world's largest observation wheel.

London Eye River Cruise Experience
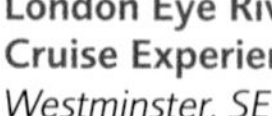

Westminster, SE1
0870 500 0600
londoneye.com
Circular cruise with fascinating live commentary.

London Wetland Centre
Barnes, SW16
(020) 8409 4400
wwt.org.uk
Europe's best urban site for watching wildlife.

Madame Tussauds and the London Planetarium
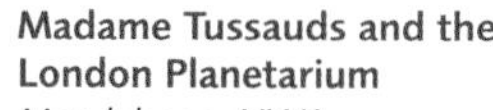
Marylebone, NW1
0870 999 0046
madame-tussauds.com/london
Meet the stars then enter the Chamber of Horrors.

National Maritime Museum

Greenwich, SE10
(020) 8858 4422
nmm.ac.uk
Over two million exhibits of seafaring history.

Royal Mews
St James Park, SW1
(020) 7766 7302
royalcollection.org.uk
One of the world's finest working stables.

Heritage

Apsley House
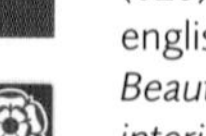
Piccadilly, W1
(020) 7499 5676
english-heritage.org.uk
Wellington's military memorabilia and dazzling art collection.

Buckingham Palace
SW1
(020) 7766 7300
royal.gov.uk
HM The Queen's official London residence.

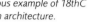

Chiswick House
W4
(020) 8995 0508
english-heritage.org.uk
Glorious example of 18thC British architecture.

Eltham Palace

SE9
(020) 8294 2548
english-heritage.org.uk
Spectacular Art Deco villa and medieval hall.

Hampton Court Palace
East Molesey, KT8
0844 482 7777
hrp.org.uk
Outstanding Tudor palace with famous maze.

Kensington Palace State Apartments
W8
0844 482 7777
hrp.org.uk
Home to the Royal Ceremonial Dress Collection.

Kenwood House

Hampstead, NW3
(020) 8348 1286
english-heritage.org.uk
Beautiful 18thC villa with fine interiors.

Tower Bridge Exhibition
SE1
(020) 7403 3761
towerbridge.org.uk
Learn all about the world's most famous bridge.

Tower of London
EC3
0870 756 6060
hrp.org.uk
Crown Jewels and 900 years of history.

Indoors

Bateaux London Restaurant Cruisers
Embankment, WC2
(020) 7695 1800
bateauxlondon.com
Luxury dining and world-class live entertainment.

BBC Television Centre Tours
Shepherd's Bush, W12
0870 603 0304
bbc.co.uk/tours
Behind the scenes of world-famous television studios.

Ben Uri Art Gallery, London Jewish Museum of Art
St John's Wood, NW8
(020) 7604 3991
benuri.org.uk
Europe's only dedicated Jewish museum of art.

BFI London IMAX Cinema
Waterloo, SE1
0870 787 2525
bfi.org.uk
The ultimate big-screen experience.

British Museum
WC1
(020) 7323 8299
britishmuseum.org
One of thc grcat museums of the world

Churchill Museum and Cabinet War Rooms
Westminster, SW1
(020) 7930 6961
iwm.org.uk
Churchill's wartime headquarters untouched since 1945.

Down House – Home of Charles Darwin
Orpington, BR6
(01689) 859119
english-heritage.org.uk
The great naturalist's home and workplace.

Hayward Gallery
South Bank, SE1
0870 380 0400
hayward.org.uk
Famous international gallery showing major exhibitions.

Imperial War Museum
Lambeth, SE1
(020) 7416 5320
iwm.org.uk
History of Britain at war since 1914.

Events 2009

New Year's Day Parade
London
londonparade.co.uk
1 Jan

Ideal Home Show
London
idealhomeshow.co.uk
20 Mar - 13 Apr

Oxford and Cambridge Boat Race
London
theboatrace.org
29 Mar

Flora London Marathon
London
london-marathon.co.uk
26 Apr

Chelsea Flower Show
London
rhs.org.uk
19 - 23 May

Wimbledon Lawn Tennis Championships
London
wimbledon.org/en_GB/index.html
Jun - Jul

The Proms
London
bbc.co.uk/proms
Jul - Sep

Notting Hill Carnival
London
rbkc.gov.uk
30 - 31 Aug

The Mayor's Thames Festival
London
thamesfestival.org
Sep

State Opening of Parliament
London
parliament.uk
Oct - Nov

Lord Mayor's Show
London
lordmayorsshow.org
Nov

Lord's Tour (MCC)
St John's Wood, NW8
(020) 7616 8595
lords.org
Guided tour of the home of cricket.

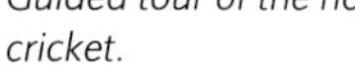

Museum of London
EC2
0870 444 3852
museumoflondon.org.uk
The world's largest urban-history museum.

National Army Museum
Chelsea, SW3
(020) 7730 0717
national-army-museum.ac.uk
The story of the British soldier.

National Portrait Gallery
WC2
(020) 7306 0055
npg.org.uk
The world's largest collection of portraits.

Natural History Museum
Kensington, SW7
(020) 7942 5000
nhm.ac.uk
World-class collections bringing the natural world to life.

Royal Air Force Museum Hendon
NW9
(020) 8205 2266
rafmuseum.org
Historic aircraft from around the world.

Royal London Hospital Archives and Museum
Whitechapel, E1
(020) 7377 7608
medicalmuseums.org
Fascinating history of Britain's largest voluntary hospital.

Royal Observatory Greenwich
SE10
(020) 8858 4422
nmm.ac.uk
Explore the history of time and astronomy.

Science Museum
Kensington, SW7
0870 870 4868
sciencemuseum.org.uk
State-of-the-art simulators, IMAX cinema and more.

Somerset House
Strand, WC2
(020) 7845 4600
somerset-house.org.uk
Arts and learning in magnificent 18thC house.

Southbank Centre
SE1
0871 663 2501
southbankcentre.co.uk
Year-round programme encompassing all the arts.

Southwark Cathedral
SE1
(020) 7367 6700
southwark.anglican.org/cathedral
London's oldest Gothic church building.

Tate Britain
Millbank, SW1
(020) 7887 8888
tate.org.uk/britain
The greatest single collection of British art.

Tate Modern
Bankside, SE1
(020) 7887 8888
tate.org.uk/modern
Britain's flagship museum of modern art.

Victoria and Albert Museum
Large Visitor Attraction of Year - Gold
Kensington, SW7
(020) 7942 2000
vam.ac.uk
World-reknowned museum, 3,000 years of art and design.

Wimbledon Lawn Tennis Museum
SW19
(020) 8946 6131
wimbledon.org/museum
Superb memorabilia and history of the game.

Outdoors

Kew Gardens (Royal Botanic Gardens)
Richmond, TW9
(020) 8332 5655
kew.org
Stunning plant collections and magnificent glasshouses.

ZSL London Zoo
Regent's Park, NW1
(020) 7722 3333
zsl.org
The hairiest and scariest animals on the planet.

ASSURANCE OF A GREAT DAY OUT
Attractions with this sign participate in the Visitor Attraction Quality Assurance Scheme which recognises high standards in all aspects of the visitor experience.

Regional contacts and information

For more information on accommodation, attractions, activities, events and holidays in London, contact Visit London. When you arrive at your destination, visit an Official Partner Tourist Information Centre for quality assured help, or email your request before you go. To search for attractions and Tourist Information Centres on the move just text INFO to 62233, and a web link will be sent to your mobile phone.

London

Go to **visitlondon.com** for all you need to know about London. Look for inspirational itineraries with great ideas for weekends and short breaks.

Or call 0870 1 LONDON (0870 1 566 366) for:

- **A London visitor information pack**
- **Visitor information on London**
  Speak to an expert for information and advice on museums, galleries, attractions, riverboat trips, sightseeing tours, theatre, shopping, eating out and much more! Or simply go to visitlondon.com.
- **Accommodation reservations**

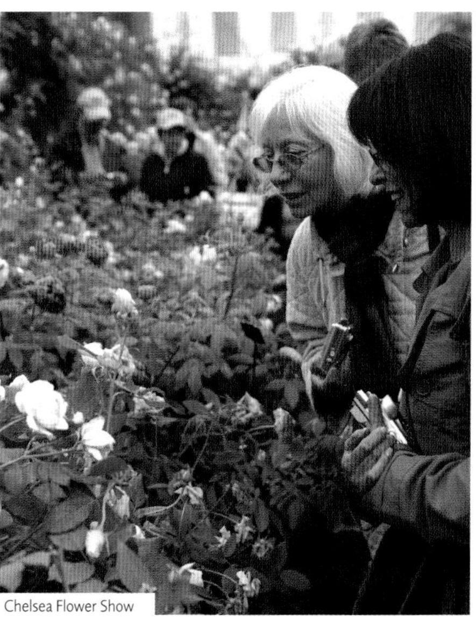

Chelsea Flower Show

Tourist Information Centres

Britain & London Visitor Centre	1 Regent Street	0870 156636	blvcenquiries@visitlondon.com
Croydon	Katharine Street	(020) 8253 1009	tic@croydon.gov.uk
Greenwich	2 Cutty Sark Gardens	0870 608 2000	tic@greenwich.gov.uk
Lewisham	199-201 Lewisham High Street	(020) 8297 8317	tic@lewisham.gov.uk
Swanley	London Road	(01322) 614660	touristinfo@swanley.org.uk

Quality visitor attractions

VisitBritain operates a Visitor Attraction Quality Assurance Service.

Participating attractions are visited annually by trained, impartial assessors who look at all aspects of the visit, from initial telephone enquiries to departure, customer service to catering, as well as all facilities and activities.

Only those attractions which have been assessed by Enjoy England and meet the standard receive the quality marque, your sign of a Quality Assured Visitor Attraction.

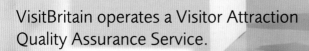

Look out for the quality marque and visit with confidence.

where to stay in
London

All place names in the blue bands are shown on the maps at the front of this guide.

A complete listing of all VisitBritain assessed parks in England appears at the back.

Accommodation symbols

Symbols give useful information about services and facilities. On page 7 you can find a key to these symbols.

LONDON SE2

★★★★★
TOURING & CAMPING PARK
(202) £14.90–£28.30
(202) £14.90–£28.30
202 touring pitches

Abbey Wood Caravan Club Site

Federation Road, Abbey Wood, London SE2 0LS **t** (020) 8311 7708

caravanclub.co.uk

open All year
payment Credit/debit cards, cash, cheques

Redeveloped to the highest standards, this site is the ideal base for exploring the capital. A green, gently sloping site with mature trees screening its spacious grounds.

SAT NAV *SE2 0LS*

Special member rates mean you can save your membership subscription in less than a week. Visit our website to find out more.

General Leisure

LONDON SE19

★★★★★
TOURING & CAMPING PARK
(126) £14.90–£28.30
(126) £14.90–£28.30
126 touring pitches

Crystal Palace Caravan Club Site

Crystal Palace Parade, London SE19 1UF **t** (020) 8778 7155

caravanclub.co.uk

open All year
payment Credit/debit cards, cash, cheques

Popular with European families in the summer, a friendly site on the edge of a pleasant park, in close proximity to all of London's attractions.

SAT NAV *SE19 1UF*

Special member rates mean you can save your membership subscription in less than a week. Visit our website to find out more.

General Leisure

South West England

Bristol, Cornwall, Devon, Dorset, Gloucestershire, Isles of Scilly, Somerset, Wiltshire

Clockwise: Porlock Bay, Somerset; Forest of Dean, Gloucestershire; Stonehenge, Wiltshire

Great days out

Go rock pooling in sandy coves. Indulge your love of cream teas and clotted cream fudge. Ramble along the South West Coast Path. Brave the waves surfing in Newquay. Wonder at the Cerne Abbas Giant and the stunning landscaped gardens at Stourhead. What will you do in South West England?

Refreshing rambles

The South West is truly a walker's paradise, from the gentle **Cotswold Hills** to the wilder beauty of **Exmoor** and **Dartmoor** National Parks. Spend a day or two rambling parts of the 101-mile **Cotswold Way** through quintessential English countryside and golden-stone villages. **The Two Moors Way** over Dartmoor and Exmoor takes you through moorland, wooded valleys, farmland and coastal towns. Gee up the pace pony trekking or mountain biking – the National Parks have plenty of space for both. Then feel the sea-salted breezes along the **South West Coast Path**. It stretches for 630 miles from Somerset to Dorset, opening up dramatic views of a shoreline organically sculpted by waves. Children just love stomping 185 million years of earth history underfoot along the **Jurassic Coast**, a World Heritage Site. They could even find a dinosaur print. Who's got the biggest feet?

Sea, surf and fun

How's this for the perfect antidote to hectic modern life? Genuine bucket-and-spade fun with the family, pure and simple. With more Blue Flag beaches than anywhere else in England, the region's sandy bays and sheltered coves are perfect getaways. Some stretches make thrilling waves for watersports: hit the hip centres of **Newquay**, **Bude**, **Croyde** and **Woolacombe**, great places to learn to surf or kitesurf. Try sailing and windsurfing in **Poole**. Devon's English Riviera – the bustling seaside towns of **Torquay**, **Paignton** and **Brixham** – is ideal for families and you can meet friendly coastal creatures like penguins and fur seals at **Living Coasts** in Torquay. Away from the beach quaint fishing villages, such as **Clovelly**, **Port Isaac** and **Beer**, are a picturesque maze of narrow streets and steep roads. And how's this for an unforgettable experience? Catch a play or musical at the open-air cliffside **Minack Theatre** at Porthcurno. The backdrop of sea vistas is breathtaking.

Torquay, Devon

Glorious gardens

The South West's balmy subtropical climate means exotic flora flourish, creating extraordinary gardens. Delight in the **Lost Gardens of Heligan** at Pentewan, neglected for years and now brought back to life complete with magical Jungle Garden. Take a helicopter ride to **Tresco**, one of the Scilly Isles, to browse some 20,000 luxuriant plants in the **Abbey Garden**. Explore the remarkable **Eden Project**, near St Austell, which features thousands of world plants in enormous glass biomes – and children become enthralled on the interactive trails. Then enjoy the pyrotechnic seasonal displays of trees and flowers at **Westonbirt Arboretum**,

Left to right: Eden Project, Cornwall; Salisbury Cathedral, Wiltshire

why not... cycle along Devon's 180-mile Tarka Trail, named after Henry Williamson's Tarka the Otter?

Gloucestershire; the clipped yews and cascades at **Forde Abbey and Gardens**, Dorset; and the eye-catching tableaux of lakeside temples at **Stourhead**, Wiltshire.

Yum yum!

Indulge yourself in the region's delicious specialities. Cornish pasties taste good washed down with a pint of sweet cider. Look out for Mendip Oggies, too: pasties made with pork, apple and cheese pastry. Devour mouthwatering scones straight from the oven and topped with rich clotted cream. And sample a different cheese every day: world-famous Cheddar, Double Gloucester, Somerset Brie, Dorset Blue Vinny and nettle-wrapped Cornish Yarg. Relish the best catches at **Rick Stein's Seafood Restaurant**, Padstow. Then finish your gourmet odyssey relaxing over a wine from **Three Choirs Vineyard**, Gloucestershire.

Mysterious and madcap

You're in just the right area for quirky customs and intriguing places. If you look hard enough you may spot the Witch of Wookey deep in **Wookey Hole Caves** where pagan and Christian legends intermingle. Ponder the mysteries of the ancient stone circles of **Stonehenge** and **Avebury** – just how were such enormous stones transported and arranged, and why? **Chipping Campden** in Gloucestershire is the location of the Cotswolds' unique version of the Olimpick Games: contests include shin-kicking, ouch! Meanwhile **Blackawton** in Devon hosts the annual International Worm Charming Festival. Seeing is believing!

Exmoor, Somerset

Splendid city highlights

Fill your days visiting attractions in Bristol and Bath, city neighbours yet so different. **Bristol's** maritime heritage has been channelled into the infectious vitality of the rejuvenated Harbourside of bars, eateries and sights. Clamber aboard Isambard Kingdom Brunel's **ss Great Britain**, the world's first great ocean liner. Treat the kids to an interactive science adventure at **Explore-at-Bristol** – freeze your shadow, fire a neuron, and get starry-eyed in the planetarium. Then revel in the Georgian elegance of **Bath** and tour the best-preserved Roman religious spa from the ancient world, beneath the watchful gaze of **Bath Abbey**. Dip your own toes – and more – into the natural thermal waters of the recently opened **Thermae Bath Spa**. Bliss!

why not... look for the Fossil Forest revealed at low tide near Little Bindon, Dorset?

Continue your journey with a trip to some of the West's other great cathedral cities. Stroll **Exeter's** historic Quayside; survey the medieval carvings of **Wells Cathedral's** majestic west front; wander the revitalised waterside of **Gloucester**; or take a guided tour of **Salisbury Cathedral**, its soaring spire the tallest in Britain.

More great days out

If you're looking for even more inspiration for great days out, add these to your love-to list. Have a fun time uncovering the history, sights and sounds of the railway at **Steam – Museum of the Great Western Railway** in Swindon, or take the kids on a wild animal safari at **Longleat**. Take a picnic to **Corfe Castle** whose evocative hilltop ruins recall a bold past. Or potter about on a driving tour – the scenic **Royal Forest Route** through the Forest of Dean and the **Romantic Road** via **Cheltenham** and **Cirencester** spring to mind. Floating skywards in a hot-air balloon over the countryside and llama-trekking also make memorable adventures!

Clockwise: Dartmoor, Devon; St Michael's Mount, Cornwall; ss Great Britain, Bristol

Destinations

Bath

Set in rolling countryside, less than two hours from London, this exquisite Georgian spa city was founded by the Romans and is now a World Heritage Site. Explore the compact city centre on foot and discover a series of architectural gems including the Roman baths and Pump Room, the 15thC Abbey, and stunning Royal Crescent. Follow in the footsteps of Romans and Celts and bathe in the naturally warm waters of the Thermae Bath Spa.

Bath

Bournemouth

Bournemouth is the perfect holiday and short-break destination, renowned for its seven miles of family-friendly, golden beaches, beautiful parks and gardens and cosmopolitan ambience. Enjoy the buzz of the town then head out and savour the beauty of the New Forest, the splendour of Dorset's spectacular World Heritage Jurassic Coastline, and the rolling countryside immortalised by Thomas Hardy.

Bristol

In bygone times, explorers and merchants set off on epic journeys from its harbour. Nowadays, Bristol's spirit of boldness and creativity expresses itself in art, architecture and an enviable quality of life. Take in Georgian terraces, waterfront arts centres, green spaces, great shopping and top-class restaurants. The city's heritage glitters with the work of historic figures such as Isambard Kingdom Brunel, and all set against a truly classic view – the River Avon and its dramatic gorge reaching almost into the heart of the city.

The Cotswolds

Escape to the rolling hills of the Cotswolds scattered with picturesque towns and villages built of distinctive honey-coloured limestone. Criss-cross the little bridges over the River Windrush in Bourton-on-the-Water; hunt for antiques in Stow-on-the-Wold; wander through the open-air street market of Moreton-in-Marsh and appreciate the beautifully preserved buildings in Chipping Campden and Tetbury.

Isles of Scilly

Just 20 minutes from Cornwall you'll find over 100 islands waiting to be explored– five of them inhabited: St Mary's, Tresco, St Martin's, St Agnes and Bryher. Discover fascinating prehistoric remains, rare species of birds and plant life, historic shipwrecks and some of the best beaches in Britain. Watersports, boat trips, wonderful gardens, including Tresco Abbey Gardens, keep everyone entertained.

Left to right: Corfe Castle, Dorset
Wells Cathedral, Somerset

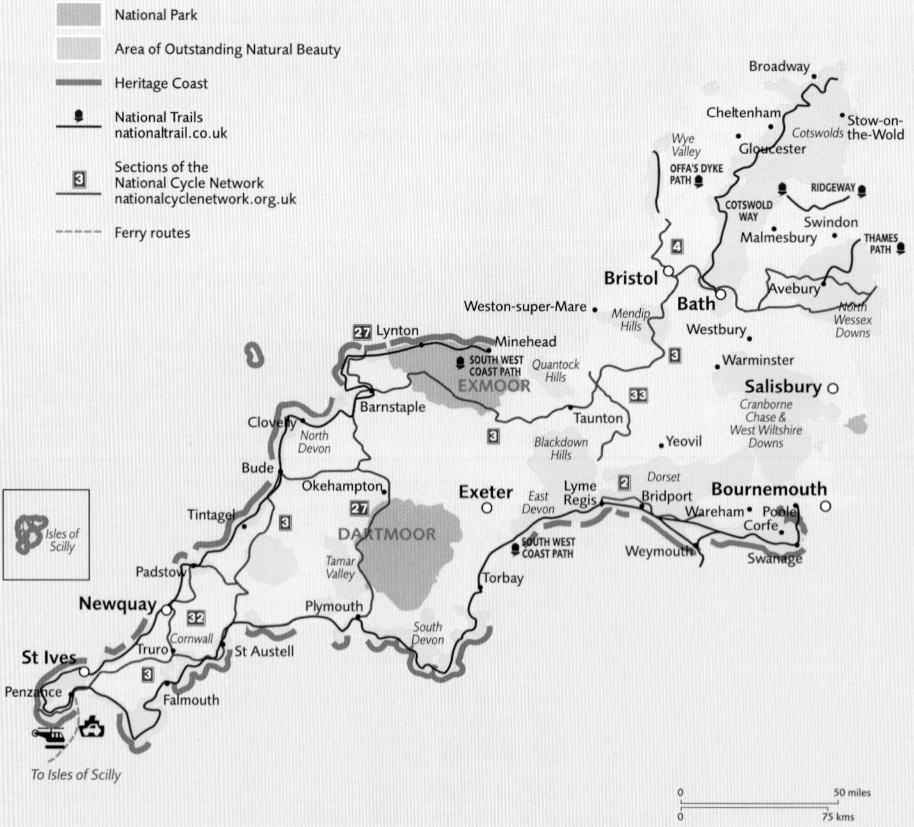

National Park
Area of Outstanding Natural Beauty
Heritage Coast
National Trails
nationaltrail.co.uk
Sections of the National Cycle Network
nationalcyclenetwork.org.uk
Ferry routes

Broadway
Cheltenham
Stow-on-the-Wold
Cotswolds
Wye Valley
Gloucester
OFFA'S DYKE PATH
RIDGEWAY
COTSWOLD WAY
Swindon
Malmesbury
THAMES PATH
Bristol
Bath
Avebury
North Wessex Downs
Weston-super-Mare
Mendip Hills
Westbury
Lynton
Minehead
SOUTH WEST COAST PATH
Quantock Hills
EXMOOR
Warminster
Salisbury
Cranborne Chase & West Wiltshire Downs
Barnstaple
Taunton
Clovelly
North Devon
Blackdown Hills
Yeovil
Bude
Okehampton
Exeter
East Devon
Lyme Regis
Dorset
Bridport
Bournemouth
Wareham
Poole
Corfe
Tintagel
DARTMOOR
SOUTH WEST COAST PATH
Weymouth
Swanage
Isles of Scilly
Padstow
Tamar Valley
Torbay
Newquay
Plymouth
Cornwall
South Devon
St Ives
Truro
St Austell
Penzance
Falmouth
To Isles of Scilly

0 50 miles
0 75 kms

Bristol

Exeter

Devon's regional capital for culture, leisure and shopping is a vibrant city, steeped in ancient history. Don't miss the superb Decorated Gothic cathedral. Stroll along the historic Quayside, once the setting for a thriving wool trade and now a bustling riverside resort. Choose from over 700 shops, join a free Red Coat-guided city tour and dine in any one of numerous acclaimed restaurants. It's also the perfect base from which to explore the sweeping National Parks of Dartmoor and Exmoor.

Newquay

A beach paradise, stretching for seven miles, makes this one of Cornwall's premier resorts. Soaring cliffs alternate with sheltered coves, and thundering surf with secluded rock pools, smugglers' caves and soft golden sands. Whatever the weather, make a splash at Waterworld, or visit Newquay Zoo, one of the best wildlife parks in the country. Newquay offers an unforgettable holiday experience.

Clockwise: Exeter; Bournemouth; The Cotswolds

Poole

Poole is fast becoming known as the St Tropez of the south coast with its award-winning beaches, beautiful harbour, exhilarating watersports and famous pottery. Follow the Cockle Trail around the old town to discover its seafaring and trading history. Take the ferry to Brownsea Island between March and October for wonderful walks and wildlife spotting. Or relax and enjoy alfresco dining overlooking the harbour.

St Ives

What was once a small, thriving fishing village is now an internationally renowned haven for artists, attracted by the unique light. Explore the narrow streets and passageways and come upon countless galleries, studios and craft shops. Don't miss Tate St Ives and the Barbara Hepworth Museum. Enjoy the natural beauty of the harbour and explore Blue Flag beaches and coastal walks. Perfectly placed for all of West Cornwall's stunning scenery and famous attractions.

Tate, St Ives

Salisbury

Nestling in the heart of southern England, Salisbury is every bit the classic English city. The majestic cathedral boasts the tallest spire in England and rises elegantly above sweeping lawns. Wander through this medieval city and you'll find first-class visitor attractions, theatre and shopping. And, of course, no trip to Salisbury would be complete without the eight-mile pilgrimage to one of the greatest prehistoric sites in the world – Stonehenge.

For lots more great ideas visit enjoyEngland.com/destinations

Visitor attractions

Family and Fun

Babbacombe Model Village
Torquay, Devon
(01803) 315315
babbacombemodelvillage.co.uk
England in miniature in four-acre gardens.

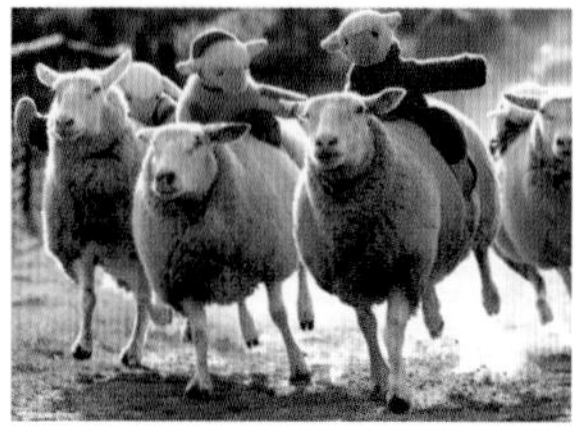

The Big Sheep
Bideford, Devon
(01237) 472366
thebigsheep.co.uk
Family fun at the sheep races.

Blue Reef Aquarium
Newquay, Cornwall
(01637) 878134
bluereefaquarium.co.uk
Close encounters with tropical sharks and rays.

Bristol Zoo Gardens
Bristol
(0117) 974 7399
bristolzoo.org.uk
Over 400 exotic and endangered species.

Cheddar Caves & Gorge
Cheddar, Somerset
(01934) 742343
cheddarcaves.com
Britain's finest caves and deepest gorge.

Combe Martin Wildlife and Dinosaur Park
Combe Martin, Devon
(01271) 882486
dinosaur-park.com
A subtropical bird, animal and dinosaur paradise.

Dairyland Farm World

Summercourt, Cornwall
(01872) 510246
dairylandfarmworld.com
Country-life park, museum and adventure playground.

Devon's Crealy Great Adventure Park
near Exeter, Devon
(01395) 233200
crealy.co.uk
All-weather attractions and friendly animals.

Farmer Palmer's Farm Park

Poole, Dorset
(01202) 622022
farmerpalmers.co.uk
Farm activities for families with young children.

Kents Cavern Prehistoric Caves
Torquay, Devon
(01803) 215136
kents-cavern.co.uk
Britain's most important Stone Age caves.

Living Coasts

Torquay, Devon
(01803) 202470
livingcoasts.org.uk
Fascinating coastal creatures in a stunning location.

Longleat
Warminster, Wiltshire
(01985) 844400
longleat.co.uk
Lions, tigers and a stately home.

The Monkey Sanctuary Trust
Looe, Cornwall
(01503) 262532
monkeysanctuary.org
Colony of woolly monkeys.

National Marine Aquarium

Plymouth, Devon
(01752) 600301
national-aquarium.co.uk
Sharks and seahorses at Britain's biggest aquarium.

Newquay Zoo
Newquay, Cornwall
(01637) 873342
newquayzoo.org.uk
Exotic animals in subtropical lakeside gardens.

Noah's Ark Zoo Farm
Wraxall, Somerset
(01275) 852606
noahsarkzoofarm.co.uk
Hands-on animal experiences for all ages.

Paignton Zoo Environmental Park
Paignton, Devon
(01803) 697500
paigntonzoo.org.uk
Gorillas and crocodiles in 75-acre botanical gardens.

Pennywell - Devon's Farm and Wildlife Centre
Lower Dean, Devon
(01364) 642023
pennywellfarm.co.uk
The South West's biggest farm-activity park.

Woodlands Leisure Park
Blackawton, Devon
(01803) 712598
woodlandspark.com
Unique combination of indoor and outdoor attractions.

Wookey Hole Caves and Papermill
near Wells, Somerset
(01749) 672243
wookey.co.uk
Spectacular caves and working Victorian papermill.

Heritage

The Bishop's Palace & Gardens
Wells, Somerset
(01749) 678691
bishopspalacewells.co.uk
Splendid medieval palace and tranquil landscaped gardens.

Bowood House and Gardens
Chippenham, Wiltshire
(01249) 812102
bowood.org
Wonderful 18thC Robert Adam house.

Corfe Castle
Corfe Castle, Dorset
(01929) 477063
nationaltrust.org.uk
Majestic ruins of a former royal castle.

Cothay Manor & Gardens
near Wellington, Somerset
(01823) 672283
cothaymanor.co.uk
Unspoilt medieval manor and romantic gardens.

Dunster Castle
Dunster, Somerset
(01643) 821314
nationaltrust.org.uk
Romantic castle and subtropical gardens.

The Fashion Museum and Assembly Rooms
Bath, Somerset
(01225) 477789
fashionmuseum.co.uk
Fine Georgian building with world-class dress collection.

Forde Abbey and Gardens
Small Visitor Attraction of the Year – Silver
Forde Abbey, Dorset
(01460) 220231
fordeabbey.co.uk
Elegant former Cistercian monastery with gardens.

Lacock Abbey
Lacock, Wiltshire
(01249) 730459
nationaltrust.org.uk
Fine country house with medieval cloisters.

Lanhydrock
Lanhydrock, Cornwall
(01208) 265950
nationaltrust.org.uk
Re-built 17thC house with magnificent illustrated ceiling.

Lulworth Castle & Park
Wareham, Dorset
0845 450 1054
lulworth.com
Idyllic castle set in extensive park.

Montacute House
Montacute, Somerset
(01935) 823289
nationaltrust.org.uk
Renaissance manor house filled with historic treasures.

Old Wardour Castle
Tisbury, Wiltshire
(01747) 870487
english-heritage.org.uk
Unusual hexagonal ruins of a 14thC castle.

Pittville Pump Room
Cheltenham, Gloucestershire
(01242) 523852
Beautiful, imposing example of Regency architecture.

Powderham Castle
Powderham, Devon
(01626) 890243
powderham.co.uk
Restored medieval castle in beautiful deer park.

Roman Baths
Bath, Somerset
(01225) 477785
romanbaths.co.uk
Magnificent Roman temple and hot-spring baths.

St Michael's Mount
Marazion, Cornwall
(01736) 710507
stmichaelsmount.co.uk
Rocky island filled with astonishing history.

Salisbury Cathedral
Salisbury, Wiltshire
(01722) 555120
salisburycathedral.org.uk
Britain's finest 13thC gothic cathedral.

Sherborne Castle
Sherborne, Dorset
(01935) 813182
sherbornecastle.com
Tudor mansion built by Sir Walter Raleigh.

Sudeley Castle, Gardens and Exhibition
Winchcombe, Gloucestershire
(01242) 602308
sudeleycastle.co.uk
Romantic castle and restored gardens.

Tintagel Castle
Tintagel, Cornwall
(01840) 770328
english-heritage.org.uk
Evocative ruined castle on wind-swept coast.

Wells Cathedral
Wells, Somerset
(01749) 674483
wellscathedral.org.uk
Superb 12thC cathedral in Early English style.

Wilton House 
Wilton, Wiltshire
(01722) 746714
wiltonhouse.com
Stunning 17thC state rooms and landscaped parkland.

Indoors

British Empire & Commonwealth Museum
Bristol
(0117) 925 4980
empiremuseum.co.uk
Explore a dramatic history and heritage.

Brunel's ss Great Britain 
Bristol
(0117) 926 0680
ssgreatbritain.org
Experience life aboard Brunel's famous steam ship.

Cheltenham Art Gallery and Museum
Cheltenham, Gloucestershire
(01242) 237431
cheltenham.artgallery.museum
World-renowned Arts and Crafts Movement collection.

The China Clay Museum
Carthew, Cornwall
(01726) 850362
wheal-martyn.com
Restored clayworks in World Heritage mining landscape.

The Dinosaur Museum
Dorchester, Dorset
(01305) 269880
thedinosaurmuseum.com
Life-sized reconstructions and hands-on displays.

Dorset County Museum
Dorchester, Dorset
(01305) 262735
dorsetcountymuseum.org
The archeology and geology of Dorset.

The Dorset Teddy Bear Museum
Dorchester, Dorset
(01305) 266040
teddybearmuseum.co.uk
Featuring a family of people-sized bears.

The Edward Jenner Museum
Berkeley, Gloucestershire
(01453) 810631
jennermuseum.com
Life-story of the smallpox vaccine pioneer.

Explore-At-Bristol
Bristol
0845 345 1235
at-bristol.org.uk
An exciting hands-on science adventure.

Fleet Air Arm Museum
Yeovilton, Somerset
(01935) 840565
fleetairarm.com
See Europe's largest collection of naval aircraft.

Geevor Tin Mine
Pendeen, Cornwall
(01736) 788662
geevor.com
The largest preserved mining site in Britain.

The Museum of East Asian Art
Bath, Somerset
(01225) 464640
meaa.org.uk
Jades, bronzes and ceramics from the East.

National Maritime Museum Cornwall
Falmouth, Cornwall
(01326) 313388
nmmc.co.uk
Enthralling exhibits for landlubbers and sailors alike.

STEAM - Museum of the Great Western Railway
Swindon, Wiltshire
(01793) 466646
swindon.gov.uk/steam
Interactive story of pioneering rail company.

Tate St Ives
St Ives, Cornwall
(01736) 796226
tate.org.uk/stives
International art in striking beach-front gallery.

The Tutankhamun Exhibition
Dorchester, Dorset
(01305) 269571
tutankhamun-exhibition.co.uk
Internationally-acclaimed exhibition with perfect reconstructions.

Outdoors

Abbey House Gardens
Malmesbury, Wiltshire
(01666) 822212
abbeyhousegardens.co.uk
Wonderful displays featuring over 10,000 plants.

Eden Project
St Austell, Cornwall
(01726) 811911
edenproject.com
A global garden for the 21st century.

Hidcote Manor Garden
near Chipping Campden, Gloucestershire
(01386) 438333
nationaltrust.org.uk
Widely celebrated Arts and Crafts garden.

Land's End
Sennen, Cornwall
0871 720 0055
landsend-landmark.co.uk
Spectacular cliffs, breathtaking vistas and multi-sensory show.

The Lost Gardens of Heligan
near St Austell, Cornwall
(01726) 845100
heligan.com
Glorious 200-acre restored garden and pleasure grounds.

The Minack Theatre and Visitor Centre
Porthcurno, Cornwall
(01736) 810181
minack.com
Open-air cliff-side theatre with breathtaking views.

Painswick Rococo Garden
Painswick, Gloucestershire
(01452) 813204
rococogarden.org.uk
A flamboyant piece of English garden design.

Pecorama
Beer, Devon
(01297) 21542
peco-uk.com
Passenger-carrying miniature railway in spectacular gardens.

RHS Garden Rosemoor
Torrington, Devon
(01805) 624067
rhs.org.uk/rosemoor
Enchanting 65-acre year-round garden.

Stonehenge and Avebury World Heritage Site
near Salisbury, Wiltshire
0870 333 1181
english-heritage.org.uk
World-famous prehistoric monument.

Stourhead House and Garden

Stourton, Wiltshire
(01747) 841152
nationaltrust.org.uk
Palladian mansion with world-renowned landscape gardens.

Thermae Bath Spa
Bath, Somerset
0844 888 0848
thermaebathspa.com
Enjoy Britain's only natural thermal waters.

Trelissick Garden
near Truro, Cornwall
(01872) 862090
nationaltrust.org.uk
Tender and exotic plants in tranquil garden.

Tresco Abbey Gardens
Isles of Scilly
(01720) 424108
tresco.co.uk
Tropical garden with species from 80 countries.

Westonbirt, The National Arboretum
Westonbirt, Gloucestershire
(01666) 880220
forestry.gov.uk/westonbirt
One of the world's finest tree collections.

Wildfowl & Wetlands Trust Slimbridge
Slimbridge, Gloucestershire
(01453) 891900
wwt.org.uk
Home to an astounding array of wildlife.

Willows & Wetlands Visitor Centre
Taunton, Somerset
(01823) 490249
englishwillowbaskets.co.uk
The art of willow growing and basketmaking.

ASSURANCE OF A GREAT DAY OUT
Attractions with this sign participate in the Visitor Attraction Quality Assurance Scheme which recognises high standards in all aspects of the visitor experience.

Events 2009

Walk Scilly
Isle of Scilly
walkscilly.co.uk
Mar

Exeter Festival of South West Food & Drink
Exeter
visitsouthwest.co.uk/exeterfoodfestival
Apr

Cheese Rolling
Brockworth
cheese-rolling.co.uk
25 May

Chippenham Folk Festival
Chippenham
chippfolk.co.uk
22 - 25 May

Annual Nettle Eating Contest
Bridport
thebottleinn.co.uk
Jun

Bristol International Festival of Kites
Bristol
kite-festival.org.uk
Aug

Spirit of the Sea
Weymouth
spiritofthesea.org.uk
Aug

Falmouth Oyster Festival
Falmouth
falmouthoysterfestival.co.uk
Oct

Bath Christmas Market
Bath
bathchristmasmarket.co.uk
Nov - Dec

Tar Barrels
Ottery St Mary
otterytourism.org.uk
5 Nov

Bridgwater Guy Fawkes Carnival
Bridgwater
bridgwatercarnival.org.uk
6 Nov

Regional contacts and information

For more information on accommodation, attractions, activities, events and holidays in South West England, contact one of the following regional or local tourism organisations. Their websites have a wealth of information and many produce free publications to help you get the most out of your visit.

South West England

Visit the following websites for further information on South West England or call **01392 360050**:

- **visitsouthwest.co.uk**
- **swcp.org.uk**
- **accessiblesouthwest.co.uk**

Publications available from South West Tourism:

- **The Trencherman's Guide to Top Restaurants in South West England**
- **Adventure South West**
  Your ultimate activity and adventure guide.
- **World Heritage Map**
  Discover our World Heritage.

Clockwise: Pedn Vounder, Cornwall; Gloucester Cathedral, Gloucestershire; Lynton, Devon

Tourist Information Centres

When you arrive at your destination, visit an Official Partner Tourist Information Centre for quality assured help with accommodation and information about local attractions and events, or email your request before you go. To search for attractions and Tourist Information Centres on the move just text INFO to 62233, and a web link will be sent to your mobile phone. To find a Tourist Information Centre by region visit enjoyEngland.com/find-tic.

Avebury	Green Street	(01672) 539425	all.tic's@kennet.gov.uk
Bath	Abbey Church Yard	0906 711 2000**	tourism@bathtourism.co.uk
Bodmin	Mount Folly Square	(01208) 76616	bodmintic@visit.org.uk
Bourton-on-the-Water	Victoria Street	(01451) 820211	bourtonvic@btconnect.com
Bridport	47 South Street	(01308) 424901	bridport.tic@westdorset-dc.gov.uk
Bristol	Harbourside	0906 711 2191**	ticharbourside@destinationbristol.co.uk
Brixham	The Quay	(01803) 211 211	holiday@torbay.gov.uk
Bude	The Crescent	(01288) 354240	budetic@visitbude.info
Burnham-on-Sea	South Esplanade	(01278) 787852	burnham.tic@sedgemoor.gov.uk
Camelford*	The Clease	(01840) 212954	manager@camelfordtic.eclipse.co.uk
Cartgate	A303/A3088 Cartgate Picnic Site	(01935) 829333	cartgate.tic@southsomerset.gov.uk
Cheddar	The Gorge	(01934) 744071	cheddar.tic@sedgemoor.gov.uk
Chippenham	Market Place	(01249) 665970	tourism@chippenham.gov.uk
Chipping Campden	High Street	(01386) 841206	information@visitchippingcampden.com
Christchurch	49 High Street	(01202) 471780	enquiries@christchurchtourism.info
Cirencester	Market Place	(01285) 654180	cirencestervic@cotswold.gov.uk
Coleford	High Street	(01594) 812388	tourism@fdean.gov.uk
Corsham	31 High Street	(01249) 714660	enquiries@corshamheritage.org.uk
Devizes	Market Place	(01380) 729408	all.tic's@kennet.gov.uk
Dorchester	11 Antelope Walk	(01305) 267992	dorchester.tic@westdorset-dc.gov.uk
Falmouth	Prince of Wales Pier	(01326) 312300	info@falmouthtic.co.uk
Frome	Justice Lane	(01373) 467271	frome.tic@ukonline.co.uk
Glastonbury	9 High Street	(01458) 832954	glastonbury.tic@ukonline.co.uk
Gloucester	28 Southgate Street	(01452) 396572	tourism@gloucester.gov.uk
Looe*	Fore Street	(01503) 262072	looetic@btconnect.com
Lyme Regis	Church Street	(01297) 442138	lymeregis.tic@westdorset-dc.gov.uk
Malmesbury	Market Lane	(01666) 823748	malmesburyip@northwilts.gov.uk
Moreton-in-Marsh	High Street	(01608) 650881	moreton@cotswold.gov.uk
Padstow	North Quay	(01841) 533449	padstowtic@btconnect.com

Paignton	The Esplanade	(01803) 211 211	holiday@torbay.gov.uk
Penzance	Station Road	(01736) 362207	pztic@penwith.gov.uk
Plymouth Mayflower	3-5 The Barbican	(01752) 306330	barbicantic@plymouth.gov.uk
St Ives	The Guildhall	(01736) 796297	ivtic@penwith.gov.uk
Salisbury	Fish Row	(01722) 334956	visitorinfo@salisbury.gov.uk
Shelton Mallet	70 High Street	(01749) 345258	sheptonmallet.tic@ukonline.co.uk
Sherborne	3 Tilton Court, Digby Road	(01935) 815341	sherborne.tic@westdorset-dc.gov.uk
Somerset	Sedgemoor Services	(01934) 750833	somersetvisitorcentre@somerset.gov.uk
Stow-on-the-Wold	The Square	(01451) 831082	stowvic@cotswold.gov.uk
Street	Farm Road	(01458) 447384	street.tic@ukonline.co.uk
Stroud	George Street	(01453) 760960	tic@stroud.gov.uk
Swanage	Shore Road	(01929) 422885	mail@swanage.gov.uk
Swindon	37 Regent Street	(01793) 530328	infocentre@swindon.gov.uk
Taunton	Paul Street	(01823) 336344	tauntontic@tauntondeane.gov.uk
Tewkesbury	100 Church Street	(01684) 855043	tewkesburytic@tewkesburybc.gov.uk
Torquay	Vaughan Parade	(01803) 211 211	holiday@torbay.gov.uk
Truro	Boscawen Street	(01872) 274555	tic@truro.gov.uk
Wadebridge	Eddystone Road	0870 1223337	wadebridgetic@btconnect.com
Wareham	South Street	(01929) 552740	tic@purbeck-dc.gov.uk
Warminster	off Station Rd	(01985) 218548	visitwarminster@btconnect.com
Wells	Market Place	(01749) 672552	touristinfo@wells.gov.uk
Weston-super-Mare	Beach Lawns	(01934) 888800	westontouristinfo@n-somerset.gov.uk
Weymouth	The Esplanade	(01305) 785747	tic@weymouth.gov.uk
Winchcombe	High Street	(01242) 602925	winchcombetic@tewkesbury.gov.uk
Yeovil	Hendford	(01935) 845946/7	yeoviltic@southsomerset.gov.uk

*seasonal opening

**calls to this number are charged at premium rate

Left to right: Jurassic Coast, Dorset; Minack Theatre, Cornwall

Country ways

The Countryside Rights of Way Act gives people new rights to walk on areas of open countryside and registered common land.

To find out where you can go and what you can do, as well as information about taking your dog to the countryside, go online at countrysideaccess.gov.uk.

And when you're out and about...

Always follow the Country Code

- Be safe – plan ahead and follow any signs
- Leave gates and property as you find them
- Protect plants and animals, and take your litter home
- Keep dogs under close control
- Consider other people

where to stay in

South West England

All place names in the blue bands are shown on the maps at the front of this guide.

A complete listing of all VisitBritain assessed parks in England appears at the back.

Accommodation symbols

Symbols give useful information about services and facilities. On page 7 you can find a key to these symbols.

ALDERHOLT, Dorset Map ref 2B3

★★★★
TOURING & CAMPING PARK

(35) £15.00–£19.00
(35) £15.00–£19.00
(50) £12.00–£18.00
35 touring pitches

Hill Cottage Farm Camping & Caravan Park

Sandleheath Road, Alderholt, Fordingbridge SP6 3EG **t** (01425) 650513
e hillcottagefarmcaravansite@supanet.com

hillcottagefarmcampingandcaravanpark.co.uk

open March to October
payment Credit/debit cards, cash, cheques

Listed in Top 100 Parks Award (Practical Caravan). Set in 40 acres of Dorset countryside on the Hampshire/Dorset border. The New Forest is just two miles away. Luxury facilities. Small lakes for coarse fishing. Rally field available with use of function room/skittle alley.

SAT NAV *SP6 3EG* **ONLINE MAP**

General Leisure

ASHBURTON, Devon Map ref 1C2

Using map references

Map references refer to the colour maps at the front of this guide.

BATH, Somerset Map ref 2B2

★★★★
TOURING & CAMPING PARK

(90) £19.50–£22.00
(90) £19.50–£22.00
(105) £7.00–£19.50
195 touring pitches

New Year party package.

Newton Mill Camping

Twaebrook Ltd, Newton Mill Camping Park, Newton Road, Bath BA2 9JF **t** (01225) 333909
e newtonmill@hotmail.com

campinginbath.co.uk

open All year
payment Credit/debit cards, cash, cheques

Situated in an idyllic hidden valley close to the city centre with easy access by frequent, local buses or nearby level, traffic-free cycle path. Superb heated amenities (5-star Loo of the Year 2008) including showers, bathrooms and private facilities. Old Mill bar/restaurant open all year. David Bellamy Gold Award for Conservation. ADAC Campingplatz Auszeichnung 2008.

SAT NAV *BA2 9JF* **ONLINE MAP**

General Leisure

BERE REGIS, Dorset Map ref 2B3

★★★
TOURING & CAMPING PARK

(71) £11.00–£16.50
(71) £11.00–£16.50
(71) £11.00–£16.50
71 touring pitches

Rowlands Wait Touring Park

Rye Hill, Bere Regis, Wareham BH20 7LP **t** (01929) 472727 **e** enquiries@rowlandswait.co.uk

rowlandswait.co.uk

open March to October
payment Credit/debit cards, cash, cheques

Set in an Area of Outstanding Natural Beauty. Modern amenity block with family/disabled facilities. Centrally situated for many attractions and places of interest. Direct access to heathland, ideal for walkers, cyclists, couples, families and nature lovers. Open winter by arrangement.

SAT NAV *BH20 7LP* **ONLINE MAP**

General Leisure

BLACKWATER, Cornwall Map ref 1B3

★★★★
HOLIDAY, TOURING & CAMPING PARK
ROSE AWARD

(30) £10.00–£15.00
(30) £10.00–£15.00
(30) £10.00–£15.00
(20) £140.00–£550.00
30 touring pitches

Trevarth Holiday Park

Blackwater, Truro TR4 8HR **t** (01872) 560266 **e** trevarth@lineone.net

trevarth.co.uk

open April to October
payment Credit/debit cards, cash, cheques

Luxury caravan holiday homes, touring and camping. A small, quiet park conveniently situated for north- and south-coast resorts. Level touring and tent pitches with electric hook-up.

SAT NAV *TR4 8HR*

General Leisure

Has every park been assessed?

All parks in this guide has been rated for quality, or is awaiting assessment, by a professional national tourist board assessor.

BLANDFORD FORUM, Dorset Map ref 2B3

★★★★
TOURING & CAMPING PARK
£12.00–£18.50
125 touring pitches

The Inside Park

Down House Estate, Blandford St Mary, Blandford Forum DT11 9AD **t** (01258) 453719
e inspark@aol.com

members.aol.com/inspark/inspark

Secluded park and woodland with facilities built into 18thC stable and coach house. Ideal location for touring the county. One-and-a-half miles south west of Blandford on road to Winterborne Stickland.

open April to October
payment Credit/debit cards, cash, cheques

General Leisure

BOURNEMOUTH, Dorset Map ref 2B3

★★★★★
HOLIDAY & TOURING PARK
ROSE AWARD
(41) £8.00–£26.00
(41) £8.00–£26.00
(75) £170.00–£895.00
41 touring pitches

Meadow Bank Holidays

Stour Way, Christchurch BH23 2PQ **t** (01202) 483597 **e** enquiries@meadowbank-holidays.co.uk

meadowbank-holiday.co.uk SPECIAL OFFERS

open March to October
payment Credit/debit cards, cash, cheques

Meadowbank Holidays operate Bournemouth's closest holiday caravan and touring park. We are superbly located on the beautiful River Stour and provide a wonderful relaxing environment for a peaceful, carefree holiday or break visiting the superb local beaches, New Forest or the famous Jurassic Coast.

SAT NAV *BH23 2PQ*

General Leisure

BRAUNTON, Devon Map ref 1C1

★★★★
TOURING & CAMPING PARK
(100) £8.00–£25.00
(40) £8.00–£25.00
(40) £6.00–£25.00
180 touring pitches

Lobb Fields Caravan and Camping Park

Saunton Road, Braunton EX33 1EB **t** (01271) 812090 **e** info@lobbfields.com

lobbfields.com

Fourteen-acre grassy park with panoramic views across the Taw Estuary. Situated one mile from Braunton centre on B3231 and 1.5 miles from Saunton beach and Biosphere reserve.

open 20 March to 25 October
payment Credit/debit cards, cash, cheques

General Leisure

BREAN, Somerset Map ref 1D1

★★★★
HOLIDAY, TOURING & CAMPING PARK
(450) £6.75–£21.50
(450) £6.75–£21.50
(150) £6.75–£18.00
450 touring pitches

Northam Farm Touring Park

Brean Sands, Burnham-on-Sea TA8 2SE **t** (01278) 751244 **e** enquiries@northamfarm.co.uk

northamfarm.co.uk

open March to October
payment Credit/debit cards, cash, cheques

Attractive and well established family-run touring park situated 200m from five miles of sandy beach. 30-acre park offering children's outdoor play areas, fishing lake, cafe, mini-supermarket, launderette, dog walks, hardstanding and grass pitches. The Seagull Inn, our own family entertainment venue and restaurant, is within 600m.

SAT NAV *TA8 2SE* **ONLINE MAP**

General Leisure

BREAN, Somerset Map ref 1D1

★★★★
HOLIDAY, TOURING & CAMPING PARK

£7.00–£15.00
£7.00–£15.00
£7.00–£15.00
(11) £170.00–£490.00
575 touring pitches

Warren Farm Holiday Centre

Warren Road, Brean Sands, Burnham-on-Sea TA8 2RP **t** (01278) 751227
e enquiries@warren-farm.co.uk

warren-farm.co.uk GUEST REVIEWS

open April to October
payment Credit/debit cards

Award-winning, family-run holiday centre close to beach. Friendly atmosphere, high standards of cleanliness, modern facilities and excellent value. Grass pitches, indoor/outdoor play facilities, pub, restaurant, nightly entertainment in high season.

General Leisure

BRIDPORT, Dorset Map ref 2A3

★★★★
HOLIDAY, TOURING & CAMPING PARK

(350) £15.00–£33.00
(50) £15.00–£33.00
(100) £15.00–£33.00
(60) £170.00–£780.00
500 touring pitches

Pitch prices include up to 6 people and club membership.

Freshwater Beach Holiday Park

Burton Bradstock, Bridport DT6 4PT **t** (01308) 897317 **e** office@freshwaterbeach.co.uk

freshwaterbeach.co.uk SPECIAL OFFERS

open Mid-March to mid-November
payment Credit/debit cards, cash, cheques

Family park with a large touring and camping field. Own private beach on Dorset's spectacular World Heritage Coastline. Surrounded by countryside and within easy reach of Dorset's features and attractions. Free nightly family entertainment and children's activities. Horse and pony rides, donkey derby, beach fishing, cliff and seaside walks.

SAT NAV *DT6 4PT* **ONLINE MAP**

General Leisure

BRIDPORT, Dorset Map ref 2A3

★★★★★
HOLIDAY, TOURING & CAMPING PARK
ROSE AWARD

£13.25–£28.00
£13.25–£28.00
(159) £13.25–£22.00
(20) £215.00–£575.00
108 touring pitches

Golden Cap Holiday Park

Seatown, Chideock, Bridport DT6 6JX **t** (01308) 422139 **e** holidays@wdlh.co.uk

wdlh.co.uk SPECIAL OFFERS

One hundred metres from beach overlooked by Dorset's highest cliff top – Golden Cap – surrounded by countryside on this Heritage Coast.

open March to November
payment Credit/debit cards, cash, cheques

General Leisure

Place index

If you know where you want to stay, the index by place name at the back of the guide will give you the page number listing accommodation in your chosen town, city or village. Check out the other useful indexes too.

BRIDPORT, Dorset Map ref 2A3

★★★★★
HOLIDAY, TOURING & CAMPING PARK
ROSE AWARD

£13.25–£24.00
£13.25–£24.00
(75) £10.25–£18.25
(18) £215.00–£575.00
120 touring pitches

Highlands End Holiday Park

Eype, Bridport DT6 6AR **t** (01308) 422139 **e** holidays@wdlh.co.uk

wdlh.co.uk SPECIAL OFFERS

Quiet, select, family park overlooking sea with exceptional views of Heritage Coast and Lyme Bay. Indoor swimming pool.

open March to November
payment Credit/debit cards, cash, cheques

General Leisure

BRIXHAM, Devon Map ref 1D2

★★★★
TOURING & CAMPING PARK

(60) £9.60–£17.20
(10) £9.60–£17.20
(60) £9.60–£17.20
(4) £205.00–£515.00
120 touring pitches

Off-peak reductions.

Galmpton Touring Park

Greenway Road, Galmpton, Brixham TQ5 0EP **t** (01803) 842066
e galmptontouringpark@hotmail.com

galmptontouringpark.co.uk

open Easter to September
payment Credit/debit cards, cash, cheques

Overlooking the River Dart with superb views from pitches. A quiet base for families and couples to explore Torbay and South Devon. Self-catering cottages available.

SAT NAV *TQ5 0EP*

General Leisure

BRIXHAM, Devon Map ref 1D2

★★★★★
TOURING & CAMPING PARK

(239) £14.90–£33.00
(239) £14.90–£33.00
on application
239 touring pitches

Hillhead Holiday Park Caravan Club Site

Hillhead, Brixham TQ5 0HH **t** (01803) 853204

caravanclub.co.uk

open March 2009 to January 2010
payment Credit/debit cards, cash, cheques

In a great location, with many pitches affording stunning sea views. Swimming pool, evening entertainment, bar, restaurant and much more!

SAT NAV *TQ5 0HH*

Special member rates mean you can save your membership subscription in less than a week. Visit our website to find out more.

General Leisure

Do you have access needs?

Look for the National Accessible Scheme symbols if you have special hearing, visual or mobility needs. An index of parks participating in the scheme can be found at the back of this guide.

BUDE, Cornwall Map ref 1C2

★★★★★
TOURING PARK

(145) £10.00–£26.00
(145) £10.00–£26.00
(145) £10.00–£26.00
145 touring pitches

Discounts for large families and longer stays. Please phone for details.

Budemeadows Touring Park

Budemeadows, Bude EX23 0NA **t** (01288) 361646 **e** holiday@budemeadows.com

budemeadows.com GUEST REVIEWS • SPECIAL OFFERS

open All year
payment Credit/debit cards, cash, cheques

Superb centre for surfing, scenery and sightseeing. All usual facilities including heated pool, licensed bar, shop, launderette, playground. Well kept and maintained grounds.

SAT NAV *EX23 0NA* ONLINE MAP

General Leisure

BUDE, Cornwall Map ref 1C2

★★★★
HOLIDAY & TOURING PARK

(20) £14.00–£21.50
£14.00–£21.50
(50) £9.50–£18.50
(130) £160.00–£900.00

Various promotions for certain times of the year – call us or see website.

Sandymouth Holiday Park

Sandymouth Bay, Bude EX23 9HW **t** (01288) 352563 **e** reception@sandymouthbay.co.uk

sandymouthbay.co.uk SPECIAL OFFERS • REAL-TIME BOOKING

open March to October
payment Credit/debit cards, cash, cheques

Friendly family park set in 24 acres of meadowland in an area rich with beautiful beaches, bustling coastal resorts and picturesque fishing villages. Inland, the rolling countryside is a fascinating contrast to the rugged coast. Licensed club, indoor pool, sauna, Black Pearl adventure play area, crazy golf, toilets and launderette.

SAT NAV *EX23 9HW*

General Leisure

BUDE, Cornwall Map ref 1C2

★★★★
HOLIDAY, TOURING & CAMPING PARK

(65) £8.50–£15.50
(65) £8.50–£15.50
(65) £8.50–£15.50
(18) £155.00–£495.00
65 touring pitches

Upper Lynstone Caravan and Camping Site

Upton, Bude EX23 0LP **t** (01288) 352017 **e** reception@upperlynstone.co.uk

upperlynstone.co.uk

open Easter to October
payment Credit/debit cards, cash, cheques

A quiet family-run park just 0.75 miles from the sandy beach and town centre. Enjoy the beauty of the coastal path from our site. Spacious camping and electric hook-up pitches. Modern, well-equipped caravans for hire. Families and couples only.

SAT NAV *EX23 0LP*

General Leisure

Look at the maps for park locations

Colour maps at the front pinpoint the location of all parks found in the regional sections.

BUDE, Cornwall Map ref 1C2

★★★★★
HOLIDAY & TOURING PARK

(50) £14.00–£24.00
(50) £14.00–£24.00
(40) £14.00–£24.00
(55) £190.00–£720.00
60 touring pitches

Wooda Farm Park

Poughill, Bude EX23 9HJ **t** (01288) 352069 **e** enquiries@wooda.co.uk

wooda.co.uk

Stunning views over Bude Bay and countryside; 1.5 miles from safe, sandy beaches. Family-owned and run with all facilities, fishing, sports barn, tennis court, woodland walks, golf. An ideal base.

open April to October
payment Credit/debit cards, cash, cheques

General Leisure

BURNHAM-ON-SEA, Somerset Map ref 1D1

★★★★★
HOLIDAY & TOURING PARK

(550) £9.00–£22.00
(100) £9.00–£22.00
(5) £225.00–£550.00

Home Farm Holiday Park

Edithmead, Highbridge TA9 4HD **t** (01278) 788888 **e** office@homefarmholidaypark.co.uk

homefarmholidaypark.co.uk REAL-TIME BOOKING

Luxury amenity blocks, electric hook-ups, hardstanding. Set in 43 acres of beautiful parkland. Outdoor swimming pool. Country club supermarket. New indoor pool for 2009.

open All year except Christmas
payment Credit/debit cards, cash, cheques

General Leisure

CAMELFORD, Cornwall Map ref 1B2

★★★
HOLIDAY, TOURING & CAMPING PARK

£19.00–£24.00
£19.00–£24.00
(38) £108.00–£610.00
(37) £210.00–£1,070.00
39 touring pitches

Juliots Well Holiday Park

Camelford PL32 9RF **t** (01840) 213302 **e** juliotswell@breaksincornwall.com

juliotswell.com

Quiet park in 31 acres of beautiful woodland and meadows. Facilities include a swimming pool, bar and restaurant. Close to beach and moor.

open All year
payment Credit/debit cards, cash, cheques

General Leisure

CHARMOUTH, Dorset Map ref 1D2

★★★
HOLIDAY, TOURING & CAMPING PARK

(300) £10.00–£19.00
(300) £10.00–£19.00
(300) £10.00–£19.00
(6) £200.00–£650.00
300 touring pitches

Manor Farm Holiday Centre

The Street, Charmouth, Bridport DT6 6QL **t** (01297) 560226 **e** enq@manorfarmholidaycentre.co.uk

manorfarmholidaycentre.co.uk

Large, open site in Area of Outstanding Natural Beauty close to the sea. From east end of Charmouth bypass, come into Charmouth and the site is 0.75 miles on the right.

open All year
payment Credit/debit cards, cash, cheques

General Leisure

CHARMOUTH, Dorset Map ref 1D2

SEADOWN HOLIDAY PARK

Bridge Road, Charmouth, Dorset DT6 6QS

Quiet family run park situated on Dorset's World Heritage Coast. The park has its own direct access to Charmouth's famous fossil beach.

T: (01297) 560154 F: (01297) 561130 www.seadownholidaypark.co.uk

What if I need to cancel?

It's advisable to check the proprietor's cancellation policy at the time of booking in case you have to change your plans.

CHARMOUTH, Dorset Map ref 1D2

★★★★★
HOLIDAY, TOURING & CAMPING PARK

(40) £12.50–£18.00
(10)
(10)
(62) £185.00–£555.00
60 touring pitches

See Ad on p184

Seadown Holiday Park

Bridge Road, Charmouth, Bridport DT6 6QS **t** (01297) 560154

seadowncaravanpark.co.uk

open Mid-March to end of October
payment Credit/debit cards, cash, cheques

Quiet, family-run park which runs alongside the River Char. It has its own direct access to Charmouth's famous fossil beach, which is situated on the World Heritage Coastline.

SAT NAV *DT6 6QS*

General Leisure

CHARMOUTH, Dorset Map ref 1D2

★★★★★
HOLIDAY, TOURING & CAMPING PARK

(186) £14.50–£28.00
£14.50–£28.00
(20) £12.50–£25.00
(3) £250.00–£650.00
206 touring pitches

Low- and mid-season offers for 1- and 2-week stays.

Wood Farm Caravan and Camping Park

Charmouth, Bridport DT6 6BT **t** (01297) 560697 **e** holidays@woodfarm.co.uk

woodfarm.co.uk

open Easter to October
payment Credit/debit cards, cash, cheques

Breathtaking views and superb facilities are both on offer at Wood Farm. Our Heritage Coast and spectacular rural scenery are just waiting to amaze you.

SAT NAV *DT6 6BT*

General Leisure

CHEDDAR, Somerset Map ref 1D1

★★★★
HOLIDAY, TOURING & CAMPING PARK
ROSE AWARD

(100) £14.00–£27.00
(20) £12.00–£20.00
(80) £14.00–£27.00
(37) £180.00–£600.00
200 touring pitches

Broadway House Holiday Touring Caravan and Camping Park

Axbridge Road, Cheddar BS27 3DB **t** (01934) 742610 **e** info@broadwayhouse.uk.com

broadwayhouse.uk.com

open March to November
payment Credit/debit cards, cash, cheques, euros

Nestling at the foot of the Mendip Hills, this family-run park is only one mile from England's Grand Canyon: Cheddar Gorge. Every facility your family could ever want: shop, bar, launderette, swimming pool, BMX track, skateboard park, nature trails, archery, caving and canoeing. Holiday caravans and lodges for hire.

SAT NAV *BS27 3DB*

General Leisure

CHRISTCHURCH, Dorset Map ref 2B3

★★★
TOURING & CAMPING PARK

(60) £13.00–£22.00
(60) £13.00–£22.00
(14) £13.00–£19.00
60 touring pitches

Harrow Wood Farm Caravan Park

Poplar Lane, Bransgore, Christchurch BH23 8JE **t** (01425) 672487
e harrowwood@caravan-sites.co.uk

caravan-sites.co.uk

Quiet site bordered by woods and meadows. Take A35 from Lyndhurst, after approximately 11 miles turn right at Cat and Fiddle pub, site approximately 1.5 miles into Bransgore, first right after school.

open 1 March to 6 January
payment Credit/debit cards, cash, cheques

General Leisure

CORFE CASTLE, Dorset Map ref 2B3

★★
HOLIDAY, TOURING & CAMPING PARK

£12.00–£20.00
£12.00–£20.00
(60) £12.00–£20.00
52 touring pitches

High season – 5% discount for 7 nights or more.

Norden Farm Campsite

Norden Farm, Wareham BH20 5DS **t** (01929) 480098 **e** nordenfarm@fsmail.net

nordenfarm.com

open March to October
payment Credit/debit cards, cash, cheques

Level fields on working farm site in the beautiful Purbeck Valley. Excellent toilet/shower facilities. Good family location. Set away from main road but with easy access. Family-run business with adjoining farm shop and bed and breakfast.

SAT NAV *BH20 5DS*

General Leisure

CORFE CASTLE, Dorset Map ref 2B3

★
CAMPING PARK

(150) £12.00
(150) £12.00

Woodyhyde Camp Site

Valley Road, Corfe Castle, Wareham BH20 5HT **t** (01929) 480274 **e** camp@woodyhyde.fsnet.co.uk

woodyhyde.co.uk

Secluded family site. Easy access to beaches and local attractions. Ideal centre for walking holidays. Steam train station nearby.

open Easter to October
payment Credit/debit cards, cash, cheques

General Leisure

COTSWOLDS

See under Moreton-in-Marsh, Tewkesbury
See also Cotswolds in South East England section

Don't forget www.

Web addresses throughout this guide are shown without the prefix www. Please include www. in the address line of your browser. If a web address does not follow this style it is shown in full.

CUBERT, Cornwall Map ref 1B2

★★★★★
HOLIDAY PARK
(22) £200.00–£575.00

Treworgans Holiday Park

Cubert, Newquay TR8 5HH **t** (01637) 830200 **e** contact-us@treworgansholidaypark.co.uk

treworgansholidaypark.co.uk SPECIAL OFFERS · REAL-TIME BOOKING

open April to October
payment Credit/debit cards, cash, cheques

Treworgans can provide a peaceful relaxing holiday. Our luxury park is located on the picturesque north Cornwall coast in a secluded hamlet. We are a quiet site and have no clubhouse or traffic noise to disturb your holiday. Separate playing field. The golden sands of Holywell Bay and Crantock are within easy reach.

SAT NAV *TR8 5HH* **ONLINE MAP**

General Leisure

DARTMOOR

See under Ashburton, Tavistock

DAWLISH, Devon Map ref 1D2

★★★★
HOLIDAY, TOURING & CAMPING PARK
ROSE AWARD

(450) £13.00–£24.00
(450) £13.00–£24.00
(450) £13.00–£24.00
(66) £179.00–£705.00
450 touring pitches

£2 off standard pitch per night, low and mid season. Senior Citizens save an extra £1 each per night (advance bookings, minimum 3 nights' stay).

Cofton Country Holidays

Cofton, Starcross, Exeter EX6 8RP **t** (01626) 890111 **e** info@coftonholidays.co.uk

coftonholidays.co.uk SPECIAL OFFERS

open Easter to October
payment Credit/debit cards, cash, cheques

A glorious corner of Devon. Family-run holiday park in 30 acres of delightful parkland. Some of the finest pitches in South Devon. Heated outdoor swimming pools. Fun-packed visitor attractions to suit all. David Bellamy Gold Conservation Award. Two minutes from Blue Flag beach.

SAT NAV *EX6 8RP* **ONLINE MAP**

General Leisure

DORCHESTER, Dorset Map ref 2B3

★★
TOURING & CAMPING PARK

(50) £7.00–£14.00
(50) £7.00–£14.00
(50) £7.00–£14.00
(3) £165.00–£275.00
50 touring pitches

Giants Head Caravan & Camping Park

Old Sherborne Road, Dorchester DT2 7TR **t** (01300) 341242 **e** holidays@giantshead.co.uk

giantshead.co.uk REAL-TIME BOOKING

Two miles north-east of Cerne Abbas, three miles south of Middlemarsh, eight miles from Dorchester.

payment Cash, cheques

General Leisure

Check the maps for park locations

Colour maps at the front pinpoint all the places where parks are featured within the regional sections of this guide. Pick your location and then refer to the place index at the back to find the page number.

DRYBROOK, Gloucestershire Map ref 2B1

★★★★
HOLIDAY, TOURING & CAMPING PARK
(20) £16.00
(20) £16.00
(35) £14.00
40 touring pitches

From 1 Apr to 30 Jun, 3 weekday nights for the price of 2.

Greenway Farm Caravan & Camping Park

Puddlebrook Road, Hawthorns, Drybrook GL17 9HW **t** (01594) 543737 **e** greenwayfarm@aic.co.uk

greenwayfarm.org GUEST REVIEWS · SPECIAL OFFERS

open All year
payment Credit/debit cards, cash, cheques

David and Lorraine welcome you to Greenway Farm, an independently owned smallholding of five acres. Situated along a quiet country lane, the site enjoys beautiful views, and with woodland walks within 100yds, you can be assured of a relaxing break in the heart of the forest.

SAT NAV *GL17 9HW* **ONLINE MAP**

General Leisure

DULVERTON, Somerset Map ref 1D1

★★★★
TOURING PARK
(64) £12.20–£25.10
(64) £12.20–£25.10
64 touring pitches

THE CARAVAN CLUB

Exmoor House Caravan Club Site

Dulverton TA22 9HL **t** (01398) 323268

caravanclub.co.uk

Very quiet and secluded, in the heart of Lorna Doone country. Shops and pubs within walking distance, Exmoor is on the doorstep. Leave your car behind and explore this walker's paradise.

open March 2009 to January 2010
payment Credit/debit cards, cash, cheques

General

DULVERTON, Somerset Map ref 1D1

★★★★★
TOURING PARK
(80) £14.00–£26.60
(80) £14.00–£26.60
80 touring pitches

Special member rates mean you can save your membership subscription in less than a week. Visit our website to find out more.

Lakeside Caravan Club Site

Higher Grants, Exebridge, Dulverton TA22 9BE **t** (01398) 324068

caravanclub.co.uk

open March to November
payment Credit/debit cards, cash, cheques

Recently redeveloped, Lakeside has splendid new facilities and all pitches (now level) boast superb views of surrounding hills and the Exe Valley. Within easy reach of the National Park and Lorna Doone country.

SAT NAV *TA22 9BE*

General Leisure

EXMOOR

See under Dulverton, Porlock, Winsford

Where can I get help and advice?

Tourist Information Centres offer friendly help with accommodation and holiday ideas as well as suggestions of places to visit and things to do. You'll find contact details at the beginning of each regional section.

EXMOUTH, Devon Map ref 1D2

EXMOUTH, Devon Map ref 1D2

★★★★★
HOLIDAY & TOURING PARK

£12.50–£18.00
(2) £155.00–£495.00
115 touring pitches

Tents/tourers/ motorhomes: 2 people, 1 week, low season £65.00.

See Ad above

Webbers Caravan & Camping Park

Castle Lane, Woodbury, Exeter EX5 1EA **t** (01395) 232276 **e** reception@webberspark.co.uk

webberspark.co.uk

open Mid-March to end of October
payment Credit/debit cards, cash, cheques

Set in a tranquil corner of East Devon, this quiet, family-run park has breathtaking views of Dartmoor and the Exe Estuary. Just a short distance from Woodbury Common, with some 3,000 acres of unspoilt open heathland to roam. Relax, and enjoy this outstanding piece of countryside.

SAT NAV *EX5 1EA*

General Leisure

FOREST OF DEAN

See under Drybrook

FOWEY, Cornwall Map ref 1B3

★★★★
TOURING & CAMPING PARK

(65) £12.00–£19.00
(65) £12.00–£19.00
(65) £12.00–£19.00
65 touring pitches

Penmarlam Caravan & Camping Park

Bodinnick by Fowey, Fowey PL23 1LZ **t** (01726) 870088 **e** info@penmarlampark.co.uk

penmarlampark.co.uk REAL-TIME BOOKING

open April to October
payment Credit/debit cards, cash, cheques, euros

A quiet, grassy site on the Fowey Estuary, an Area of Outstanding Natural Beauty. Choose from our lawned, sheltered field or enjoy breathtaking views from the upper field. Shop and off-licence, immaculately clean heated amenity block, electric hook-ups and serviced pitches, Wi-Fi internet access, boat launching and storage adjacent.

SAT NAV *PL23 1LZ* **ONLINE MAP**

General Leisure

What shall we do today?

For ideas on places to visit, see the beginning of this regional section or go online at visitbritain.com.

GLASTONBURY, Somerset Map ref 2A2

★★★★★
TOURING & CAMPING PARK

(60) £13.50–£21.00
(20) £13.50–£21.00
(20) £13.50–£21.00
100 touring pitches

The Old Oaks Touring Park

Wick, Glastonbury BA6 8JS **t** (01458) 831437 **e** info@theoldoaks.co.uk

theoldoaks.co.uk

An award-winning park, exclusively for adults, set in tranquil, unspoilt countryside with panoramic views, offering spacious, landscaped pitches and excellent amenities.

open 1 March to 20 November
payment Credit/debit cards, cash, cheques

General Leisure

GREAT TORRINGTON, Devon Map ref 1C2

★★★★
HOLIDAY PARK

(9) £155.00–£425.00
(4) £155.00–£425.00

Greenways Valley Holiday Park

Caddywell Lane, Great Torrington, Devon EX38 7EW **t** (01805) 622153
e enquiries@greenwaysvalley.co.uk

greenwaysvalley.co.uk

Small peaceful park with spacious chalets and modern caravans. Cycle the Tarka Trail or walk the many footpaths. Explore a different part of Devon.

open March to October
payment Credit/debit cards, cash, cheques

General Leisure

HAYLE, Cornwall Map ref 1B3

★★★★
HOLIDAY, TOURING & CAMPING PARK

£8.00–£24.50
£8.00–£24.50
£8.00–£24.50
£85.00–£725.00
84 touring pitches

Beachside Holiday Park

Lethlean Lane, Phillack, Hayle TR27 5AW **t** (01736) 753080 **e** reception@beachside.demon.co.uk

beachside.co.uk

Beachside is a family holiday park amidst sand dunes beside the sea in the famous St Ives Bay. Our location is ideal for the beach and for touring the whole of West Cornwall.

open Easter to October
payment Credit/debit cards, cash, cheques

General Leisure

HOLSWORTHY, Devon Map ref 1C2

★★
HOLIDAY, TOURING & CAMPING PARK

(5) £4.00–£6.00
(5) £4.00–£6.00
(15) £4.00–£6.00
(1) £150.00–£400.00

Noteworthy Caravan & Camping Site

Bude Road, Holsworthy EX22 7JB **t** (01409) 253731 & 07811 000071
e enquiries@noteworthy-devon.co.uk

noteworthy-devon.co.uk

Rural caravan and camping site, self-contained park on the Devon/Cornwall border. Four miles Holsworthy, six miles Bude.

open All year
payment Cash

General Leisure

Where can I find accessible accommodation?

If you have special hearing, visual or mobility needs, there's an index of National Accessible Scheme participants featured in this guide. For more accessible accommodation buy a copy of Easy Access Britain available online at visitbritaindirect.com, and from Tourism for All on 0845 124 997 or visit tourismforall.org.uk.

KENTISBEARE, Devon Map ref 1D2

★★★★
HOLIDAY & TOURING PARK
ROSE AWARD

£12.50–£18.00
£12.50–£18.00
£10.50–£14.00
(26) £195.00–£460.00
80 touring pitches

Club members £1 per night discount on pitch fees. Short breaks available in holiday homes all season. Pet-free and non-smoking holiday homes available.

Forest Glade Holiday Park

Kentisbeare, Cullompton EX15 2DT **t** (01404) 841381 **e** enquiries@forest-glade.co.uk

forest-glade.co.uk SPECIAL OFFERS

open Mid-March to end of October
payment Credit/debit cards, cash, cheques

Free indoor heated pool on small, family-owned park surrounded by forest with deer. Large, flat, sheltered pitches. Luxury, all-serviced holiday homes for hire.

SAT NAV *EX15 2DT*

General Leisure

LACOCK, Wiltshire Map ref 2B2

★★★★★
TOURING & CAMPING PARK

(39) £12.50–£14.50
(39) £12.50–£14.50
(4) £12.50–£14.50
43 touring pitches

Piccadilly Caravan Park Ltd

Folly Lane (West), Lacock, Chippenham SN15 2LP **t** (01249) 730260 **e** piccadillylacock@aol.com

This well-maintained and peaceful site stands in open countryside 0.5 miles from the historic National Trust village of Lacock.

open April to October
payment Cash, cheques

General Leisure

LANDRAKE, Cornwall Map ref 1C2

★★★★
TOURING & CAMPING PARK

(60) £13.90–£19.80
(60) £13.90–£19.80
(20) £3.50–£19.80
60 touring pitches

See our newly designed website for our latest special offers.

Dolbeare Park, Caravan & Camping

St Ive Road, Landrake, Saltash PL12 5AF **t** (01752) 851332 **e** reception@dolbeare.co.uk

dolbeare.co.uk GUEST REVIEWS · SPECIAL OFFERS · REAL-TIME BOOKING

open All year
payment Credit/debit cards, cash

Friendly, well-maintained park which offers you that personal touch. Set amidst beautiful rolling countryside, an ideal base from which to explore both Devon and Cornwall. One mile from A38. Beaches 20 minutes, Plymouth 20 minutes, Eden Project 40 minutes.

SAT NAV *PL12 5AF* **ONLINE MAP**

General Leisure

LAND'S END, Cornwall Map ref 1A3

★★★★
TOURING & CAMPING PARK

£9.00–£16.50
£9.00–£16.50
£9.00–£16.50
105 touring pitches

Cardinney Caravan & Camping Park

Penberth Valley, St Buryan, Penzance TR19 6HX **t** (01736) 810880 **e** cardinney@btinternet.com

cardinney-camping-park.co.uk

Quiet, family-run site set in rural area. Peaceful, central for the Land's End peninsula.

payment Credit/debit cards, cash, cheques

General Leisure

LANIVET, Cornwall Map ref 1B2

★★★
HOLIDAY PARK
(5) £150.00–£330.00

Weekend and mini-breaks subject to availability.

Kernow Caravan Park

Clann Lane, Lanivet, Bodmin PL30 5HD **t** (01208) 831343

open March to October
payment Cash, cheques

Kernow Caravan Park is quiet and peaceful, in a tranquil setting. Personally supervised by a Cornish family. An ideal touring location to visit Eden Project, Heligan Lost Gardens, Lanhydrock, Camel Trail, Saints Way or Wenford Steam Railway. Site is a few minutes' walk from Lanivet village shop, pub, fish and chip restaurant.

SAT NAV *PL30 5HD*

General

LOOE, Cornwall Map ref 1C2

★★★★
HOLIDAY, TOURING & CAMPING PARK
(100) £9.50–£18.00
(40) £9.50–£18.00
(100) £9.50–£18.00
(100) £120.00–£460.00
240 touring pitches

Various promotions for certain times of the year – call us or see website.

Tencreek Caravan Park

Polperro Road, Looe PL13 2JR **t** (01503) 262447 **e** reception@tencreek.co.uk

dolphinholidays.co.uk SPECIAL OFFERS • REAL-TIME BOOKING

open All year
payment Credit/debit cards, cash, cheques

Lying close to the South Cornwall coast, in a rural but not isolated position, Tencreek Holiday Park is ideal for exploring Cornwall and South Devon. Tencreek is the closest park to Looe and lies in Daphne du Maurier Country; beyond are Bodmin Moor, Dartmoor, traditional Cornish towns and picturesque beaches and ports.

SAT NAV *PL13 2JR*

General Leisure

MAWGAN PORTH, Cornwall Map ref 1B2

★★★★★
HOLIDAY, TOURING & CAMPING PARK
ROSE AWARD
(30) £11.00–£25.00
(30) £11.00–£25.00
(80) £11.00–£25.00
(40) £250.00–£700.00
110 touring pitches

Out-of-season discounts on 2-week holidays, 2-person-only holidays, and for early payment.

Sun Haven Valley Country Holiday Park

Mawgan Porth, Cornwall TR8 4BQ **t** (01637) 860373 **e** sunhaven@hotmail.co.uk

sunhavenvalley.com SPECIAL OFFERS

open All year
payment Credit/debit cards, cash

Immaculately maintained luxury family site in beautiful countryside just ten minutes' walk from a large sandy beach. Touring campsite from May to October plus spacious chalets and static caravans available to hire all year round.

SAT NAV *TR8 4BQ*

General Leisure

Do you have access needs?

Look for the National Accessible Scheme symbols if you have special hearing, visual or mobility needs.

MEVAGISSEY, Cornwall Map ref 1B3

★★★★★
HOLIDAY, TOURING & CAMPING PARK
ROSE AWARD

(189) £7.00–£30.00
(189) £7.00–£30.00
(189) £7.00–£30.00
(38) £149.00–£999.00
189 touring pitches

Please visit the website for special offers.

Sea View International

Boswinger, Gorran, St Austell PL26 6LL **t** (01726) 843425 **e** holidays@seaviewinternational.com

seaviewinternational.com SPECIAL OFFERS • REAL-TIME BOOKING

open Mid-March to October
payment Credit/debit cards, cash, cheques

Close to Eden Project and New Maritime Museum. AA's best campsite many times. 3.5 miles south west of Mevagissey, parkland setting with panoramic views. Luxury caravans and chalets, mains services, colour television etc. Statics: mid-March to end of October. Touring: May to end of September.

SAT NAV *PL26 6LL*

General Leisure

MODBURY, Devon Map ref 1C3

★★★★
TOURING PARK

(112) £12.20–£25.10
(112) £12.20–£25.10
112 touring pitches

THE CARAVAN CLUB

Broad Park Caravan Club Site

Higher East Leigh, Modbury, Ivybridge PL21 0SH **t** (01548) 830714

caravanclub.co.uk

open March to November
payment Credit/debit cards, cash, cheques

Situated between moor and sea, this makes a splendid base from which to explore South Devon. Head for Dartmoor, or seek out the small villages of the South Hams.

SAT NAV *PL21 0SH*

Midweek discount: pitch fee for standard pitches for stays on any Tue, Wed or Thu night outside peak season dates will be reduced by 50%.

General

MOORSHOP, Devon Map ref 1C2

★★★★
TOURING & CAMPING PARK

(80) £6.00–£12.00
(10) £6.00–£12.00
(40) £5.00–£12.00
(4) £150.00–£480.00
100 touring pitches

Higher Longford Caravan & Camping Park

Moorshop, Tavistock PL19 9LQ **t** (01822) 613360 **e** stay@higherlongford.co.uk

higherlongford.co.uk

Beautiful, quiet family-run park with scenic views of Dartmoor. Spacious pitches, electric hook-ups, grass, hardstanding and multiserviced pitches available all year. Modern, clean and warm facilities. Dogs welcome. Ideal for Devon, Cornwall and Dartmoor.

open All year
payment Credit/debit cards, cash, cheques

General Leisure

It's all quality-assessed accommodation

Our commitment to quality involves wide-ranging accommodation assessment. Ratings and awards were correct at the time of going to press but may change following a new assessment. Please check at time of booking.

MORETON-IN-MARSH, Gloucestershire Map ref 2B1

★★★★★
TOURING PARK

(184) £14.90–£28.30
(184) £14.90–£28.30
184 touring pitches

THE CARAVAN CLUB

Moreton-in-Marsh Caravan Club Site

Bourton Road, Moreton-in-Marsh GL56 0BT **t** (01608) 650519

caravanclub.co.uk

open All year
payment Credit/debit cards, cash, cheques

An attractive, well-wooded site within easy walking distance of the market town of Moreton-in-Marsh. On-site facilities include crazy golf, volleyball and boules. Large dog-walking area.

SAT NAV *GL56 0BT*

Special member rates mean you can save your membership subscription in less than a week. Visit our website to find out more.

General Leisure

MORTEHOE, Devon Map ref 1C1

★★★★
HOLIDAY, TOURING & CAMPING PARK

(25) £13.00–£19.50
£12.00–£19.50
(150) £12.00–£17.00
(24) £230.00–£550.00

North Morte Farm Caravan and Camping Park

North Morte Road, Mortehoe, Woolacombe EX34 7EG **t** (01271) 870381
e info@northmortefarm.co.uk

northmortefarm.co.uk

Set in beautiful countryside overlooking Rockham Bay, close to village of Mortehoe, and Woolacombe.

open April to September
payment Credit/debit cards, cash, cheques

General Leisure

NEWQUAY, Cornwall Map ref 1B2

★★★★★
HOLIDAY, TOURING & CAMPING PARK
ROSE AWARD

(378) £10.50–£19.00
(378) £10.50–£19.00
(170) £10.50–£19.00
(280) £200.00–£1,050.00
378 touring pitches

See our website for seasonal offers, 3-/4-night short breaks, holiday homes for all budgets and our range of touring/camping options.

Hendra Holiday Park

Newquay TR8 4NY **t** (01637) 875778 **e** enquiries@hendra-holidays.com

hendra-holidays.com SPECIAL OFFERS

open Easter to October
payment Credit/debit cards, cash, cheques, euros

Award-winning Hendra is ideal for families and couples and offers superb-quality holiday homes and touring/camping pitches. With entertainment, indoor and outdoor play areas and amusements, children's club, cafes and restaurant, and Oasis Fun Pool complex. An ideal location for exploring Cornwall – you'll have your best holiday ever!

SAT NAV *TR8 4NY* **ONLINE MAP**

General
Leisure

Remember to check when booking

Please remember that all information in this guide has been supplied by the proprietors well in advance of publication. Since changes do sometimes occur it's a good idea to check details at the time of booking.

NEWQUAY, Cornwall Map ref 1B2

★★★★★
HOLIDAY PARK
ROSE AWARD

£9.00–£14.90
£9.00–£14.90
£9.00–£14.90
(5) £229.00–£660.00
395 touring pitches

Newperran Holiday Park

Rejerrah, Newquay TR8 5QJ **t** (01872) 572407 **e** holidays@newperran.co.uk

newperran.co.uk REAL-TIME BOOKING

Peaceful family holiday park renowned for its spacious perimeter pitching, with breathtaking open countryside and sea views. Caravans, motor homes, tents and holiday caravans for hire.

open Easter to October
payment Credit/debit cards, cash, cheques

General Leisure

NEWQUAY, Cornwall Map ref 1B2

★★★★
HOLIDAY, TOURING & CAMPING PARK
ROSE AWARD

£11.00–£37.00
£10.00–£37.00
£8.00–£29.00
(18) £269.00–£675.00
200 touring pitches

Porth Beach Tourist Park

Porth, Newquay TR7 3NH **t** (01637) 876531 **e** info@porthbeach.co.uk

porthbeach.co.uk SPECIAL OFFERS

open March to October
payment Credit/debit cards, cash, cheques

Situated in a valley with small stream running down one side, and only 100m from Porth Beach – the perfect family beach. Premium pitches have all facilities. All 18 static caravans were brand new for 2008 season. Bookings only accepted from families or couples (maximum three couples).

SAT NAV *TR7 3NH* **ONLINE MAP**

General Leisure

NEWQUAY, Cornwall Map ref 1B2

★★★★
HOLIDAY, TOURING & CAMPING PARK

£13.00–£17.00
(19) £200.00–£675.00
98 touring pitches

Riverside Holiday Park

Gwills Lane, Newquay TR8 4PE **t** (01637) 873617 **e** info@riversideholidaypark.co.uk

riversideholidaypark.co.uk

Peaceful riverside family park. Two miles to Newquay. Sheltered, level touring pitches, luxury lodges and caravans. Covered, heated pool and bar.

open March to October
payment Credit/debit cards, cash, cheques

General Leisure

NEWQUAY, Cornwall Map ref 1B2

★★★
HOLIDAY, TOURING & CAMPING PARK

(63) £15.00–£19.00
(2) £15.00–£19.00
(12) £12.00–£16.00
75 touring pitches

Trekenning Tourist Park

Newquay TR8 4JF **t** (01637) 880462 **e** holidays@trekenning.co.uk

trekenning.co.uk

Set in beautiful Cornish countryside and only minutes from Cornwall's finest beaches and attractions. A must for caravanners and campers. Great for surfing and rambling; golf, fishing and horse-riding also nearby.

open All year
payment Credit/debit cards, cash, cheques

General Leisure

Fancy a cycling holiday?

For a fabulous freewheeling break, seek out accommodation participating in our Cyclists Welcome scheme. Look out for the symbol and plan your route online at nationalcyclenetwork.org.

NEWQUAY, Cornwall Map ref 1B2

★★★★
TOURING & CAMPING PARK

(140) £8.50–£14.50
(140) £8.50–£14.50
(140) £8.50–£14.50
140 touring pitches

Free-night offers early and late season. Conditions apply.

Treloy Touring Park

Newquay TR8 4JN **t** (01637) 872063 & (01637) 876279 **e** treloy.tp@btconnect.com

treloy.co.uk

open April to September
payment Credit/debit cards, cash, cheques

A family-run park catering exclusively for touring caravans, tents and motor homes. We aim to offer fun and enjoyable holidays for families and couples, in a pleasant, relaxed setting with clean, modern facilities. Nearby is Treloy Golf Club and driving range. Coarse fishing available at Porth Reservoir, one mile away.

SAT NAV *TR8 4JN*

General Leisure

NEWTON ABBOT, Devon Map ref 1D2

★★★★★
TOURING & CAMPING PARK

(135) £13.00–£25.00
£13.00–£25.00
£12.00–£24.00

Early- and late-season bookings. Book for 7 days and only pay for 5. Details on request.

Dornafield

Two Mile Oak, Newton Abbot TQ12 6DD **t** (01803) 812732 **e** enquiries@dornafield.com

dornafield.com REAL-TIME BOOKING

payment Credit/debit cards, cash, cheques

Beautiful 14thC farmhouse located in 30 acres of glorious South Devon countryside. So quiet and peaceful, yet so convenient for Torbay and Dartmoor. Superb facilities to suit the discerning caravanner, including many hardstanding, all-service pitches. Shop, games room, adventure play area, tennis and golf. Our brochure is only a phone call away.

SAT NAV *TQ12 6DD*

General Leisure

PADSTOW, Cornwall Map ref 1B2

★★★★
TOURING & CAMPING PARK

£10.00–£16.00
£10.00–£16.00
£10.00–£16.00
30 touring pitches

The Laurels Touring Park

Padstow Road, Whitecross, Wadebridge PL27 7JQ **t** (01209) 313474
e info@thelaurelsholidaypark.co.uk

thelaurelsholidaypark.co.uk GUEST REVIEWS · SPECIAL OFFERS

payment Credit/debit cards, cash, cheques

Voted one of 100 top UK touring parks 2007. Top-quality select park with beautiful well-cared for grounds, boasting a host of established shrubs and flowers. Most electric serviced pitches have hedged boundary. Excellent amenity block, launderette and washing up area, free hot water. Wet suit dunking/drying area, play park, dog walk.

SAT NAV *PL27 7JQ* **ONLINE MAP**

General Leisure

What do the star ratings mean?

Detailed information about star ratings can be found at the back of this guide.

PADSTOW, Cornwall Map ref 1B2

★★★★★
HOLIDAY, TOURING & CAMPING PARK
ROSE AWARD

(118) £12.00–£43.00
(118) £12.00–£43.00
(124) £12.00–£43.00
(51) £190.00–£920.00
126 touring pitches

Mother Iveys Bay Caravan Park

Trevose Head, Padstow PL28 8SL **t** (01841) 520990 **e** info@motheriveysbay.com

motheriveysbay.com

Situated on the coast with spectacular sea views and our own private sandy beach, perfect for traditional family holidays.

open 15 March to 2 November
payment Credit/debit cards, cash, cheques

General Leisure

PADSTOW, Cornwall Map ref 1B2

★★★★
TOURING & CAMPING PARK

(180) £10.00–£18.50
(180) £10.00–£18.50
(180) £10.00–£18.50
180 touring pitches

Padstow Touring Park

Padstow PL28 8LE **t** (01841) 532061 **e** mail@padstowtouringpark.co.uk

padstowtouringpark.co.uk

Located one mile from Padstow with footpath access. Quiet family park with panoramic views. Sandy beaches two miles. Some en suite pitches. Easy access from main road.

open All year
payment Credit/debit cards, cash, cheques

General Leisure

PAIGNTON, Devon Map ref 1D2

★★★★★
HOLIDAY, TOURING & CAMPING PARK
ROSE AWARD

£14.25–£36.50
£14.25–£36.50
£11.00–£30.00
(189) £165.00–£980.00
175 touring pitches

Special discounts for over-50s and under-5s in holiday caravans. 7 nights touring for 6. Specific dates apply.

Beverley Park

Goodrington Road, Paignton TQ4 7JE **t** (01803) 843887 **e** info@beverley-holidays.co.uk

beverley-holidays.co.uk

open All year except Christmas and New Year
payment Credit/debit cards

Superb luxury holiday park overlooking Torbay with fabulous sea views. South West Tourism 'Caravan Park of the Year' 2004/2005. David Bellamy Gold Conservation Award. Indoor/outdoor pools, tennis, gym, crazy golf, playground, restaurant, bar, shop, plus golf, watersports, and unlimited coastal walks nearby. Less than one mile to the beach.

SAT NAV *TQ4 7JE*

General Leisure

PAIGNTON, Devon Map ref 1D2

★★★★
HOLIDAY, TOURING & CAMPING PARK

(80) £9.00–£15.00
(80) £9.00–£15.00
(80) £9.00–£15.00
(18) £155.00–£475.00
80 touring pitches

Higher Well Farm Holiday Park

Waddeton Road, Stoke Gabriel, Totnes TQ9 6RN **t** (01803) 782289 **e** higherwell@talk21.com

higherwellfarmholidaypark.co.uk

Secluded farm park with static caravans and separate area welcoming touring caravans, tents and motor homes. Within one mile of Stoke Gabriel and the River Dart. Four miles to Paignton.

payment Credit/debit cards, cash, cheques

General Leisure

WALKERS WELCOME WELCOME WALKERS

Do you like walking?

Walkers feel at home in accommodation participating in our Walkers Welcome scheme. Look out for the symbol. Consider walking all or part of a long-distance route – go online at nationaltrail.co.uk.

PAIGNTON, Devon Map ref 1D2

★★★★
HOLIDAY, TOURING & CAMPING PARK

£12.00–£28.00
£12.00–£28.00
£11.50–£25.00
(60) £165.00–£655.00
260 touring pitches

£20 off per week in a caravan for 2 people. 7 nights touring for 6 – specific dates apply.

Whitehill Country Park

Stoke Road, Paignton TQ4 7PF **t** (01803) 782338 **e** info@whitehill-park.co.uk

whitehill-park.co.uk

open Easter to September
payment Credit/debit cards

Beautifully situated in rolling Devon countryside yet within easy reach of the sea, the bright lights of Torbay, and Dartmoor. Outdoor swimming pool, play area, craft room, table tennis, amusements, cycle and walking trails, bar and restaurant.

SAT NAV *TQ4 7PF*

General Leisure

PENZANCE, Cornwall Map ref 1A3

★★★★
HOLIDAY, TOURING & CAMPING PARK

£11.00–£15.00
£11.00–£15.00
£9.00–£12.50
(5) £160.00–£340.00
102 touring pitches

Camping – 7 nights for the price of 6 (low/mid-season). Short breaks for static holiday homes (except Jul & Aug).

Tower Park Caravans & Camping

St Buryan, Penzance TR19 6BZ **t** (01736) 810286 **e** enquiries@towerparkcamping.co.uk

towerparkcamping.co.uk

open March to January
payment Credit/debit cards, cash, cheques

A peaceful, family-run campsite in the heart of the Land's End peninsula ideally situated for beaches, the coast path and the Minack Theatre. Large, level pitches for tents and tourers, static holiday caravans for hire. Five-minute level walk from St Buryan village with pub, shop and post office.

SAT NAV *TR19 6BZ* **ONLINE MAP**

General Leisure

PLYMOUTH, Devon Map ref 1C2

★★★★
HOLIDAY & TOURING PARK

(58) £7.60–£18.80
(58) £7.60–£18.80
58 touring pitches

Plymouth Sound Caravan Club Site

Bovisand Lane, Down Thomas, Plymouth PL9 0AE **t** (01752) 862325

caravanclub.co.uk

open March to October
payment Credit/debit cards, cash, cheques

Within easy reach of the historic port. Superb views over the Sound. Close to the South West Coast Path and lovely beaches.

SAT NAV *PL9 0AE*

Special member rates mean you can save your membership subscription in less than a week. Visit our website to find out more.

General Leisure

Using map references

Map references refer to the colour maps at the front of this guide.

POLRUAN-BY-FOWEY, Cornwall Map ref 1B3

★★★★
HOLIDAY, TOURING & CAMPING PARK

(7) £10.00–£18.00
(7) £10.00–£18.00
(40) £7.50–£15.50
(10) £165.00–£470.00
47 touring pitches

Polruan Holidays (Camping & Caravanning)

Townsend, Polruan PL23 1QH **t** (01726) 870263 **e** polholiday@aol.com

polruanholidays.co.uk

Small, peaceful, coastal holiday park surrounded by sea, river and National Trust farmland. Walking, sailing, fishing, boating and beaches nearby.

payment Cash, cheques

General Leisure

PORLOCK, Somerset Map ref 1D1

★★★★
HOLIDAY, TOURING & CAMPING PARK

(54) £10.00–£17.00
(54) £10.00–£17.00
(66) £10.00–£15.00
(19) £170.00–£400.00
120 touring pitches

Burrowhayes Farm Caravan and Camping Site and Riding Stables

West Luccombe, Porlock, Minehead TA24 8HT **t** (01643) 862463 **e** info@burrowhayes.co.uk

burrowhayes.co.uk

open Mid-March to end of October
payment Credit/debit cards, cash, cheques

Popular family site in delightful National Trust setting on Exmoor, just two miles from Porlock. Surrounding moors and woods provide a walker's paradise. Children can play and explore safely. Riding stables offer pony-trekking for all abilities. Heated shower block with disabled and baby-changing facilities, laundrette and pot wash.

SAT NAV *TA24 8HT*

General Leisure

PORLOCK, Somerset Map ref 1D1

★★★★
HOLIDAY, TOURING & CAMPING PARK
ROSE AWARD

Min £12.00
Min £12.00
Min £11.00
(9) £285.00–£465.00
40 touring pitches

Porlock Caravan Park

Highbank TA24 8ND **t** (01643) 862269 **e** info@porlockcaravanpark.co.uk

porlockcaravanpark.co.uk

Quiet, select site, ideal for walking, touring and beaches. Five acres, grassy, level and sheltered. A39 from Minehead, in Porlock village take B3225 to Porlock Weir, site signposted.

open Mid-March to mid-January
payment Credit/debit cards, cash, cheques

General Leisure

PORTHTOWAN, Cornwall Map ref 1B3

★★★★
TOURING & CAMPING PARK

(22) £8.50–£15.00
(6) £8.50–£15.00
(22) £8.50–£15.00
80 touring pitches

Off-peak special offers – see our website for details.

Porthtowan Tourist Park

Mile Hill, Porthtowan, Truro TR4 8TY **t** (01209) 890256 **e** admin@porthtowantouristpark.co.uk

porthtowantouristpark.co.uk

open April to September
payment Cash, cheques

This quiet, family-run park offers plenty of space and level pitches. Superb new toilet/laundry facilities with family rooms. Close to a sandy surfing beach, coastal path and Portreath to Devoran cycle trail, it is an excellent base from which to discover the delights of Cornwall. David Bellamy Silver Conservation Award.

SAT NAV *TR4 8TY*

General Leisure

PORTREATH, Cornwall Map ref 1B3

★★★
TOURING & CAMPING PARK
£9.00–£14.50
£9.00–£14.50
£9.00–£14.50
60 touring pitches

Cambrose Touring Park

Portreath Road, Cambrose, Redruth TR16 4HT **t** (01209) 890747
e cambrosetouringpark@supanet.com

cambrosetouringpark.co.uk

Six acres of well-sheltered land in a valley. Excellent suntrap. Most roads are tarmac finished. Facilities for the disabled.

open April to October
payment Credit/debit cards, cash, cheques

General Leisure

PORTREATH, Cornwall Map ref 1B3

★★★★★
HOLIDAY VILLAGE
(58) £445.00–£1,795.00

Gwel an Mor

Tregea Hill, Portreath TR16 4PE **t** (023) 8064 2610 **e** hannah@gwelanmor.com

gwelanmor.co.uk SPECIAL OFFERS

open All year
payment Credit/debit cards, cash, cheques

Gwel an Mor, a new, luxury development of three-bedroom Scandinavian-style lodges, each offering three spacious bedrooms, the master bedroom with en suite facilities. Health and beauty spa, heated indoor swimming pool, sauna, steam room, croquet lawn, restaurant and bar.

SAT NAV *TR16 4PE*

General Leisure

PORTREATH, Cornwall Map ref 1B3

★★★★
HOLIDAY, TOURING & CAMPING PARK
(38) £8.50–£14.00
(3) £8.50–£14.00
(35) £8.50–£14.00
(20) £140.00–£575.00

Tehidy Holiday Park

Harris Mill, Illogan, Redruth TR16 4JQ **t** (01209) 216489 **e** holiday@tehidy.co.uk

tehidy.co.uk GUEST REVIEWS · REAL-TIME BOOKING

open March to November
payment Credit/debit cards, cash, cheques

Holiday Park of the Year 2008 – Shires Magazine. David Bellamy Conservation Award 2007. Nestled in a wooded valley. Near broad sandy beaches, hidden coves and the crystal-clear ocean. An ideal base for exploring the rich and diverse Cornish countryside. Children's play area, shop/off licence, payphone, games room. Toilet block with laundrette. Park contains six cottages.

SAT NAV *TR16 4JQ*

General Leisure

REDRUTH, Cornwall Map ref 1B3

★★★★
HOLIDAY, TOURING & CAMPING PARK

(25) £10.00–£16.00
(25) £10.00–£16.00
(50) £10.00–£16.00
(16) £230.00–£580.00
25 touring pitches

Lanyon Holiday Park

Loscombe Lane, Four Lanes, Redruth TR16 6LP **t** (01209) 313474 **e** info@lanyonholidaypark.co.uk

lanyonholidaypark.co.uk GUEST REVIEWS • SPECIAL OFFERS • REAL-TIME BOOKING

open All year
payment Credit/debit cards, cash, cheques

High quality, well-maintained family-owned park in the heart of the beautiful Cornish countryside with distant views to the coast. All electric-serviced pitches are large, most with hedged boundary, ideal for RVs. Modern amenity block with free hot water. Covered, heated swimming pool, games room, children's play area, bar/restaurant.

SAT NAV *TR16 6LP* **ONLINE MAP**

General Leisure

ROSUDGEON, Cornwall Map ref 1B3

★★★★
HOLIDAY, TOURING & CAMPING PARK
ROSE AWARD

(25) £14.50–£22.00
(25) £14.50–£22.00
(50) £10.00–£22.00
(9) £220.00–£515.00
50 touring pitches

No single-sex groups or large parties.

Kenneggy Cove Holiday Park

Higher Kenneggy, Rosudgeon, Penzance TR20 9AU **t** (01736) 763453
e enquiries@kenneggycove.co.uk

kenneggycove.co.uk

open 17 May to 4 October
payment Cash, cheques, euros

Flat, lawned pitches in a beautiful garden setting with panoramic sea views. Twelve minutes' walk to South West Coast Path and secluded, sandy beach. Home-made breakfasts available. Please note: this is a quiet site, operating a policy of no noise between 2200 and 0800. German and French spoken.

SAT NAV *TR20 9AU*

General Leisure

RUAN MINOR, Cornwall Map ref 1B3

★★★★
HOLIDAY, TOURING & CAMPING PARK

(15) £12.00–£17.00
(15) £12.00–£17.00
(20) £10.00–£15.00
(14) £99.00–£419.00
35 touring pitches

Silver Sands Holiday Park

Gwendreath, Nr Kennack Sands, Ruan Minor, Helston TR12 7LZ **t** (01326) 290631
e enquiries@silversandsholidaypark.co.uk

silversandsholidaypark.co.uk

open Easter to end of September
payment Credit/debit cards, cash, cheques

A quiet family-run park set in nine acres of landscaped grounds, offering peace and tranquillity. The large, well-spaced touring emplacements are individually marked and bounded by trees and shrubs. A short, enchanting woodland walk through the Lizard nature reserve brings you to award-winning sandy beaches. David Bellamy Gold Conservation Award.

SAT NAV *TR12 7LZ* **ONLINE MAP**

General Leisure

Has every park been assessed?

All parks in this guide has been rated for quality, or is awaiting assessment, by a professional national tourist board assessor.

For **key to symbols** see page 7

ST AGNES, Cornwall Map ref 1B3

★★★★
TOURING & CAMPING PARK

(70) £15.00–£21.00
(70) £15.00–£21.00
(70) £15.00–£21.00
70 touring pitches

Beacon Cottage Farm Touring Park

Beacon Drive, St Agnes TR5 0NU **t** (01872) 552347 **e** beaconcottagefarm@lineone.net

beaconcottagefarmholidays.co.uk GUEST REVIEWS • SPECIAL OFFERS

Peaceful, secluded park on a working farm in an Area of Outstanding Natural Beauty. Pitches in six small, landscaped paddocks. Beautiful sea views, lovely walks, ten minutes' walk to sandy beach.

open April to October
payment Credit/debit cards, cash, cheques

General Leisure

ST AUSTELL, Cornwall Map ref 1B3

ST AUSTELL, Cornwall Map ref 1B3

★★★★★
HOLIDAY, TOURING & CAMPING PARK

£12.00–£26.00
£12.00–£26.00
£12.00–£26.00
(40) £250.00–£650.00
45 touring pitches

Short-break offers in static vans. 7 nights for the price of 5 in the touring meadow.

River Valley Holiday Park

Pentewan Road, London Apprentice, St Austell PL26 7AP **t** (01726) 73533

cornwall-holidays.co.uk REAL-TIME BOOKING

open April to October
payment Credit/debit cards, cash, cheques

Stay at River Valley and you will enjoy our high standards. Quality caravans to hire, or bring your own and stay in our level, sheltered meadow. Surrounded by woodlands and bordered by a river with lots of walks. Indoor swimming pool, cycle trail to the beach, immaculate toilet block.

SAT NAV *PL26 7AP* **ONLINE MAP**

General Leisure

ST IVES, Cornwall Map ref 1B3

★★★★★
TOURING & CAMPING PARK

£13.00–£29.00
£13.00–£29.00
£13.00–£28.00
240 touring pitches

Polmanter Touring Park

St Ives TR26 3LX **t** (01736) 795640 **e** reception@polmanter.com

polmanter.com REAL-TIME BOOKING

Family park in lovely countryside with sea views, within walking distance of St Ives and beaches. Heated toilets/showers. Hard-standings.

open April to October
payment Credit/debit cards, cash, cheques

General Leisure

Look at the maps for park locations

Colour maps at the front pinpoint the location of all parks found in the regional sections.

ST JUST IN ROSELAND, Cornwall Map ref 1B3

★★★★★
TOURING & CAMPING PARK

(84) £15.00–£21.00
(50) £15.00–£21.00
(35) £15.00–£21.00
84 touring pitches

Trethem Mill Touring Park

Trethem, St Just in Roseland TR2 5JF **t** (01872) 580504 **e** reception@trethem.com

trethem.com

open April to mid-October
payment Credit/debit cards

We offer peace and tranquillity with an exceptional standard of facilities. Cornwall Tourism Awards: 'Consistent winners offering consistent quality.' Say hello to a new experience.

SAT NAV *TR2 5JF* **ONLINE MAP**

General Leisure

ST MERRYN, Cornwall Map ref 1B2

★★★★
HOLIDAY, TOURING & CAMPING PARK

£8.00–£12.00
£8.00–£12.00
£8.00–£12.00
(3) £175.00–£450.00
70 touring pitches

Trevean Farm

St Merryn, Padstow PL28 8PR **t** (01841) 520772 **e** trevean.info@virgin.net

Small, pleasant farm site one mile from the sea. Ideally situated for beaches, walking and many visitor attractions.

open Easter to October
payment Cash, cheques, euros

General Leisure

SALCOMBE, Devon Map ref 1C3

★★★
HOLIDAY, TOURING & CAMPING PARK

(20) £10.00–£19.00
(20) £10.00–£19.00
(50) £8.00–£19.00
(10) £110.00–£530.00
70 touring pitches

Special rates, low season only for couples over 50 – from £60 per week (incl electric).

Bolberry House Farm Caravan & Camping Park

Bolberry, Malborough TQ7 3DY **t** (01548) 561251 **e** bolberry.house@virgin.net

bolberryparks.co.uk

open April to October
payment Cash, cheques

Beautiful coastal area, our friendly family-run park is situated between the sailing paradise of Salcombe and the old fishing village of Hope Cove. It is peaceful and mostly level with good facilities. Children's play area. Good access to coastal footpaths. Sandy beaches nearby. Small shop (high season only).

SAT NAV *TQ7 3DY*

General Leisure

SALCOMBE REGIS, Devon Map ref 1D2

★★★★
TOURING & CAMPING PARK

(100) £11.60–£17.90
(100) £11.60–£17.90
(100) £11.60–£17.90
100 touring pitches

Kings Down Tail Caravan & Camping Park

Salcombe Regis, Sidmouth EX10 0PD **t** (01297) 680313 **e** info@kingsdowntail.co.uk

kingsdowntail.co.uk

Level, grassy, sheltered park. Central area for East Devon coast and countryside access. Three miles east of Sidmouth. Adjacent A352, opposite Branscombe water tower, not in any village.

open 15 March to 15 November
payment Credit/debit cards, cash, cheques

General Leisure

SALISBURY PLAIN

See under Warminster

SIDBURY, Devon Map ref 1D2

★★★★★
TOURING PARK
(117) £12.20–£25.10
(117) £12.20–£25.10
117 touring pitches

Putts Corner Caravan Club Site

Sidbury, Sidmouth EX10 0QQ **t** (01404) 42875

caravanclub.co.uk

open March to November
payment Credit/debit cards, cash, cheques

A quiet site in pretty surroundings, with a private path to the local pub. Bluebells create a sea of blue in spring, followed by foxgloves.

SAT NAV *EX10 0QQ*

Special member rates mean you can save your membership subscription in less than a week. Visit our website to find out more.

General Leisure

SWANAGE, Dorset Map ref 2B3

★★★★
HOLIDAY, TOURING & CAMPING PARK
£17.50–£38.00
£17.50–£38.00
£5.50–£10.00
(140) £181.00–£723.00
77 touring pitches

Ulwell Cottage Caravan Park

Ulwell BH19 3DG **t** (01929) 422823 **e** enq@ulwellcottagepark.co.uk

ulwellcottagepark.co.uk

open 1 March to 7 January
payment Credit/debit cards, cash, cheques

Quiet site in picturesque setting adjoining Purbeck Hills. One and a half miles from Swanage and two miles from Studland, the entrance is on the Swanage to Studland road.

SAT NAV *BH19 3DG*

General Leisure

TAUNTON, Somerset Map ref 1D1

★★★
TOURING & CAMPING PARK
(20) £10.00–£12.50
(10) £10.00–£12.50
(10) £10.00–£12.50
(2) £120.00–£175.00
30 touring pitches

Ashe Farm Caravan and Campsite

Thornfalcon, Taunton TA3 5NW **t** (01823) 443764 **e** camping@ashe-farm.fsnet.co.uk

Quiet farm site, lovely views, easy access. Central for touring. Easy reach coast and hills. Family run and informal.

open April to October
payment Cash, cheques

General Leisure

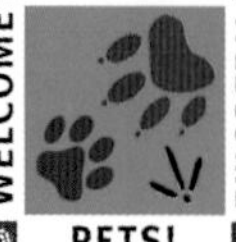

Where is my pet welcome?

Want to take your cherished companion with you on holiday? Proprietors participating in our Welcome Pets! scheme go out of their way to make special provision for you and your pet. Look out for the symbol.

TAUNTON, Somerset Map ref 1D1

★★★★
TOURING & CAMPING PARK

(30) £12.00–£15.00
(30) £12.00–£15.00
(10) £10.00–£13.00
40 touring pitches

Holly Bush Park

Culmhead, Taunton TA3 7EA **t** (01823) 421515 **e** info@hollybushpark.com

hollybushpark.com

A small, clean, quiet and friendly park. Ideal for walking, relaxing or touring. Excellent local inn 150 yds. Opposite woodlands and in an Area of Outstanding Natural Beauty.

open All year
payment Credit/debit cards, cash, cheques

General Leisure

TAVISTOCK, Devon Map ref 1C2

★★★★
HOLIDAY, TOURING & CAMPING PARK
ROSE AWARD

(40) £11.25–£16.75
(40) £11.25–£16.75
(40) £11.25–£16.75
(12) £240.00–£485.00
120 touring pitches

Holiday let: £15 off 2-week booking. £10 Senior Citizen discount.

Harford Bridge Holiday Park

Peter Tavy, Tavistock PL19 9LS **t** (01822) 810349 **e** enquiry@harfordbridge.co.uk

harfordbridge.co.uk

open All year
payment Credit/debit cards, cash, cheques

Beautiful, level, sheltered park set in Dartmoor with delightful views of Cox Tor. The River Tavy forms a boundary, offering riverside and other spacious, level camping pitches. Luxury, self-catering caravan holiday homes. Ideal for exploring Devon and Cornwall, walking the moor or just relaxing on this beautiful park.

SAT NAV *PL19 9LS*

General Leisure

TAVISTOCK, Devon Map ref 1C2

★★★★
HOLIDAY, TOURING & CAMPING PARK
ROSE AWARD

(40) £13.00–£15.00
(40) £13.00–£15.00
(40) £13.00–£15.00
(7) £170.00–£465.00
40 touring pitches

£25 discount for 2-week booking in holiday homes. 20% discount for 2 sharing on weekly bookings in holiday accommodation (off-peak).

Langstone Manor Caravan and Camping Park

Moortown, Tavistock PL19 9JZ **t** (01822) 613371 **e** jane@langstone-manor.co.uk

langstone-manor.co.uk

payment Credit/debit cards, cash, cheques

Fantastic location with direct access onto moor. Peace and quiet, with secluded pitches. Bar and restaurant. Excellent base for South Devon and Cornwall. Discover Dartmoor's secret!

SAT NAV *PL19 9JZ*

General Leisure

Looking for an ideal family break?

For accommodation offering additional facilities and services for a range of ages and family units, look out for the Families Welcome symbol. Owners of these properties will go out of their way to welcome families.

For **key to symbols** see page 7

TEIGNGRACE, Devon Map ref 1D2

★★★★
TOURING & CAMPING PARK

(25) £8.50–£14.00
(25) £8.50–£14.00
£8.50–£14.00
25 touring pitches

Twelve Oaks Farm Caravan Park

Teigngrace, Newton Abbot TQ12 6QT **t** (01626) 352769 **e** info@twelveoaksfarm.co.uk

twelveoaksfarm.co.uk

A working farm specialising in Charolais beef cattle. Friendly, personal service. Luxury showers and toilets, heated swimming pool. Coarse fishing.

open All year
payment Credit/debit cards, cash, cheques

General Leisure

TEWKESBURY, Gloucestershire Map ref 2B1

★★★★
TOURING & CAMPING PARK

(157) £12.20–£25.10
(157) £12.20–£25.10
on application
157 touring pitches

Special member rates mean you can save your membership subscription in less than a week. Visit our website to find out more.

Tewkesbury Abbey Caravan Club Site

Gander Lane, Tewkesbury GL20 5PG **t** (01684) 294035

caravanclub.co.uk

open March to November
payment Credit/debit cards, cash, cheques

Impressive location next to Tewkesbury Abbey. Only a short walk into the old town of Tewkesbury where there is much to explore.

SAT NAV *GL20 5PG*

General Leisure

TINTAGEL, Cornwall Map ref 1B2

★★★★★
TOURING & CAMPING PARK

(142) £14.00–£26.60
(142) £14.00–£26.60
on application
142 touring pitches

Special member rates mean you can save your membership subscription in less than a week. Visit our website to find out more.

Trewethett Farm Caravan Club Site

Trethevy, Tintagel PL34 0BQ **t** (01840) 770222

caravanclub.co.uk

open March to November
payment Credit/debit cards, cash, cheques

Cliff-top site with breathtaking views. Walk to Boscastle, with its pretty harbour and quayside, or Tintagel to see its dramatic castle. Non-members welcome.

SAT NAV *PL34 0BQ*

General Leisure

What if I need to cancel?

It's advisable to check the proprietor's cancellation policy at the time of booking in case you have to change your plans.

TORQUAY, Devon Map ref 1D2

★★★★
HOLIDAY, TOURING & CAMPING PARK

(160) £7.00–£19.00
(30) £7.00–£19.00
(10) £7.00–£17.00
(3) £200.00–£480.00
200 touring pitches

Widdicombe Farm Touring Park

Marldon, Paignton TQ3 1ST **t** (01803) 558325 **e** info@widdicombefarm.co.uk

widdicombefarm.co.uk

Select, family-run caravan park, the nearest to Torquay's town and beaches. Luxurious facilities, restaurant, bar with entertainment. Adult-only areas. Reputation for cleanliness and friendliness. Phone for bargain-break offers.

open Mid-March to mid-October
payment Credit/debit cards, cash, cheques

General Leisure

TOTNES, Devon Map ref 1D2

★★★★
TOURING & CAMPING PARK

£10.50–£16.50
£10.50–£16.50
£10.50–£16.50
85 touring pitches

Broadleigh Farm Park

Coombe House Lane, Aish, Stoke Gabriel, Totnes TQ9 6PU **t** (01803) 782309
e enquiries@broadleighfarm.co.uk

gotorbay.com/accommodation

Situated in beautiful South Hams village of Stoke Gabriel close to the River Dart and Torbay's wonderful, safe beaches. Many local walks. Bus stop at end of lane. Dartmoor within easy reach by car.

open March to October
payment Cash, cheques

General Leisure

TRURO, Cornwall Map ref 1B3

★★★★
TOURING PARK

(40) £10.50–£13.50
(5) £10.50–£13.50
(15) £10.50–£13.50
60 touring pitches

Summer Valley Touring Park

Shortlanesend, Truro TR4 9DW **t** (01872) 277878 **e** res@summervalley.co.uk

summervalley.co.uk

Situated in a sheltered valley surrounded by woods and farmland, we have been awarded for our peaceful, rural environment. We have the ideal site for visiting the gardens in spring.

open April to October
payment Credit/debit cards, cash, cheques

General Leisure

WAREHAM, Dorset Map ref 2B3

Using map references

The map references refer to the colour maps at the front of this guide. The first figure is the map number, the letter and figure that follow indicate the grid reference on the map.

WAREHAM, Dorset Map ref 2B3

★
HOLIDAY, TOURING & CAMPING PARK
(40) £8.00–£28.00
(40) £8.00–£28.00
(40) £8.00–£28.00
40 touring pitches

Luckford Wood Farm Caravan & Camping Park

Luckford Wood House, East Stoke, Wareham BH20 6AW **t** (01929) 463098 & 07888 719002
e luckfordleisure@hotmail.co.uk

luckfordleisure.co.uk REAL-TIME BOOKING

open March to November
payment Credit/debit cards, cash, cheques, euros

Old-fashioned camping around a camp fire with a relaxed, traditional feel. Central position makes Luckford Wood an ideal location for you to enjoy the Jurassic Coastline, wonderful beaches and bays, coastal and inland walks, many exciting places to explore. Country-house accommodation available. Telephone for details.

SAT NAV *BH20 6AW* **ONLINE MAP**

General Leisure

WARMINSTER, Wiltshire Map ref 2B2

★★★★★
TOURING PARK
(165) £14.90–£28.30
(165) £14.90–£28.30
165 touring pitches

THE CARAVAN CLUB

Longleat Caravan Club Site

Longleat, Warminster BA12 7NL **t** (01985) 844663

caravanclub.co.uk

Close to Longleat House, this is the only site where you can hear lions roar at night! Cafés, pubs and restaurants within walking distance. Non-members welcome.

open March to November
payment Credit/debit cards, cash, cheques

General Leisure

WARMWELL, Dorset Map ref 2B3

★★★★
HOLIDAY, TOURING & CAMPING PARK
(37) £12.95–£15.95
(9) £12.95–£15.95
(5) £10.50–£13.50
40 touring pitches

Warmwell Caravan Park

Warmwell, Dorchester DT2 8JD **t** (01305) 852313 **e** stay@warmwellcaravanpark.co.uk

warmwellcaravanpark.co.uk

The park is set in the heart of Thomas Hardy country, close to Dorchester and Weymouth. Adults-only touring area.

open March to January
payment Credit/debit cards, cash, cheques

General Leisure

WATERGATE BAY, Cornwall Map ref 1B2

★★★★
HOLIDAY, TOURING & CAMPING PARK
(171) £10.00–£17.50
(171) £10.00–£17.50
(171) £10.00–£17.50
(2) £175.00–£500.00
171 touring pitches

Watergate Bay Touring Park

Watergate Bay TR8 4AD **t** (01637) 860387 **e** email@watergatebaytouringpark.co.uk

watergatebaytouringpark.co.uk GUEST REVIEWS

Half a mile from Watergate Bay's sand, surf and cliff walks. Rural location in an Area of Outstanding Natural Beauty. Personally supervised by resident owners.

open March to October
payment Credit/debit cards, cash, cheques

General
Leisure

WATERROW, Somerset Map ref 1D1

★★★★★
TOURING & CAMPING PARK

(38) £13.00–£20.00
(38) £13.00–£20.00
(7) £13.00–£20.00
(1) £270.00–£415.00
45 touring pitches

Waterrow Touring Park

Waterrow, Taunton TA4 2AZ **t** (01984) 623464 **e** taylor@waterrowpark.u-net.com

waterrowpark.co.uk

A gently sloping, grassy site with landscaped hardstandings in the peaceful Tone Valley. An ideal base from which to explore this beautiful unspoilt area. One holiday caravan for hire. Adults only.

open All year
payment Credit/debit cards, cash, cheques

General Leisure

WEMBURY, Devon Map ref 1C3

★★★★
HOLIDAY PARK

(56) £255.00–£865.00

Promotions include Midsummer Bargain Weekend and Midweek Breaks, Senior Citizens and second week discounts.

Churchwood Valley Holiday Cabins

Churchwood Valley, Wembury Bay, Plymouth PL9 0DZ **t** (01752) 862382
e churchwoodvalley@btconnect.com

churchwoodvalley.com SPECIAL OFFERS

open April to mid-January
payment Credit/debit cards, cash, cheques

Churchwood Valley is a haven of peace! Set in a beautiful wooded valley, close to beaches, coastal walks and glorious countryside. Comfortable timber cabins, each with its own secluded patio. Wildlife abounds and the walks are stunning. Pets welcome.

SAT NAV *PL9 0DZ* **ONLINE MAP**

General Leisure

WESTON-SUPER-MARE, Somerset Map ref 1D1

★★★★
HOLIDAY, TOURING & CAMPING PARK

(120) £12.00–£22.00
(120) £12.00–£22.00
(120) £12.00–£22.00
120 touring pitches

Country View Holiday Park

29 Sand Road, Sand Bay, Weston-super-Mare BS22 9UJ **t** (01934) 627595 **e** giles@cvhp.co.uk

cvhp.co.uk

Country View is a beautifully kept site surrounded by the countryside and just 200yds from the Sand Bay beach. Heated pool, bar, shop and children's play area. Fantastic new toilet and shower facilities. New and used holiday homes for sale.

open All year
payment Cash, cheques

General Leisure

WESTON-SUPER-MARE, Somerset Map ref 1D1

★★★
TOURING & CAMPING PARK

(57) £10.00–£17.00
(5) £10.00–£17.00
(25) £8.00–£15.00
87 touring pitches

Dulhorn Farm Camping Site

Weston Road, Lympsham, Weston-super-Mare BS24 0JQ **t** (01934) 750298

A family site on a working farm set in the countryside, approximately four miles from the beach, midway between Weston and Burnham. Ideal for touring. Easily accessible from M5.

open March to October
payment Credit/debit cards, cash, cheques

General Leisure

What if I need to cancel?

It is advisable to check the proprietor's cancellation policy in case you have to change your plans at a later date.

WEYMOUTH, Dorset Map ref 2B3

★★★★
TOURING PARK
(120) £10.60–£23.20
(120) £10.60–£23.20
120 touring pitches

Midweek discount: pitch fee for standard pitches for stays on any Tue, Wed or Thu night outside peak season dates will be reduced by 50%.

Crossways Caravan Club Site

Crossways, Dorchester DT2 8BE **t** (01305) 852032

caravanclub.co.uk

open March to October
payment Credit/debit cards, cash, cheques

Set in 35 acres of woodland. Dorchester is nearby, also Weymouth's award-winning, sandy beach. Visit Lawrence of Arabia's house at Cloud's Hill. If you want to leave the car behind for the day, the railway station is just five minutes' walk from the site.

SAT NAV *DT2 8BE*

General Leisure

WIMBORNE MINSTER, Dorset Map ref 2B3

★★★★★
TOURING & CAMPING PARK
(60) £18.00–£24.00
(60) £18.00–£24.00
(25) £18.00–£24.00
85 touring pitches

7-night booking outside peak times – 1 night free.

Wilksworth Farm Caravan Park

Cranborne Road, Furzehill, Wimborne BH21 4HW **t** (01202) 885467
e rayandwendy@wilksworthfarmcaravanpark.co.uk

wilksworthfarmcaravanpark.co.uk

open April to October
payment Credit/debit cards, cash, cheques

A popular and attractive park set in the grounds of a Grade II* Listed farmhouse, tranquilly placed in the heart of rural Dorset. Facilities include an outdoor heated swimming pool, large play area, completely refurbished toilet block, cafe, takeaway, shop and games room. Close to Kingston Lacy, Poole and Bournemouth.

SAT NAV *BH21 4HW*

General Leisure

WINSFORD, Somerset Map ref 1D1

★★★★
TOURING & CAMPING PARK
(22) £12.00–£15.00
(22) £12.00–£15.00
(22) £12.00–£15.00
44 touring pitches

10% discount for 1 week or more, paid 14 days in advance.

Halse Farm Caravan & Tent Park

Winsford, Minehead TA24 7JL **t** (01643) 851259 **e** brit@halsefarm.co.uk

halsefarm.co.uk

open 20 March to 31 October.
payment Credit/debit cards, cash, cheques

Exmoor National Park, small, peaceful, working farm with spectacular views. Paradise for walkers and country lovers. David Bellamy Gold Conservation Award.

SAT NAV *TA24 7JL* **ONLINE MAP**

General Leisure

WOOL, Dorset Map ref 2B3

★★★★
TOURING & CAMPING PARK

(95) £9.00–£15.25
(95) £9.00–£15.25
(95) £9.00–£15.25
95 touring pitches

Whitemead Caravan Park

East Burton Road, Wool, Wareham BH20 6HG **t** (01929) 462241 **e** whitemeadcp@aol.com

whitemeadcaravanpark.co.uk

Within easy reach of beaches and beautiful countryside, this friendly site is maintained to a high standard of cleanliness. Turn west off the A352 near Wool level crossing.

open 18 March to 31 October
payment Cash, cheques

General Leisure

YEOVIL, Somerset Map ref 2A3

★★★★
HOLIDAY, TOURING & CAMPING PARK

(30) £17.00
(30) £17.00
(20) £17.00
(2) £375.00–£800.00
50 touring pitches

Long Hazel Park

High Street, Sparkford, Yeovil BA22 7JH **t** (01963) 440002 **e** longhazelpark@hotmail.com

sparkford.f9.co.uk/lhi.htm

Adult-only park in a village location just off A303T. Level, landscaped grounds. Hardstandings, full disabled facilities. Two lodges for hire. Pub/restaurant, shop, post office, services and bus stop 200m.

open All year
payment Cash, cheques, euros

General Leisure

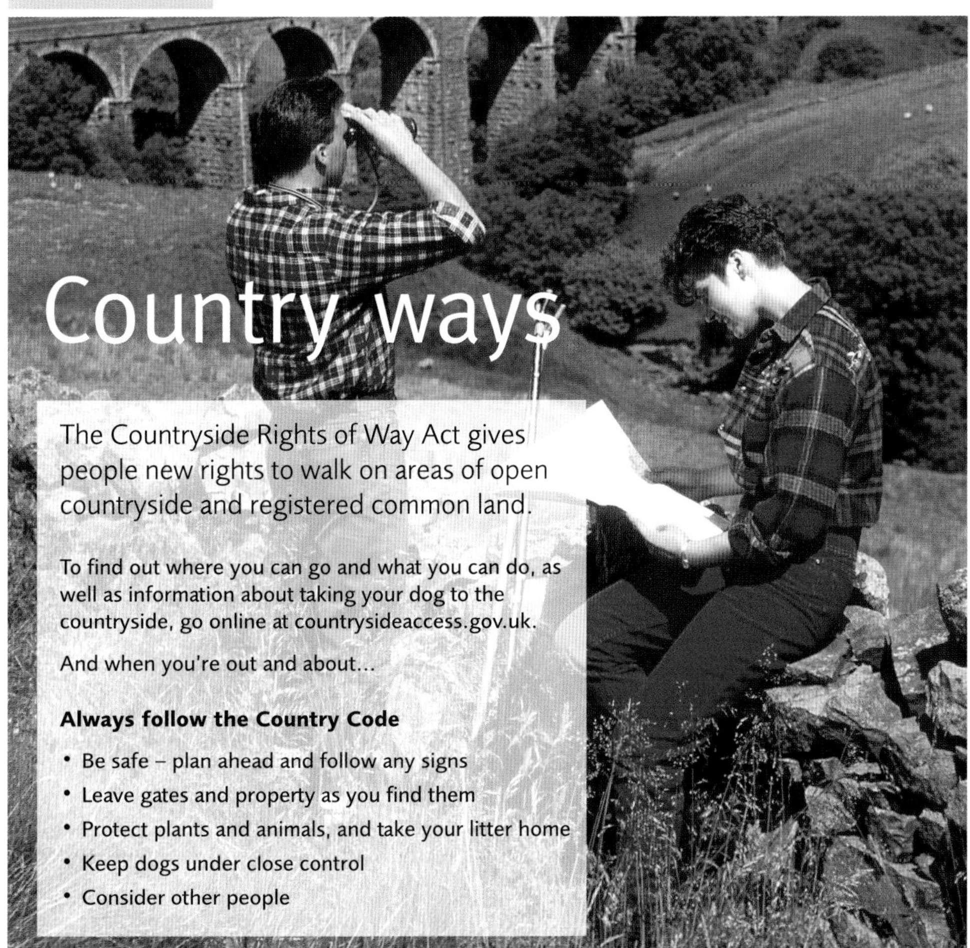

Country ways

The Countryside Rights of Way Act gives people new rights to walk on areas of open countryside and registered common land.

To find out where you can go and what you can do, as well as information about taking your dog to the countryside, go online at countrysideaccess.gov.uk.

And when you're out and about...

Always follow the Country Code

- Be safe – plan ahead and follow any signs
- Leave gates and property as you find them
- Protect plants and animals, and take your litter home
- Keep dogs under close control
- Consider other people

Scotland

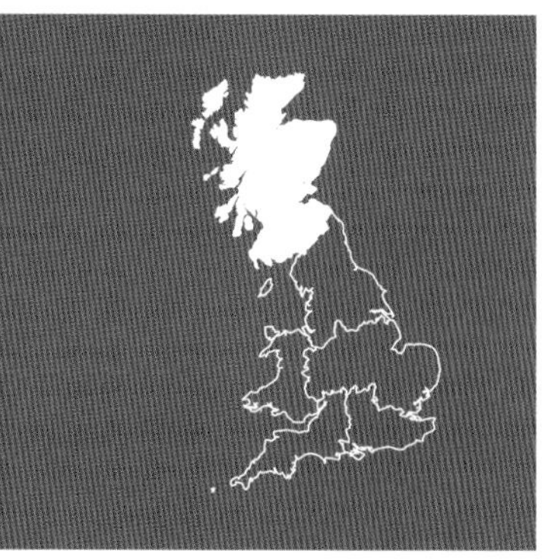

Clockwise: Cairngorms, Highlands; St Andrews, Fife; Loch Laich, Argyll and Bute

Great days out

Relax, recharge and rediscover yourself! Scotland's natural paradise of dramatic mountains, lochs and glens is the ideal escape from too-busy living. Climb mighty Munros and dawdle around romantic castles. Then soak up Scotland's world-class culture in its historic cities or at festival time.

Mountains and eagles

As the sun sinks, streaking the sky with flame, you spot the red deer stags in silhouette. An unforgettable experience, and just one reason to escape to Scotland. The country's ancient geology has created the most amazingly diverse landscapes, of mountain, loch and coast. Wildlife thrives and so will you. Start with the magical corner of **Dumfries and Galloway**, meandering along deserted beaches. Follow the **Fife Coastal Walk** to spot seabirds and grey seals, stopping off at quaint fishing villages like Pittenweem.

Glencoe, Highlands

Scenery and fauna are at their most spectacular in Scotland's two National Parks: **Loch Lomond & The Trossachs**, and the Arctic plateau of the **Cairngorms**. Journey through heather-clad peaks on The Trossachs Trail. Then look out for red squirrels, deer, golden eagles and ospreys in the **Highlands**, where land and sea collide to create stunning perspectives.

Adventures before tee-time

Opportunities for outdoor adventure are breathtaking, literally! If you're up for it, tackle a Munro – Scottish mountains over 3,000ft. **Ben Nevis**, Britain's highest mountain at 4,408ft, throws down the gauntlet to climbers, and the Nevis Range is a blast for mountain biking and winter skiing. Or, for something gentler, pedal the **Great Glen Cycle Route** along canal towpaths, forestry roads and quiet lanes.

Take to the waters sailing – **Argyll's** west coast is good for novices and old seadogs alike. Atlantic and North Sea swells all around the coast provide great breakers for surfing, and inland rivers give canoeists and white-water rafters a brilliant adrenalin rush. Find a peaceful stretch for fishing: the **River Tweed** is a classic. And there's no place like the home of golf for a round or two. Scotland has over 550 courses, including world-famous **St Andrews**, where you can also browse the **British Golf Museum**.

Keys to the castles

Scotland's tumultuous past is vividly etched on its landscapes in the shape of immense castles. View the ancient crowning site of Scottish kings at **Scone Palace** and hear tales of the Atholl Highlanders private army at **Blair Castle**. Follow in the steps of ill-fated Mary Queen of Scots to grand old **Stirling Castle**, or relax at **Balmoral** as Queen Victoria did. Words simply can't capture **Eilean Donan Castle**, you just have to see for yourself the striking ruin amid mountains mirrored in the waters of the loch. And at **Urquhart Castle** keep one eye out for the Loch Ness monster!

Left to right: Edinburgh Festival; Eilean Donan Castle, Highlands

why not... cruise the Caledonian Canal and lochs linking Scotland's east and west coasts?

Tales of two cities

Scotland's great cities beckon. Get 'three in one' in **Edinburgh**, whose World Heritage Site embraces the medieval Old Town, the Georgian New Town and award-winning modern architecture. Follow the cobbled **Royal Mile** to magnificent **Edinburgh Castle** – check out those Crown Jewels for sparkle! Then take your pick of top museums and galleries, and share the kids' excitement in **Our Dynamic Earth**: flying over glaciers, encountering a tropical rainstorm and discovering the new Earthscape Scotland gallery. Come for August's celebrated arts and fringe festivals or the **Edinburgh Military Tattoo** – there's always something happening in the 'Festival City'.

Change scene, change mood and hit **Glasgow**: Scotland's largest city has reinvented itself as a buzzing cultural hotspot. Charles Rennie Mackintosh led the way with his streamlined building designs – visit the refurbished **Kelvingrove Art Gallery and Museum** to learn more about him and the Glasgow Style. Among 30-plus galleries and museums, Clydebuilt **Scottish Maritime Museum** reveals the city's shipping heritage. For R&R you can't beat the **Merchant City** quarter, an irresistible mix of sublime shopping and eateries. Do you fancy Scottish, Italian, or noodles in a Pop Art-decorated café?

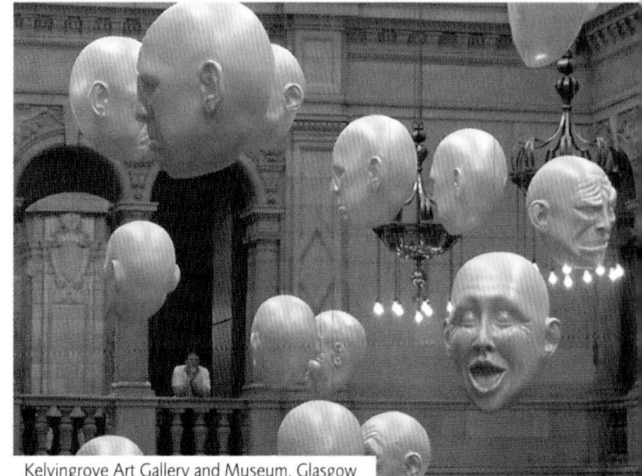

Kelvingrove Art Gallery and Museum, Glasgow

Flings and drams

Brush up on national poet Robert Burns, recalled at venues throughout the **Scottish Borders** in May each year. Watch caber tossing, dancing and games at Highland Gatherings from Cowal to Tomintoul and all points in between. If bagpipes and fiddles are less your thing, there's also plenty of rock 'n' pop, or gigs at **Murrayfield** stadium. Keep energy levels up by tucking into a food festival, or toast some colourful occasions with a dram of 'uisge beatha', the 'water of life'. **Aberdeen** is a fine place from which to tour distilleries on the world's only **Malt Whisky Trail**.

why not... enjoy Sir Walter Scott's favourite picnic spot, Scott's View onto the Eildon Hills?

Island life

And just when you think you've 'done' Scotland, think again: you've countless islands to experience. Conveniently reached by air or ferry, they nevertheless remain worlds apart, each with its own unique character, crafts and traditions. Find dreamy beaches and a warm Gaelic welcome in the **Outer Hebrides**. Follow romantic tales of Bonnie Prince Charlie to **Skye**. Off Scotland's northeast tip, the archipelago of **Orkney** offers a scattering of 70 or so islands and skerries (small, rocky isles). Step back 5,000 years on mainland Orkney to **Skara Brae** Neolithic village complete with homes featuring stone beds. Then catch the ferry and ramble the **Eday Heritage Walk** past standing stones and ancient cairns. Puffins by the million await birdwatchers in **Shetland**, where Viking influences live on through the fire festival of Up Helly Aa and the famous Shetland knitwear.

Clockwise: Skara Brae, Orkney; Highland Games; Shetland

Destinations

Duthie Park, Aberdeen

Aberdeen

Prosperous and cosmopolitan, the 'Granite City' can hold its own as a cultural and academic centre. You'll find spectacular architecture, captivating museums, a wealth of art and culture and a lively social scene. The famous 'Granite Mile', Union Street, is the gateway to over 800 shops, restaurants and bars. Wander the cobbled lanes of Old Aberdeen and soak up the life and colour of the historic harbour. Find flower-filled parks and even a two-mile sweep of golden, sandy beach.

Dundee

The 'City of Discovery' is Scotland's sunniest city. You'll find superb shopping and a lively pub and club scene. Step into a bygone age on Captain Scott's famous polar exploration ship Discovery or check out the hip and exciting Dundee Contemporary Arts, a stunning complex on Nethergate. Enjoy panoramic views from Dundee Law – the plug of an extinct volcano – and nearby Broughty Ferry has one of the cleanest beaches in the UK.

Edinburgh

One of the most visited cities in Europe, the capital of Scotland is historic, cosmopolitan and cultured. Its magnificent castle dominates the city-centre skyline. The Old and New Towns are a World Heritage Site: explore the winding alleys of the medieval Old Town and the neoclassical buildings and broad, straight streets of the New Town. Edinburgh is not called the Festival City lightly, as its incredible calendar of annual events clearly shows.

Glasgow

Glasgow, Scotland's capital of style, is positively oozing with things to see and do. From superb shopping and a vibrant nightlife, to some of the best free museums and galleries in the country. At The Lighthouse, a Charles Rennie Mackintosh conversion, you'll find dynamic art and architecture exhibitions and a stunning, uninterrupted view over the city. Or take a stroll through the city's West End, a bohemian district of cafés, bars, clubs and boutiques.

Inverness

Visit Inverness for the perfect cocktail of city life and adventure sports enjoyed in the great outdoors. Crowned by a Gothic red sandstone castle, the compact city centre is lavishly decorated with flowers. You'll find great shopping, food and drink and plenty of places to relax. See the tropical gardens at the Floral Hall, head out to Culloden, site of the famous battle, or go monster-spotting on nearby Loch Ness.

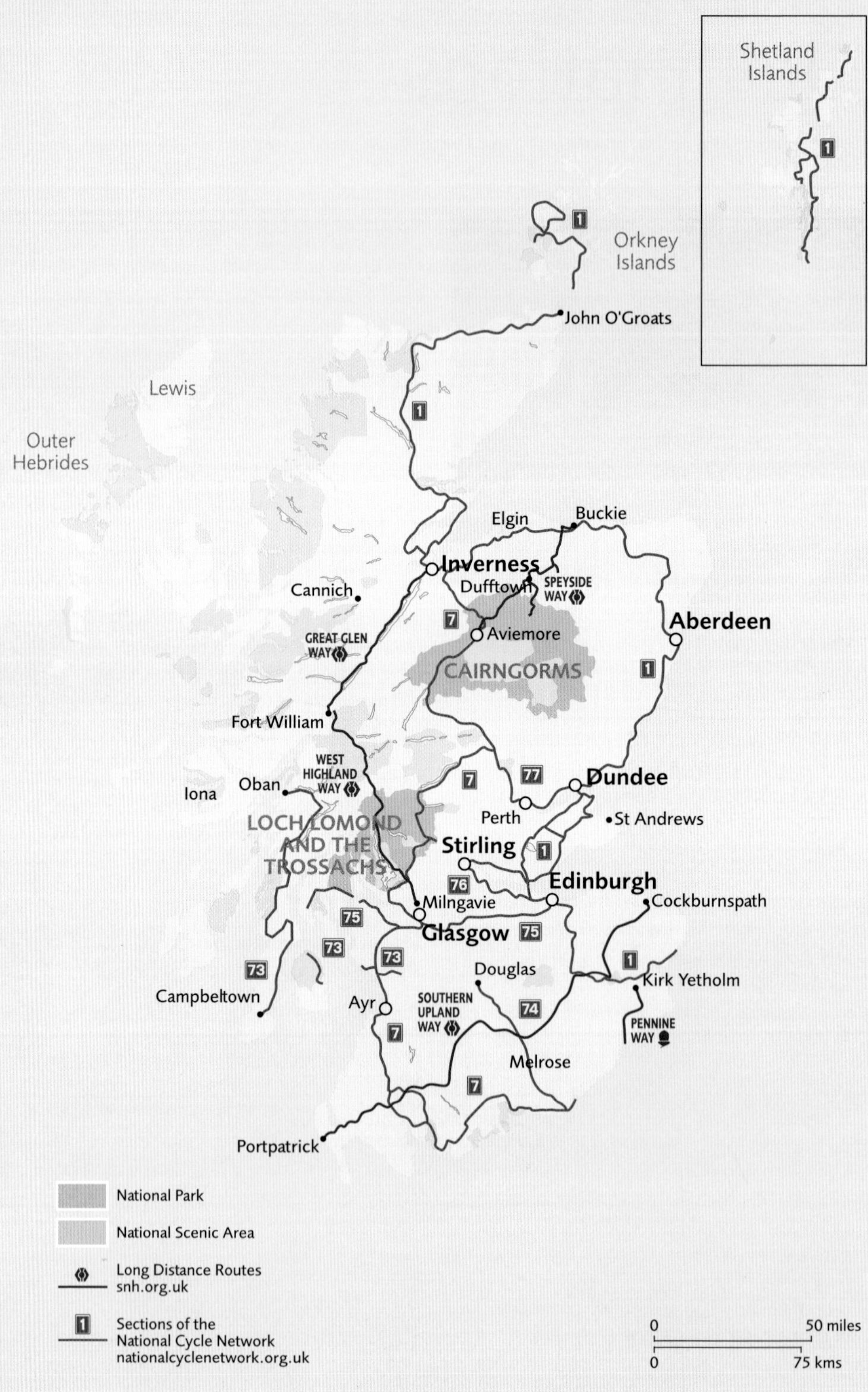
Shetland Islands
1
Orkney Islands
John O'Groats
Lewis
Outer Hebrides
Elgin
Buckie
Inverness
Dufftown
SPEYSIDE WAY
Cannich
7
Aviemore
Aberdeen
GREAT GLEN WAY
CAIRNGORMS
Fort William
WEST HIGHLAND WAY
77
Dundee
Iona
Oban
Perth
St Andrews
LOCH LOMOND AND THE TROSSACHS
Stirling
76
Edinburgh
Milngavie
Cockburnspath
75
Glasgow
73
Douglas
Kirk Yetholm
Campbeltown
Ayr
SOUTHERN UPLAND WAY
74
PENNINE WAY
Melrose
Portpatrick
National Park
National Scenic Area
Long Distance Routes snh.org.uk
Sections of the National Cycle Network nationalcyclenetwork.org.uk
0
50 miles
0
75 kms

Lewis

Lewis

Lewis forms part of a chain of islands with spectacular silver beaches, culture and wildlife. Fish in freshwater and sea lochs, take a boat trip to spot whales, dolphins, seals and puffins, or a guided walk to see otters, buzzards and deer. In the main town of Stornoway, visit Lewis Castle for great views of the port, and the Nan Eilean museum for the history of the Outer Hebrides. Gain a fascinating insight into the traditional island dwellings at the cottage museum of Arnol Blackhouse and experience the atmosphere surrounding the Calanais Standing Stones that are older than Stonehenge.

Clockwise: Glasgow; Edinburgh; Inverness

Orkney

The island's history goes back more than 4,500 years to Neolithic times – discover it for yourself at stunning Skara Brae. Spectacular wildlife abounds: listen to the sea cliffs resounding with the calls of auks and kittiwakes and see rare birds of prey on the moorlands. Learn about the Viking invasions and see the magnificent St Magnus Cathedral in Kirkwall, the islands' capital. Follow the Orkney Craft Trail which includes the world-renowned Orcadian jewellery or sample whisky from Highland Park, the most northerly of whisky distilleries.

Stirling Castle

Stirling

Stirling may be Scotland's youngest city, but, as the centre of Braveheart country, you can touch and feel the sense of history that marks it out as unique. Take in the magnificent view from the ramparts of the cliff-top castle, or meander along the compact heritage mile of the Old Town, boasting the finest concentration of historic buildings in Scotland. Modern Stirling has a bustling centre with a cosmopolitan edge, quality local attractions and a café culture.

For lots more great ideas go to visitbritain.com/destinations and visitscotland.com

Visitor attractions

Family and Fun

Edinburgh Dungeon
Edinburgh
(0131) 240 1001
thedungeons.com
From local legends to world-famous vampires.

Historic Paddle Steamer 'Maid of the Loch'
Balloch, West Dunbartonshire
(01389) 711865
maidoftheloch.com
The ongoing restoration of a historic craft.

Our Dynamic Earth
Edinburgh
(0131) 550 7800
dynamicearth.co.uk
Discover our planet's past, present and future.

The Royal Yacht Britannia
Leith Docks, Edinburgh
(0131) 555 5566
Award-winning tour of a unique royal residence.

Scottish Sea Life Sanctuary
Barcaldine, Argyll and Bute
(01631) 720386
sealsanctuary.co.uk
Marine marvels from around our shores.

Heritage

Balmoral Castle
Balmoral, Aberdeenshire
(01339) 742534
balmoralcastle.com
Scottish holiday home of the Royal Family.

Blair Castle
Blair Atholl, Perth and Kinross
(01796) 481207
blair-castle.co.uk
Ancient seat of the Dukes of Atholl.

Edinburgh Castle
Edinburgh
(0131) 225 9846
edinburghcastle.gov.uk
Magnificent fortress dominating the capital's skyline.

National Wallace Monument
Causewayhead, Stirling
(01786) 472140
nationalwallacemonument.com
Spectacular tower commemorating Scotland's 'Braveheart'.

Palace of Holyroodhouse
Edinburgh
(0131) 556 5100
royalcollection.org.uk
HM The Queen's official residence in Scotland.

Robert Burns Centre
Dumfries, Dumfries & Galloway
(01387) 264808
dumgal.gov.uk/museums
Compelling exhibition featuring original manuscripts and memorabilia.

Scone Palace
Scone, Perth and Kinross
(01738) 552300
scone-palace.co.uk
The ancient crowning place of Scottish kings.

Stirling Castle
Stirling
(01786) 450000
historic-scotland.gov.uk
Historic fortress perched on dramatic volcanic crag.

Urquhart Castle
near Drumnadrochit, Highland
(01456) 450551
historic-scotland.gov.uk
Magnificent ruins on banks of Loch Ness.

Indoors

Auld Reekie Tours
Edinburgh
(0131) 557 4700
auldreekietours.co.uk
The scariest ghost tours in the world.

British Golf Museum
St Andrews, Fife
(01334) 460046
britishgolfmuseum.co.uk
Unsurpassed collection of golfing memorabilia.

Clydebuilt Scottish Maritime Museum
Glasgow
(0141) 886 1013
scottishmaritimemuseum.org
Interactive history of Glasgow's emblematic river.

Glasgow Cathedral
Glasgow
(0141) 552 6891
glasgowcathedral.org.uk
Splendid Gothic building founded by St Mungo.

Hunterian Art Gallery
Glasgow
(0141) 330 4221
hunterian.gla.ac.uk
Distinguished gallery housing the Mackintosh Collection.

Hunterian Museum
Glasgow
(0141) 330 4221
hunterian.gla.ac.uk
A million items from meteorites to mummies.

John Paul Jones Cottage
Kirkbean, Dumfries & Galloway
(01387) 880613
jpj.demon.co.uk
Traditional cottage home of naval hero.

The National Gallery Complex
Edinburgh
(0131) 624 6200
nationalgalleries.org
Interconnected galleries housing outstanding art collections.

Scottish Maritime Museum
Irvine, North Ayrshire
(01294) 278283
scottishmaritimemuseum.org
Harbourside museum featuring historic vessels and tools.

Scottish National Portrait Gallery
Edinburgh
(0131) 624 6200
natgalscot.ac.uk
Portraits of those who shaped Scottish history.

World Famous Old Blacksmith's Shop Centre
Gretna Green, Dumfries & Galloway
(01461) 338224
gretnagreen.com
World-famous marriage venue for eloping couples.

Outdoors

Glasgow Botanic Gardens
Glasgow
(0141) 276 1614
glasgow.gov.uk
Renowned collections of tropical plants.

ASSURANCE OF A GREAT DAY OUT
Attractions with this sign participate in the Visitor Attraction Quality Assurance Scheme which recognises high standards in all aspects of the visitor experience.

Go Ape!
Aberfoyle, Stirling
0845 643 9215
goape.co.uk
Rope bridges, swings and zip slides.

Mercat Walking Tours of Edinburgh
Edinburgh
(0131) 225 5445
mercattours.com
The dark, magical history of the city.

Royal Botanic Garden
Edinburgh
(0131) 552 7171
rbge.org.uk
Plant treasures from around the globe.

The Tall Ship at Glasgow Harbour
Glasgow
(0141) 222 2513
thetallship.com
Historic Clydebuilt ship restored to former glory.

Events 2009

Celtic Connections
Glasgow
celticconnections.com
14 Jan - 1 Feb

Up-Helly-Aa
Shetland Islands
visitshetland.com
27 Jan

Gourock Highland Games
Gourock
inverclyde.gov.uk
10 May

Edinburgh International Film Festival
Edinburgh
edfilmfest.org.uk
17 - 28 Jun*

The Open Golf Championships 2009
Turnberry
opengolf.com
16 - 19 Jul

The Gathering
Edinburgh
clangathering.org
25 Jul - 26 Sep

Langholm Common Riding
Langholm
langholm-online.co.uk
31 Jul

Edinburgh Military Tattoo
Edinburgh
edintattoo.co.uk
7 - 29 Aug

Piping Live!
Glasgow
pipingfestival.co.uk
10 - 16 Aug

Edinburgh International Festival
Edinburgh
eif.co.uk
14 Aug - 6 Sep

Scottish International Storytelling Festival
Edinburgh
scottishstorytellingcentre.co.uk
23 Oct - 1 Nov

** provisional date at time of going to press*

Regional contacts and information

For more information on accommodation, attractions, activities, events and holidays in Scotland, contact the regional tourism organisation below. The website has a wealth of information and you can order or download publications.

Scotland

The following is a selection of publications available online from **VisitScotland.com** or by calling the information and booking service on **0845 22 55 121**:

Where to Stay Hotels & Guest Houses £8.99

Over 3,000 places to stay in Scotland – from luxury town houses and country hotels to budget-priced guesthouses. Details of prices and facilities, with location maps.

Where to Stay Bed & Breakfast £6.99

Over 2,000 Bed and Breakfast establishments throughout Scotland offering inexpensive accommodation – the perfect way to enjoy a budget trip and meet Scottish folk in their own homes. Details of prices and facilities, with location maps.

Where to Stay Caravan & Camping £4.99

Over 280 parks detailed with prices, available facilities and lots of other useful information. Also includes caravan homes for hire, with location maps.

Where to Stay Self Catering £5.99

Over 3,400 cottages, apartments and chalets to let – many in scenic areas. Details of prices and facilities, with location maps.

Touring Guide to Scotland £7.99

A fully revised edition of this popular guide which now lists over 1,700 things to do and places to visit in Scotland. Easy to use index and locator maps. Details of opening hours, admission charges, general description and information on disabled access.

Touring Map of Scotland £4.99

An up-to-date touring map of Scotland. Full colour with comprehensive motorway and road information, the map details over 20 categories of tourist information and names over 1,500 things to do and places to visit in Scotland.

Loch Lomond

Visitor Information Centres

When you arrive at your destination, visit a Visitor Information Centre for help with accommodation and information about local attractions and events. Alternatively call **0845 22 55 121** to receive information and book accommodation before you go.

Aberdeen	23 Union Street
Aberfeldy	The Square
Aberfoyle	Trossachs Discovery Centre
Abington	Junction 13, M74 Services
Alford*	Old Station Yard
Alva	Sterling Mills Outlet Village
Anstruther*	Scottish Fisheries Museum
Arbroath	Fishmarket Quay
Ardgartan*	By Arrochar
Aviemore	Grampian Road
Ayr	22 Sandgate
Ballater	Station Square
Balloch	The Old Station Building
Banchory*	Bridge Street
Banff*	Collie Lodge
Biggar*	155 High Street
Blairgowrie	26 Wellmeadow
Bo'ness*	Union Street
Bowmore	The Square
Braemar	Mar Road
Brechin	Pictavia Centre
Brodick	The Pier
Callander	Rob Roy Centre
Campbeltown	The Pier
Castlebay*	Main Street
Castle Douglas*	Market Hill Car Park
Craignure	The Pier
Crail*	Crail Museum, 62 Marketgate
Crathie*	The Car Park
Crieff	High Street
Daviot Wood*	Picnic Area, A9
Drumnadrochit	The Car Park
Dufftown*	The Square
Dumbarton*	Milton, A82 Northbound
Dumfries	64 Whitesands
Dunbar*	141 High Street
Dundee	21 Castle Street
Dunfermline	1 High Street
Dunkeld	The Cross
Dunoon	7 Alexandra Parade
Dunvegan	2 Lochside
Durness*	Sangomore
Edinburgh	Princess Mall, 3 Princes Street
Edinburgh Airport	Main Concourse
Elgin	17 High Street
Eyemouth*	Auld Kirk, Manse Road
Falkirk	The Falkirk Wheel
Fort William	15 High Street
Fraserburgh*	3 Saltoun Square
Glasgow	11 George Square
Glasgow Airport	International Arrivals Hall
Grantown on Spey*	54 High Street
Gretna	Gretna Gateway Outlet Village
Hawick	Tower Mill
Helensburgh*	The Clock Tower
Huntly*	9a The Square
Inveraray	Front Street
Inverness	Castle Wynd
Inverurie*	18 High Street
Jedburgh	Murrays Green
Kelso	The Square

Killin	Breadalbane Folklore Centre
Kirkcaldy	339 High Street
Kirkcudbright	Harbour Square
Kirkwall	6 Broad Street
Lanark	Horsemarket, Ladyacre Road
Largs*	Main Street
Lerwick	The Market Cross
Lochboisdale*	Pier Road
Lochgilphead	Lochnell Street
Lochinver*	Kirk Lane
Lochmaddy*	Pier Road
Melrose	Abbey Street
Moffat*	Churchgate
Newtongrange*	Scottish Mining Museum
Newton Stewart*	Dashwood Square
North Berwick	Quality Street
Oban	Argyll Square
Paisley	9A Gilmour Street
Peebles	High Street
Perth	West Mill Street
Pitlochry	22 Atholl Road
Portree	Bayfield Road
Rothesay	Winter Gardens
St Andrews	70 Market Street
Selkirk*	Halliwells House
Southwaite	M6 Service Area
Stirling	41 Dumbarton Road
Stirling (Pirnhall)	Junction 9, M9 Services
Stonehaven*	66 Allardice Street
Stornoway	26 Cromwell Street
Stranraer	Burns House, 28 Harbour Street
Stromness	Ferry Terminal Building
Strontian*	Acharacle
Sumburgh	Sumburgh Airport
Tarbert (Harris)*	Pier Road
Tarbert (Loch Fyne)*	Harbour Street
Tarbet (Loch Lomond)*	Main Street
Thurso*	Riverside Road
Tobermory*	The Pier
Tomintoul*	The Square
Tyndrum	Main Street
Ullapool*	Argyle Street

* seasonal opening

Clockwise: Dunnottar Castle, Aberdeenshire; Italian Chapel, Orkney; The Falkirk Wheel

Ratings you can trust

When you're looking for a place to stay, you need a rating system you can trust. The British Graded Holiday Parks Scheme, operated jointly by VisitBritain, VisitScotland and Visit Wales, gives you a clear guide as to what to expect.

Based on the internationally recognised rating of one to five stars, the system puts great emphasis on quality and reflects customer expectations.

Parks are visited annually by professional assessors who award a rating based on cleanliness, environment and the quality of services and facilities provided.

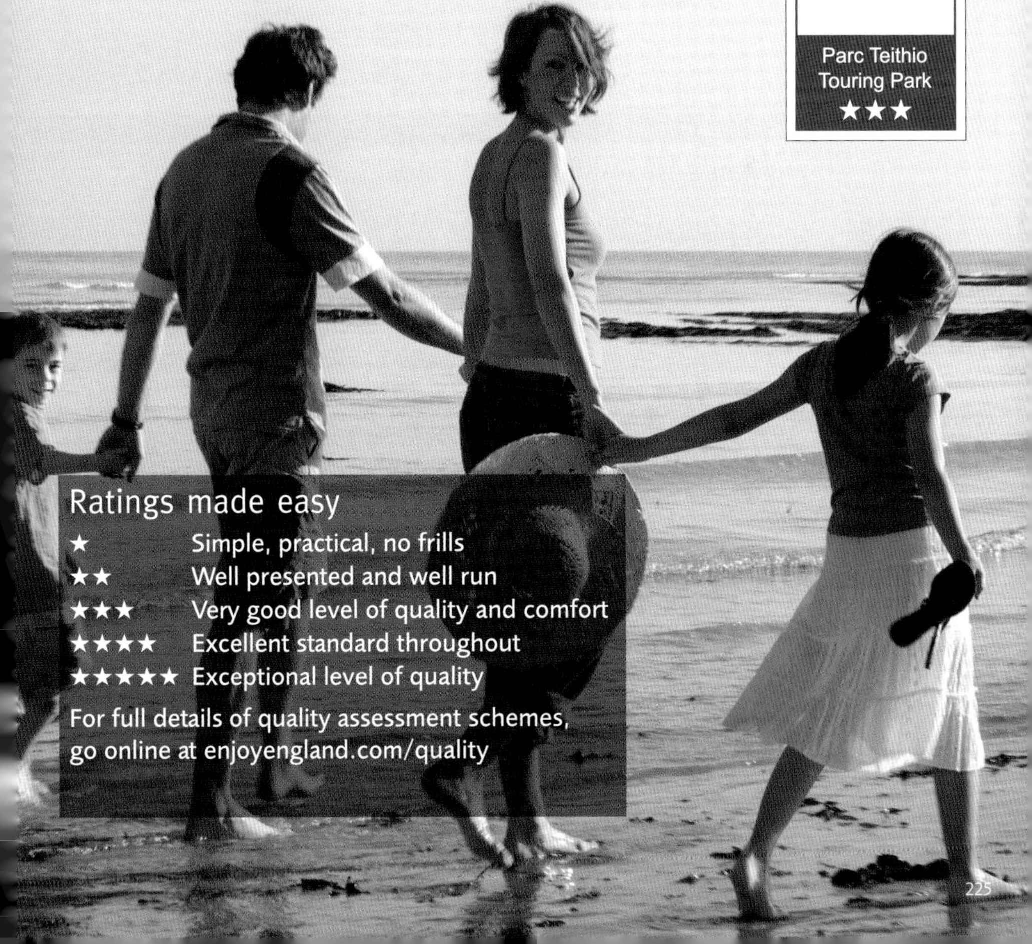

Cymru
Wales
Parc Teithio
Touring Park
★★★

Ratings made easy

★ Simple, practical, no frills
★★ Well presented and well run
★★★ Very good level of quality and comfort
★★★★ Excellent standard throughout
★★★★★ Exceptional level of quality

For full details of quality assessment schemes, go online at enjoyengland.com/quality

where to stay in

Scotland

All place names in the blue bands are shown on the maps at the front of this guide.

Accommodation symbols

Symbols give useful information about services and facilities. On page 7 you can find a key to these symbols.

ABINGTON, South Lanarkshire Map ref 6C2

★★★★
HOLIDAY PARK
THISTLE AWARD

£11.00–£16.00
£11.00–£16.00
(8) £6.00–£16.00
(3) £160.00–£374.00
50 touring pitches

Mount View Caravan Park

Abington ML12 6RW **t** (01864) 502808 **e** info@mountviewcaravanpark.co.uk

A developing park, surrounded by the Southern Uplands and handily located between Carlisle and Glasgow. It is an excellent stopover site for those travelling between Scotland and the South. The West Coast railway passes beside the park.

open March to October
payment Credit/debit cards, cash, cheques

General Leisure

AYR, South Ayrshire Map ref 6B2

★★★★
HOLIDAY PARK

(20) £12.50–£18.00
(8) £11.00–£16.50
(8) £11.00–£18.00
(10) £170.00–£550.00
36 touring pitches

Heads of Ayr Caravan Park

Dunure Road, Ayr KA7 4LD **t** (01292) 442269 **e** stay@headsofayr.com

headsofayr.com

Situated five miles south of Ayr on the A719. Facilities include bar, shop, laundry, play area and beach. Seasonal entertainment. Caravans to hire. Tourers and tents welcome.

open March to October
payment Cash, cheques

General Leisure

BALLOCH, West Dunbartonshire Map ref 6B2

★★★★★
HOLIDAY PARK
THISTLE AWARD

£18.00–£22.00
£18.00–£22.00
(6) £195.00–£550.00
120 touring pitches

Lomond Woods Holiday Park

Tullichewan, Old Luss Road, Balloch, Loch Lomond G83 8QP **t** (01389) 755000
e lomondwoods@holiday-parks.co.uk

holiday-parks.co.uk SPECIAL OFFERS · REAL-TIME BOOKING

Beside Loch Lomond and at the gateway to the National Park, this superbly appointed, family-run park offers pine lodges and caravans for holiday hire and sunny, secluded pitches for touring caravans and motor homes.

open All year
payment Credit/debit cards, cash, cheques

General Leisure

What shall we do today?

For ideas on places to visit, see the beginning of this regional section or go online at visitbritain.com.

BALMACARA, Highland Map ref 7B3

★★★★
TOURING PARK
(40) on application
(40) on application
(5) on application
45 touring pitches

Reraig Caravan Site

Balmacara, Kyle of Lochalsh IV40 8DH **t** (01599) 566215 **e** warden@reraig.com

reraig.com

Small family-run site, four miles from bridge to Isle of Skye. Booking not necessary. No awnings during July and August. Tents: only small tents permitted. No youth groups. Prices on application, or see our website.

open May to September
payment Credit/debit cards, cash, cheques

General

BOAT OF GARTEN, Highland Map ref 7C3

★★★★
HOLIDAY PARK
(3) £250.00–£375.00

Loch Garten Lodges & Caravan Park

Loch Garten Road, Boat of Garten PH24 3BY **t** (01479) 831769 **e** m.ireland@totalise.co.uk

lochgarten.co.uk

Close by the ospreys on the outskirts of Boat of Garten beside the Speyside Way. A quiet location with squirrels, deer and rampant bird life. This is luxury in a wilderness setting. Self catering at its most comfortable.

open All year
payment Cash, cheques

General Leisure

BRAEMAR, Aberdeenshire Map ref 7C3

★★★★
TOURING PARK
(97) £12.20–£25.10
(97) £12.20–£25.10
97 touring pitches

The Invercauld Caravan Club Site

Glenshee Road, Braemar, Ballater AB35 5YQ **t** (01342) 326944

caravanclub.co.uk

open December 2008 to October 2009
payment Credit/debit cards, cash, cheques

Set on the edge of Braemar village, gateway to the Cairngorms. Ideal centre for mountain lovers. See red deer, capercaillie and golden eagles.

SAT NAV *AB35 5YQ*

Special member rates mean you can save your membership subscription in less than a week. Visit our website to find out more.

General Leisure

CALLANDER, Stirling Map ref 6B1

★★★★★
HOLIDAY PARK
(128) Min £18.00
(128) Min £18.00
128 touring pitches

Reduced rates for the over 50s. Winner – Calor Gas Best Park in Britain 2003.

Gart Caravan Park

Stirling Road, Callander FK17 8LE **t** (01877) 330002 **e** enquiries@theholidaypark.co.uk

theholidaypark.co.uk

open 1 April to 15 October
payment Credit/debit cards, cash, cheques

A peaceful and spacious park maintained to a very high standard with modern, heated shower block facilities. The ideal centre for cycling, walking and fishing.

SAT NAV *FK17 8LE*

General Leisure

CALLANDER, Stirling Map ref 6B1

★★★★
TOURING PARK
(50) £10.50–£12.50
(50) £10.50–£12.50
(50) £9.00–£12.50
50 touring pitches

Keltie Bridge Caravan Park

Keltie Bridge, Callander FK17 8LQ **t** (01877) 330606 **e** stay@keltiebridge.co.uk

ukparks.co.uk/keltie

Flat, grassy park in Scotland's new Loch Lomond and The Trossachs National Park. Top-quality shower block. Easily accessible from central Scotland's motorways.

open Easter to October
payment Cash, cheques

General

DIRLETON, East Lothian Map ref 6D2

★★★★★
TOURING PARK
(116) £14.00–£26.60
(116) £14.00–£26.60
116 touring pitches

Yellowcraig Caravan Club Site

Dirleton, North Berwick EH39 5DS **t** (01620) 850217

caravanclub.co.uk

open March to November
payment Credit/debit cards, cash, cheques

This is a great choice for family holidays with acres of golden sands and rock pools close by. Pitching areas separated by sandy dunes, shrubs and roses.

SAT NAV *EH39 5DS*

Special member rates mean you can save your membership subscription in less than a week. Visit our website to find out more.

General Leisure

DUMFRIES, Dumfries & Galloway Map ref 6C3

★★★
HOLIDAY PARK
(10) £12.00–£16.00
(10) £12.00–£20.00
(10) £10.00–£18.00
(2) £190.00–£280.00
30 touring pitches

Barnsoul Farm

Irongray, Shawhead, Dumfries DG2 9SQ **t** (01387) 730249 **e** barnsouldg@aol.com

barnsoulfarm.co.uk

Barnsoul is one of Galloway's most scenic farms. Acres of meadows, ponds, woodlands and heath. Two 2,500-year-old hill forts. Famous timber wigwam bunkhouses.

open March to October
payment Cash, cheques

General Leisure

DUNBAR, East Lothian Map ref 6D2

★★★★
HOLIDAY PARK
THISTLE AWARD
(53) £12.50–£24.00
(53) £12.50–£24.00
(53) £12.50–£24.00
(5) £255.00–£565.00
53 touring pitches

See website for special offers.

Belhaven Bay Caravan and Camping Park

Belhaven Bay, Dunbar EH42 1TU **t** (01368) 865956 **e** belhaven@meadowhead.co.uk

meadowhead.co.uk GUEST REVIEWS • SPECIAL OFFERS

open 20 March to 3 January
payment Credit/debit cards, cash, cheques, euros

Bordered by one of Britain's cleanest beaches and a tranquil pond. Set on the edge of the John Muir Country Park but only 30 minutes to Edinburgh's city centre! Perfect for a quiet and relaxing break.

SAT NAV *EH42 1TU* **ONLINE MAP**

General Leisure

DUNKELD, Perth and Kinross Map ref 6C1

★★★★
TOURING PARK
£13.00–£14.00
£13.00–£14.00
(15) £11.00–£14.00
50 touring pitches

Inver Mill Farm Caravan Park

Inver, Dunkeld PH8 0JR **t** (01350) 727477 **e** invermill@talk21.com

visitdunkeld.com/perthshire-caravan-park.htm

We are situated in a very tranquil, scenic and beautiful part of Perthshire, an ideal location to explore a large part of Scotland.

open March to October
payment Cash, cheques

General Leisure

EDINBURGH, Edinburgh Map ref 6C2

EDINBURGH, Edinburgh Map ref 6C2

★★★★★
TOURING PARK
(80) £15.00–£18.00
(40) £15.00–£18.00
(28) £15.00–£18.00
(12) £300.00–£800.00
108 touring pitches

See Ad above

Drummohr Caravan Park

Levenhall, Musselburgh, Edinburgh EH21 8JS **t** (0131) 665 6867

drummohr.org

payment Credit/debit cards, cash, cheques

Premier park close to Princes Street, Edinburgh and the coast of East Lothian. Excellent bus service to city with many retail outlets in the area.

SAT NAV *EH21 8JS*

General Leisure

EDINBURGH, Edinburgh Map ref 6C2

★★★★★
TOURING PARK
(197) £14.00–£26.60
(197) £14.00–£26.60
197 touring pitches

Special member rates mean you can save your membership subscription in less than a week. Visit our website to find out more.

Edinburgh Caravan Club Site

35-37 Marine Drive, Edinburgh EH4 5EN **t** (0131) 312 6874

open All year
payment Credit/debit cards, cash, cheques

Situated to the north of the city on the Firth of Forth, the site provides easy access to Edinburgh. It's a historic setting – yet Edinburgh is a friendly, modern, cosmopolitan city with something for everyone.

SAT NAV *EH4 5EN*

General Leisure

Do you have access needs?

Look for the National Accessible Scheme symbols if you have special hearing, visual or mobility needs.

EDINBURGH, Edinburgh Map ref 6C2

★★★★
TOURING PARK
(50) £12.00–£16.00
(50) £12.00–£16.00
(10) £10.00–£14.00
60 touring pitches

Linwater Caravan Park

West Clifton, East Calder EH53 0HT **t** (0131) 333 3326 **e** linwater@supanet.com

linwater.co.uk GUEST REVIEWS

A peaceful park seven miles west of Edinburgh. Excellent facilities. Ideal for visiting Edinburgh, Royal Highland Showground, Falkirk Wheel, or as a stop-over on your way north or south.

open 13 March to 1 November
payment Credit/debit cards, cash, cheques, euros

General Leisure

EDINBURGH, Edinburgh Map ref 6C2

★★★★
HOLIDAY PARK
THISTLE AWARD
(100) £11.80–£27.25
(100) £11.80–£27.25
(150) £11.80–£27.25
(19) £267.00–£690.00
250 touring pitches

Please see website for special promotions and details on our new wigwams too!

Mortonhall Caravan Park

38 Mortonhall Gate, Frogston Road East, Edinburgh EH16 6TJ **t** (0131) 664 1533
e mortonhall@meadowhead.co.uk

meadowhead.co.uk GUEST REVIEWS · SPECIAL OFFERS

open 20 March to 3 January
payment Credit/debit cards, cash, cheques

Our park is in unrivalled, historic, landscaped grounds only four miles from the heart of Edinburgh. Great new wcs and showers. Wonderful walks with vistas over Edinburgh and views of highland cattle. Fine fare at the Stable Bar or nearby coffee shop. Efficient bus routes connect us to the city centre.

SAT NAV *EH16 6TJ* **ONLINE MAP**

General Leisure

FORDOUN, Aberdeenshire Map ref 6D1

★★★
HOLIDAY PARK
(11) £10.00–£11.50
(11) £10.00–£11.50
(11) £7.00–£10.00
(3) £250.00
11 touring pitches

Brownmuir Caravan Park

Fordoun, Laurencekirk AB30 1SJ **t** (01561) 320786 **e** brownmuircaravanpark@talk21.com

brownmuircaravanpark.co.uk REAL-TIME BOOKING

A quiet park set in the Howe-of-the-Mearns not far from Royal Dee Side, ideal for cycling and fishing. Top golf courses are nearby. Children's play area on site.

open April to October
payment Cash, cheques

General Leisure

FORT WILLIAM, Highland Map ref 6B1

★★★★★
TOURING PARK
(99) £14.00–£26.60
(99) £14.00–£26.60
99 touring pitches

Bunree Caravan Club Site

Onich, Fort William PH33 6SE **t** (01855) 821283

caravanclub.co.uk

open March 2009 to January 2010
payment Credit/debit cards, cash, cheques

Your van can be parked almost at the water's edge of Loch Linnhe for wonderful views of the mountains across the water. This site is breathtaking. Try a visit to Ben Nevis or Glencoe.

SAT NAV *PH33 6SE*

General Leisure

FORT WILLIAM, Highland Map ref 6B1

★★★★★
HOLIDAY PARK

£13.00–£19.00
£13.00–£19.00
(300) £10.20–£15.50
(22) £235.00–£525.00
250 touring pitches

Glen Nevis Caravan & Camping Park

Glen Nevis, Fort William PH33 6SX **t** (01397) 702191 **e** holidays@glen-nevis.co.uk

glen-nevis.co.uk

Our award-winning touring caravan and camping park has a magnificent location in one of Scotland's most famous highland glens at the foot of mighty Ben Nevis, Britain's highest mountain.

payment Credit/debit cards, cash, cheques

General Leisure

FORT WILLIAM, Highland Map ref 6B1

★★★★★
HOLIDAY PARK

(65) £10.50–£12.50
(65) £10.50–£12.50
(15) £6.00–£10.50
(60) £250.00–£899.00
80 touring pitches

Discounts for senior citizen groups and for 2nd week. Rallies – no charge for awnings.

Linnhe Lochside Holidays

Corpach, Fort William PH33 7NL **t** (01397) 772376 **e** relax@linnhe-lochside-holidays.co.uk

linnhe-lochside-holidays.co.uk

open 15 December to 31 October
payment Credit/debit cards, cash, cheques

Almost a botanical garden. Winner of 'Best Park in Scotland 1999' award. Free fishing. Colour brochure sent with pleasure. Also self-catering.

SAT NAV *PH33 7NL*

General Leisure

GLENCOE, Highland Map ref 6B1

★★★★★
HOLIDAY PARK
THISTLE AWARD

Min £17.00
Min £17.00
Min £15.00
£270.00–£450.00
60 touring pitches

Invercoe Caravan & Camping Park

Invercoe, Glencoe PH49 4HP **t** (01855) 811210 **e** holidays@invercoe.co.uk

invercoe.co.uk

open All year
payment Credit/debit cards, cash, cheques

Situated on the shores of Loch Leven and surrounded by spectacular scenery, Invercoe is a small, award-winning, family-run park and is an excellent base for exploring the West Highlands. Booking advisable during high season (minimum three nights).

SAT NAV *PH49 4HP*

General Leisure

Don't forget www.

Web addresses throughout this guide are shown without the prefix www. Please include www. in the address line of your browser. If a web address does not follow this style it is shown in full.

GRANTOWN-ON-SPEY, Highland Map ref 7C3

★★★★★
HOLIDAY PARK
(136) £15.00–£23.00
(136) £15.00–£23.00
(40) £10.00–£17.00
136 touring pitches

Grantown on Spey Caravan Park

Seafield Avenue, Grantown on Spey PH26 3JQ **t** (01479) 872474 **e** warden@caravanscotland.com

caravanscotland.com

open All year
payment Credit/debit cards, cash, cheques

A scenic park in a mature setting near the river and town, surrounded by hills, mountains, moors and woodland. The park is very well landscaped, and is in a good location for golf, fishing, mountaineering, walking, sailing and canoeing.

SAT NAV *PH26 3JQ*

General Leisure

INVERNESS, Highland Map ref 7C3

★★★★
HOLIDAY PARK
£11.00–£15.00
£11.00–£15.00
(30) £8.00–£10.00
(11) £160.00–£300.00
45 touring pitches

Auchnahillin Caravan and Camping Park

Daviot East, Inverness IV2 5XQ **t** (01463) 772286 **e** info@auchnahillin.co.uk

auchnahillin.co.uk

Warm welcome awaits at friendly, informal, family-run park. Ten acres, peaceful, scenic, rural location but convenient for many attractions, ideal base for touring. Refurbished amenities, small shop, play area, launderette.

open March to October
payment Credit/debit cards, cash, cheques

General Leisure

JOHN O' GROATS, Highland Map ref 7D1

★★★
TOURING PARK
(90) Min £10.00
(90) Min £10.00
(90) Min £10.00
90 touring pitches

John O' Groats Caravan Park

John O' Groats, Wick KW1 4YR **t** (01955) 611329 & (01955) 611744
e info@johnogroatscampsite.co.uk

johnogroatscampsite.co.uk

On seashore overlooking Orkney Islands (day trips available). Hotel restaurant 400m, harbour 150m, sea birds 3km. Cliff scenery.

open April to September
payment Cash, cheques

General Leisure

KIRKPATRICK FLEMING, Dumfries & Galloway Map ref 6C3

★★★
HOLIDAY PARK
(35) £10.00
(5) £10.00
(40) £8.50–£16.00
(3) £210.00–£400.00
80 touring pitches

King Robert the Bruce's Cave

Cove Estate, Lockerbie DG11 3AT **t** (01461) 800285 **e** enquiries@brucescave.co.uk

The lovely wooded grounds of an old castle and mansion are the setting for this pleasant park. The mature woodland is a haven for wildlife, and there is a riverside walk to Robert the Bruce's cave. Luxury holiday apartments available to let.

open All year
payment Credit/debit cards, cash, cheques

General Leisure

Place index

If you know where you want to stay, the index by place name at the back of the guide will give you the page number listing accommodation in your chosen town, city or village. Check out the other useful indexes too.

LAURENCEKIRK, Aberdeenshire Map ref 6D1

★★★★
HOLIDAY PARK
(25) £11.00–£12.00
(25) £11.00–£12.00
(25) £8.00–£9.00
(1) £220.00–£250.00
25 touring pitches

Dovecot Caravan Park

Northwaterbridge, Laurencekirk AB30 1QL **t** (01674) 840630 **e** adele@dovecotcaravanpark.co.uk

dovecotcaravanpark.co.uk

Dovecot is a peaceful, rural site located halfway between Dundee and Aberdeen. Ideal location for touring. Sandy beaches eight miles and Angus Glens on our doorstep.

open April to mid-October
payment Cash, cheques

General Leisure

LINLITHGOW, West Lothian Map ref 6C2

★★★★
TOURING PARK
(36) £13.50–£16.00
(36) £13.50–£16.00
(20) £11.85–£19.40
56 touring pitches

1 Sep – 18 Dec 2008 and 4 Jan – 2 Apr 2009: 10% discount for Senior Citizens aged 65+ (proof required) and 10% discount for 7-night stay if paid in advance (excl Senior Citizens).

Beecraigs Caravan and Camping Site

Beecraigs Country Park, The Park Centre, Linlithgow EH49 6PL **t** (01506) 844516
e mail@beecraigs.com

beecraigs.com

open All year
payment Credit/debit cards, cash, cheques

Open all year. Situated near historic Linlithgow town. On-site facilities include electric hook-ups, barbecues, play area, modern toilet facilities with privacy cubicles, baby-change and laundry. Pets welcome. Leaflets available. Great for exploring central Scotland and the Lothians.

SAT NAV *EH49 6PL*

General Leisure

LOCKERBIE, Dumfries & Galloway Map ref 6C3

★★★★★
HOLIDAY PARK
(100) £9.00–£19.00
(100) £9.00–£19.00
(30) £8.00–£16.00
130 touring pitches

Hoddom Castle Caravan Park

Hoddom, Lockerbie DG11 1AS **t** (01576) 300251 **e** hoddomcastle@aol.com

hoddomcastle.co.uk

Part of 10,000-acre estate. Beautiful, peaceful, award-winning park. Own 9-hole golf course. Salmon, seatrout and coarse fishing. Nature trails and walks in surrounding countryside.

open April to October
payment Credit/debit cards, cash, cheques

General Leisure

MELROSE, Scottish Borders Map ref 6C2

★★★★★
TOURING PARK
(60) £14.00–£26.60
(60) £14.00–£26.60
on application
60 touring pitches

Special member rates mean that you can save your membership subscription in less than a week. Visit our website to find out more.

Gibson Park Caravan Club Site

High Street, Melrose TD6 9RY **t** (01896) 822969

caravanclub.co.uk

open All year
payment Credit/debit cards, cash, cheques

Peaceful, award-winning site on edge of town. Adjacent tennis courts and playing fields. Melrose Abbey, where Robert the Bruce's head is buried, is within walking distance. Non-members welcome.

SAT NAV *TD6 9RY*

General Leisure

NORTH BERWICK, East Lothian Map ref 6D2

★★★★
HOLIDAY PARK
THISTLE AWARD

(147) £13.50–£24.00
(147) £13.50–£24.00
(40) £13.50–£24.00
(10) £290.00–£660.00
147 touring pitches

See website for special offers.

Tantallon Caravan Park

Dunbar Road, North Berwick EH39 5NJ **t** (01620) 893348 **e** tantallon@meadowhead.co.uk

meadowhead.co.uk GUEST REVIEWS · SPECIAL OFFERS

open 20 March to 3 January
payment Credit/debit cards, cash, cheques, euros

Relaxing park that's ideal for exploring the classy golfing capital of North Berwick and East Lothian beyond. Overlooks Glen Golf Course with views of the Forth, Bass Rock, Isle of May and Fife. Local bus and trains connect us to Edinburgh.

SAT NAV *EH39 5NJ* **ONLINE MAP**

General Leisure

OBAN, Argyll and Bute Map ref 6B1

★★★
HOLIDAY PARK

(50) £14.00–£19.00
(50) £14.00–£19.00
(50) £11.00–£12.00
(17) £250.00–£450.00
150 touring pitches

Oban Caravan & Camping Park

Gallanach Road, Oban PA34 4QH **t** (01631) 562425 **e** info@obancaravanpark.com

obancaravanpark.com

open Easter to October
payment Credit/debit cards, cash, cheques

A beautiful coastal tourist park in a very attractive location. Close to the ferries to the Isles. This family park is an ideal boating centre, and offers two large rally areas in addition to the touring pitches, one with hardstandings and many electric hook-ups.

SAT NAV *PA34 4QH* **ONLINE MAP**

General Leisure

PARTON, Dumfries & Galloway Map ref 6C3

★★★★
HOLIDAY PARK

(52) £16.00–£18.00
(4) £16.00–£18.00
(50) £12.00–£16.00
(10) £260.00–£480.00
56 touring pitches

Short breaks for static holiday homes Mar-Jul, Sep-Nov.

Loch Ken Holiday Park

Parton, Castle Douglas DG7 3NE **t** (01644) 470282 **e** penny@lochkenholidaypark.co.uk

lochkenholidaypark.co.uk

open March to November
payment Credit/debit cards, cash, cheques

A popular park situated on the shores of Loch Ken. There is a natural emphasis on water activities; excellent fishing, sailing, water-skiing. Family-owned and run. It is in a beautiful spot, opposite the RSPB reserve. An uncommercialised, natural, peaceful place for a relaxing family holiday. David Bellamy Gold Conservation Award.

SAT NAV *DG7 3NE*

General Leisure

What do the star ratings mean?

Detailed information about star ratings can be found at the back of this guide.

PORT LOGAN, Dumfries & Galloway Map ref 6B3

★★★★
TOURING PARK
(158) £10.60–£23.20
(158) £10.60–£23.20
158 touring pitches

New England Bay Caravan Club Site

Port Logan, Stranraer DG9 9NX **t** (01776) 860275

caravanclub.co.uk

open March to November
payment Credit/debit cards, cash, cheques

On the edge of Luce Bay, an ideal site for children with direct access to a safe, clean, sandy beach. Sailing, sea-angling, golf, green bowling, pony-trekking.

SAT NAV *DG9 9NX*

Special member rates mean you can save your membership subscription in less than a week. Visit our website to find out more.

THE CARAVAN CLUB

General Leisure

STEPPS, North Lanarkshire Map ref 6B2

★★★
HOLIDAY PARK
(14) £14.25–£15.75
(13) £14.25–£15.75
(30) £12.25–£14.25
(17) £160.00–£530.00
27 touring pitches

Craigendmuir Caravan and Camping Park

Craigendmuir Park, Stepps G33 6AF **t** (0141) 779 4159 **e** info@craigendmuir.co.uk

craigendmuir.co.uk

Craigendmuir Park offers substantial touring caravan and camping areas, together with fully equipped chalets, static caravans and holiday homes.

open All year
payment Credit/debit cards, cash, cheques

General Leisure

THURSO, Highland Map ref 7C1

★★★★★
TOURING PARK
(57) £12.20–£25.10
(57) £12.20–£25.10
57 touring pitches

Dunnet Bay Caravan Club Site

Dunnet, Thurso KW14 8XD **t** (01847) 821319

caravanclub.co.uk

open April to October
payment Credit/debit cards, cash, cheques

A good place for those who like to be solitary. Views to Dunnet Head, northernmost point of mainland Britain. Good for bird-watching and fishing.

SAT NAV *KW14 8XD*

Special member rates mean you can save your membership subscription in less than a week. Visit our website to find out more.

General Leisure

Do you have access needs?

Look for the National Accessible Scheme symbols if you have special hearing, visual or mobility needs. An index of parks participating in the scheme can be found at the back of this guide.

Wales

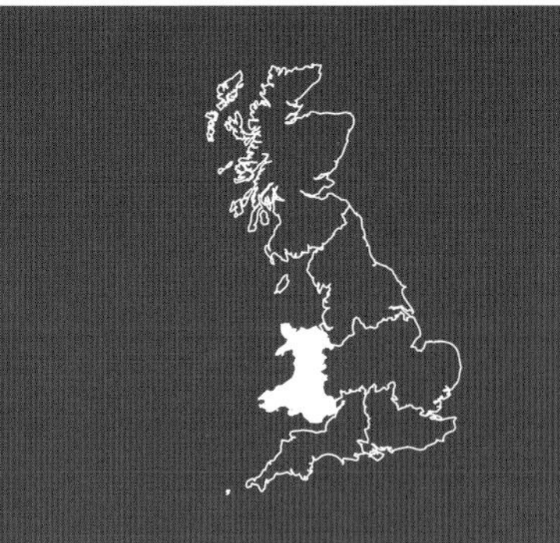

Clockwise: Whitesands Bay, Pembrokeshire; Brecon Beacons, Powys; Caernarfon Castle, Gwynedd

Great days out

For a small country Wales is big on things to see and do. We're not just talking about mountains, valleys and beaches – culture, exercise, adventure and tranquillity are here too. Land of legend, land of song, it's rich with heritage, and it looks forward with exciting city living and attractions.

Breathing spaces

Fill your lungs with fresh air and feast your eyes on the exhilarating scenery! A quarter of Wales is covered by **National Parks** and **Areas of Outstanding Natural Beauty**. And that's a lot of space to explore, as well as stretches of **Heritage Coast** and hundreds of nature and wildlife reserves. Savour the contrasts in the three National Parks: conquer Snowdonia's **Mount Snowdon** by foot, or railway, it'll certainly put you in high spirits. Ramble the famous Welsh 'green, green grass' in the **Brecon Beacons** – there are plenty of ups and downs for mountain bikers, too, or take a leap paragliding. What a buzz! Mosey along to **Pembrokeshire Coast's** big beaches and little coves, ideal for family fun and wildlife watching.

Snowdon Mountain Railway, Snowdonia

Take a dip

Did you know: Wales has lots of water! To swim, paddle, surf, sail, coasteer, white-water raft and fish – 750 miles of coast, nearly 500 lakes and reservoirs, and around 15,000 miles of rivers and canals. Saddle up and gallop over the beach on **Carmarthen Bay**, spot bottlenose dolphins along the coast of **Cardigan Bay**. And don't forget seaside treats like cockles and laverbread. Another day, simply relax on a canal boat, or ambling the river meadows, woods and villages of the **Wye Valley**. In many places you can even play a round of golf beside the sea – Llyn's amazing clifftop Nefyn & District course, Gwynedd, is unforgettable.

Iron ring or fairytale?

Throughout Wales you'll encounter prehistoric, Roman and Norman sites, but nothing tells the story of the land's turbulent and thrilling past like its castles. There were around 641 at the last count ranging from war-torn ruins to whimsical fancies. Seek out King Edward I's 13thC 'iron ring' of fortresses in the north, including the World Heritage Sites of **Caernarfon** and **Beaumaris**. You simply have to admire the ingenious 'walls within walls' design of Beaumaris – state of the defensive art at the time. Castles like **Chirk** near Wrexham, transformed from a 14thC fortress into an elegant mansion home, reveal how life has changed. And turreted **Castell Coch**, hidden in woodlands overlooking a gorge in the Taff Valley, is the ultimate fairytale castle: a flamboyant Victorian vision of the Middle Ages replete with dazzling interiors and fantastic furnishings.

Left to right: National Botanic Garden of Wales, Carmarthenshire; Powis Castle, Powys

did you know... the unique Snowdon Lily has survived on Mount Snowdon for 10,000 years?

Inspiring gardens

Wales' gardens dazzle, too, showcasing a breathtaking diversity. Include on your must-see list the world-famous Italianate terraces with enormous clipped yews and statuary beneath medieval **Powis Castle**. Stroll the enchanting cloister, pool and walled gardens at **Aberglasney**, tucked away in the lovely Tywi Valley and an inspiration to poets since 1477. The woods and lakes at exotic **Portmeirion Village and Gardens** are wonderfully relaxing. And there's something for everyone at the **National Botanic Garden of Wales**, Llanarthne – from Bog and Japanese gardens to an Apothecaries' Garden. Travel through continents in a few steps in the Great Glasshouse, past thousands of Mediterranean-climate plants.

Capital attractions

Join the cafe culture and enjoy shopping in one of the many attractive arcades in Cardiff. Check out sporting fixtures or concerts at the iconic **Millennium Stadium**, too. Wales' capital is a sassy place, no more so than along the revitalised waterfront of **Cardiff Bay** – take a look at superb landmarks like the **Millennium Centre** for arts and performance plus the Senedd, Wales' National Assembly. Drop into historic **Cardiff Castle** or the treasure-filled **National Museum and Gallery**, and do browse the speciality shops of the glass-canopied Victorian and Edwardian arcades. Welsh kilt, anyone?

Millennium Centre, Cardiff

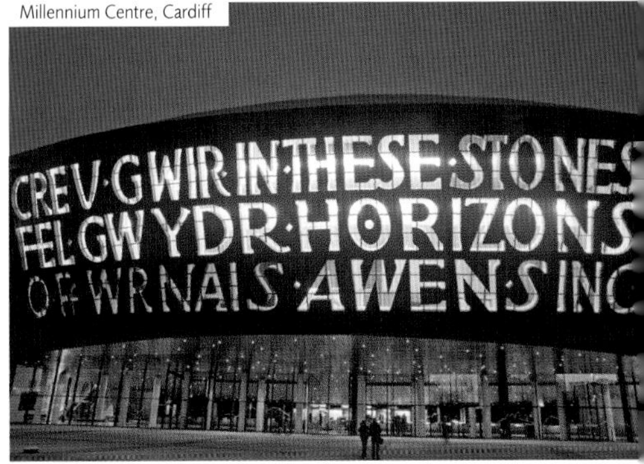

Iechyd da!

It means 'cheers' or 'good health' (say, 'yekkee-da') – you'll hear it in friendly pubs up and down. Welsh is a Celtic language and a lyrical, living part of the country's heritage, making the principality just that bit different. For a colourful celebration of Welsh culture visit the **National Eisteddfod**, on the outskirts of Bala in 2009. Or head for **Swansea**, sandy city by the sea, and share the life of its world-famous son at the Dylan Thomas Centre.

Music, of course, resounds countrywide – join the cosmopolitan gathering at **Llangollen International Musical Eisteddfod** in July, or tap your foot to the super-cool sounds of **Brecon Jazz** in August. And make time to discover a land of legends. Begin at **St Davids**, Britain's smallest city, where the relics of Wales' patron saint are said to rest in the 12thC cathedral. Then get on the trail of King Arthur, wizards and dragons...

Family favourites

Wherever you go, there's plenty to enthral children (and fascinate parents, too). Wander around more than 40 authentic buildings from different eras at the **Museum of Welsh Life**, St Fagans, and see how people in the past worked and played. Tour underground at **Big Pit**, Blaenavon, to get a taste of mining, or take a scenic ride on the narrow-gauge **Ffestiniog Railway** – one of the charming Great Little Trains of Wales.

At the **Centre for Alternative Technology**, Machynlleth, you'll find the village of the future with lots of child-friendly exhibits and events throughout the year. Try the Carbon Gym to assess how 'green' your lifestyle is! For the wackiest day out, watch the extraordinary **World Bog Snorkelling Championships** near Llanwrtyd Wells on August Bank Holiday Monday. Muddee!

why not... enjoy some of Britain's best sunsets, at Whitesands Bay, Pembrokeshire?

Clockwise: St Davids Cathedral, Pembrokeshire; Ffestiniog Railway, Gwynedd; World Bog Snorkelling Championship, Powys

Destinations

Aberystwyth

This established and cosmopolitan holiday resort is home to many of Wales' cultural institutions – start by tracing your Welsh ancestors in Wales' literary treasure, the National Library of Wales. Situated on spectacular coastline, it's an ideal base for exploring hidden coves, sandy beaches and the striking and unspoilt countryside on its doorstep. Enjoy secluded walks along the Rheidiol and Ystwyth valleys or take a steam train from Aberystwyth up to the mysteriously named Devils Bridge, passing through some of the most rugged terrain of any railway in the United Kingdom.

Bangor

This university and cathedral city is located in a breathtaking landscape, with Snowdonia National Park to the south and the Isle of Anglesey to the north. The city centre combines historic atmosphere with the best of modern amenities. Visit the cathedral, founded on one of the earliest Christian settlements in Britain, or the restored Victorian pier, extending out into the Menai Straits and surrounded by traditional pubs and restaurants, or head further afield to explore local villages.

Caernarfon

This market town has a long and fascinating history: make its striking castle, built by Edward I, your first port of call. It's undoubtedly one of the most architecturally impressive castles in the country. Discover other evidence of the town's historical past including prehistoric remains and the ruins of Segontium, a Roman military fort. Take a ride on the scenic Welsh Highland Railway and explore the magnificent Snowdonia National Park.

Cardiff

The capital city of Wales has plenty to keep you entertained. One of the UK's top shopping destinations, it's a true shoppers' paradise – from pedestrian Queen Street to the city's network of Victorian and Edwardian arcades. You can find great gifts including handmade Welsh textiles, love spoons and rugby shirts in the arcades, as well as plenty of places to enjoy a drink and a bite to eat. Stroll through the regenerated Cardiff Bay and catch a performance at the spectacular Wales Millennium Centre. Cardiff Castle and the National Museum Wales are just two of the great attractions to visit in and around the city.

Cardiff Castle

Carmarthen

Legend suggests this is the birthplace of the wizard Merlin. Explore the remains of the Norman Castle, sample local delicacies such as Carmarthenshire Ham and Penclawdd Cockles in the indoor market, or visit on a Wednesday to experience the lively Farmers Market. The nearby National Botanic Garden of Wales is a must-see, where the largest single-span glasshouse in the world houses many endangered plant species. Aberglasney Gardens is also worthy of a visit – the secret past of this historic garden is only now being rediscovered.

For lots more great ideas visit visitbritain.com/destinations and visitwales.com

Clockwise: Gower Peninsular; Swansea; Celtic Manor Resort, Newport

Swansea

Wales' 'City by the Sea' is the only place in the UK where you can shop, eat out and enjoy a vibrant arts, entertainment and club scene yet be so close to an Area of Outstanding Natural Beauty. Visit the stunning new National Waterfront Museum or sample local delicacies such as cockles and laverbread at the largest indoor market in Wales. If you're looking for sun, sand and watersports, the beaches stretch from Swansea Bay to the rugged beauty of the Gower Peninsula.

Tenby

Tenby is a town steeped in ancient history, with a medieval heart, yet is a thoroughly modern holiday destination. With its miles of European Blue Flag-winning beaches, picturesque working harbour and rich heritage, Tenby mixes cosmopolitan style with traditional seaside fun. Take time out from the beach to wander the town walls, dating back as far as 1260, and to explore a wealth of historic buildings. What's more you are only minutes away from some of Pembrokeshire's finest attractions and the sweeping landscapes of the Pembrokeshire Coast National Park.

Newport

Newport is a city of contrasts – where medieval cathedral and castle rub shoulders with exuberant Victorian architecture, and Roman walls and amphitheatre contrast with high-tech developments. Visit one of the last working transporter bridges in the world, tour the fascinating Roman site at Caerleon, or take in a show at the impressive new Riverfront Arts Centre. For golf lovers, there's the world-class Celtic Manor Resort, venue for the 2010 Ryder Cup.

St Davids

Britain's smallest city, located in the Pembrokeshire Coast National Park, has been a favourite destination for pilgrims, travellers and artists through the ages. Visit the starkly beautiful cathedral, reputedly founded on the site of St Davids 6th-century monastery and enjoy fresh local food in the highly-rated refectory. Walk coastal paths amid some of the finest natural scenery in Europe, relax on unspoilt beaches or take a boat trip to spot dolphins and whales.

Tenby

Visitor attractions

Family and Fun

Anglesey Sea Zoo
Brynsiencyn, Isle of Anglesey
(01248) 430411
angleseyseazoo.co.uk
Wales' largest marine aquarium.

Big Pit National Mining Museum of Wales
Blaenavon, Torfaen
(01495) 790311
museumwales.ac.uk/en/bigpit
Travel 300ft underground guided by an ex-miner.

Ffestiniog Railway
Porthmadog, Gwynedd
(01766) 516000
festrail.co.uk
Heritage rail journey from coast to mountains.

Gower Heritage Centre
Parkmill, Swansea
(01792) 371206
gowerheritagecentre.co.uk
Family attraction on the beautiful Gower peninsula.

King Arthur's Labyrinth
Corris, Gwynedd
(01654) 761584
kingarthurslabyrinth.com
An underground boat trip through spectacular caverns.

National Showcaves for Wales
near Abercraf, Powys
(01639) 730284
showcaves.co.uk
Spectacular caves and children's dinosaur park.

Welsh Highland Railway
Porthmadog, Gwynedd
(01766) 51600
25miles of scenic 2ft steam rail travel from Caernarfon to Porthmadog.

Heritage

Abergavenny Museum & Castle
Abergavenny, Monmouthshire
(01873) 854282
abergavennymuseum.co.uk
Local museum in grounds of ruined fortress.

Beaumaris Castle
Beaumaris, Isle of Anglesey
(01443) 336000
cadw.wales.gov.uk
Awesome, unfinished masterpiece begun in 1295.

Caernarfon Castle and Town Walls
Caernarfon, Gwynedd
(01286) 677617
cadw.wales.gov.uk
Medieval fortress, now a World Heritage Site.

Carew Castle & Tidal Mill
Carew, near Tenby, Pembrokeshire
(01646) 651782
carewcastle.com
From Norman fortification to Elizabethan country house.

Castell Coch
Cardiff
(029) 2050 0200
cadw.wales.gov.uk
The ultimate fairytale castle.

Chirk Castle and Gardens
Chirk, Wrexham
(01691) 777701
nationaltrust.org
Magnificent medieval fortress of the Welsh Marches.

Powis Castle and Garden
Welshpool, Powys
(01938) 551929
nationaltrust.org.uk
Wander the world-famous terraced garden.

St Davids Cathedral
St Davids, Pembrokeshire
(01437) 720199
stdavidscathedral.org.uk
Majestic 12thC cathedral with 6thC roots.

Indoors

Cardiff Bay Visitor Centre
Cardiff
(029) 2046 3833
cardiffharbour.com
Interactive attraction housed in stunning 'Tube' building.

Ceredigion Museum
Aberystwyth, Ceredigion
(01970) 633088
museum.ceredigion.gov.uk
A fascinating chronicle of local life.

Dylan Thomas Centre
Swansea
(01792) 463980
dylanthomas.com
The life of Swansea's world-famous son.

Inigo Jones Slate Works
Caernarfon, Gwynedd
(01286) 830242
inigojones.co.uk
Engrave your own piece of slate.

The Museum of Modern Art, Wales
Machynlleth, Powys
(01654) 703355
momawales.org.uk
Beautiful galleries set in historic market town.

National Museum Wales
Cardiff
(029) 2039 7951
museumwales.ac.uk
Dazzling displays of art and natural history.

National Waterfront Museum
Swansea
(01792) 638950
waterfrontmuseum.co.uk
Inspirational museum of industrial and maritime history.

Swansea Museum
Swansea
(01792) 653763
swansea.gov.uk/swanseamuseum
Treasure house of the ordinary and extraordinary.

Tenby Museum & Art Gallery
Tenby, Pembrokeshire
(01834) 842809
tenbymuseum.org.uk
Discover the culture and heritage of Pembrokeshire.

Outdoors

Aberdulais Falls
Aberdulais, Neath Port Talbot
(01639) 636674
nationaltrust.org.uk
Famous waterfalls and fascinating industrial site.

Aberglasney Gardens
Llangathen, Carmarthenshire
(01558) 668998
aberglasney.org
Spectacular gardens set in beautiful Tywi valley.

Hafod Eryri
Snowdon Summit, Gwynedd
0871 720 0033
The new £8.3m visitor centre on the summit of Snowdon, Wales' highest mountain.

Museum of Welsh Life
St Fagans, Cardiff
(029) 2057 3500
nmgw.ac.uk
One of Europe's foremost open-air museums.

National Botanic Garden of Wales
Llanarthney, Carmarthenshire
(01558) 668768
gardenofwales.org.uk
Beautiful 500-acre gardens with Foster's Great Glasshouse.

Portmeirion Village and Gardens
Portmeirion, Gwynedd
(01766) 770000
portmeirion-village.com
Italianate resort village built by Clough Williams-Ellis.

ASSURANCE OF A GREAT DAY OUT
Attractions with this sign participate in a quality assurance scheme.

Events 2009

St David's Day (Dydd Gwyl Dewi Sant)
1 Mar

Hay Festival of Literature
Hay-on-Wye
hayfestival.com
21 - 31 May

Celtic Manor Resort Wales Open
Newport
walesopen.com
4 - 7 Jun

Ryder Cup Wales Seniors Open
Royal Porthcawl Golf Club
rydercupwales2010.com
19 - 21 Jun

Llangollen International Musical Eisteddfod
Llangollen
international-eisteddfod.co.uk
7 - 12 Jul

The Ashes 2009 Series England v Australia
Swalec Stadium, Cardiff
glamorgancricket.com
8 - 12 Jul

Royal Welsh Show
Builth Wells
rwas.co.uk
20 - 23 Jul

National Eisteddfod of Wales
Bala
eisteddfod.org.uk
1 - 8 Aug

Brecon Jazz Festival
Brecon
breconjazz.co.uk
7 - 9 Aug

Bryn Terfel's Faenol Festival
Faenol Estate, Near Bangor
brynfest.com
28 - 31 Aug

Abergavenny Food Festival
Abergavenny
abergavennyfoodfestival.com
19 - 20 Sep

Dylan Thomas Festival
Swansea
dylanthomas.com
27 Oct - 9 Nov

Wales Rally GB
Cardiff, South & Mid Wales
walesrallygb.com
End of October

Regional contacts and information

For more information on accommodation, attractions, activities, events and holidays in Wales, contact the regional tourism organisation below. The website has a wealth of information and you can order or download publications.

Wales

For any further information contact:

Visit Wales
Brunel House, 2 Fitzalan Road,
Cardiff CF24 0UY
t 0870 121 1251
0870 121 1255 (minicom)
w visitwales.com

Clockwise: Ogmore Castle, Glamorgan; Plas Newydd, Denbighshire; Snowdonia; Mumbles, Swansea

Tourist Information Centres

When you arrive at your destination, visit a Tourist Information Centre for help with accommodation and information about local attractions and events, or email your request before you go.

Aberaeron	The Quay	(01545) 570602	aberaerontic@ceredigion.gov.uk
Aberdulais Falls	The National Trust	(01639) 636674	aberdulaistic@nationaltrust.org.uk
Aberdyfi*	The Wharf Gardens	(01654) 767321	tic.aberdyfi@eryri-npa.gov.uk
Abergavenny	Monmouth Road	(01873) 853254	abergavennyic@breconbeacons.org
Aberystwyth	Terrace Road	(01970) 612125	aberystwythtic@ceredigion.gov.uk
Bala*	Pensarn Road	(01678) 521021	bala.tic@gwynedd.gov.uk
Bangor*	Deiniol Road	(01248) 352786	bangor.tic@gwynedd.gov.uk
Barmouth	Station Road	(01341) 280787	barmouth.tic@gwynedd.gov.uk
Barry Island*	The Promenade	(01446) 747171	barrytic@valeofglamorgan.gov.uk
Beddgelert*	Canolfan Hebog	(01766) 890615	tic.beddgelert@eryri-npa.gov.uk
Betws y Coed	Royal Oak Stables	(01690) 710426	tic.byc@eryri-npa.gov.uk
Blaenau Ffestiniog*	Unit 3, High Street	(01766) 830360	tic.blaenau@eryri-npa.gov.uk
Blaenavon*	Church Road	(01495) 742333	blaenavon.tic@torfaen.gov.uk
Borth*	Cambrian Terrace	(01970) 871174	borthtic@ceredigion.gov.uk
Brecon	Cattle Market Car park	(01874) 622485	brectic@powys.gov.uk
Bridgend	Bridgend Designer Outlet	(01656) 654906	bridgendtic@bridgend.gov.uk
Builth Wells	The Groe Car Park	(01982) 553307	builtic@powys.gov.uk
Caerleon	5 High Street	(01633) 422656	caerleon.tic@newport.gov.uk
Caernarfon	Castle Street	(01286) 672232	caernarfon.tic@gwynedd.gov.uk
Caerphilly	The Twyn	(029) 2088 0011	tourism@caerphilly.gov.uk
Cardiff	The Old Library	0870 121 1258	visitor@cardiff.gov.uk
Cardigan	Bath House Road	(01239) 613230	cardigantic@ceredigion.gov.uk
Carmarthen	113 Lammas Street	(01267) 231557	carmarthentic@carmarthenshire.gov.uk
Chepstow	Bridge Street	(01291) 623772	chepstow.tic@monmouthshire.gov.uk
Conwy	Castle Buildings	(01492) 592248	conwytic@conwy.gov.uk
Dolgellau	Eldon Square	(01341) 422888	tic.dolgellau@eryri-npa.gov.uk
Fishguard Harbour	The Parrog	(01348) 872037	fishguardharbour.tic@pembrokeshire.gov.uk
Fishguard Town	Market Square	(01437) 776636	fishguard.tic@pembrokeshire.gov.uk
Harlech*	High Street	(01766) 780658	tic.harlech@eryri-npa.gov.uk
Haverfordwest	Old Bridge	(01437) 763110	haverfordwest.tic@pembrokeshire.gov.uk

Holyhead	Stena Line, Terminal 1	(01407) 762622	holyhead@nwtic.com
Knighton	West Street	(01547) 528753	oda@offasdyke.demon.co.uk
Llanberis*	41b High Street	(01286) 870765	llanberis.tic@gwynedd.gov.uk
Llandovery	Kings Road	(01550) 720693	llandovery.ic@breconbeacons.org
Llandudno	Mostyn Street	(01492) 876413	llandudnotic@conwy.gov.uk
Llanelli	North Dock	(01554) 777744	DiscoveryCentre@ carmarthenshire.gov.uk
Llanfairpwllgwyngyll	Station Site	(01248) 713177	llanfairpwll@nwtic.com
Llangollen	Castle Street	(01978) 860828	llangollen@nwtic.com
Machynlleth	Penrallt Street	(01654) 702401	mactic@powys.gov.uk
Merthyr Tydfil	14a Glebeland Street	(01685) 379884	tic@merthyr.gov.uk
Milford Haven*	94 Charles Street	(01646) 690866	milford.tic@pembrokeshire.gov.uk
Mold	Earl Road	(01352) 759331	mold@nwtic.com
Monmouth	Agincourt Square	(01600) 713899	monmouth.tic@monmouthshire.gov.uk
Mumbles	Mumbles Road	(01792) 361302	info@mumblestic.co.uk
New Quay*	Church Street	(01545) 560865	newquaytic@ceredigion.gov.uk
Newport	John Frost Square	(01633) 842962	newport.tic@newport.gov.uk
Newport (pembs)*	Long Street	(01239) 820912	newportTIC@pembrokeshirecoast.org.uk
Oswestry Mile End	Mile End Services	(01691) 662488	tic@oswestry-bc.gov.uk
Oswestry Town	2 Church Terrace	(01691) 662753	ot@oswestry-welshborders.org.uk
Pembroke*	Commons Road	(01646) 622388	pembroke.tic@pembrokeshire.gov.uk
Penarth*	Penarth Pier	(029) 2070 8849	penarthtic@valeofglamorgan.gov.uk
Porthcawl*	John Street	(01656) 786639	porthcawltic@bridgend.gov.uk
Porthmadog	High Street	(01766) 512981	porthmadog.tic@gwynedd.gov.uk
Presteigne*	Broad Street	(01544) 260650	presteignetic@powys.gov.uk
Pwllheli	Station Square	(01758) 613000	pwllheli.tic@gwynedd.gov.uk
Rhyl	West Parade	(01745) 355068	rhyl.tic@denbighshire.gov.uk
St Davids	1 High Street	(01437) 720392	enquiries@ stdavids.pembrokeshirecoast.org.uk
Saundersfoot*	Harbour Car Park	(01834) 813672	saundersfoot.tic@pembrokeshire.gov.uk
Swansea	Plymouth Street	(01792) 468321	tourism@swansea.gov.uk
Tenby	Unit 2, The Gateway Complex	(01834) 842402	tenby.tic@pembrokeshire.gov.uk
Tywyn*	High Street	(01654) 710070	tywyn.tic@gwynedd.gov.uk
Welshpool	Church Street	(01938) 552043	weltic@powys.gov.uk
Wrexham	Lambpit Street	(01978) 292015	tic@wrexham.gov.uk

* seasonal opening

where to stay in
Wales

All place names in the blue bands are shown on the maps at the front of this guide.

Accommodation symbols

Symbols give useful information about services and facilities. On page 7 you can find a key to these symbols.

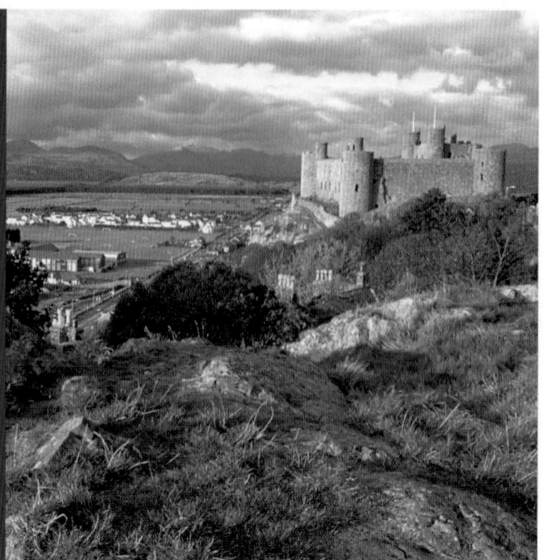

ABERAERON, Ceredigion Map ref 8A2

★★★★
HOLIDAY, TOURING & CAMPING PARK
£15.00–£24.00
£15.00–£24.00
£15.00–£24.00
100 touring pitches

Aeron Coast Caravan Park

North Road, Aberaeron SA46 0JF **t** (01545) 570349 **e** enquiries@aeroncoast.co.uk

aeroncoast.co.uk REAL-TIME BOOKING

open March to October
payment Credit/debit cards, cash, cheques

We are privileged to be part of Aberaeron with its picturesque harbour, shops and restaurants. River and coastal walks. Quiet out of high season but good leisure provision for families in school holidays including entertainment every evening. Apart from laundry, all facilities on-site including entertainment are free of charge.

SAT NAV *SA46 0JF* **ONLINE MAP**

General Leisure

ABERGAVENNY, Monmouthshire Map ref 8B3

★★★★
TOURING PARK
(53) £12.20–£25.10
(53) £12.20–£25.10
on application
53 touring pitches

Pandy Caravan Club Site

Pandy NP7 8DR **t** (01342) 326944 **e** natalie.tiller@caravanclub.co.uk

caravanclub.co.uk

open March to October
payment Credit/debit cards, cash, cheques

Attractively landscaped site where you can fish (by permit from the site), pony trek or walk on Offa's Dyke or in the Brecon Beacons National Park.

SAT NAV *NP7 8DR*

Special member rates mean you can save your membership subscription in less than a week. Visit www.caravan club.co.uk to find out more.

General

AMROTH, Pembrokeshire Map ref 8A3

★★★★★
HOLIDAY, TOURING & CAMPING PARK
£14.50–£22.50
£14.50–£22.50
(60) £14.50–£22.50
(13) £255.00–£650.00
60 touring pitches

Little Kings Park

Amroth Road, Ludchurch, Narberth SA67 8PG **t** (01834) 831330 **e** littlekingspark@btconnect.com

littlekings.co.uk

open March to mid-November
payment Credit/debit cards, cash, cheques

Quiet park with view across open land to sea. Beach 1.5 miles. Covered, heated pool, bar/restaurant, two toilet blocks, laundry, shop, mains hook-up, games room, children's play area, dog walk.

SAT NAV *SA67 8PG*

General Leisure

AMROTH, Pembrokeshire Map ref 8A3

★★★★★
HOLIDAY PARK
(12) £120.00–£630.00

Fortnightly bookings: 5% discount; couples only: 10% discount Mar, Apr, May, late Sep, Oct (but not school holidays).

Pendeilo Dragon Award Caravans

Pendeilo Leisure Park, Amroth, Narberth SA67 8PR **t** (01834) 831259 **e** pendeiloholidays@aol.com

pendeilo.co.uk

open March to October
payment Credit/debit cards, cash, cheques

This is an award-winning park set amid the beautiful countryside of the Pembrokeshire Coast National Park and yet only five minutes' drive from the wide expanse of Amroth's clean, golden sands. Choose from two- and three-bedroom static caravans or cosy cottage for two. Central heating and double glazing available on top-of-range homes.

SAT NAV *SA67 8PR*

General Leisure

BALA, Gwynedd Map ref 8B1

★★★★
TOURING & CAMPING PARK
(70) £16.00–£20.00
(15) £16.00–£20.00
(80) £12.00–£16.00
£250.00–£550.00

Glanllyn Lakeside Caravan & Camping Park

Llanuwchllyn, Bala LL23 7SS **t** (01678) 540227 **e** info@glanllyn.com

glanllyn.com

Sixteen acres of level parkland with mature trees, and a meandering river, situated on the shore of Wales' largest natural lake in the Snowdonia National Park.

open Mid-March to mid-October
payment Credit/debit cards, cash, cheques

General Leisure

BEAUMARIS, Isle of Anglesey Map ref 8A1

★★★★
HOLIDAY, TOURING & CAMPING PARK
(55) £16.00–£18.00
(2) £16.00–£18.00
(20) £16.00–£19.50
(2) £175.00–£320.00
99 touring pitches

Kingsbridge Touring and Camping

Camp Road, Llanfaes, Anglesey LL58 8LR **t** (01248) 490636 **e** info@kingsbridgecaravanpark.co.uk

kingsbridgecaravanpark.co.uk

A quiet, family-run park located in an Area of Outstanding Natural Beauty. We aim to provide first-class facilities for those wishing to escape the hectic pace of modern living.

payment Cash, cheques

General Leisure

For **key to symbols** see page 7

BENLLECH, Isle of Anglesey Map ref 8A1

★★★★
TOURING PARK
(52) £12.20–£25.10
(52) £12.20–£25.10
52 touring pitches

Penrhos Caravan Club Site

Brynteg, Benllech LL78 7JH **t** (01248) 852617

caravanclub.co.uk

open March to October
payment Credit/debit cards, cash, cheques

An ideal site for a family holiday, five minutes' drive from a safe, sandy beach.

SAT NAV *LL78 7JH*

Special member rates mean you can save your membership subscription in less than a week. Visit our website to find out more.

General Leisure

BRECON, Powys Map ref 8B3

★★★★
HOLIDAY, TOURING & CAMPING PARK
(60) £12.00–£16.00
(10) £12.00–£16.00
(40) £12.00–£14.00
110 touring pitches

Anchorage Caravan Park

Bronllys, Brecon LD3 0LD **t** (01874) 711246

anchoragecp.co.uk

High-standard family-run park. Panoramic views of the Brecon Beacons National Park. Ideal for touring and walking mid and south Wales.

open All year
payment Cash, cheques

General  Leisure

BRECON, Powys Map ref 8B3

★★★★★
TOURING & CAMPING PARK
(130) £17.00–£21.00
(130) £17.00–£21.00
on application
130 touring pitches

Brynich Caravan Club Site

Brecon LD3 7SH **t** (01874) 623325

caravanclub.co.uk

open March to November
payment Credit/debit cards, cash, cheques

Situated near the foothills of the Brecon Beacons, Brynich is well located with excellent facilities. It boasts some of the best views of the central Beacons, including Pen-y-Fan, Cribyn and Corn Du and is the ideal base for touring the towns and countryside of mid and south Wales.

SAT NAV *LD3 7SH*

Special member rates mean you can save your membership subscription in less than a week. Visit our website to find out more.

WALKERS WELCOME CYCLISTS WELCOME

THE CARAVAN CLUB

General Leisure

BROAD HAVEN, Pembrokeshire Map ref 8A3

★★★★★
TOURING & CAMPING PARK
(62) £14.00–£16.00
(10) £14.00–£16.00
(10) £14.00–£17.50
(1) £250.00–£420.00
72 touring pitches

Creampots Touring Caravan & Camping Park

Broadway, Broad Haven, Haverfordwest SA62 3TU **t** (01437) 781776 **e** creampots@btconnect.com

creampots.co.uk GUEST REVIEWS

Peaceful, quiet, immaculate, friendly, family-run park in countryside, close to the National Park and only 1.5 miles from Broad Haven and Littlehaven's safe sandy beaches. Ideal central location. Large pitches.

open March to November
payment Credit/debit cards, cash, cheques

General Leisure

CAERNARFON, Gwynedd Map ref 8A1

CAERNARFON, Gwynedd Map ref 8A1

★★★
TOURING & CAMPING PARK

(30) £12.00–£17.00
(5) £12.00–£17.00
(25) £9.00–£17.00
60 touring pitches

Cwm Cadnant Valley

Llanberis Road, Caernarfon LL55 2DF **t** (01286) 673196 **e** visitwales@cadnantvalley.co.uk

cwmcadnant.co.uk

A ten-minute stroll to Caernarfon town and castle. Hot showers available and toilet block. A quiet family site with children's play area and friendly atmosphere.

open March to November
payment Credit/debit cards, cash

General Leisure

COLWYN BAY, Conwy Map ref 8B1

★★★★★
TOURING PARK

(120) £18.00–£21.00
(10) £18.00–£21.00
130 touring pitches

Bron-Y-Wendon Touring Caravan Park

Wern Road, Llanddulas, Colwyn Bay LL22 8HG **t** (01492) 512903 **e** stay@northwales-holidays.co.uk

northwales-holidays.co.uk

Award-winning park, all pitches overlooking the sea. Ideally situated for touring Snowdonia, Llandudno, Chester. Leave the A55 at Llanddulas, junction 23 (A547), and follow Tourist Information signs to the park.

open All year
payment Credit/debit cards, cash, cheques

General Leisure

CONWY Map ref 8B1

★★★
TOURING PARK

(320) £8.85–£26.10
(25) £8.85–£26.10
(50) £7.00–£26.10
320 touring pitches

Conwy Touring Park

Trefriw Road, Conwy LL32 8UX **t** (01492) 592856 **e** sales@conwytouringpark.co.uk

conwytouringpark.co.uk

Set in spectacular scenery, the perfect location for touring Snowdonia and coastal resorts. Sheltered, wooded site with splendid views. Excellent children's facilities. Special offers. Storage and servicing available.

open Easter to September
payment Credit/debit cards, cash, cheques

General Leisure

Check the maps for park locations

Colour maps at the front pinpoint all the places where parks are featured within the regional sections of this guide. Pick your location and then refer to the place index at the back to find the page number.

CROSS INN, Ceredigion Map ref 8A2

★★★★
HOLIDAY PARK
(35) £20.50–£26.50
(35) £20.50–£26.50
(50) £18.00–£24.00
(8) £130.00–£545.00
30 touring pitches

Pencnwc Holiday Park

Cross Inn, Llandysul SA44 6NL **t** (01545) 560479 **e** holidays@pencnwc.co.uk

pencnwc.co.uk GUEST REVIEWS

Two miles from New Quay, this tranquil area has gained a reputation as West Wales' best kept secret. Pencnwc, a family-owned park, has an atmosphere of warmth and friendliness.

open All year
payment Credit/debit cards, cash, cheques

General Leisure

CWMCARN, Newport Map ref 8B3

★★★
TOURING & CAMPING PARK
(23) £9.50–£11.00
(23) £9.50–£11.00
(27) £7.00–£16.00
27 touring pitches

Cwmcarn Forest Drive and Campsite

Nantcarn Road, Cwmcarn, Cross Keys, Newport NP11 7FA **t** (01495) 272001
e cwmcarn-vc@caerphilly.gov.uk

caerphilly.gov.uk/visiting

Set amongst rolling hills and green forests, this quiet campsite is close to Cardiff, Newport and Brecon Beacons. Ideal base for touring. Mountain-bike trails, walking routes, visitor centre, cafe and gift shop on-site.

open All year except Christmas and New Year
payment Credit/debit cards, cash, cheques

General Leisure

FISHGUARD, Pembrokeshire Map ref 8A2

★★★★
HOLIDAY, TOURING & CAMPING PARK
£14.00–£16.00
£14.00–£16.00
(30) £13.00–£15.00
(14) £220.00–£499.00
20 touring pitches

Fishguard Bay Caravan & Camping Park

Garn Gelli, Fishguard SA65 9ET **t** (01348) 811415 **e** enquiries@fishguardbay.com

fishguardbay.com

Enjoy your stay on this beautiful stretch of Pembrokeshire National Park coastline. Ideal centre for walking and touring. Quiet, family-run park.

open March to November
payment Credit/debit cards, cash, cheques

General Leisure

FISHGUARD, Pembrokeshire Map ref 8A2

★★★★
TOURING PARK
(19) £13.00–£14.00
(20) £13.00–£14.00
(8) £10.00–£13.00
28 touring pitches

Gwaun Vale Touring Park

Llanychaer, Fishguard SA65 9TA **t** (01348) 874698 **e** info@gwaunvale.co.uk

gwaunvale.co.uk

Situated in the beautiful Gwaun Valley, overlooking Pembrokeshire National Park. Ideal for walking, sightseeing or just relaxing. Close to Irish ferry.

payment Cash, cheques

General Leisure

Don't forget www.

Web addresses throughout this guide are shown without the prefix www. Please include www. in the address line of your browser. If a web address does not follow this style it is shown in full.

FRESHWATER EAST, Pembrokeshire Map ref 8A3

★★★★
TOURING & CAMPING PARK

(130) £12.20–£25.10
(130) £12.20–£25.10
on application
130 touring pitches

Midweek discount: pitch fee for standard pitches for stays on any Tue, Wed or Thu night outside peak season dates will be reduced by 50%.

THE CARAVAN CLUB

Freshwater East Caravan Club Site

Trewent Hill, Freshwater East, Pembroke SA71 5LN **t** (01646) 672341

caravanclub.co.uk

open March to October
payment Credit/debit cards, cash, cheques

Only a few minutes from a beautiful stretch of beach, this hill-bottom site is flanked by trees on one side with a selection of grass or hardstanding pitches. This location offers fantastic walks with magnificent cliff-top views.

SAT NAV *SA71 5LN*

General Leisure

LLANABER, Gwynedd Map ref 8A2

★★★★★
TOURING & CAMPING PARK

(70) £23.00–£32.00
(70) £23.00–£32.00
(30) £15.00–£27.00
100 touring pitches

Trawsdir Touring & Camping Park

Trawsdir Touring Caravan and Camping Park, Llanaber LL42 1RR **t** (01341) 280999
e enquiries@barmouthholidays.co.uk

barmouthholidays.co.uk

open 1 March to 6 January
payment Credit/debit cards, cash, cheques

Trawsdir is a luxury site situated on the mid-Wales coast with magnificent views over Cardigan Bay and the Lleyn Peninsula. £500,000 upgrade in 2007. Just a few minutes' walk from miles of beautiful sandy beach. Ideal for families and couples. Booking required.

SAT NAV *LL42 1RR* **ONLINE MAP**

General Leisure

LLANELLI, Carmarthenshire Map ref 8A3

★★★★★
TOURING PARK

(130) £14.00–£26.60
(130) £14.00–£26.60
130 touring pitches

Special member rates mean you can save your membership subscription in less than a week. Visit our website to find out more.

THE CARAVAN CLUB

Pembrey Country Park Caravan Club Site

Factory Road, Llanelli SA16 0EJ **t** (01342) 326944 **e** natalie.tiller@caravanclub.co.uk

open March 2009 to January 2010
payment Credit/debit cards, cash, cheques

Situated on the edge of a 520-acre country park with a vast range of outdoor sporting activities, and including use of a seven-mile stretch of safe, sandy beach, only a mile away.

SAT NAV *SA16 0EJ*

General Leisure

Using map references

Map references refer to the colour maps at the front of this guide.

LLANGADOG, Carmarthenshire Map ref 8B3

★★★★
TOURING & CAMPING PARK

(60) £9.50–£11.50
(60) £9.50–£11.50
(28) £9.00–£11.50
88 touring pitches

Abermarlais Caravan Park

Llangadog SA19 9NG **t** (01550) 777868 & (01550) 777797

abermarlaiscaravanpark.co.uk

open 16 March to 16 November
payment Credit/debit cards, cash, cheques

A tranquil site in a beautiful woodland valley at the western end of the Brecon Beacons National Park, ideal for nature lovers and bird-watchers. The site's facilities are of the highest standard with excellent shower and toilet block. Camp shop and reception with comprehensive selection of groceries, gas, etc.

SAT NAV *SA19 9NG*

General Leisure

LLANGORSE, Powys Map ref 8B3

★★★
HOLIDAY, TOURING & CAMPING PARK

(20) £11.00–£13.00
(20) £11.00–£13.00
(40) £11.00–£13.00
(10) £215.00–£395.00
20 touring pitches

Lakeside Caravan Park

Llangorse Lake, Llangorse LD3 7TR **t** (01874) 658226 **e** holidays@llangorselake.co.uk

llangorselake.co.uk

Lakeside Caravan Park is surrounded by the Brecon Beacons National Park and is adjacent to Llangorse Common, which leads down to Llangorse Lake.

open All year except Christmas and New Year
payment Credit/debit cards, cash, cheques

General Leisure

LLIGWY BAY, Isle of Anglesey Map ref 8A1

★★★★★
HOLIDAY PARK

(4) £140.00–£575.00

Minffordd Caravan Park

Lligwy, Dulas LL70 9HJ **t** (01248) 410678 **e** enq@minffordd-holidays.com

minffordd-holidays.com

Beautiful, small, family-run garden park near Lligwy beach. Parking alongside each caravan, one of which is designed for physically disabled guests. Many local walks and cycle routes. Ideal countryside for birdwatchers.

open 22 March to November
payment Cash, cheques

General Leisure

NEWPORT, Newport Map ref 8B3

★★★★★
TOURING & CAMPING PARK

(80) £12.20–£25.10
(80) £12.20–£25.10
80 touring pitches

Tredegar House & Park Caravan Club Site

Coedkernew, Newport NP10 8TW **t** (01342) 326944 **e** natalie.tiller@caravanclub.co.uk

caravanclub.co.uk

open All year
payment Credit/debit cards, cash, cheques

High-standard site within the park, bordering one of the ornamental lakes. Just off the M4, seven miles from Cardiff. Non-members welcome.

SAT NAV *NP10 8TW*

Special member rates mean you can save your membership subscription in less than a week. Visit our website to find out more.

General Leisure

ST DAVIDS, Pembrokeshire Map ref 8A3

★★★★
HOLIDAY, TOURING & CAMPING PARK
(26) £11.50–£15.50
(15) £9.50–£15.50
(69) £9.50–£13.00
(9) £200.00–£400.00
110 touring pitches

Caerfai Bay Caravan and Tent Park

St Davids, Haverfordwest SA62 6QT **t** (01437) 720274 **e** info@caerfaibay.co.uk

caerfaibay.co.uk

A quiet, family-run park. Turn off A487 (Haverfordwest to St Davids) in St Davids at Visitor Centre. The park is at road end, one mile, on the right. Signposted. No dogs in tent fields during school summer holidays.

open April to mid-November
payment Credit/debit cards, cash, cheques

General Leisure

SAUNDERSFOOT, Pembrokeshire Map ref 8A3

★★★★★
HOLIDAY PARK
(8) £150.00–£525.00

Pinewood Caravan Park

Cliff Road, Wisemans Bridge, Narberth SA67 8NU **t** (01834) 811082
e info@pinewoodholidaypark.co.uk

pinewoodholidaypark.co.uk

Peaceful location. Owners live on site. 350yds to the beach at Wiseman's Bridge.

payment Cash, cheques

General Leisure

SWANSEA, Swansea Map ref 8B3

★★★★
TOURING PARK
(135) £12.20–£25.50
(135) £12.20–£25.50
135 touring pitches

Gowerton Caravan Club Site

Pont-Y-Cob Road, Swansea SA4 3QP **t** (01342) 326944 **e** natalie.tiller@caravanclub.co.uk

caravanclub.co.uk

open March to November
payment Credit/debit cards, cash, cheques

A level, well-designed site within an easy drive of the whole range of superb beaches on the Gower Peninsula, such as Oxwich and Caswell Bay.

SAT NAV *SA4 3QP*

Special member rates mean you can save your membership subscription in less than a week. Visit our website to find out more.

General Leisure

Enjoy England assessed accommodation

On the following pages you will find an exclusive listing of every park in England assessed under the British Graded Holiday Parks Scheme.

The information includes brief contact details together with its star rating and classification. The listing also shows if an establishment has a National Accessible rating or participates in the Welcome schemes: Cyclists Welcome, Walkers Welcome, Welcome Pets! and Families Welcome (see the front of the guide for further information).

Parks are listed by region and then alphabetically by place name. They may be located in, or a short distance from, the places in the blue bands.

More detailed information on all the places shown in black can be found in the regional sections (where parks have paid to have their details included). To find these entries please refer to the park index at the back of this guide.

The list which follows was compiled slightly later than the regional sections. For this reason you may find that, in a few instances, a star rating may differ between the two sections. This list contains the most up-to-date information and was correct at the time of going to press. Please note that it does not include parks in Scotland and Wales.

NORTHERN ENGLAND

ACASTER MALBIS
North Yorkshire

Moor End Farm ★★★★
Holiday, Touring & Camping Park
Moor End, Acaster Malbis, York YO23 2UQ
t (01904) 706727
e moorendfarm@acaster99.fsnet.co.uk
w ukparks.co.uk/moorend

AINSDALE
Merseyside

Willowbank Holiday Home & Touring Park ★★★★★
Holiday & Touring Park
Willowbank Caravan Park, Coastal Road, Ainsdale PR8 3ST
t (01704) 571566
e info@willowbankcp.co.uk
w willowbankcp.co.uk

ALLERSTON
North Yorkshire

Vale of Pickering Caravan Park ★★★★★
Touring & Camping Park
Allerston, Pickering YO18 7PQ
t (01723) 859280
e tony@valeofpickering.co.uk
w valeofpickering.co.uk

ALLONBY
Cumbria

Manor House Caravan Park ★★★
Holiday, Touring & Camping Park
Edderside Road, Allonby, Maryport CA15 6RA
t (01900) 881236
e holidays@manorhousepark.co.uk
w manorhousepark.co.uk

Spring Lea Caravan Park ★★★★
Holiday, Touring & Camping Park
Main Road, Allonby, Maryport CA15 6QF
t (01900) 881331

ALNWICK
Northumberland

Alnwick Rugby Football Club ★
Touring & Camping Park
Greensfield, Alnwick NE66 1BG
t (01665) 602342
w alnwickrugby.com

AMBLE
Northumberland

Amble Links Holiday Park ★★★★
Holiday Park
Links Road, Morpeth NE65 0SD
t (01665) 710530
e amble@parkleisure.co.uk
w amblelinksholidaypark.co.uk

AMBLESIDE
Cumbria

Skelwith Fold Caravan Park ★★★★★
Holiday & Touring Park
Ambleside, Cumbria, Ambleside LA22 0HX
t (015394) 32277
e info@skelwith.com
w skelwithfold.co.uk

APPLEBY-IN-WESTMORLAND
Cumbria

Wild Rose Park ★★★★★
Holiday, Touring & Camping Park
Ormside, Appleby-in-Westmorland CA16 6EJ
t (017683) 51077

ARMATHWAITE
Cumbria

Englethwaite Hall Caravan Club Site ★★★★
Touring Park
Armathwaite, Carlisle CA4 9SY
t (01228) 560202
e enquiries@caravanclub.co.uk
w caravanclub.co.uk

ASHINGTON
Northumberland

Wansbeck Riverside Park Caravan & Camp Site ★★
Touring & Camping Park
Wansbeck Riverside Park, Ashington NE63 8TX
t (01670) 812323
e http://wansbeckcaravan@aol.com
w wansbeck.gov.uk

BAMBURGH
Northumberland

Bradford Kaims Caravan Park ★★★
Holiday, Touring & Camping Park
Bradford House, Belford NE70 7JT
t (01668) 213432
e lwrob@tiscali.co.uk
w bradford-leisure.co.uk

Glororum Caravan Park ★★★
Holiday & Touring Park
Glororum, Bamburgh NE69 7AW
t (01668) 214457
e info@glororum-caravanpark.co.uk
w glororum-caravanpark.co.uk

Meadowhead's Waren Caravan and Camping Park ★★★★ ROSE AWARD
Holiday, Touring & Camping Park
Waren Mill, Belford NE70 7EE
t (01668) 214366
e waren@meadowhead.co.uk
w meadowhead.co.uk

BARDSEY
West Yorkshire

Haighfield Caravan Park ★★★★★ ROSE AWARD
Holiday Park
5 Blackmoor Lane, Bardsey, Leeds LS17 9DY
t (01937) 574658
e haighfield@aol.com
w haighfieldcaravanpark.co.uk

BARMSTON
East Riding of Yorkshire

Barmston Beach Holiday Park ★★★★ ROSE AWARD
Holiday Park
Sands Lane, Barmston, Hornsea YO25 8PJ
t (01442) 830185
e angie.pyle@park-resorts.com
w park-resorts.com

BASSENTHWAITE
Cumbria

Bassenthwaite Lakeside Lodges ★★★★★ ROSE AWARD
Holiday Park
Scarness, Keswick CA12 4QZ
t (017687) 76641
e enquiries@bll.ac
w bll.ac

BEADNELL
Northumberland

Beadnell Bay Camping & Caravanning Site ★★
Touring & Camping Park
Chathill NE67 5BX
t (01665) 720586
w campingandcaravanningclub.co.uk

BEAL
Northumberland

Haggerston Castle Holiday Park ★★★★★ ROSE AWARD
Holiday, Touring & Camping Park
Haggerston Castle, Haggerston TD15 2PA
t (01289) 381333
e enquiries@british-holidays.co.uk
w haggerstoncastle-park.co.uk

BEAMISH
Durham

Bobby Shafto Caravan Park ★★★★
Holiday, Touring & Camping Park
Cranberry Plantation, Stanley DH9 0RY
t (0191) 370 1776
e info@bobbyshaftocaravanpark.co.uk
w bobbyshaftocaravanpark.co.uk

BEDALE
North Yorkshire

Pembroke Caravan Park ★★★★
Touring & Camping Park
19 Low Street, Leeming Bar, Northallerton DL7 9BW
t (01677) 422652

BELFORD
Northumberland

South Meadows Caravan Park ★★★★★
Holiday, Touring & Camping Park
South Meadows, Belford NE70 7DP
t (01668) 213326
e g.mcl@btinternet.com
w southmeadows.co.uk

BELLINGHAM
Northumberland

Bellingham Camping & Caravanning Club Site ★★★★
Touring & Camping Park
Tweed House, The Croft, Hexham NE48 2JY
t (01434) 220175
w campingandcaravanningclub.co.uk

Demesne Farm Campsite & Bunkhouse ★★★
Touring & Camping Park
Demesne Farm, Hexham NE48 2BS
t (01434) 220258
e stay@demesnefarmcampsite.co.uk
w demesnefarmcampsite.co.uk

BERWICK-UPON-TWEED
Northumberland

Beachcomber Campsite ★★
Touring & Camping Park
Goswick, Berwick-upon-Tweed TD15 2RW
t (01289) 381217
e johngregson@micro-plus-web.net
w lindisfarne.org.uk/beachcomber

Berwick Holiday Park ★★★★★ ROSE AWARD
Holiday Park
Magdalene Fields, Berwick-upon-Tweed TD15 1NE
t (01289) 307113
e berwick@bourne-leisure.co.uk
w british-holidays.co.uk

Seaview Caravan Club Site ★★★★
Touring & Camping Park
Billendean Road, Berwick-upon-Tweed TD15 1QU
t (01289) 305198
e enquiries@caravanclub.co.uk
w caravanclub.co.uk

BEVERLEY
East Riding of Yorkshire

Barmston Farm Holiday Park ★★★★★
Holiday Park
Barmston Farm, Barmston Lane, Beverley HU17 0TP
t (01482) 863566 & 07970 042587
e enquiry@barmstonfarm.co.uk
w barmstonfarm.co.uk

BLACKHALL COLLIERY
Durham

Crimdon Dene Holiday Park ★★★★
Holiday & Touring Park
Coast Road, Hartlepool TS27 4BN
t 0871 664 9737
e holidaysales.crimdondene@park-resorts.com
w park-resorts.com

BLACKPOOL
Lancashire

Marton Mere Holiday Village ★★★★
Holiday & Touring Park
Mythop Road, Blackpool FY4 4XN
t (01253) 767544
w martonmere-park.co.uk

Newton Hall Holiday Park ★★★★
Holiday Park
Staining Road, Blackpool FY3 0AX
t (01253) 882512
e reception@newtonhall.net
w partingtons.com

Sunset Park ★★★★★
Holiday Park
Enjoy England Awards for Excellence Winner
Sower Carr Lane, Hambleton FY6 9EQ
t (01253) 700222
e sales@sunsetpark.co.uk
w sunsetpark.co.uk

Windy Harbour Holiday Centre ★★★
Holiday, Touring & Camping Park
Windy Harbour Road, Singleton FY6 8NB
t (01253) 883064
e info@windyharbour.net
w windyharbour.net

BOLTON ABBEY
North Yorkshire

Strid Wood Caravan Club Site ★★★★★
Touring Park
Skipton BD23 6AN
t (01756) 710433
w caravanclub.co.uk

BOOT
Cumbria

Camping & Caravanning Club Site – Eskdale ★★★★
Camping Park
Boot, Holmrook, Eskdale CA18 1SR
t (01946) 723253
w campingandcaravanningclub.co.uk

BOTHEL
Cumbria

Skiddaw View at Stay Lakeland ★★★★ **ROSE AWARD**
Holiday Park
Bothel, Bassenthwaite, Keswick CA13 9QW
t 0845 468 0936
e info@staylakeland.co.uk
w skiddawview.co.uk

BOUTH
Cumbria

Black Beck Caravan Park ★★★★★ **ROSE AWARD**
Holiday & Touring Park
Bouth, Ulverston LA12 8JN
t (01229) 861274
e reception@blackbeck.com

BRANDESBURTON
East Riding of Yorkshire

Dacre Lakeside Park ★★★★
Holiday & Touring Park
Leven Road, Brandesburton, Hornsea YO25 8RT
t 0800 180 4556
e chalets@dacrepark.co.uk
w dacrepark.co.uk

Fosse Hill Caravan Park ★★★
Touring & Camping Park
Catwick Lane, Brandesburton, Hornsea YO25 8SB
t (01964) 542608
e tony@fossehill.co.uk
w fossehill.co.uk

BRAYSTONES
Cumbria

Tarnside Caravan Park ★★★
Holiday, Touring & Camping Park
Braystones, Beckermet, Egremont CA21 2YL
t (01946) 822777
e tom@seacote.com
w tarnsidepark.co.uk

BRIDLINGTON
East Riding of Yorkshire

North Bay Leisure Limited ★★★★ **ROSE AWARD**
Holiday Park
Lime Kiln Lane, Bridlington YO16 6TG
t (01262) 673733
e enquiries@northbayleisure.co.uk
w northbayleisure.co.uk

The Poplars Touring Park ★★★★
Touring & Camping Park
45 Jewison Lane, Sewerby, Bridlington YO15 1DX
t (01262) 677251
w thepoplars.co.uk

South Cliff Caravan Park ★★★★
Holiday, Touring & Camping Park
Wilsthorpe, Bridlington YO15 3QN
t (01262) 671051
e southcliff@eastriding.gov.uk
w southcliff.co.uk

BURTON-IN-LONSDALE
North Yorkshire

Gallaber Farm Caravan Park ★★★★
Holiday, Touring & Camping Park
Gallaber Farm, Burton in Lonsdale, Lancaster LA6 3LU
t (01524) 261361
e gallaber@btopenworld.com
w gallaber.btinternet.co.uk

BURY
Greater Manchester

Burrs Country Park Caravan Club Site ★★★★★
Touring Park
Woodhill Road, Bury BL8 1BN
t (0161) 761 0489
w caravanclub.co.uk

CABUS
Lancashire

Claylands Caravan Park ★★★★
Holiday, Touring & Camping Park
Weavers Lane, Garstang PR3 1AJ
t (01524) 791242
e alan@claylandscaravanpark.co.uk
w claylandscaravanpark.co.uk

CAPERNWRAY
Lancashire

Old Hall Caravan Park ★★★★★
Holiday & Touring Park
Capernwray, Carnforth LA6 1AD
t (01524) 733276
w oldhall.uk.com

CARLISLE
Cumbria

Dandy Dinmont Caravan & Camping Site ★★★★
Touring & Camping Park
Blackford, Carlisle CA6 4EA
t (01228) 674611
e dandydinmont@btopenworld.com
w caravan-camping-carlisle.itgo.com

CARNFORTH
Lancashire

Netherbeck Holiday Home Park ★★★★★
Holiday Park
North Road, Carnforth LA5 9NG
t (01524) 735101
e info@netherbeck.co.uk
w netherbeck.co.uk

CASTLESIDE
Durham

Manor Park Caravan Park ★★
Holiday, Touring & Camping Park
Broadmeadows, Rippon Burn, Consett DH8 9HD
t (01207) 501000

CAYTON BAY
North Yorkshire

Cayton Bay Holiday Park ★★★★
Holiday Park
Mill Lane, Cayton Bay, Scarborough YO11 3NJ
t (01723) 583111
e holidaysales.caytonbay@park-resorts.com
w park-resorts.com

Cliff Farm Caravan Park ★★★★★
Holiday Park
Mill Lane, Cayton Bay, Scarborough YO11 3NN
t (01723) 582239

CHESTER
Cheshire

Chester Fairoaks Caravan Club Site ★★★★★
Touring & Camping Park
Rake Lane, Little Stanney, Chester CH2 4HS
t (0151) 355 1600
w caravanclub.co.uk

Manor Wood Country Caravan Park ★★★★★
Holiday, Touring & Camping Park
Manor Wood, Coddington, Chester CH3 9EN
t (01829) 782990 & 07762 817827
e info@manorwoodcaravans.co.uk
w cheshire-caravan-sites.co.uk

CHRISTLETON
Cheshire

Parkfields Farm Camping Site ★★
Touring Park
Plough Lane, Christleton CH3 7BA
t 07914 734260

CLAXTON
North Yorkshire

Foxhill Park ★★★
Holiday, Touring & Camping Park
Claxton To Harton Lodge Road, Claxton, Malton YO60 7RX
t (01904) 468355
e enquiries@foxhillpark.com

CLITHEROE
Lancashire

Camping & Caravanning Club Site – The Clitheroe ★★★★
Touring & Camping Park
Edisford Road, Clitheroe BB7 3LA
t (01200) 425294
w campingandcaravanningclub.co.uk

Look out for parks participating in the National Accessible Scheme

COCKERHAM
Lancashire

Moss Wood Caravan Park ★★★★★
Holiday & Touring Park
Crimbles Lane, Cockerham LA2 0ES
t (01524) 791041
w mosswood.co.uk

COCKERMOUTH
Cumbria

Violet Bank Holiday Home Park ★★★★ ROSE AWARD
Holiday Park
Simonscales Lane, Cockermouth CA13 9TG
t (01900) 822169
e john@justsearching.co.uk
w violetbank.co.uk

CONISTON
Cumbria

Crake Valley Holiday Park ★★★★★ ROSE AWARD
Holiday Park
Lake Bank, Water Yeat, Ulverston LA12 8DL
t (01229) 885203
e crakevalley@coniston1.fslife.co.uk
w crakevalley.co.uk

Park Coppice Caravan Club Site ★★★★
Touring & Camping Park
Park Gate, Coniston LA21 8LA
t (015394) 41555
w caravanclub.co.uk

CONSTABLE BURTON
North Yorkshire

Constable Burton Hall Caravan Park ★★★★
Touring Park
Constable Burton, Leyburn DL8 5LJ
t (01677) 450428

CORBRIDGE
Northumberland

Well House Farm – Corbridge ★★★
Touring & Camping Park
Newton, Stocksfield NE43 7UY
t (01661) 842193
e info@wellhousefarm.co.uk
w wellhousefarm.co.uk

COTHERSTONE
Durham

Doe Park Caravan Site ★★★★
Touring Park
Barnard Castle DL12 9UQ
t (01833) 650302

CRASTER
Northumberland

Proctors Stead Caravan Site ★★★
Holiday, Touring & Camping Park
Dunstan Village, Alnwick NE66 3TF
t (01665) 576613

CRESSWELL
Northumberland

Cresswell Towers Holiday Park ★★★★
Holiday Park
Morpeth NE61 5JT
t 0871 664 9734
e holidaysales.cresswelltowers@park-resorts.com
w park-resorts.com

Golden Sands Holiday Park ★★★★★ ROSE AWARD
Holiday Park
Beach Road, Cresswell NE61 5LF
t (01670) 860256
e enquiries@northumbrianleisure.co.uk
w northumbrianleisure.co.uk

CROPTON
North Yorkshire

Spiers House Caravan & Camping Site
Rating Applied For
Holiday, Touring & Camping Park
Forestry Commission, Cropton, Pickering YO18 8ES
t (0131) 314 6453
e fe.holidays@forestry.gov.uk
w forestholidays.co.uk

DALTON PIERCY
Tees Valley

Ashfield Caravan Park ★★★★
Touring & Camping Park
Hartlepool TS27 3HY
t (01429) 269969
e info@ashfield-caravanpark.co.uk
w ashfield-caravanpark.co.uk

DARLINGTON
Tees Valley

Newbus Grange Country Park ★★★★
Touring & Camping Park
Hurworth Road, Neasham DL2 1PE
t (01325) 720973
e newbusgrangecp@btconnect.com
w newbusgrangecountrypark.co.uk

DELAMERE
Cheshire

Delamere Forest Camping & Caravanning Club Site ★★★★
Touring & Camping Park
Station Road, Delamere CW8 2HZ
t 0845 130 7633
w campingandcaravanningclub.co.uk

DUNNINGTON
North Yorkshire

Ashfield Caravan Park ★★★★
Touring & Camping Park
Hagg Lane, York YO19 5PE
t (01904) 489147
w ashfieldtouringcaravanpark.co.uk

DUNSTAN
Northumberland

Dunstan Hill Camping & Caravan Club ★★★★
Touring & Camping Park
Dunstan Hill, Dunstan NE66 3TQ
t (01665) 576310
w campingandcaravanningclub.co.uk

DURHAM

Finchale Abbey Caravan Park ★★★★
Touring Park
Finchale Abbey Farm, Finchale Abbey, Durham DH1 5SH
t (0191) 386 6528 & 07989 854704
e godricawatson@hotmail.com
w finchaleabbey.co.uk

Grange Caravan Club Site ★★★★★
Touring & Camping Park
Meadow Lane, Durham DH1 1TL
t (0191) 384 4778
w caravanclub.co.uk

Strawberry Hill Farm Camping & Caravanning Park ★★★★ ROSE AWARD
Holiday, Touring & Camping Park
Running Waters, Old Cassop, Durham DH6 4QA
t (0191) 372 3457
e info@strawberryhf.co.uk
w strawberry-hill-farm.co.uk

EAST ORD
Northumberland

Ord House Country Park ★★★★★
Holiday, Touring & Camping Park
East Ord, Berwick-upon-Tweed TD15 2NS
t (01289) 305288
e enquiries@ordhouse.co.uk
w ordhouse.co.uk

EBCHESTER
Durham

Byreside Caravan Site ★★★★
Touring & Camping Park
Hamsterley Colliery, Newcastle upon Tyne NE17 7RT
t (01207) 560280
w byresidecaravansite.co.uk

ESCRICK
North Yorkshire

The Hollicarrs ★★★★★
Holiday Park
Riccall Road, York YO19 6EA
t 0800 980 8070
e sales@thehollicarrs.com
w thehollicarrs.com

FARNHAM
North Yorkshire

Kingfisher Caravan & Camping Park ★★★★
Holiday, Touring & Camping Park
Low Moor Lane, Scotton, Knaresborough HG5 9JB
t (01423) 869411

FILEY
North Yorkshire

Filey Brigg Caravan & Camping Park ★★★★
Touring & Camping Park
Church Cliff Drive, North Cliff, Arndale, Filey YO14 9ET
t (01723) 513852
e fileybrigg@scarborough.gov.uk
w scarborough.gov.uk

Orchard Farm Holiday Village ★★★★★
Holiday Park
Stonegate, Hunmanby, Filey YO14 0PU
t (01723) 891582

Primrose Valley Holiday Park ★★★★★
Holiday & Touring Park
Primrose Valley, Filey YO14 9RF
t (01723) 513771
w primrosevalley-park.co.uk

FLAMBOROUGH
East Riding of Yorkshire

Thornwick & Sea Farm Holiday Centre ★★★★ ROSE AWARD
Holiday, Touring & Camping Park
North Marine Road, Flamborough, Bridlington YO15 1AU
t (01262) 850369
e enquiries@thornwickbay.co.uk
w thornwickbay.co.uk

FLEETWOOD
Lancashire

Broadwater Caravan Park
Rating Applied For
Holiday, Touring & Camping Park
Fleetwood Road, Fleetwood FY7 8JX
t (01253) 872796
e reception@broad-water.co.uk
w partingtons.com

Cala Gran ★★★★
Holiday Park
Fleetwood Road, Blackpool FY7 8JY
t (01253) 872555
e enquiries@british-holidays.co.uk
w calagran-park.co.uk

FLOOKBURGH
Cumbria

Lakeland Leisure Park ★★★★
Holiday, Touring & Camping Park
Moor Lane, Flookburgh, Grange-over-Sands LA11 7LT
t (015395) 58556
e sioned.richards@bourne-leisure.co.uk
w haven.com/lakeland

FOLLIFOOT
North Yorkshire

Great Yorkshire Showground Caravan Club ★★★★
Touring Park
Wetherby Road, Harrogate HG3 1TZ
t (01423) 560470
e enquiries@caravanclub.co.uk
w caravanclub.co.uk

FRODSHAM
Cheshire

Ridgeway Country Holiday Park ★★★★
Holiday Park
The Ridgeway, Frodsham WA6 6XQ
t (01928) 734981
e sue@ridgewaypark.com
w ridgewaypark.com

FROSTERLEY
Durham

Heatherview Leisure Park ★★★★★
Holiday Park
Park Leisure 2000, Bishop Auckland DL13 2PS
t (01388) 528728
e heatherview@parkleisure.co.uk
w heatherview.co.uk

Kingfisher Country Park ★★★★★
Holiday Park
Landieu, Bishop Auckland DL13 2SJ
t (01388) 527230
e kingfisher@parkleisure.co.uk
w kingfisherpark.co.uk

GILCRUX
Cumbria

The Beeches Caravan Park ★★★★
Holiday Park
Gilcrux, Wigton, Cockermouth CA7 2QX
t (01697) 321555
e holiday@thebeechescaravanpark.com
w thebeechescaravanpark.com

GILLING WEST
North Yorkshire

Hargill House Caravan Club Site ★★★★
Touring Park
Gilling West, Richmond DL10 5LJ
t (01342) 336732
e enquiries@caravanclub.co.uk
w caravanclub.co.uk

GRANGE-OVER-SANDS
Cumbria

Greaves Farm Caravan Park ★★★★ ROSE AWARD
Holiday & Touring Park
Field Broughton, Grange-over-Sands LA11 6HR
t (015395) 36329 & (015395) 36587

Meathop Fell Caravan Club Site ★★★★★
Touring Park
Meathop, Grange-over-Sands LA11 6RB
t (015395) 32912
w caravanclub.co.uk

GREENHEAD
Northumberland

Roam-n-Rest Caravan Park ★★★
Touring & Camping Park
Raylton House, Brampton CA8 7HA
t (01697) 747213

GRISTHORPE BAY
North Yorkshire

Blue Dolphin Holiday Park ★★★★
Holiday, Touring & Camping Park
Gristhorpe Bay, Filey YO14 9PU
t (01723) 513771
w bluedolphin-park.co.uk

HALTWHISTLE
Northumberland

Haltwhistle Camping & Caravanning Club Site ★★★★
Touring & Camping Park
Park Burnfoot Farm, Haltwhistle NE49 0JP
t (01434) 320106
w campingandcaravanningclub.co.uk

HARDEN
West Yorkshire

Harden & Bingley Holiday Park ★★★★
Holiday & Touring Park
Goit Stock Private Estate, Goit Stock Lane, Bradford BD16 1DF
t (01535) 273810
e pauldavisdunham@tiscali.co.uk
w ukparks.co.uk/harden

HARMBY
North Yorkshire

Lower Wensleydale Caravan Club Site ★★★
Touring & Camping Park
Harmby, Leyburn DL8 5NU
t (01969) 623366
e enquiries@caravanclub.co.uk
w caravanclub.co.uk

HARROGATE
North Yorkshire

High Moor Farm Park ★★★★★
Holiday & Touring Park
Skipton Road, Felliscliffe, Harrogate HG3 2LT
t (01423) 563637
e highmoorfarmpark@btconnect.com

Reynard Crag Park ★★★★
Holiday Park
Reynard Crag Lane, Burstwith, Harrogate HG3 2JQ
t (01423) 772828
e reynardcrag@btconnect.com
w reynardcragpark.co.uk

Ripley Caravan Park ★★★★★
Holiday, Touring & Camping Park
Knaresborough Road, Ripley, Knaresborough HG3 3AU
t (01423) 770050

Rudding Holiday Park ★★★★★ ROSE AWARD
Holiday, Touring & Camping Park
Follifoot, Harrogate HG3 1JH
t (01423) 870439
e holiday-park@ruddingpark.com
w ruddingpark.com

Warren Forest Caravan Park ★★★★★
Holiday Park
Warsill, Harrogate HG3 3LH
t (01765) 620683
e enquiries@warrenforestpark.co.uk
w warrenforestpark.co.uk

HAWES
North Yorkshire

Bainbridge Ings Caravan and Camping Site ★★★
Holiday, Touring & Camping Park
Hawes DL8 3NU
t (01969) 667354
e janet@bainbridge-ings.co.uk
w bainbridge-ings.co.uk

Honeycott Caravan Park ★★★★
Holiday Park
Ingleton Road, Hawes DL8 3LH
t (01969) 667310
e info@honeycott.co.uk
w honeycott.co.uk

HAWKSHEAD
Cumbria

The Croft Caravan and Camp Site ★★★★
Holiday, Touring & Camping Park
North Lonsdale Road, Hawkshead, Ambleside LA22 0NX
t (015394) 36374
e enquiries@hawkshead-croft.com
w hawkshead-croft.com

HAWORTH
West Yorkshire

Upwood Holiday Park ★★★★
Holiday, Touring & Camping Park
Blackmoor Road, Oxenhope, Haworth, Keighley BD22 9SS
t (01535) 644242
e info@upwoodpark.co.uk
w upwoodpark.co.uk

HAYDON BRIDGE
Northumberland

Poplars Riverside Caravan Park ★★★★
Holiday, Touring & Camping Park
East Lands Ends, Haydon Bridge, Hexham NE47 6BY
t (01434) 684427

HEBDEN BRIDGE
West Yorkshire

Lower Clough Foot Caravan Club Site ★★★★★
Touring Park
Cragg Vale, Hebden Bridge HX7 5RU
t (01422) 882531
w caravanclub.co.uk

HELMSLEY
North Yorkshire

Foxholme Touring Caravan Park ★★★★★
Touring & Camping Park
Harome, Helmsley YO62 5JG
t (01439) 770416

Golden Square Caravan & Camping Park ★★★★★
Touring & Camping Park
Oswaldkirk, Helmsley YO62 5YQ
t (01439) 788269
e barbara@goldensquarecaravanpark.freeserve.co.uk
w goldensquarecaravanpark.com

HEXHAM
Northumberland

Fallowfield Dene Caravan and Camping Park ★★★★
Touring & Camping Park
Acomb, Hexham NE46 4RP
t (01434) 603553
e den@fallowfielddene.co.uk
w fallowfielddene.co.uk

Heathergate Country Park ★★★★★
Holiday Park
Lowgate, Hexham NE46 2NN
t (01434) 609030
e info@heathergate.co.uk
w heathergate.co.uk

Hexham Racecourse Caravan Site ★★★
Touring & Camping Park
Yarridge Road, High Yarridge, Hexham NE46 2JP
t (01434) 606847
e hexrace@aol.com
w hexham-racecourse.co.uk

HEYSHAM
Lancashire

Ocean Edge Leisure Park ★★★
Holiday, Touring & Camping Park
Moneyclose Lane, Morecambe LA3 2XA
t 0870 774 4024
e enquiries@southlakelandparks.co.uk
w southlakelandparks.co.uk

Look out for parks participating in the National Accessible Scheme

HIGH BENTHAM
North Yorkshire

Riverside Caravan Park ★★★★★
Holiday, Touring & Camping Park
Wenning Avenue, Lancaster LA2 7LW
t (01524) 261272
e info@riversidecaravanpark.co.uk
w riversidecaravanpark.co.uk

HINDERWELL
North Yorkshire

Serenity Touring Caravan & Camping Park ★★★★
Touring & Camping Park
Saltburn-by-the-Sea TS13 5JH
t (01947) 841122

HOLMFIRTH
West Yorkshire

Holme Valley Camping and Caravan Park ★★★★
Touring & Camping Park
Thongsbridge, Holmfirth HD9 7TD
t (01484) 665819
e enquiries@holmevalleycamping.com
w holmevalleycamping.com

HOLMROOK
Cumbria

Seven Acres Caravan Park ★★★
Holiday, Touring & Camping Park
Holmrook, Ravenglass, St Bees CA19 1YD
t (01946) 822777
e reception@seacote.com
w sevenacrespark.co.uk

HORNSEA
East Riding of Yorkshire

Longbeach Leisure Park
Rating Applied For
Holiday, Touring & Camping Park
South Cliff, Hornsea HU18 1TL
t (01964) 532506
w longbeach-leisure.co.uk

HUTTON-LE-HOLE
North Yorkshire

Hutton le Hole Caravan Park ★★★★
Touring & Camping Park
Westfield Lodge, Hutton-le-Hole, Kirkbymoorside YO62 6UG
t (01751) 417261
e rwstrickland@farmersweekly.net
w westfieldlodge.co.uk

INGLETON
North Yorkshire

Parkfoot Holiday Homes ★★★★★
Holiday Park
Bentham Road, Carnforth LA6 3HR
t (01524) 261833
e parkfoot.ingleton@virgin.net
w parkfoot.co.uk

KEARBY WITH NETHERBY
North Yorkshire

Maustin Park ★★★★★ **ROSE AWARD**
Holiday, Touring & Camping Park
Wharfe Lane, Kearby, Wetherby LS22 4DA
t (0113) 288 6234
e info@maustin.co.uk
w maustin.co.uk

KENDAL
Cumbria

Camping & Caravanning Club Site – Kendal ★★★★
Touring Park
Millcrest, Shap Road, Kendal LA9 6NY
t 0845 130 7633
w campingandcaravanningclub.co.uk

Low Park Wood Caravan Club Site ★★★★
Touring Park
Sedgwick, Kendal LA8 0JZ
t (015395) 60186
e enquiries@caravanclub.co.uk
w caravanclub.co.uk

Waters Edge Caravan Park ★★★★
Holiday, Touring & Camping Park
Crooklands, Milnthorpe LA7 7NN
t (015395) 67708
w watersedgecaravanpark.co.uk

KESWICK
Cumbria

Camping & Caravanning Club Site – Derwentwater ★★★
Holiday & Touring Park
Crow Park Road, Keswick CA12 5EN
t 0845 130 7633
w campingandcaravanningclub.co.uk

Camping & Caravanning Club Site – Keswick ★★★
Touring & Camping Park
Crow Park Road, Keswick CA12 5EP
t 0845 130 7633
w campingandcaravanningclub.co.uk

Castlerigg Farm Camping and Caravan Site ★★★★
Touring & Camping Park
Castlerigg, Keswick CA12 4TE
t (017687) 72479
e info@castleriggfarm.com
w castleriggfarm.com

Castlerigg Hall Caravan & Camping Park ★★★★
Holiday, Touring & Camping Park
Castlerigg Hall, Keswick CA12 4TE
t (017687) 74499
e info@castlerigg.co.uk
w castlerigg.co.uk

Low Briery Holiday Village ★★★★ **ROSE AWARD**
Holiday Park
Penrith Road, Keswick CA12 4RN
t (017687) 72044
e lowbriery@wyrenet.co.uk
w keswick.uk.com

Scotgate Holiday Park ★★★
Holiday, Touring & Camping Park
Braithwaite, Keswick CA12 5TF
t (017687) 78343
e info@scotgateholidaypark.co.uk
w scotgateholidaypark.co.uk

KIRKBY LONSDALE
Cumbria

Woodclose Caravan Park ★★★★★
Holiday, Touring & Camping Park
Kirkby Lonsdale LA6 2SE
t (01524) 271597
e info@woodclosepark.com
w woodclosepark.com

KIRKBY STEPHEN
Cumbria

Pennine View Caravan Park ★★★★★
Touring & Camping Park
Station Road, Kirkby Stephen CA17 4SZ
t (017683) 71717

KIRKHAM
Lancashire

Mowbreck Holiday & Residential Park ★★★★★
Holiday Park
Mowbreck Lane, Wesham PR4 3HA
t (01772) 682494
e info@mowbreckpark.co.uk
w mowbreckpark.co.uk

KNARESBOROUGH
North Yorkshire

Knaresborough Caravan Club Site ★★★★★
Touring Park
New Road, Scotton, Knaresborough HG5 9HH
t (01342) 336732
w caravanclub.co.uk

LAMPLUGH
Cumbria

Dockray Meadow Caravan Club Site ★★★★
Touring Park
Lamplugh CA14 4SH
t (01946) 861357
w caravanclub.co.uk

Inglenook Caravan Park ★★★★
Holiday, Touring & Camping Park
Lamplugh, Workington CA14 4SH
t (01946) 861240

LANCASTER
Lancashire

New Parkside Farm Caravan Park ★★★
Touring & Camping Park
Denny Beck, Caton Road LA2 9HH
t (01524) 770723

Wyreside Lakes Fishery ★★★★
Touring & Camping Park
Sunnyside Farmhouse, Gleaves Hill Road, Lancaster LA2 9DG
t (01524) 792093
e wyreside2003@yahoo.co.uk
w wyresidelakes.co.uk

LANGTHORPE
North Yorkshire

Old Hall Holiday Park ★★★★
Holiday & Touring Park
Skelton Road, Langthorpe, Boroughbridge, Harrogate YO51 9BZ
t (01423) 323190
e phil.brierley@which.net
w yhcparks.info

LARTINGTON
Durham

Camping & Caravanning Club Site – Barnard Castle ★★★★★
Touring & Camping Park
Dockenflats Lane, Barnard Castle DL12 9DG
t (01833) 630228
w campingandcaravanningclub.co.uk

LEEDS
West Yorkshire

St Helena's Caravan Site ★★★★
Holiday, Touring & Camping Park
Otley Old Road, Leeds LS18 5HZ
t (0113) 284 1142

LITTLE WEIGHTON
East Riding of Yorkshire

Croft Park ★★★★★
Touring & Camping Park
55 Rowley Road, Little Weighton, Beverley HU20 3XJ
t (01482) 840600
e steve@croftpark.fsnet.co.uk
w croftpark.net

LOFTHOUSE
North Yorkshire

Studfold Farm Caravan and Camping Park ★★★★
Touring & Camping Park
Studfold Farm, Lofthouse, Pateley Bridge HG3 5SG
t (01423) 755084
e ianwalker@studfold.fsnet.co.uk
w studfoldfarm.co.uk

LONG PRESTON
North Yorkshire

Gallaber Park ★★★★
Holiday & Touring Park
Long Preston, Settle BD23 4QF
t (01729) 851397
e info@gallaberpark.com
w gallaberpark.com

LONGHORSLEY Northumberland

Forget-Me-Not Holiday Park ★★★★
Holiday, Touring & Camping Park
Croftside, Morpeth NE65 8QY
t (01670) 788364
e info@forget-me-notholidaypark.co.uk
w forget-me-notholidaypark.co.uk

LONGRIDGE Lancashire

Beacon Fell View ★★★
Holiday, Touring & Camping Park
110 Higher Road, Longridge PR3 2TF
t (01772) 783233
e info@hagansleisure.co.uk
w hagansleisure.co.uk

LOUGHRIGG Cumbria

Neaum Crag ★★★★★
Holiday Park
Loughrigg, Ambleside LA22 9HG
t (015394) 33221
e neaumcrag@ktdbroadband.com
w neaumcrag.co.uk

LYTHAM ST ANNES Lancashire

Eastham Hall Caravan Park ★★★★
Holiday & Touring Park
Saltcotes Road, Blackpool FY8 4LS
t (01253) 737907
e ehcplytham@aol.com
w ukparks.co.uk/easthamhall

MALTON North Yorkshire

Wolds Way Caravan & Camping ★★★★
Touring & Camping Park
West Farm, West Knapton, Malton YO17 8JE
t (01944) 728463
e knapton.wold.farms@farming.co.uk
w ryedalesbest.co.uk

MARKINGTON North Yorkshire

Yorkshire Hussar Inn & Caravan Park ★★★★
Holiday, Touring & Camping Park
J S Brayshaw Caravans Ltd, High Street, Markington, Nr Harrogate HG3 3NR
t (01765) 677327
e yorkshirehussar@yahoo.co.uk
w yorkshire-hussar-inn.co.uk

MARSDEN West Yorkshire

Standedge Caravan & Campsite ★★★
Touring & Camping Park
The Carriage House, Manchester Road, Marsden HD7 6NL
t (01484) 844419
e info@carriage-house.co.uk
w carriage-house.co.uk

MASHAM North Yorkshire

Black Swan Holiday Park ★★★★
Holiday, Touring & Camping Park
Rear Black Swan Hotel, Masham HG4 4NF
t (01765) 689477
e info@blackswanholiday.co.uk
w blackswanholiday.co.uk

MELKRIDGE Northumberland

Hadrian's Wall Caravan & Camping Site ★★★
Touring & Camping Park
Melkridge Tilery, Haltwhistle NE49 9PG
t (01434) 320495
e info@romanwallcamping.co.uk
w romanwallcamping.co.uk

MILNTHORPE Cumbria

Fell End Caravan Park ★★★★★
Holiday, Touring & Camping Park
Slack Head Road, Hale, Milnthorpe LA7 7BS
t (01524) 781918
e enquiries@pureleisuregroup.com
w fellendcaravanpark.co.uk

MORECAMBE Lancashire

Regent Leisure Park ★★★★
Holiday Park
Westgate, Morecambe LA3 3DF
t 0870 774 4024
e enquiries@southlakelandparks.co.uk
w southlakelandparks.co.uk

Venture Caravan Park ★★★★
Holiday, Touring & Camping Park
Langridge Way, Westgate LA4 4TQ
t (01524) 412986
e mark@venturecaravanpark.co.uk
w venturecaravanpark.co.uk

Westgate Caravan Park ★★★★
Holiday & Touring Park
Westgate, Morecambe LA3 3DE
t (01524) 411448
w westgatecaravanpark.co.uk/

NAWTON North Yorkshire

Wrens of Ryedale Caravan & Camp Site ★★★★
Touring & Camping Park
Gale Lane, Nawton, York YO62 7SD
t (01439) 771260
e dave@wrensofryedale.fsnet.co.uk
w wrensofryedale.co.uk

NETHER KELLET Lancashire

The Hawthorns Caravan Park ★★★★★
Holiday Park
Nether Kellet, Carnforth LA6 1EA
t (01524) 732079
w hawthornscaravanpark.co.uk

NEW HUTTON Cumbria

Ashes Exclusively Adult Caravan Park ★★★★★
Touring Park
New Hutton, Kendal LA8 0AS
t (01539) 731833
e info@ashescaravanpark.co.uk
w ashescaravanpark.co.uk

NEWBIGGIN-BY-THE-SEA Northumberland

Church Point Holiday Park ★★★★
Holiday Park
High Street, Newbiggin-by-the-Sea NE64 6DP
t (01670) 817443
e holidaysales.churchpoint@park-resorts.com
w park-resorts.com

NEWBY BRIDGE Cumbria

Newby Bridge Country Caravan Park ★★★★★
ROSE AWARD
Holiday Park
Canny Hill, Newby Bridge LA12 8NF
t (015395) 31030
e info@cumbriancaravans.co.uk
w cumbriancaravans.co.uk

NEWLANDS Cumbria

Low Manesty Caravan Club Site ★★★★
Touring Park
Manesty, Keswick CA12 5UG
t (017687) 77275
e enquiries@caravanclub.co.uk
w caravanclub.co.uk

NEWTON-LE-WILLOWS North Yorkshire

Lindale Holiday Park – Dell Lodges ★★★★
ROSE AWARD
Holiday Park
Lindale Holiday Park Luxury Pine Lodge, Bedale DL8 1TA
t (01677) 450842
e info@lindalepark.co.uk
w lindalepark.co.uk

NORTH SEATON Northumberland

Sandy Bay Holiday Park ★★★
Holiday & Touring Park
Ashington NE63 9YD
t 0871 664 9764
e holidaysales.sandybay@park-resorts.com
w park-resorts.com

NORTHALLERTON North Yorkshire

Cote Ghyll Caravan & Camping Park ★★★★★
ROSE AWARD
Holiday, Touring & Camping Park
Osmotherley, Northallerton DL6 3AH
t (01609) 883425
e hills@coteghyll.com
w coteghyll.com

NOSTELL West Yorkshire

Nostell Priory Holiday Home Park ★★★★★
Holiday, Touring & Camping Park
Nostell Priory Estate, Wakefield WF4 1QE
t (01924) 863938
e info@nostellprioryholidaypark.co.uk
w nostellprioryholidaypark.co.uk

ORTON Cumbria

Westmorland Touring & Caravan Park ★★★★
Holiday & Touring Park
Orton, Penrith CA10 3SB
t (01539) 711322
e caravans@westmorland.com
w westmorland.com

OTTERBURN Northumberland

Border Forest Caravan Park
Rating Applied For
Holiday, Touring & Camping Park
Cottonshopeburnfoot, Newcastle-upon-Tyne NE19 1TF
t (01830) 520259
e borderforest@btinternet.com
w borderforestcaravanpark.co.uk

Look out for parks participating in the National Accessible Scheme

OVINGHAM
Northumberland

The High Hermitage Caravan Park ★★★
Holiday, Touring & Camping Park
The Hermitage, Main Road, Prudhoe NE42 6HH
t (01661) 832250
e highhermitage@onetel.com
w highhermitagecaravanpark.co.uk

PATRINGTON
East Riding of Yorkshire

Patrington Haven Leisure Park ★★★★★
Holiday Park
Patrington Haven, Hull HU12 0PT
t (01964) 630071
e guy@phlp.co.uk
w phlp.co.uk

PAYTHORNE
Lancashire

Twynghyll Leisure Park ★★★★
Holiday Park
Gisburn BB7 4JD
t (01200) 445465
e twynghll@parkleisure.co.uk
w twynghyll.co.uk

PENRITH
Cumbria

Flusco Wood Caravan Park ★★★★★
Holiday & Touring Park
Flusco, Penrith CA11 0JB
t (017684) 80020
e admin@fluscowood.co.uk
w fluscowood.co.uk

Lowther Holiday Park ★★★★★
Holiday, Touring & Camping Park
Eamont Bridge, Penrith CA10 2JB
t (01768) 863631
e info@lowther-holidaypark.co.uk
w lowther-holidaypark.co.uk

Troutbeck Head Caravan Club Site ★★★★★
Holiday, Touring & Camping Park
Troutbeck, Penrith CA11 0SS
t (017684) 83521
e enquiries@caravanclub.co.uk
w caravanclub.co.uk

PICKERING
North Yorkshire

Wayside Caravan Park ★★★★
Holiday, Touring & Camping Park
Pickering YO18 8PG
t (01751) 472608
e waysideparks@freenet.co.uk
w waysideparks.co.uk

PLANTATION BRIDGE
Cumbria

Camping & Caravanning Club Site – Windermere ★★★★★
Holiday, Touring & Camping Park
Ashes Lane, Staveley, Windermere LA8 9JS
t 0845 130 7633
w campingandcaravanningclub.co.uk

POCKLINGTON
East Riding of Yorkshire

South Lea Caravan Park ★★★★
Touring & Camping Park
The Balk, York YO42 2NX
t (01759) 303467
e southlea@fsmail.net
w south-lea.co.uk

POOLEY BRIDGE
Cumbria

Waterside House Campsite ★★★★
Camping Park
Waterside House, Howtown, Penrith CA10 2NA
t (017684) 86332
e enquire@watersidefarm-campsite.co.uk
w watersidefarm-campsite.co.uk

POULTON-LE-FYLDE
Lancashire

Poulton Plaiz Holiday Park ★★★★
Holiday, Touring & Camping Park
Garstang Road West, Poulton-le-Fylde FY6 8AR
t (01253) 888930
e info@poultonplaiz.co.uk

POWBURN
Northumberland

River Breamish Caravan Club Site ★★★★★
Touring & Camping Park
Powburn, Alnwick NE66 4HY
t (01665) 578320
w caravanclub.co.uk

RAMSHAW
Durham

Craggwood Caravan Park ★★★
Holiday & Touring Park
Gordon Lane, Ramshaw DL14 0NS
t (01388) 835866
e billy6482@btopenworld.com
w craggwoodcaravanpark.co.uk

RAVENGLASS
Cumbria

Camping & Caravanning Club Site – Ravenglass ★★★★
Touring & Camping Park
Ravenglass, Cumbria, Ravenglass CA18 1SR
t (01229) 717250
w campingandcaravanningclub.co.uk

REIGHTON GAP
North Yorkshire

Reighton Sands Holiday Park ★★★
Holiday, Touring & Camping Park
Reighton Gap, Filey YO14 9SJ
t (01723) 513771
w reightonsands-park.co.uk

RIMINGTON
Lancashire

Rimington Caravan Park ★★★★★
Holiday & Touring Park
Hardacre Lane, Gisburn, Nr Clitheroe BB7 4EE
t (01200) 445355
e rimingtoncaravanpark@btinternet.com
w rimingtoncaravanpark.co.uk

RIPON
North Yorkshire

River Laver Holiday Park ★★★★★
Holiday & Touring Park
Studley Road, Ripon HG4 2QR
t (01765) 690508
e riverlaver@lineone.net
w riverlaver.co.uk

Sleningford Watermill Caravan & Camping Park ★★★★★
Touring & Camping Park
North Stainley, Ripon HG4 3HQ
t (01765) 635201
e sleningford@hotmail.co.uk
w sleningfordwatermill.co.uk

Woodhouse Farm Caravan & Camping Park ★★★★
Holiday, Touring & Camping Park
Winksley, Ripon HG4 3PG
t (01765) 658309
e woodhouse.farm@talk21.com
w woodhousewinksley.com

ROCHDALE
Greater Manchester

Gelder Wood Country Park ★★★★★
Touring & Camping Park
Oak Leigh Cottage, Ashworth Road, Rochdale OL11 5UP
t (01706) 364858
e gelderwood@aol.com

Hollingworth Lake Caravan Park ★★★
Holiday, Touring & Camping Park
Roundhouse Farm, Hollingworth Lake, Littleborough OL15 0AT
t (01706) 378661

ROECLIFFE
North Yorkshire

Camping & Caravanning Club Site – Boroughbridge ★★★★★
Touring & Camping Park
Bar Lane, Roecliffe, Harrogate YO51 9LS
t (01423) 322683
w campingandcaravanningclub.co.uk

ROOS
East Riding of Yorkshire

Sand-le-Mere Caravan & Leisure Park ★★★★ ROSE AWARD
Holiday & Touring Park
Seaside Lane, Tunstall HU12 0JQ
t (01964) 670403
e info@sand-le-mere.co.uk
w sand-le-mere.co.uk

ROTHBURY
Northumberland

Coquetdale Caravan Park ★★★
Holiday & Touring Park
Whitton, Morpeth NE65 7RU
t (01669) 620549
e enquiry@coquetdalecaravanpark.co.uk
w coquetdalecaravanpark.co.uk

Nunnykirk Caravan Club Site ★★★★
Touring Park
Nunnykirk Caravan Park, Nunnykirk NE61 4PZ
t (01669) 620762
e enquiries@caravanclub.co.uk
w caravanclub.co.uk

RUDSTON
East Riding of Yorkshire

Thorpe Hall Caravan & Camping Site ★★★★
Touring & Camping Park
Thorpe Hall, Rudston, Driffield YO25 4JE
t (01262) 420393
e caravansite@thorpehall.co.uk
w thorpehall.co.uk

ST BEES
Cumbria

Seacote Park ★★★★ ROSE AWARD
Holiday, Touring & Camping Park
The Beach, St Bees CA27 0ET
t (01946) 822777
e reception@seacote.com
w seacote.com

ST MICHAEL'S ON WYRE
Lancashire

Wyreside Farm Park ★★★
Holiday, Touring & Camping Park
Allotment Lane, St Michaels PR3 0TZ
t (01995) 679797
e penny.wyresidefarm@freenet.co.uk
w riverparks.co.uk

SALTWICK BAY
North Yorkshire

Whitby Holiday Park – Touring Park ★★★★
Holiday & Touring Park
Whitby Holiday Park, Saltwick Bay, Whitby YO22 4JX
t (01947) 602664
e info@whitbyholidaypark.co.uk
w whitbypark.co.uk

SCARBOROUGH
North Yorkshire

Browns Caravan Park ★★★★★
Holiday & Touring Park
Mill Lane, Cayton Bay, Scarborough YO11 3NN
t (01723) 582303
e info@brownscaravan.co.uk
w brownscaravan.co.uk

Camping & Caravanning Club Site – Scarborough ★★★★★
Touring Park
Field Lane, Burniston Road, Scarborough YO13 0DA
t (01423) 322683
w campingandcaravanningclub.co.uk

Cayton Village Caravan Park ★★★★★
Touring & Camping Park
Mill Lane, Cayton Bay, Scarborough YO11 3NN
t (01723) 583171
e info@caytontouring.co.uk
w caytontouring.co.uk

Crows Nest Caravan Park ★★★★ ROSE AWARD
Holiday Park
Gristhorpe, Filey YO14 9PS
t (01723) 582206
e enquiries@crowsnestcaravanpark.com
w crowsnestcaravanpark.com

Flower of May Holiday Parks Ltd ★★★★★ ROSE AWARD
Holiday, Touring & Camping Park
Lebberston, Scarborough YO11 3NU
t (01723) 584311
e info@flowerofmay.com
w flowerofmay.com

Jasmine Park ★★★★★
Holiday, Touring & Camping Park
Cross Lane, Snainton, Scarborough YO13 9BE
t (01723) 859240
e enquiries@jasminepark.co.uk
w jasminepark.co.uk

Lebberston Touring Park ★★★★★
Touring Park
Lebberston, Scarborough YO11 3PE
t (01723) 585723
e info@lebberstontouring.co.uk
w lebberstontouring.co.uk

Scalby Close Park ★★★★ ROSE AWARD
Holiday, Touring & Camping Park
Burniston Road, Scarborough YO13 0DA
t (01723) 365908

SCARISBRICK
Lancashire

Hurlston Hall Country Caravan Park ★★★★
Holiday & Touring Park
Hurlston Lane, Scarisbrick L40 8HB
t (01704) 841064

SEAHOUSES
Northumberland

Seafield Caravan Park ★★★★★ ROSE AWARD
Holiday & Touring Park
Enjoy England Awards for Excellence Winner
Seafield Road, Seahouses NE68 7SP
t (01665) 720628
e info@seafieldpark.co.uk
w seafieldpark.co.uk

Springhill Farm Holiday Accomodation
Rating Applied For
Holiday, Touring & Camping Park
Springhill Farmhouses, Seahouses NE68 7UR
t (01665) 721820
e enquiries@springhill-farm.co.uk
w springhill-farm.co.uk

SETTLE
North Yorkshire

Langcliffe Park ★★★★
Holiday, Touring & Camping Park
Settle BD24 9LX
t (01729) 822387
e info@langcliffe.com
w langcliffe.com

SHERIFF HUTTON
North Yorkshire

Camping & Caravanning Club Site – Sheriff ★★★★
Touring & Camping Park
Bracken Hill, Sheriff Hutton, Malton YO60 6QG
t (01347) 878660
e info@campingandcaravanningclub.co.uk
w campingandcaravanningclub.co.uk

SILLOTH
Cumbria

Seacote Caravan Park ★★★★
Holiday & Touring Park
Skinburness Road, Silloth CA7 4QJ
t (01697) 331121
e seacote@bfcltd.co.uk
w seacotecaravanpark.co.uk

Solway Holiday Village ★★
Holiday, Touring & Camping Park
Skinburness Drive, Silloth CA7 4QQ
t (01697) 331236
e solway@hagansleisure.co.uk
w hagansleisure.co.uk

Stanwix Park Holiday Centre ★★★★★ ROSE AWARD
Holiday, Touring & Camping Park
Greenrow, Silloth CA7 4HH
t (01697) 332666
e enquiries@stanwix.com
w stanwix.com

Tanglewood Caravan Park ★★★
Holiday, Touring & Camping Park
Causewayhead, Silloth CA7 4PE
t (01697) 331253
e tanglewoodcaravanpark@hotmail.com
w tanglewoodcaravanpark.co.uk

SILVERDALE
Lancashire

Far Arnside Caravan Park ★★★★★
Holiday Park
Holgates Caravan Parks, Middlebarrow Plain, Carnforth LA5 0SH
t (01524) 701508
e caravan@holgates.co.uk
w holgates.co.uk

Holgates Caravan Park ★★★★★ ROSE AWARD
Holiday, Touring & Camping Park
Cove Road, Silverdale, Carnforth LA5 0SH
t (01524) 701508
e caravan@holgates.co.uk
w holgates.co.uk

SKIPSEA
East Riding of Yorkshire

Far Grange Park ★★★★★
Holiday Park
Hornsea Road, Driffield YO25 8SY
t (01262) 468010
e andy.such@bourne-leisure.co.uk
w fargrangepark.co.uk

Skipsea Sands Holiday Village ★★★★ ROSE AWARD
Holiday, Touring & Camping Park
Mill Lane, Skipsea, Hornsea YO25 8TZ
t (01262) 468210
e info@skipseasands.co.uk
w hoseasons.co.uk

Skirlington Leisure Park ★★★★★ ROSE AWARD
Holiday, Touring & Camping Park
Hornsea Road, Skipsea, Hornsea YO25 8SY
t (01262) 468213
e enquiries@skirlington.com
w skirlington.com

SKIRLAUGH
East Riding of Yorkshire

Burton Constable Holiday Park&Arboretum ★★★★★
Holiday, Touring & Camping Park
The Old Lodges, Sproatley, Hornsea HU11 4LN
t (01964) 562508
e info@burtonconstable.co.uk
w burtonconstable.co.uk

SLINGSBY
North Yorkshire

Robin Hood Caravan & Camping Park ★★★★★ ROSE AWARD
Holiday, Touring & Camping Park
Green Dyke Lane, Slingsby, York YO62 4AP
t (01653) 628391
e info@robinhoodcaravanpark.co.uk
w robinhoodcaravanpark.co.uk

Slingsby Camping & Caravanning Club ★★★★★
Touring & Camping Park
Railway Street, York, Malton YO62 4AA
t (01653) 628335
w campingandcaravanningclub.co.uk

SNEATON
North Yorkshire

Low Moor Caravan Club Site ★★★★
Touring Park
Sneaton, Whitby YO22 5JE
t (01947) 810505
e enquiries@caravanclub.co.uk
w caravanclub.co.uk

STAINFORTH
North Yorkshire

Knight Stainforth Hall Caravan & Camping ★★★★
Holiday, Touring & Camping Park
Little Stainforth, Settle BD24 0DP
t (01729) 822200
e info@knightstainforth.co.uk
w knightstainforth.co.uk

STIRTON
North Yorkshire

Tarn House Caravan Park
Rating Applied For
Holiday, Touring & Camping Park
Stirton BD23 3LQ
t (01756) 795309
w partingtons.com

STOCKTON-ON-TEES
Tees Valley

White Water Caravan Club Park ★★★★★
Touring & Camping Park
Tees Barrage, Stockton-on-Tees TS18 2QW
t (01642) 634880
w caravanclub.co.uk

Look out for parks participating in the National Accessible Scheme

STONEHAUGH
Northumberland

Stonehaugh Campsite ★★
Touring & Camping Park
The Old Farmhouse, Stonehaugh Shields NE48 3BU
t (01434) 230798
e carole.townsend@btconnect.com
w stonehaugh.fsbusiness.co.uk

STRENSALL
North Yorkshire

Moorside Caravan Park ★★★★
Touring Park
Lords Moor Lane, Strensall, York YO32 5XJ
t (01904) 491208
w moorsidecaravanpark.co.uk

THIRSK
North Yorkshire

Thirsk Racecourse Caravan Club Site ★★
Touring & Camping Park
Thirsk Racecourse, Station Road, Thirsk YO7 1QL
t (01845) 525266
e enquiries@caravanclub.co.uk
w caravanclub.co.uk

York House Caravan Park ★★★★
Holiday, Touring & Camping Park
Balk, Thirsk YO7 2AQ
t (01423) 323190
e phil.brierley@which.net
w yhcparks.info

THORNE
South Yorkshire

Elder House Touring Park ★★★★
Touring Park
Sandtoft Road, Thorne Levels, Doncaster DN8 5TD
t (01405) 813173

THORNTON DALE
North Yorkshire

Overbrook Caravan Park ★★★★
Touring Park
Maltongate, Pickering YO18 7SE
t (01751) 474417
w overbrookcaravanpark.co.uk

THRESHFIELD
North Yorkshire

Long Ashes Park ★★★★
Holiday Park
Threshfield, Skipton-on-Swale BD23 5PN
t (01756) 752261
e info@longashespark.co.uk
w longashespark.co.uk

Wood Nook Caravan Park ★★★★
Holiday, Touring & Camping Park
Skirethorns, Threshfield, Skipton BD23 5NU
t (01756) 752412
e enquiries@woodnook.net
w woodnook.net

THURSTASTON
Merseyside

Wirral Country Park Caravan Club Site ★★★★
Touring & Camping Park
Station Road, Thurstaston CH61 0HN
t (0151) 648 5228
e enquiries@caravanclub.co.uk
w caravanclub.co.uk

TOSSIDE
Lancashire

Crowtrees Park ★★★★★ **ROSE AWARD**
Holiday Park
Tosside, Skipton BD23 4SD
t (01729) 840278
e hol@crowtreespark.co.uk
w crowtreespark.co.uk

TROUTBECK
Cumbria

Camping & Caravanning Club Site – Troutbeck ★★★★
Holiday, Touring & Camping Park
Hutton Moor End, Troutbeck, Penrith CA11 0SX
t (017687) 79615
e troutbeck@campingandcaravanningclub.co.uk
w campingandcaravanningclub.co.uk

ULLSWATER
Cumbria

Quiet Site Caravan Park ★★★★★
Holiday, Touring & Camping Park
Ullswater, Penrith CA11 0LS
t 07768 727016
e info@thequietsite.fsnet.co.uk
w thequietsite.co.uk

Waterfoot Caravan Park ★★★★★
Holiday & Touring Park
Pooley Bridge, Penrith CA11 0JF
t (017684) 86302
e enquiries@waterfootpark.co.uk
w waterfootpark.co.uk

ULVERSTON
Cumbria

Bardsea Leisure Park ★★★★
Holiday & Touring Park
Priory Road, Ulverston LA12 9QE
t (01229) 584712

WASDALE
Cumbria

Church Stile Holiday Park ★★★★
Holiday, Touring & Camping Park
Church Stile Farm, Wasdale CA20 1ET
t (01946) 726252
e churchstile@campfarm.fsnet.co.uk
w churchstile.com

WEST BRADFORD
Lancashire

Three Rivers Woodland Park ★★★
Holiday, Touring & Camping Park
Eaves Hall Lane, West Bradford, Clitheroe BB7 3JG
t (01200) 423523
w threeriverspark.co.uk

WHINFELL
Cumbria

Center Parcs Whinfell Forest ★★★★★
Forest Holiday Village
Penrith CA10 2DW
t 0870 067 3030
w centerparcs.co.uk/villages/whinfell/index.jsp

WHITBY
North Yorkshire

Flask Holiday Home Park ★★★★ **ROSE AWARD**
Holiday Park
Robin Hood's Bay, Fylingdales, Whitby YO22 4QH
t (01947) 880592
e info@flaskinn.com
w flaskinn.com

High Straggleton Farm Caravan Site ★★
Holiday & Camping Park
High Straggleton Farm, Sandsend Road, Whitby YO21 3SR
t (01947) 602373
e derekatkinson@farmersweekly.net
w highstraggleton.co.uk

Ladycross Plantation Caravan Park ★★★★★
Touring & Camping Park
Whitby YO21 1UA
t (01947) 895502
e enquiries@ladycrossplantation.co.uk
w ladycrossplantation.co.uk

Middlewood Farm Holiday Park ★★★★★ **ROSE AWARD**
Holiday, Touring & Camping Park
Middlewood Lane, Fylingthorpe, Robin Hood's Bay, Whitby YO22 4UF
t (01947) 880414
e info@middlewoodfarm.com
w middlewoodfarm.com

Northcliffe & Seaview Holiday Parks ★★★★★
Holiday & Touring Park
Bottoms Lane, High Hawsker, Whitby YO22 4LL
t (01947) 880477
e enquiries@northcliffe-seaview.com
w northcliffe-seaview.com

Partridge Nest Farm Holiday Caravans ★★★
Holiday Park
Eskdaleside, Sleights, Whitby YO22 5ES
t (01947) 810450
e barbara@partridgenestfarm.com
w partridgenestfarm.com

Sandfield House Farm Caravan Park ★★★★★
Touring Park
Sandsend Road, Whitby YO21 3SR
t (01947) 602660
e info@sandfieldhousefarm.co.uk
w sandfieldhousefarm.co.uk

WHITEGATE
Cheshire

Lamb Cottage Caravan Park ★★★★★
Holiday & Touring Park
Dalefords Lane, Whitegate CW8 2BN
t (01606) 882302
w lambcottage.co.uk

WHITLEY BAY
Tyne and Wear

Whitley Bay Holiday Park ★★★★
Holiday Park
The Links, Newcastle-upon-Tyne NE16 4BR
t 0871 664 9800
e holidaysales.whitleybay@park-resorts.com
w park-resorts.com

WILSTHORPE
East Riding of Yorkshire

The White House Caravan Park ★★★★★
Holiday Park
Wilsthorpe, Bridlington YO15 3QN
t (01262) 673894

WINDERMERE
Cumbria

Braithwaite Fold Caravan Club Site ★★★★
Touring Park
Glebe Road, Bowness-on-Windermere, Windermere LA23 3HB
t (015394) 42177
e enquiries@caravanclub.co.uk
w caravanclub.co.uk

Fallbarrow Park ★★★★★ ROSE AWARD
Holiday & Touring Park
Rayrigg Road, Bowness-on-Windermere, Windermere LA23 3DL
t (015395) 69835
w southlakelandparks.co.uk

Hill of Oaks and Blakeholme Caravans ★★★★★
Holiday & Touring Park
Newby Bridge, Nr Ulverston LA12 8NR
t (015395) 31578
e enquiries@hillofoaks.co.uk
w hillofoaks.co.uk

Limefitt Park ★★★★★ ROSE AWARD
Holiday, Touring & Camping Park
Patterdale Road, Windermere LA23 1PA
t (015395) 69835
e enquiries@southlakelandparks.co.uk
w southlakelandparks.co.uk

Park Cliffe Camping & Caravan Estate ★★★★★
Holiday, Touring & Camping Park
Birks Road, Windermere LA23 3PG
t (015395) 31344
e info@parkcliffe.co.uk
w parkcliffe.co.uk

White Cross Bay Holiday Park and Marina ★★★★★
Holiday & Touring Park
Ambleside Road, Troutbeck Bridge, Windermere LA23 1LF
t (015395) 69835
e enquiries@southlakelandparks.co.uk
w southlakelandparks.co.uk

WINSFORD Cheshire

Elm Cottage Caravan Park ★★★
Touring & Camping Park
Chester Lane, Little Budworth, Winsford CW7 2QJ
t (01829) 760544
e chris@elmcottagecp.co.uk
w elmcottagecp.co.uk

Lakeside Caravan Park ★★★★
Holiday Park
Stocks Hill, Winsford CW7 4EF
t (01606) 861043
e enquiries@thornleyleisure.co.uk

WINSTON Durham

Winston Caravan Park ★★★
Holiday & Touring Park
Front Street, Darlington DL2 3RH
t (01325) 730228
e m.willetts@ic24.net
w touristnetuk.com/ne/winston

WITHERNSEA East Riding of Yorkshire

Willows Holiday Park ★★★★
Holiday, Touring & Camping Park
Hollym Road, Withernsea HU19 2PN
t (01964) 612233
e info@highfield-caravans.co.uk
w highfield-caravans.co.uk

Withernsea Sands Holiday Village ★★★★
Holiday Park
North Road, Withernsea HU19 2BS
t 0871 644 9704
e angie.pyle@park-resorts.com
w park-resorts.com

WOMBLETON North Yorkshire

Wombleton Caravan Park ★★★★★
Touring & Camping Park
Moorfield Lane, York YO62 7RY
t (01751) 431684
e info@wombletoncaravanpark.co.uk
w wombletoncaravanpark.co.uk

WREA GREEN Lancashire

Ribby Hall Village ★★★★
Holiday Village
Ribby Road, Wrea Green, Preston PR4 2PR
t 0800 085 1717
e enquiries@ribbyhall.co.uk
w ribbyhall.co.uk

YORK North Yorkshire

Alders Caravan Park ★★★★★
Touring & Camping Park
Home Farm, Monk Green, Alne, York YO61 1RY
t (01347) 838722
e enquiries@homefarmalne.co.uk
w alderscaravanpark.co.uk

Allerton Park Caravan Park ★★★★ ROSE AWARD
Holiday, Touring & Camping Park
Allerton Park, Knaresborough HG5 0SE
t (01423) 330569
e enquiries@yorkshireholidayparks.co.uk
w yorkshireholidayparks.co.uk

Beechwood Grange Caravan Club Site ★★★★★
Touring Park
Malton Road, York YO32 9TH
t (01904) 424637
w caravanclub.co.uk

Goosewood Holiday Park ★★★★★ ROSE AWARD
Holiday & Touring Park
Sutton on the Forest, York, Easingwold YO61 1ET
t (01347) 810829
e enquiries@goosewood.co.uk
w goosewood.co.uk

Rowntree Park Caravan Club Site ★★★★★
Touring & Camping Park
Terry Avenue, York YO23 1JQ
t (01904) 658997
w caravanclub.co.uk

Weir Caravan Park ★★★★ ROSE AWARD
Holiday & Touring Park
Buttercrambe Road, Stamford Bridge, York YO41 1AN
t (01759) 371377
e enquiries@yorkshireholidayparks.co.uk
w yorkshireholidayparks.co.uk

YCP York Caravan Park and Storage ★★★★★
Touring Park
Stockton Lane, York YO32 9UB
t (01904) 424222
e mail@yorkcaravanpark.com
w yorkcaravanpark.com

York Touring Caravan Site ★★★★
Touring & Camping Park
Towthorpe Lane, Towthorpe, York YO32 9ST
t (01904) 499275
e info@yorkcaravansite.co.uk
w yorkcaravansite.co.uk

CENTRAL ENGLAND

ALREWAS Staffordshire

Kingfisher Holiday Park ★★★★★ ROSE AWARD
Holiday Park
Fradley Junction, Alrewas, Lichfield DE13 7DN
t (01283) 790407
e mail@kingfisherholidaypark.com
w kingfisherholidaypark.com

ALSOP-EN-LE-DALE Derbyshire

Rivendale Caravan and Leisure Park ★★★★
Holiday, Touring & Camping Park
Buxton Road, Alsop-en-le-Dale, Ashbourne DE6 1QU
t (01335) 310311
e enqs@rivendalecaravanpark.co.uk
w rivendalecaravanpark.co.uk

AMBERGATE Derbyshire

The Firs Caravan Club Site
Rating Applied For
Touring & Camping Park
Crich Lane, Belper DE56 2JH
t (01773) 852913
w caravanclub.co.uk

ANDERBY CREEK Lincolnshire

Anderby Springs Caravan Estate ★★★
Holiday Park
The White House, Anderby Creek, Skegness PE24 5XW
t (01754) 872265
w ukparks.co.uk/anderby

ASHBOURNE Derbyshire

Blackwall Plantation Caravan Club Site ★★★★
Touring Park
Kirk Ireton, Ashbourne DE6 3JL
t (01335) 370903
e enquiries@caravanclub.co.uk
w caravanclub.co.uk

Callow Top Holiday Park ★★★★
Holiday, Touring & Camping Park
Buxton Road, Sandybrook, Ashbourne DE6 2AQ
t (01335) 344020
e enquiries@callowtop.co.uk
w callowtop.co.uk

Look out for parks participating in the National Accessible Scheme

ASTON CANTLOW
Warwickshire

Island Meadow Caravan Park ★★★
Holiday, Touring & Camping Park
The Mill House, Aston Cantlow B95 6JP
t (01789) 488273
e holiday@islandmeadowcaravanpark.co.uk
w islandmeadowcaravanpark.co.uk

ATTLEBOROUGH
Norfolk

Oak Tree Park ★★★★
Touring Park
Norwich Road, Attleborough NR17 2JX
t (01953) 455565
e oaktree.cp@virgin.net

BACTON
Norfolk

Castaways Holiday Park
Rating Applied For
Holiday, Touring & Camping Park
Paston Road, Norwich NR12 0JB
t (01692) 650436
e castaways.bacton@hotmail.co.uk
w castawaysholidaypark.co.uk

The Red House Chalet and Caravan Park ★★★
Holiday Park
Paston Road, Norwich NR12 0JB
t (01692) 650815

BACTON-ON-SEA
Norfolk

Cable Gap Holiday Park ★★★★★ **ROSE AWARD**
Holiday Park
Coast Road, Bacton, Norwich NR12 0EW
t (01692) 650667
e holiday@cablegap.co.uk
w cablegap.co.uk

BAKEWELL
Derbyshire

Chatsworth Park Caravan Club Site ★★★★★
Touring Park
Chatsworth, Bakewell DE45 1PN
t (01246) 582226
w caravanclub.co.uk

BANHAM
Norfolk

Applewood Caravan & Camping Park ★★★★
Touring Park
Banham Zoo, Banham NR16 2HE
t (01953) 715318
e info@banhamzoo.co.uk
w banhamzoo.co.uk

BARTON-UPON-HUMBER
Lincolnshire

Silver Birches Tourist Park ★★★
Touring & Camping Park
Waterside Road, Barton-upon-Humber DN18 5BA
t (01652) 632509
e info@silverbirchescaravanpark.co.uk

BAWBURGH
Norfolk

Norfolk Showground Caravan Club Site ★★★★
Touring Park
Royal Norfolk Agricultural Association Showground, Long Lane, Bawburgh, Norwich NR9 3LX
t (01603) 742708
e enquiries@caravanclub.co.uk
w caravanclub.co.uk

BEESTON REGIS
Norfolk

Beeston Regis Caravan Park ★★★
Holiday, Touring & Camping Park
Cromer Road, Cromer NR27 9QZ
t (01263) 823614
e info@beestonregis.co.uk
w beestonregis.co.uk

BELPER
Derbyshire

Broadholme Lane Caravan Park ★★★
Touring Park
Broadholme Lane, Belper DE56 2JF
t (01773) 823517
w broadholme-caravanpark.co.uk

BELTON
Norfolk

Wild Duck Holiday Park ★★★★
Holiday Park
Howards Common, Belton, Great Yarmouth NR31 9NE
t (01493) 780268
e austin.james@bourne-leisure.co.uk
w havenholidayhomes.co.uk

BENHALL
Suffolk

Whitearch (Touring Caravan) Park ★★★
Holiday Park
Main Road, Saxmundham IP17 1NA
t (01728) 604646

BIRMINGHAM
West Midlands

Chapel Lane Caravan Club Site ★★★★★
Touring Park
Chapel Lane, Wythall, Birmingham B47 6JX
t (01564) 826483
w caravanclub.co.uk

BLACKSHAW MOOR
Staffordshire

Blackshaw Moor Caravan Club Site ★★★★★
Touring Park
Blackshaw Moor, Leek ST13 8TW
t (01538) 300203
w caravanclub.co.uk

BODYMOOR HEATH
West Midlands

Kingsbury Camping & Caravan Club ★★★★★
Touring & Camping Park
Bodymoor Heath Lane, Bodymoor Heath, Sutton Coldfield B76 0DY
t (01827) 874101
w campingandcaravanningclub.co.uk

BOSTON
Lincolnshire

Orchard Park ★★★
Holiday, Touring & Camping Park
Frampton Lane, Hubberts Bridge, Boston PE20 3QU
t (01205) 290368
e davidmay@orchardholidaypark.fsnet.co.uk
w orchardpark.co.uk

BRENTWOOD
Essex

Kelvedon Hatch Camping & Caravanning Club Site ★★★★
Touring & Camping Park
Warren Lane, Brentwood CM15 0JG
t (01277) 372773
w campingandcaravanningclub.co.uk

BREWOOD
Staffordshire

Homestead Caravan Park ★★★★
Holiday Park
Shutt Green, Brewood, Wolverhampton ST19 9LX
t (01902) 851302
e info@caravanparkstaffordshire.co.uk
w caravanparkstaffordshire.co.uk

BRIDGNORTH
Shropshire

Park Grange Holidays ★★★★
Holiday Park
Morville, Bridgnorth WV16 4RN
t (01746) 714285
e info@parkgrangeholidays.co.uk
w parkgrangeholidays.co.uk

Stanmore Hall Touring Park ★★★★★
Touring Park
Stourbridge Road, Bridgnorth WV15 6DT
t (01746) 761761
e stanmore@morris-leisure.co.uk
w morris-leisure.co.uk

BUCKLESHAM
Suffolk

The Oaks Caravan Park ★★★★
Holiday & Touring Park
Chapel Road, Bucklesham, Ipswich IP10 0BT
t (01394) 448837
w oakscaravanpark.co.uk

Westwood Caravan Park ★★★★
Holiday, Touring & Camping Park
Old Felixstowe Road, Ipswich IP10 0BT
t (01473) 659637
e info@westwoodcaravanpark.co.uk
w westwoodcaravanpark.co.uk

BUNGAY
Suffolk

Outney Meadow Caravan Park ★★★
Touring & Camping Park
Outney Meadow, Bungay NR35 1HG
t (01986) 892338
e c.r.hancy@ukgateway.net
w outneymeadow.co.uk

BURGH CASTLE
Norfolk

Burgh Castle Marina & Caravan Park ★★★
Holiday, Touring & Camping Park
Butt Lane, Burgh Castle, Great Yarmouth NR31 9PZ
t (01493) 780331
e info@burghcastlemarina.co.uk
w burghcastlemarina.co.uk

BURGH-LE-MARSH
Lincolnshire

Sycamore Farm Park ★★★
Holiday, Touring & Camping Park
Chalk Lane, Skegness PE24 5HN
t (01754) 810833
e lloyd@sycamorefarm.net
w sycamorefarm.net

Sycamore Lakes Touring Site ★★★★
Touring & Camping Park
Skegness Road, Burgh-le-Marsh PE24 5LN
t (01754) 811411
w sycamorelakes.co.uk

BURGH ST PETER
Norfolk

Waveney River Centre ★★★★
Holiday Park
Staithe Road, Beccles NR34 0BT
t (01502) 677343
e info@waveneyrivercentre.co.uk
w waveneyrivercentre.co.uk

BURNHAM DEEPDALE
Norfolk

Deepdale Camping ★★★★
Camping Park
Deepdale Farm, Burnham Deepdale PE31 8DD
t (01485) 210256
e info@deepdalefarm.co.uk
w deepdalefarm.co.uk

BUXTON
Derbyshire

Cold Springs Caravan & Camp Site ★★
Touring & Camping Park
Cold Springs Farm, Manchester Road, Buxton SK17 6SS
t (01298) 22762

Cottage Farm Caravan Park ★★★
Touring & Camping Park
Beech Croft, Blackwell, Buxton SK17 9TQ
t (01298) 85330
e mail@cottagefarmsite.co.uk
w cottagefarmsite.co.uk

Grin Low Caravan Club Site ★★★★★
Touring & Camping Park
Grin Low Road, Ladmanlow, Buxton SK17 6UJ
t (01298) 77735
w caravanclub.co.uk

Lime Tree Park ★★★★ ROSE AWARD
Holiday, Touring & Camping Park
Dukes Drive, Buxton SK17 9RP
t (01298) 22988
e info@limetreeparkbuxton.co.uk
w limetreeparkbuxton.co.uk

Longnor Wood Caravan & Camping Park ★★★★
Touring Park
Newtown, Longnor, Buxton SK17 0NG
t (01298) 83648
e info@longnorwood.co.uk
w longnorwood.co.uk

Newhaven Caravan and Camping Park ★★★
Holiday, Touring & Camping Park
Newhaven, Nr Buxton SK17 0DT
t (01298) 84300
e bobmacara@ntlworld.com
w newhavencaravanpark.co.uk

CAISTER-ON-SEA
Norfolk

Caister Holiday Park ★★★
Holiday Park
Ormesby Road, Caister-on-Sea, Great Yarmouth NR30 5NQ
t (01493) 728931
w havenholidays.com

Eastern Beach Caravan Park ★★★★
Holiday Park
Manor Road, Caister-on-Sea, Great Yarmouth NR30 5HH
t (01493) 720367
w easternbeachcaravanpark.co.uk

Elm Beach Caravan Park ★★★★
Holiday Park
Manor Road, Caister-on-Sea, Great Yarmouth NR30 5HG
t (01493) 721630
e enquiries@elmbeachcaravanpark.com
w elmbeachcaravanpark.com

Wentworth Holidays ★★★
Holiday Park
9 Bultitudes Loke, Great Yarmouth NR30 5DH
t (01493) 720382

CALIFORNIA
Norfolk

Beachside Holidays (Norfolk) ★★★★
Holiday Park
Wakefield Court, California, Great Yarmouth NR29 3QT
t (01493) 730279
e holidays@theseaside.org
w beachside-holidays.co.uk

CAMBRIDGE
Cambridgeshire

Appleacre Park ★★
Touring Park
London Road, Royston SG8 7RU
t (01763) 208354
e ajbearpark@aol.com
w appleacrepark.co.uk

Cherry Hinton Caravan Club Site ★★★★★
Touring & Camping Park
Lime Kiln Road, Cherry Hinton, Cambridge CB1 8NQ
t (01223) 244088
w caravanclub.co.uk

Highfield Farm Touring Park ★★★★★
Touring & Camping Park
Long Road, Comberton, Cambridge CB23 7DG
t (01223) 262308
e enquiries@highfieldfarmtouringpark.co.uk
w highfieldfarmtouringpark.co.uk

CHAPEL ST LEONARDS
Lincolnshire

Tomlinsons Leisure Park ★★★★ ROSE AWARD
Holiday Park
South Road, Chapel St Leonards, Skegness PE24 5TL
t (01754) 872241
w tomlinsons-leisure.co.uk

CHEDDLETON
Staffordshire

Glencote Caravan Park ★★★★★
Holiday, Touring & Camping Park
Station Road, Cheddleton, Leek ST13 7EE
t (01538) 360745
e canistay@glencote.co.uk
w glencote.co.uk

CLACTON-ON-SEA
Essex

Highfield Grange Holiday Park ★★★★
Holiday Park
London Road, Clacton-on-Sea CO16 9QY
t 0871 664 9746
e holidaysales.highfieldgrange@park-resorts.com
w park-resorts.com

Valley Farm Holiday Park ★★★★ ROSE AWARD
Holiday Park
Valley Road, Clacton-on-Sea CO15 6LY
t 0871 664 9788
e holidaysales.valleyfarm@park-resorts.com
w park-resorts.com

CLIPPESBY
Norfolk

Clippesby Hall ★★★★★
Holiday Park
Hall Lane, Great Yarmouth NR29 3BL
t (01493) 367800
w clippesby.com

CORTON
Suffolk

Broadland Sands Holiday Park ★★★★ ROSE AWARD
Holiday Park
Coast Road, Lowestoft NR32 5LG
t (01502) 730939
e admin@broadlandsands.co.uk
w broadlandsands.co.uk

CROFT
Lincolnshire

Pine Trees Caravan Park ★★★
Touring Park
Croft Bank, Skegness PE24 4RE
t (01754) 762949
e pinetreesholidays@yahoo.co.uk
w pinetreesholidays.co.uk

CROMER
Norfolk

Forest Park Caravan Site ★★★★
Touring & Camping Park
Northrepps Road, Northrepps, Cromer NR27 0JR
t (01263) 513290

Seacroft Caravan Club Site ★★★★
Touring & Camping Park
Runton Road, Cromer NR27 9NH
t (01263) 514938
w caravanclub.co.uk

DERBY
Derbyshire

Elvaston Castle Caravan Club Site ★★★
Touring Park
Borrowash Road, Elvaston, Derby DE72 3EP
t (01332) 571342
e enquiries@caravanclub.co.uk
w caravanclub.co.uk

DUNWICH
Suffolk

Cliff House Holiday Park ★★★★
Holiday Park
Minsmere Road, Dunwich, Saxmundham IP17 3DQ
t (01728) 648282
e info@cliffhouseholidays.co.uk
w cliffhouseholidays.co.uk

EARDISLAND
Herefordshire

Arrow Bank Holiday Park ★★★★
Holiday, Touring & Camping Park
Nun House Farm, Eardisland, Leominster HR6 9BG
t (01544) 388312
e enquiries@arrowbankholidaypark.co.uk
w arrowbankholidaypark.co.uk

EAST FIRSBY
Lincolnshire

Manor Farm Caravan & Camping Site ★★★
Touring & Camping Park
Manor Farm, East Firsby, Market Rasen LN8 2DB
t (01673) 878258
e info@lincolnshire-lanes.com
w lincolnshire-lanes.com

EAST HARLING
Norfolk

The Dower House Touring Park ★★★★
Touring & Camping Park
Thetford Forest, East Harling, Norwich NR16 2SE
t (01953) 717314

EAST MERSEA
Essex

Coopers Beach Holiday Park ★★★★
Holiday Park
East Mersea, Colchester CO5 8TN
t (01206) 383236

Cosway Holiday Home Park ★★★★★
Holiday Park
Fen Lane, East Mersea, Colchester CO5 8UA
t (01206) 383252

Look out for parks participating in the National Accessible Scheme

Fen Farm Camping & Caravan Site ★★★★
Holiday Park
Moore Lane, East Mersea, Colchester CO5 8UA
t (01206) 383275
w mersea-island.com/fenfarm

EAST RUNTON
Norfolk

Woodhill Park ★★★★ ROSE AWARD
Holiday, Touring & Camping Park
Cromer Road, East Runton, Cromer NR27 9PX
t (01263) 512242
e info@woodhill-park.com
w woodhill-park.com

ELLESMERE
Shropshire

Fernwood Caravan Park ★★★★★
Holiday & Touring Park
Lyneal, Ellesmere SY12 0QF
t (01948) 710221
e enquiries@fernwoodpark.co.uk
w fernwoodpark.co.uk

ELVEDEN
Suffolk

Center Parcs Elveden Forest ★★★★★
Forest Holiday Village
Brandon IP27 0YZ
t 0870 067 3030
w centerparcs.co.uk/villages/elveden/index.jsp

EVESHAM
Worcestershire

The Ranch Caravan Park ★★★★★
Holiday & Touring Park
Station Road, Honeybourne, Evesham WR11 7PR
t (01386) 830744
e enquiries@ranch.co.uk
w ranch.co.uk

FAKENHAM
Norfolk

Fakenham Racecourse ★★★
Touring Park
The Racecourse, Fakenham NR21 7NY
t (01328) 862388
e caravan@fakenhamracecourse.co.uk
w fakenhamracecourse.co.uk

The Old Brick Kilns ★★★★★
Touring & Camping Park
Little Barney Lane, Fakenham NR21 0NL
t (01328) 878305
e enquiries@old-brick-kilns.co.uk
w old-brick-kilns.co.uk

FELIXSTOWE
Suffolk

Felixstowe Beach Holiday Park
Rating Applied For
Holiday, Touring & Camping Park
Walton Avenue, Felixstowe IP11 2HA
t (01394) 283393
e christinajones@parkholidayuk.com
w parkholidaysuk.com

Peewit Caravan Park ★★★★
Touring & Camping Park
Walton Avenue, Felixstowe IP11 2HB
t (01394) 284511
e peewitpark@aol.com
w peewitcaravanpark.co.uk

Suffolk Sands Holiday Park
Rating Applied For
Holiday, Touring & Camping Park
Carr Road, Felixstowe IP11 2TS
t (01394) 273434

FINESHADE
Northamptonshire

Top Lodge Caravan Club Site ★★★★
Touring Park
Fineshade, Duddington, Corby NN17 3BB
t (01780) 444617
w caravanclub.co.uk

FLAGG
Derbyshire

Knotlow Farm ★★
Touring & Camping Park
Flagg, Buxton SK17 9QP
t (01298) 85313

Pomeroy Caravan & Camping Park ★★
Touring & Camping Park
Street House Farm, Pomeroy, Buxton SK17 9QG
t (01298) 83259

FLEET HARGATE
Lincolnshire

Delph Bank Caravan Park ★★★★
Touring & Camping Park
Old Main Road, Fleet Hargate PE12 8LL
t (01406) 422910
e enquiries@delphbank.co.uk
w delphbank.co.uk

FOLKINGHAM
Lincolnshire

Low Farm Touring Park ★★★
Touring Park
Spring Lane, Folkingham NG34 0SJ
t (01529) 497322

FOXHALL
Suffolk

Low House Touring Caravan Centre ★★★
Holiday Park
Bucklesham Road, Ipswich IP10 0AU
t (01473) 659437

GOLDHANGER
Essex

Osea Leisure Park ★★★★
Holiday Park
Goldhanger Road, Maldon CM9 4SA
t (01621) 854695
w osealeisure.com

GREAT HOCKHAM
Norfolk

Camping & Caravan Club Site – Thetford Forest ★★★★
Holiday, Touring & Camping Park
Puddledock Farm, Thetford IP24 1PA
t (01953) 498455
w campingandcaravanningclub.co.uk

GREAT SHELFORD
Cambridgeshire

Cambridge Camping & Caravanning Club Site ★★★★
Touring Park
19 Cabbage Moor, Cambridge CB2 5NB
t (01223) 841185
w campingandcaravanningclub.co.uk

GREAT YARMOUTH
Norfolk

Breydon Water Holiday Park (Bure Village) ★★★★
Holiday, Touring & Camping Park
Butt Lane, Burgh Castle, Great Yarmouth NR31 9PY
t 0871 664 9710
e holidaysales.breydonwater@park-resorts.com
w park-resorts.com

Cherry Tree Holiday Park ★★★★ ROSE AWARD
Holiday Park
Mill Road, Great Yarmouth NR31 9QR
t (01493) 780229
w parkdeanholidays.co.uk

The Grange Touring Park ★★★★
Holiday Park
Yarmouth Road, Ormesby St Margaret, Great Yarmouth NR29 3QG
t (01493) 730306
e info@grangetouring.co.uk
w grangetouring.co.uk

Grasmere Caravan Park ★★★
Touring Park
Bultitudes Loke, Yarmouth Road, Caister-on-Sea, Great Yarmouth NR30 5DH
t (01493) 720382
w grasmere-wentworth.co.uk

Great Yarmouth Caravan Club Site ★★★★
Holiday Park
Great Yarmouth Racecourse, Jellicoe Road, Great Yarmouth NR30 4AU
t (01493) 855223
w caravanclub.co.uk

Hopton Holiday Village ★★★★
Holiday Park
Warren Lane, Hopton, Great Yarmouth NR31 9BW
t (01502) 730214

Potters Leisure Resort ★★★★★
Holiday Village
Coast Road, Hopton-on-Sea, Great Yarmouth NR31 9BX
t (01502) 730345
e potters@pottersholidays.com
w pottersholidays.com

Seacroft (Hemsby) Summerfields Holiday Village ★★★★
Holiday Park
Beach Road, Scratby, Great Yarmouth NR29 3NW
t (01493) 731419

Seashore Holiday Park ★★★
Holiday Park
North Denes, Great Yarmouth NR30 4HG
t (01493) 851131

Vauxhall Holiday Park ★★★★★
Holiday & Touring Park
Acle New Road, Great Yarmouth NR30 1TB
t (01493) 857231

HADFIELD
Derbyshire

Camping & Caravanning Club Site – Crowden ★★
Touring & Camping Park
Crowden, Glossop SK13 1HZ
t (01457) 866057
w campingandcaravanningclub.co.uk

HANLEY SWAN
Worcestershire

Blackmore Camping & Caravanning Club Site ★★★★★
Touring & Camping Park
Camp Site No 2, Hanley Swan WR8 0EE
t (01684) 310280
w campingandcaravanningclub.co.uk

HANWORTH
Norfolk

Deer's Glade Caravan & Camping Park ★★★★★
Touring & Camping Park
White Post Road, Hanworth, Norwich NR11 7HN
t (01263) 768633
e info@deersglade.co.uk
w deersglade.co.uk

HAUGHTON
Shropshire

Ebury Hill Camping & Caravanning Club Site
★★★★
Touring & Camping Park
Ebury Hill, Haughton, Telford TF6 6BU
t (01743) 709334
w campingandcaravanning club.co.uk

HAYFIELD
Derbyshire

Camping & Caravanning Club Site – Hayfield ★★★
Camping Park
Kinder Road, Hayfield, High Peak SK22 2LE
t (01663) 745394
w campingandcaravanning club.co.uk

HEACHAM
Norfolk

Heacham Beach Holiday Park ★★★★
Holiday Park
South Beach Road, Heacham, King's Lynn PE31 7BD
t 0871 664 9743
e holidaysales. heachambeach@park-resorts. com
w park-resorts.com

Meadows Caravan Park
★★★★
Holiday Park
Lamsey Lane, Norflolk PE31 7LA
t (01553) 636243
e mcdonnellcaravans@fsmail. net
w mcdonnellcaravans.co.uk

HEMINGFORD ABBOTS
Cambridgeshire

Quiet Waters Caravan Park
★★★★
Holiday, Touring & Camping Park
Hemingford Abbots, Huntingdon PE28 9AJ
t (01480) 463405
e quietwaters.park@ btopenworld.com
w quietwaterscaravanpark.co. uk

HEMSBY
Norfolk

Newport Caravan Park (Norfolk) ★★★★
Holiday, Touring & Camping Park
Newport Road, Hemsby, Great Yarmouth NR29 4NW
t (01493) 730405
e enquiries@ newportcaravanpark.co.uk
w newportcaravanpark.co.uk

HEREFORD
Herefordshire

Lucksall Caravan & Camping Park ★★★★★
Holiday & Touring Park
Mordiford, Hereford HR1 4LP
t (01432) 870213
e enquiries@lucksallpark.co. uk
w lucksallpark.co.uk

HERTFORD
Hertfordshire

Hertford Camping & Caravanning Club Site
★★★★
Touring & Camping Park
Mangrove Road, Hertford SG13 8AJ
t (01992) 586696
w campingandcaravanning club.co.uk

HOPTON HEATH
Shropshire

Ashlea Pools Country Park-Log Cabins ★★★★★ ROSE AWARD
Holiday Park
Hopton Heath, Craven Arms SY7 0QD
t (01547) 530430
e ashleapools@surfbay.dircon. co.uk
w ashleapools.co.uk

HORNCASTLE
Lincolnshire

Ashby Park ★★★★
Holiday, Touring & Camping Park
Horncastle, West Ashby LN9 5PP
t (01507) 527966
e ashbypark@btconnect.com
w ukparks.co.uk/ashby

Elmhirst Lakes Caravan Park
★★★★
Holiday Park
Elmhirst Road, Horncastle LN9 5LU
t (01507) 527533
e info@elmhirstlakes.co.uk
w elmhirstlakes.co.uk

HUMBERSTON
North East Lincolnshire

Beachcomber ★★★
Holiday Park
208 North Sea Lane, Grimsby DN36 4ET
t (01472) 812666
e enquiries@ beachcomberholidaypark.co.uk
w beachcomberholidaypark. co.uk

Thorpe Park Holiday Centre
★★★★
Holiday Park
Cleethorpes DN35 0PW
t (01442) 868325
e theresa.ludlow@bourne-leisure.co.uk
w british-holidays.co.uk

HUNSTANTON
Norfolk

Manor Park Holiday Village
★★★★
Holiday & Touring Park
Manor Road, Hunstanton PE36 5AZ
t (01485) 532300
e info@manor-park.co.uk
w manor-park.co.uk

Searles Leisure Resort ★★★★★ ROSE AWARD
Holiday, Touring & Camping Park
South Beach Road, Hunstanton PE36 5BB
t (01485) 534211
e bookings@searles.co.uk
w searles.co.uk

HUNTINGDON
Cambridgeshire

Grafham Water Caravan Club Site ★★★★
Holiday & Touring Park
Church Road, Grafham, Huntingdon PE28 0BB
t (01480) 810264
w caravanclub.co.uk

Houghton Mill Caravan Club Site ★★★★
Touring Park
Mill Street, Huntingdon PE28 2AZ
t (01480) 466716
e enquiries@caravanclub.co. uk
w caravanclub.co.uk

INGOLDMELLS
Lincolnshire

Coastfield Caravan Park
★★★
Holiday Park
Vickers Point, Roman Bank, Ingoldmells, Skegness PE25 1JU
t (01754) 872592

Country Meadows ★★★★
Holiday & Touring Park
Anchor Lane, Ingoldmells PE25 1LZ
t (01754) 874455
e brochure@ countrymeadows.co.uk
w countrymeadows.co.uk

Golden Beach Holiday Park
★★★★
Holiday Park
Roman Bank, Ingoldmells, Skegness PE25 1LT
t (01754) 873000

Kingfisher Park ★★★
Holiday Park
Sea Lane, Ingoldmells PE25 1PG
t (01754) 872465
e kingfisherpark@e-lindsey. gov.uk

JAYWICK
Essex

Martello Beach Holiday Park
★★★★
Holiday, Touring & Camping Park
Belsize Avenue, Jaywick, Clacton-on-Sea CO15 2LF
t 0871 664 9782
e holidaysales.martellobeach@ park-resorts.com
w park-resorts.com

KESSINGLAND
Suffolk

Alandale Park ★★
Holiday Park
Bethel Drive, Lowestoft NR33 7SD
t (01502) 740610

Heathland Beach Caravan Park ★★★★★ ROSE AWARD
Holiday, Touring & Camping Park
London Road, Lowestoft NR33 7PJ
t (01502) 740337
e heathlandbeach@btinternet. com
w heathlandbeach.co.uk

Kessingland Beach Holiday Park ★★★
Holiday, Touring & Camping Park
Beach Road, Kessingland NR33 7RW
t 0871 664 9749

Kessingland Camping & Caravanning Club Site
★★★★
Touring & Camping Park
Whites Lane, Lowestoft NR33 7TF
t (01502) 742040
w campingandcaravanning club.co.uk

KINNERLEY
Shropshire

Camping & Caravanning Club Site – Oswestry
★★★★★
Touring & Camping Park
Cranberry Moss, Kinnerley, Oswestry SY10 8DY
t (01743) 741118
e oswestry.site@ campingandcaravanningclub. co.uk
w campingandcaravanning club.co.uk

KIRKBY-ON-BAIN
Lincolnshire

Camping & Caravanning Club Site – Woodhall Spa
★★★★★
Touring & Camping Park
Wellsyke Lane, Kirkby-on-Bain LN10 6YU
t (01526) 352911
w campingandcaravanning club.co.uk

Look out for parks participating in the National Accessible Scheme

LEEK
Staffordshire

Leek Camping & Caravanning Club Site ★★★★
Touring & Camping Park
Blackshaw Grange, Leek ST13 8TL
t 0845 130 7633
w campingandcaravanning club.co.uk

LEOMINSTER
Herefordshire

Fairview Caravan Park ★★★★
Holiday Park
The Willows, Hatfield, Leominster HR6 0SF
t (01568) 760428
e fairviewcaravanpark@ supanet.com

LINCOLN
Lincolnshire

Hartsholme Country Park ★★★
Touring Park
Skellingthorpe Road, Lincoln LN6 0EY
t (01522) 873578
e hartsholmecp@lincoln.gov. uk
w lincoln.gov.uk

LITTLE CORNARD
Suffolk

Willowmere Caravan Park ★★★
Touring & Camping Park
Bures Road, Little Cornard, Sudbury CO10 0NN
t (01787) 375559

LITTLE TARRINGTON
Herefordshire

Hereford Camping & Caravanning Club Site ★★★★★
Touring & Camping Park
The Millpond, Little Tarrington HR1 4JA
t (01432) 890243
e enquiries@millpond.co.uk
w campingandcaravanning club.co.uk

LOUGHTON
Essex

Debden House Camp Site ★★
Touring & Camping Park
Debden Green, Loughton IG10 2NZ
t (020) 8508 3008
e debdenhouse@newham. govt.uk
w debdenhouse.com

LOWESTOFT
Suffolk

Beach Farm Residential & Holiday Park Limited ★★★
Holiday Park
Arbor Lane, Lowestoft NR33 7BD
t (01502) 572794
e beachfarmpark@aol.com
w beachfarmpark.co.uk

LUDLOW
Shropshire

Orleton Rise Holiday Home Park ★★★★★
Holiday & Touring Park
Green Lane, Orleton, Ludlow SY8 4JE
t (01584) 831617

MABLETHORPE
Lincolnshire

Camping & Caravanning Club Site – Mablethorpe ★★★★
Touring & Camping Park
Highfield, 120 Church Lane, Mablethorpe LN12 2NU
t (01507) 472374
w campingandcaravanning club.co.uk

Golden Sands Holiday Park ★★★
Holiday & Touring Park
Quebec Road, Mablethorpe LN12 1QJ
t (01507) 477871
w goldensands-park.co.uk

Grange Leisure Park ★★
Holiday & Touring Park
Alford Road, Mablethorpe LN12 1NE
t (01507) 427814

Holivans ★★★
Touring Park
Quebec Road, Mablethorpe LN12 1QH
t (01507) 473327
e holivans@enterprise.net
w holivans.co.uk

Trusthorpe Springs Leisure Park ★★
Holiday & Touring Park
Mile Lane, Trusthorpe, Mablethorpe LN12 2QQ
t (01507) 441384
e d.brailsford@ukonline.co.uk

MALDON
Essex

Herbage Park Holiday Lodges
Rating Applied For
Holiday, Touring & Camping Park
Herbage Park, Herbage Park Road, Maldon CM9 6RW
t 0845 017 7787
w herbagepark.com

MARKET BOSWORTH
Leicestershire

Bosworth Water Trust ★★★
Touring & Camping Park
Wellesborough Road, Market Bosworth CV13 6PD
t (01455) 291876
e info@bosworthwatertrust. co.uk
w bosworthwatertrust.co.uk

MARKET HARBOROUGH
Leicestershire

Brook Meadow ★★
Holiday & Camping Park
Welford Road, Sibbertoft, Market Harborough LE16 9UJ
t (01858) 880886
e brookmeadow@farmline. com
w brookmeadow.co.uk

MERIDEN
West Midlands

Somers Wood Caravan Park ★★★★★
Touring Park
Somers Road, Meriden, Coventry CV7 7PL
t (01676) 522978
e enquiries@somerswood.co. uk
w somerswood.co.uk

MERSEA ISLAND
Essex

Waldegraves Holiday Park ★★★★
Holiday, Touring & Camping Park
Waldegraves Lane, Mersea Island, Colchester CO5 8SE
t (01206) 382898
e holidays@waldegraves.co.uk
w waldegraves.co.uk

MILDENHALL
Suffolk

Round Plantation Caravan Club Site ★★★★
Touring Park
Brandon Road, Bury St Edmunds IP28 7JE
t (01638) 713089
e enquiries@caravanclub.co. uk
w caravanclub.co.uk

MOIRA
Leicestershire

Conkers, National Forest Camping Site ★★★★
Touring & Camping Park
Bath Lane, Moira, Ashby-de-la-Zouch DE12 6BD
t 0870 770 6141
e customerservices@yha.org. uk
w campingandcaravanning club.co.uk

MUMBY
Lincolnshire

Inglenook Caravan Park ★★★
Touring Park
Hogsthorpe Road, Mumby, Alford LN13 9SE
t (01507) 490365
e pulse@lincolnshiretourism. com

MUNDESLEY
Norfolk

Sandy Gulls Cliff Top Touring Park ★★★
Holiday & Touring Park
Cromer Road, Mundesley, Norwich NR11 8DF
t (01263) 720513

MUTFORD
Suffolk

Beulah Hall Caravan Park ★★★
Touring & Camping Park
Beulah Hall, Dairy Lane, Beccles NR34 7QJ
t (01502) 476609
e beulah.hall@btinternet.com

NEWARK
Nottinghamshire

Milestone Caravan Park ★★★★★
Touring Park
Great North Road, Cromwell, Newark NG23 6JE
t (01636) 821244
e enquiries@ experiencenottinghamshire. com

NORMANBY
Lincolnshire

Normanby Hall Country Park Accommodation ★★★
Touring Park
Normanby, Scunthorpe DN15 9HU
t (01724) 720588
e normanby.hall@northlincs. gov.uk
w northlincs.gov.uk/normanby

NORTH RUNCTON
Norfolk

Kings Lynn Caravan & Camping Park ★★★
Touring Park
New Road, King's Lynn PE33 0RA
t (01553) 840004

NORTH SCARLE
Lincolnshire

Lowfields Country Holiday Fishing Retreat
Rating Applied For
Holiday, Touring & Camping Park
Eagle Road, Lincoln LN6 9EN
t (01522) 778717
e lowretreat@aol.com
w lowfields-retreat.co.uk

NORTH WALSHAM
Norfolk

Two Mills Touring Park ★★★★★
Touring Park
Yarmouth Road, North Walsham NR28 9NA
t (01692) 405829

NORWICH
Norfolk

Norwich Camping & Caravanning Club Site ★★★
Holiday Park
Martineau Lane, Norwich NR1 2HX
t (01603) 620060
w campingandcaravanning club.co.uk

Reedham Ferry Touring & Camping Park ★★★
Holiday, Touring & Camping Park
Ferry Road, Reedham, Norwich NR13 3HA
t (01493) 700999

OULTON BROAD
Suffolk

Broadland Holiday Village ★★★★★ ROSE AWARD
Holiday Park
Marsh Road, Lowestoft
NR33 9JY
t (01502) 573033
e info@broadlandvillage.co.uk
w broadlandvillage.co.uk

OVERSTRAND
Norfolk

Ivy Farm Holiday Park ★★★★
Holiday, Touring & Camping Park
Overstrand, Cromer NR27 0AB
t (01263) 579239
e enquiries@ivy-farm.co.uk
w ivy-farm.co.uk

PAKEFIELD
Suffolk

Pakefield Caravan Park ★★★
Holiday Park
Arbor Lane, Lowestoft
NR33 7BQ
t (01502) 561136

PEMBRIDGE
Herefordshire

Townsend Touring Park ★★★★★
Touring & Camping Park
East Street, Pembridge, Leominster HR6 9HB
t (01544) 388527
e info@townsendfarm.co.uk
w townsend-farm.co.uk

PENTNEY
Norfolk

Pentney Park Caravan Site ★★★★
Touring & Camping Park
Main Road, Pentney, King's Lynn PE32 1HU
t (01760) 337479
e holidays@pentney.demon.co.uk
w pentney-park.co.uk

PETERBOROUGH
Cambridgeshire

Ferry Meadows Caravan Club Site ★★★★★
Holiday Park
Ham Lane, Peterborough
PE2 5UU
t (01733) 233526
w caravanclub.co.uk

PETERCHURCH
Herefordshire

Poston Mill Park C & C ★★★★★
Holiday & Touring Park
Enjoy England Awards for Excellence Winner
Peterchurch, Golden Valley
HR2 0SF
t (01981) 550225
e info@poston-mill.co.uk
w bestparks.co.uk

PRESTHOPE
Shropshire

Presthope Caravan Club Site ★★★
Touring Park
Stretton Road, Much Wenlock
TF13 6DQ
t (01746) 785234
w caravanclub.co.uk

RIPLEY
Derbyshire

Golden Valley Caravan & Camping ★★★★
Touring & Camping Park
The Tanyard, Coach Road, Golden Valley, Ripley
DE55 4ES
t (01773) 513881
e enquiries@goldenvalleycaravanpark.co.uk
w goldenvalleycaravanpark.co.uk

ROMSLEY
Worcestershire

Clent Hills Camping & Caravanning Club Site ★★★★
Touring Park
Fieldhouse Lane, Romsley, Bromsgrove B62 0NH
t (01562) 710015
w campingandcaravanningclub.co.uk

ROSS-ON-WYE
Herefordshire

Broadmeadow Caravan Park ★★★★★
Touring & Camping Park
Broadmeadows, Ross-on-Wye
HR9 7BW
t (01989) 768076
e broadm4811@aol.com

RUFFORD
Nottinghamshire

Center Parcs Sherwood Forest ★★★★★
Forest Holiday Village
Newark NG22 9DN
t 0870 067 3030
w centerparcs.co.uk/villages/sherwood/index.jsp

RUGELEY
Staffordshire

Camping & Caravanning Club Site – Cannock Chase ★★★★
Touring & Camping Park
Old Youth Hostel, Wandon, Rugeley WS15 1QW
t (01889) 582166
w campingandcaravanningclub.co.uk

Silver Trees Holiday Park ★★★★ ROSE AWARD
Holiday Park
Stafford Brook Road, Penkridge Bank, Rugeley WS15 2TX
t (01889) 582185
e info@silvertreesholidaypark.co.uk
w silvertreesholidaypark.co.uk

SAHAM HILLS
Norfolk

Lowe Caravan Park ★★★★
Touring & Camping Park
Ashdale, Hills Road, Saham Hills, Thetford IP25 7EZ
t (01953) 881051
w lowecaravanpark.co.uk

ST NEOTS
Cambridgeshire

St Neots Camping & Caravanning Club Site ★★★★
Touring Park
Hardwick Road, Eynesbury, St Neots PE19 2PR
t (01480) 474404
w campingandcaravanningclub.co.uk

ST OSYTH
Essex

Oaklands Holiday Park ★★★
Holiday Park
Colchester Road, Clacton-on-Sea CO16 8HW
t (01255) 820432

The Orchards Holiday Village ★★★
Holiday Park
Point Clear, Clacton-on-Sea
CO16 8LJ
t (01255) 820651

St Osyth Beach Holiday Park
Rating Applied For
Holiday, Touring & Camping Park
Beach Road, Clacton-on-Sea
CO16 8SG
t 0845 815 9795

Seawick Holiday Park
Rating Applied For
Holiday, Touring & Camping Park
Beach Road, Clacton-on-Sea
CO16 8SG
t (01255) 820416

SALTFLEET
Lincolnshire

Sunnydale Holiday Park ★★★★ ROSE AWARD
Holiday & Touring Park
Sea Lane, Saltfleet, Louth
LN11 7RP
t (01507) 338100
w gbholidayparks.co.uk

SANDRINGHAM
Norfolk

Sandringham Camping & Caravanning Club Site ★★★★★
Touring Park
The Sandringham Estate, Double Lodges, Hunstanton
PE36 6EA
t (01485) 542555
w campingandcaravanningclub.co.uk

The Sandringham Estate Caravan Club Site ★★★★★
Touring Park
Glucksburgh Woods, Sandringham PE35 6EZ
t (01553) 631614
e enquiries@caravanclub.co.uk
w caravanclub.co.uk

SCRATBY
Norfolk

California Cliffs Holiday Park ★★★★
Holiday Park
Rottenstone Lane, Scratby, Great Yarmouth NR29 3QU
t 0871 664 9716
e holidaysales.californiacliffs@park-resorts.com
w park-resorts.com

Green Farm Caravan Park ★★★★★
Holiday & Touring Park
Beach Road, Great Yarmouth
NR29 3NW
t (01493) 730440
e contact@greenfarmcaravanpark.com
w greenfarmcaravanpark.com

Scratby Hall Caravan Park ★★★★
Touring & Camping Park
Thoroughfare Lane, Great Yarmouth NR29 3PH
t (01493) 730283

SCUNTHORPE
Lincolnshire

Brookside Caravan Park ★★★★★
Touring Park
Stather Road, Burton upon Stather, Scunthorpe
DN15 9DH
t (01724) 721369
e brooksidecp@aol.com
w brooksidecaravanpark.co.uk

SHADWELL
Norfolk

Thorpe Woodland Caravan & Camping Site
Rating Applied For
Holiday, Touring & Camping Park
Shadwell, Thetford IP24 2RX
t (01842) 751042
e thorpewoodland.site@forestholidays.co.uk
w forestholidays.co.uk

SHOBDON
Herefordshire

Pearl Lake Leisure Park ★★★★★
Holiday Park
Shobdon, Leominster
HR6 9NQ
t (01568) 708326
e info@pearllake.co.uk
w bestparks.co.uk

Look out for parks participating in the National Accessible Scheme

SHREWSBURY
Shropshire

Beaconsfield Farm Caravan Park ★★★★★
ROSE AWARD
Holiday & Touring Park
Upper Battlefield, Shrewsbury SY4 4AA
t (01939) 210370
e mail@beaconsfield-farm.co.uk
w beaconsfield-farm.co.uk

Oxon Hall Touring Park ★★★★★
Holiday & Touring Park
Welshpool Road, Oxon, Shrewsbury SY3 5FB
t (01743) 340868
e oxon@morris-leisure.co.uk
w morrisleisure.com

SKEGNESS
Lincolnshire

Bryanston Kenmore Southview
Rating Applied For
Holiday, Touring & Camping Park
Burgh Road, Skegness PE25 2LA
t (01754) 896000
e holidays@southview-leisure.com
w southview-leisure.com

Butlins at Skegness Butlins Limited ★★★★
Holiday Village
Roman Bank, Skegness PE25 1NJ
t (01754) 762311

Butlins Skegness – Luxury Family Caravans ★★★
Holiday & Touring Park
Butlins Skyline Caravan Park, Ingoldmells PE25 1NJ
t 0870 145 0050
e butlins.webmaster@bourne-leisure.co.uk
w butlins.com/skegness

Manor Farm Caravan Park ★★
Touring & Camping Park
Sea Road, Anderby PE24 5YB
t (01507) 490372
e skegnessinfo@e-lindsey.gov.uk

Richmond Holiday Centre ★★★
Holiday & Touring Park
Richmond Drive, Skegness PE25 3TQ
t (01754) 762097
e sales@richmondholidays.com
w richmondholidays.com

Skegness Sands Touring Site ★★★★
Holiday & Touring Park
Skegness Sands, Winthorpe Avenue, Skegness PE25 1QZ
t (01754) 761484
e info@skegnesssands.co.uk
w skegnesssands.co.uk

Skegness Water Leisure Park ★★★
Holiday, Touring & Camping Park
Walls Lane, Ingoldmells, Skegness PE25 1JF
t (01754) 899400
e enquiries@skegnesswaterleisurepark.co.uk
w skegnesswaterleisurepark.co.uk

Walsh's Holiday Park ★★★
Holiday Park
Roman Bank, Skegness PE25 1QP
t (01754) 764485

SNETTISHAM
Norfolk

Diglea Caravan & Camping Park ★★★
Holiday, Touring & Camping Park
Beach Road, King's Lynn PE31 7RA
t (01485) 541367

SOUTHMINSTER
Essex

Eastland Meadows Country Park ★★★
Holiday Park
East End Road, Bradwell-on-Sea, Southminster CM0 7PP
t (01621) 776577
e enquiries@eastlamdmeadows.co.uk
w eastlandmeadows.co.uk

Waterside Holiday Park ★★★
Holiday & Touring Park
Main Road, St Lawrence Bay, Southminster CM0 7LY
t 0871 664 9794
e holidaysales.waterside@park-resorts.com
w park-resorts.com

SPANBY
Lincolnshire

Highfields Country Holiday Fishing Retreat
Rating Applied For
Holiday, Touring & Camping Park
Mareham Lane, Sleaford NG34 0AT
t (01529) 241185
e info@highretreat.co.uk
w highfields-retreat.co.uk

STANHOE
Norfolk

The Rickels Caravan and Camping Park ★★★★
Touring Park
Bircham Road, Stanhoe, King's Lynn PE31 8PU
t (01485) 518671

STAVELEY
Derbyshire

Poolsbrook Country Park Caravan Club Site
Rating Applied For
Holiday, Touring & Camping Park
Staveley, Chesterfield S43 3LS
t (01246) 470659
w caravanclub.co.uk

STEEPLE
Essex

Steeple Bay Holiday Park
Rating Applied For
Holiday, Touring & Camping Park
Canney Road, Southminster CM0 7RS
t (01621) 773991

STOKE-ON-TRENT
Staffordshire

Star Caravan & Camping Park ★★★★★
ROSE AWARD
Holiday, Touring & Camping Park
Star Road, Cotton, Alton Towers Area ST10 3BZ
t (01538) 702219
w starcaravanpark.co.uk

STOURPORT-ON-SEVERN
Worcestershire

Lickhill Manor Caravan Park ★★★★★
Holiday Park
Stourport-on-Severn DY13 8RL
t (01299) 871041
e excellent@lickhillmanor.co.uk
w lickhillmanor.co.uk

STRATFORD-UPON-AVON
Warwickshire

Dodwell Park ★★★
Touring & Camping Park
Evesham Rd, Stratford-upon-Avon CV37 9SR
t (01789) 204957
e enquiries@dodwellpark.co.uk
w dodwellpark.co.uk

SUTTON IN ASHFIELD
Nottinghamshire

Teversal Camping & Caravanning Club Site ★★★★★
Touring & Camping Park
Silverhill Lane, Teversal, Sutton in Ashfield NG17 3JJ
t (01623) 551838
e stay@shardaroba.co.uk
w campingandcaravanningclub.co.uk

SUTTON-ON-SEA
Lincolnshire

Cherry Tree Site ★★★★
Touring Park
Huttoft Road, Sutton-on-Sea LN12 2RU
t (01507) 441626
e info@cherrytreesite.co.uk
w cherrytreesite.co.uk

SUTTON ST EDMUND
Lincolnshire

Orchard View Caravan & Camping Park ★★★
Holiday, Touring & Camping Park
102 Broadgate, Sutton St Edmund, Spalding PE12 0LT
t (01945) 700482
e raymariaorchardview@btinternet.com

SWADLINCOTE
Derbyshire

Beehive Farm Woodland Lakes ★★★
Touring & Camping Park
Rosliston, Swadlincote DE12 8HZ
t (01283) 763981
e info@beehivefarm-woodlandlakes.co.uk
w beehivefarm-woodlandlakes.co.uk

SWAFFHAM
Norfolk

The Covert Caravan Club Site ★★★★
Touring Park
High Ash, Thetford IP26 5BZ
t (01842) 878356
e enquiries@caravanclub.co.uk
w caravanclub.co.uk

SYMONDS YAT WEST
Herefordshire

Sterrett's Caravan Park ★★★★
Holiday & Touring Park
Symonds Yat West, Ross-on-Wye HR9 6BY
t (01600) 890886
w ukparks.co.uk/sterretts

TANSLEY
Derbyshire

Lickpenny Caravan Park ★★★★
Touring Park
Lickpenny Lane, Tansley, Matlock DE4 5GF
t (01629) 583040
e lickpenny@btinternet.com
w lickpennycaravanpark.co.uk

Packhorse Farm Bungalow C&C ★★★
Touring Park
Packhorse Farm, Foxholes Lane, Matlock DE4 5LF
t (01629) 580950

TATTERSETT
Norfolk

Greenwoods Campsite ★★★
Touring Park
Old Fakenham Road, King's Lynn PE31 8RS
t (01485) 528310
e webmaster@greenwoodscampsite.co.uk
w greenwoodscampsite.co.uk

THORNHAM
Norfolk

The Haven Caravan Park
★★★★
Holiday Park
Church Street, Hunstanton
PE36 6NJ
t (01553) 636243
e mcdonnellcaravans@fsmail.net
w mcdonnellcaravans.co.uk

TRUSTHORPE
Lincolnshire

Seacroft Holiday Estate
★★★★ **ROSE AWARD**
Holiday & Touring Park
Sutton Road, Trusthorpe, Mablethorpe LN12 2PN
t (01507) 472421
e info@seacroftcaravanpark.co.uk
w seacroftcaravanpark.co.uk

Sutton Springs Holiday Estate ★★★
Holiday Park
Sutton Road, Trusthorpe, Mablethorpe LN12 2PZ
t (01507) 441333
e d.brailsford@ukonline.co.uk

UPPER SHERINGHAM
Norfolk

Woodlands Caravan Park
★★★★
Holiday & Touring Park
Holt Road, Upper Sheringham, Sheringham NR26 8TU
t (01263) 823802
e info@woodlandscaravanpark.co.uk
w woodlandscaravanpark.co.uk

UTTOXETER
Staffordshire

Uttoxeter Racecourse Caravan Club Site ★★
Touring Park
Uttoxeter Racecourse, Wood Lane, Uttoxeter ST14 8BD
t (01889) 564172
e enquiries@caravanclub.co.uk
w caravanclub.co.uk

WALTHAM CROSS
Hertfordshire

Camping & Caravanning Club Site – Theobalds Park
★★★
Holiday Park
Bulls Cross Ride, Waltham Cross EN7 5HS
t (01992) 620604
w campingandcaravanningclub.co.uk

WALTON-ON-THE-NAZE
Essex

Naze Marine Holiday Park
★★★
Holiday Park
Hall Lane, Walton-on-the-Naze CO14 8HL
t 0871 664 9755
e holidaysales.nazemarine@park-resorts.com
w park-resorts.com

WARWICK
Warwickshire

Warwick Racecourse ★★★
Touring Park
Hampton Street, Warwick CV34 6HN
t (01926) 495448
e enquiries@caravanclub.co.uk
w caravanclub.co.uk

WEELEY
Essex

Homestead Lake Park
★★★★
Holiday, Touring & Camping Park
Thorpe Road, Clacton-on-Sea CO16 9JN
t (01255) 833492

Weeley Bridge Holiday Park
★★★★
Holiday Park
Clacton Road, Weeley, Clacton-on-Sea CO16 9DH
t 0871 664 9797
e holidaysales.weeleybridge@park-resorts.com
w park-resorts.com

WELLS-NEXT-THE-SEA
Norfolk

Pinewoods Holiday Park
★★★★
Holiday Park
Beach Road, Wells-next-the-Sea NR23 1DR
t (01328) 713200
e pinewoods@lineone.net

WEST ROW
Suffolk

The Willows ★★★
Touring & Camping Park
Hurdle Drove, West Row, Bury St Edmunds IP28 8RB
t (01638) 715963
e tedandsue@hotmail.co.uk

WEST RUNTON
Norfolk

West Runton Camping & Caravanning Club Site
★★★★
Touring & Camping Park
Holgate Lane, Cromer NR27 9NW
t (01263) 837544
w campingandcaravanningclub.co.uk

WEYBOURNE
Norfolk

Kelling Heath Holiday Park
★★★★★ **ROSE AWARD**
Holiday, Touring & Camping Park
Sandy Hill Lane, Weybourne, Holt NR25 7HW
t (01263) 512242
e info@kellingheath.co.uk
w kellingheath.co.uk

WHATSTANDWELL
Derbyshire

Birchwood Farm Caravan Park ★★
Holiday, Touring & Camping Park
Wirksworth Road, Whatstandwell, Matlock DE4 5HS
t (01629) 822280
e carol@birchwoodfcp.co.uk
w birchwoodfcp.co.uk

WHISSENDINE
Rutland

Greendale Farm Caravan & Camping Park ★★★★
Touring & Camping Park
Pickwell Lane, Whissendine, Oakham LE15 7LB
t (01664) 474516
e enq@rutlandgreendale.co.uk
w rutlandgreendale.co.uk

WISBECH
Cambridgeshire

Virginia Lake Caravan Park
★★★★
Holiday Park
Smeeth Road, St Johns Fen End, Wisbech PE14 8JF
t (01945) 430167
e louise@virginialake.co.uk
w virginialake.co.uk

WOLVERLEY
Worcestershire

Wolverley Camping & Caravanning Club Site ★★★
Touring & Camping Park
Brown Westhead Park, Wolverley, Kidderminster DY10 3PX
t (01562) 850909
w campingandcaravanningclub.co.uk

WOODBRIDGE
Suffolk

Forest Camping ★★★
Touring & Camping Park
Tangham Campsite, Rendlesham Forest Centre, Woodbridge IP12 3NF
t (01394) 450707
e admin@forestcamping.co.uk
w forestcamping.co.uk

WOODHALL SPA
Lincolnshire

Bainland Country Park
★★★★★ **ROSE AWARD**
Holiday, Touring & Camping Park
Horncastle Road, Woodhall Spa LN10 6UX
t (01526) 352903
e bookings@bainland.co.uk
w bainland.co.uk

WORKSOP
Nottinghamshire

Clumber Park Caravan Club Site ★★★★★
Touring Park
Lime Tree Avenue, Clumber Park, Worksop S80 3AE
t (01909) 484758
w caravanclub.co.uk

WORTWELL
Norfolk

Little Lakeland Caravan Park
★★★★
Holiday & Touring Park
Wortwell, Harleston IP20 0EL
t (01986) 788646

WYRE PIDDLE
Worcestershire

Rivermead Holiday Home Park ★★★★★
Holiday Park
Church Street, Wyre Piddle, Pershore WR10 2JF
t (01386) 561250
e enquiries@rivermeadcaravanpark.co.uk
w rivermeadcaravanpark.co.uk

WYTON
Cambridgeshire

Wyton Lakes Holiday Park
★★★★
Holiday Park
Banks End, Wyton, Huntingdon PE28 2AA
t (01480) 412715
e loupeter@supanet.com
w wytonlakes.com

YOULGREAVE
Derbyshire

Bakewell Camping & Caravaning Club ★★★
Touring & Camping Park
Hopping Farm, Youlgreave, Bakewell DE45 1NA
t 0870 243 3331
w campingandcaravanningclub.co.uk

Look out for parks participating in the National Accessible Scheme

SOUTH EAST ENGLAND

ANDOVER
Hampshire

Wyke Down Touring Caravan & Camping Park
★★★
Touring & Camping Park
Picket Piece, Andover
SP11 6LX
t (01264) 352048
e p.read@wykedown.co.uk
w wykedown.co.uk

APSE HEATH
Isle of Wight

Old Barn Touring Park
★★★★
Touring & Camping Park
Cheverton Farm, Newport Road, Sandown PO36 9PJ
t (01983) 866414
e oldbarn@weltinet.com
w oldbarntouring.co.uk

Village Way Caravan & Camping Site ★★★
Holiday, Touring & Camping Park
Newport Road, Sandown
PO36 9PJ
t (01983) 863279
e info@islandbreaks.co.uk

ARRETON
Isle of Wight

Perreton Farm ★★
Holiday Park
East Lane, Arreton, Newport
PO30 3DL
t (01983) 865218
e roger.perreton@virgin.net
w islandbreaks.co.uk

ASHFORD
Kent

Broadhembury Holiday Park
★★★★★
Holiday, Touring & Camping Park
Steeds Lane, Kingsnorth, Ashford TN26 1NQ
t (01233) 620859
e holidaypark@broadhembury.co.uk
w broadhembury.co.uk

ASHURST
Hampshire

Forestry Commission Ashurst Caravan & Camping Site ★★★
Touring & Camping Park
Lyndhurst Road, Ashurst, Southampton SO40 7AR
t (0131) 314 6505
e fe.holidays@forestry.gov.uk
w forestholidays.co.uk

ATHERFIELD BAY
Isle of Wight

Chine Farm Camping Site
★★
Touring & Camping Park
Military Road, Atherfield Bay
PO38 2JH
t (01983) 740901
e jill@chine-farm.co.uk
w chine-farm.co.uk

BANBURY
Oxfordshire

Bo Peep Caravan Park
★★★★
Holiday & Touring Park
Aynho Road, Banbury
OX17 3NP
t (01295) 810605
e warden@bo-peep.co.uk
w bo-peep.co.uk

BATTLE
East Sussex

Crowhurst Park ★★★★★
ROSE AWARD
Holiday Park
Telham Lane, Battle TN33 0SL
t (01424) 773344
e enquiries@crowhurstpark.co.uk
w crowhurstpark.co.uk

Normanhurst Court Caravan Club Site ★★★★★
Touring Park
Stevens Crouch, Battle
TN33 9LR
t (01424) 773808
e enquiries@caravanclub.co.uk
w caravanclub.co.uk

BEACONSFIELD
Buckinghamshire

Highclere Farm Camp Site
★★★★
Touring & Camping Park
Newbarn Lane, Beaconsfield
HP9 2QZ
t (01494) 874505
e enquiries@highclerefarmpark.co.uk
w highclerefarmpark.co.uk

BEMBRIDGE
Isle of Wight

Sandhills Holiday Park ★★★
Holiday Park
Whitecliff Bay, Bembridge
PO35 5QB
t (01983) 872277
e enquiries@sandhillsholidaypark.com
w sandhillsholidaypark.com

Whitecliff Bay Holiday Park
★★★
Holiday Park
Hillway Road, Bembridge
PO35 5PL
t (01983) 872671
e holiday@whitecliff-bay.com
w whitecliff-bay.com

BEXHILL-ON-SEA
East Sussex

Cobbs Hill Farm Caravan & Camping Park ★★★★
Holiday, Touring & Camping Park
Watermill Lane, Sidley, Bexhill-on-Sea TN39 5JA
t (01424) 213460
e cobbshillfarmuk@hotmail.com
w cobbshillfarm.co.uk

BIDDENDEN
Kent

Woodlands Park ★★★★
Touring & Camping Park
Tenterden Road, Ashford
TN27 8BT
t (01580) 291216
e woodlandsp@aol.com
w campingsite.co.uk

BIRCHINGTON
Kent

Quex Caravan Park
★★★★★
Holiday & Touring Park
Park Road, Birchington
CT7 0BL
t (01843) 841273
e info@keatfarm.co.uk
w keatfarm.co.uk

Two Chimneys Holiday Park
★★★★★
Holiday, Touring & Camping Park
Shottendane Road, Birchington
CT7 0HD
t (01843) 841068
e info@twochimneys.co.uk
w twochimneys.co.uk

BOGNOR REGIS
West Sussex

Butlins Bognor Regis Resort
★★★★
Holiday Village
Upper Bognor Road, Bognor Regis PO21 1JJ
t 0845 070 4754
w butlins.com

Copthorne Caravans
★★★★ **ROSE AWARD**
Holiday Park
Rose Green Road, Bognor Regis PO21 3ER
t (01243) 262408
e copthornecaravans@dsl.pipex.com

Riverside Caravan Centre (Bognor) ★★★★★
Holiday Park
Shripney Road, Bognor Regis
PO22 9NE
t (01243) 865823
e info@rivcentre.co.uk
w rivcentre.co.uk

Rowan Park Caravan Club Site ★★★★★
Touring & Camping Park
Rowan Way, Bognor Regis
PO22 9RP
t (01243) 828515
e enquiries@caravanclub.co.uk
w caravanclub.co.uk

BRIGHSTONE
Isle of Wight

Grange Farm Brighstone Bay
★★★
Holiday & Touring Park
Grange Chine, Military Road, Newport PO30 4DA
t (01983) 740296
e grangefarm@brighstonebay.fsnet.co.uk
w brighstonebay.fsnet.co.uk

BRIGHTON & HOVE
East Sussex

Sheepcote Valley Caravan Club Site ★★★★★
Touring & Camping Park
East Brighton Park, Brighton
BN2 5TS
t (01273) 626546
w caravanclub.co.uk

BROCKENHURST
Hampshire

Black Knowl (New Forest)
★★
Touring & Camping Park
Aldridge Hill, Brockenhurst
SO42 7QD
t (01590) 623600
w caravanclub.co.uk

Forestry Commission Hollands Wood Caravan & Camping Site ★★★
Holiday, Touring & Camping Park
Lyndhurst Road, Brockenhurst
SO42 7QH
t (0131) 314 6505
e fe.holidays@forestry.gov.uk
w forestholidays.co.uk

Forestry Commission Roundhill Caravan & Camping Site ★★★
Holiday, Touring & Camping Park
Beaulieu Road, Brockenhurst
SO42 7QL
t (0131) 314 6505
e fe.holidays@forestry.gov.uk
w forestholidays.co.uk

BROOK
Isle of Wight

Compton Farm ★★
Holiday Park
Brook, Newport PO30 4HF
t (01983) 740215
e info@islandbreaks.co.uk

BURFORD
Oxfordshire

Burford Caravan Club Site
★★★★★
Touring Park
Bradwell Grove, Burford
OX18 4JJ
t (01993) 823080
w caravanclub.co.uk

CAMBER
East Sussex

Camber Sands Holiday Park ★★★★
Holiday Park
New Lydd Road, Camber TN31 7RT
t 0871 664 9718
e holidaysales.cambersands@park-resorts.com
w park-resorts.com

CANTERBURY
Kent

Camping & Caravanning Club Site – Canterbury ★★★★
Touring & Camping Park
Bekesbourne Lane, Canterbury CT3 4AB
t (01227) 463216
w campingandcaravanningclub.co.uk

Yew Tree Park ★★★★
Holiday, Touring & Camping Park
Stone Street, Petham, Canterbury CT4 5PL
t (01227) 700306
e info@yewtreepark.com
w yewtreepark.com

CAPEL LE FERNE
Kent

Little Satmar Holiday Park ★★★★
Holiday, Touring & Camping Park
Winehouse Lane, Capel le Ferne, Folkestone CT18 7JF
t (01303) 251188
w katefarm.co.uk

Varne Ridge Holiday Park ★★★★★
Holiday & Touring Park
145 Old Dover Road, Capel le Ferne, Folkestone CT18 7HX
t (01303) 251765
e info@varne-ridge.co.uk
w varne-ridge.co.uk

CHADLINGTON
Oxfordshire

Camping & Caravanning Club Site – Chipping Norton ★★★★
Touring & Camping Park
Chipping Norton Road, Chadlington OX7 3PE
t (01608) 641993
w campingandcaravanningclub.co.uk

CHERTSEY
Surrey

Chertsey Camping & Caravanning Club Site ★★★★
Touring & Camping Park
Bridge Road, Chertsey KT16 8JX
t (01932) 562405
w campingandcaravanningclub.co.uk

CHICHESTER
West Sussex

Bell Caravan Park ★★
Holiday, Touring & Camping Park
Bell Lane, Birdham, Chichester PO20 7HY
t (01243) 512264

Wicks Farm Holiday Park ★★★★★
Holiday & Camping Park
Redlands Lane, West Wittering, Chichester PO20 8QE
t (01243) 513116
e wicks.farm@virgin.net
w wicksfarm.co.uk

COLWELL BAY
Isle of Wight

Colwell Bay Caravan Park ★★★★
Holiday Park
Madeira Lane, Colwell PO40 9SR
t (01983) 752403
e james.bishop1@tinyworld.co.uk
w isleofwight-colwellbay.co.uk

COWES
Isle of Wight

Sunnycott Caravan Park ★★★★
Holiday Park
Rew Street, Cowes PO31 8NN
t (01983) 292859
e info@sunnycottcaravanpark.co.uk
w sunnycottcaravanpark.co.uk

CROWBOROUGH
East Sussex

Norman's Bay Camping & Caravanning Club ★★★★
Touring & Camping Park
Pevensey, Pevensey BN24 6PR
t 0845 130 7633
w campingandcaravanningclub.co.uk

CROWMARSH GIFFORD
Oxfordshire

Bridge Villa Caravan & Camping Site ★★★★
Touring & Camping Park
The Street, Crowmarsh Gifford OX10 8HB
t (01491) 836860
e bridge.villa@btinternet.com

DORNEY REACH
Berkshire

Amerden Caravan & Camping Park ★★★★
Touring & Camping Park
Old Marsh Lane, Dorney Reach, Maidenhead SL6 0EE
t (01628) 627461
e beverly@amerdencaravanpark.co.uk

DYMCHURCH
Kent

Dymchurch Caravan Park ★★★★
Holiday Park
St Marys Road, Dymchurch, Romney Marsh TN29 0PW
t (01303) 872303

E & J Piper Caravan Park ★★★★
Holiday Park
St Marys Road, Dymchurch, Romney Marsh TN29 0PN
t (01303) 872103

New Beach Holiday Village ★★★★ **ROSE AWARD**
Holiday, Touring & Camping Park
Hythe Road, Dymchurch, Romney Marsh TN29 0JX
t (01303) 872233 & (01303) 872234
e newbeachholiday@aol.com

EAST COWES
Isle of Wight

Waverley Park Holiday Centre ★★★★
Holiday, Touring & Camping Park
51 Old Road, East Cowes PO32 6AW
t (01983) 293452
e holidays@waverley-park.co.uk
w waverley-park.co.uk

EAST HORSLEY
Surrey

Horsley Camping & Caravanning Club Site ★★★★
Touring & Camping Park
Ockham Road North, Leatherhead KT24 6PE
t (01483) 283273
w campingandcaravanningclub.co.uk

EASTBOURNE
East Sussex

Fairfields Farm Caravan & Camping Park ★★★
Touring & Camping Park
Eastbourne Road, Westham, Pevensey BN24 5NG
t (01323) 763165
e enquiries@fairfieldsfarm.com
w fairfieldsfarm.com

EASTCHURCH
Kent

Ashcroft Coast Holiday Park ★★★★
Holiday Park
Plough Road, Eastchurch, Sheerness ME12 4JH
t 0871 664 9701
e holidaysales.ashcroftcoast@park-resorts.com
w park-resorts.com

Shurland Dale Holiday Park ★★★★★
Holiday Park
Warden Road, Eastchurch, Sheerness ME12 4EN
t 0871 664 9769
e holidaysales.shurland@park-resorts.com
w park-resorts.com

Warden Springs Holiday Park ★★★★
Holiday, Touring & Camping Park
Thorn Hill Road, Eastchurch, Sheerness ME12 4HF
t 0871 664 9790
e holidayparks.wardensprings@park-resorts.com
w park-resorts.com

FOLKESTONE
Kent

Black Horse Farm Caravan Club Site ★★★★★
Touring & Camping Park
385 Canterbury Road, Densole, Folkestone CT18 7BG
t (01303) 892665
w caravanclub.co.uk

Camping & Caravanning Club Site – Folkestone ★★★★★
Touring & Camping Park
The Warren, Folkestone CT19 6NQ
t (01303) 255093
w campingandcaravanningclub.co.uk

FORDINGBRIDGE
Hampshire

Sandy Balls Holiday Centre ★★★★★ **ROSE AWARD**
Holiday Park
Godshill, Fordingbridge SP6 2JZ
t 0845 270 2248
e post@sandy-balls.co.uk
w sandy-balls.co.uk

FRESHWATER
Isle of Wight

Heathfield Farm Camping ★★★★
Touring & Camping Park
Heathfield Road, Freshwater PO40 9SH
t (01983) 756756
e web@heathfieldcamping.co.uk
w heathfieldcamping.co.uk

FRITHAM
Hampshire

Forestry Commission Ocknell/ Longbeech Caravan & Camping Site
Rating Applied For
Holiday, Touring & Camping Park
Fritham, Lyndhurst SO43 7HH
t (0131) 314 6505
e fe.holidays@forestry.gov.uk
w forestholidays.co.uk

GOSPORT
Hampshire

Kingfisher Caravan Park ★★★
Holiday, Touring & Camping Park
Browndown Road, Stokes Road, Gosport PO13 9BG
t (023) 9250 2611
e info@kingfisher-caravan-park.co.uk
w kingfisher-caravan-park.co.uk

Look out for parks participating in the National Accessible Scheme

GRAFFHAM
West Sussex

Graffham Camping & Caravanning Club Site ★★★★
Touring & Camping Park
Great Bury, Graffham, Petworth GU28 0QJ
t 0845 130 7633
w campingandcaravanning club.co.uk

HAILSHAM
East Sussex

Peel House Farm Caravan Park (Touring) ★★★★
Holiday, Touring & Camping Park
Sayerland Lane, Polegate, Hailsham BN26 6QX
t (01323) 845629
e peelhocp@tesco.net

HAMBLE
Hampshire

Riverside Holidays ★★★
Holiday, Touring & Camping Park
Satchell Lane, Hamble SO31 4HR
t (023) 8045 3220
e enquiries@riversideholidays.co.uk
w riversideholidays.co.uk

HASTINGS
East Sussex

Coghurst Hall Holiday Park
Rating Applied For
Holiday, Touring & Camping Park
Ivyhouse Lane, Hastings TN35 4NP
t (01424) 757955

Combe Haven Holiday Park ★★★★
Holiday Park
Harley Shute Road, St Leonards-on-Sea TN38 8BZ
t (01424) 427891

Hastings Touring Park ★★★★
Holiday, Touring & Camping Park
Barley Lane, Hastings TN35 5DX
t (01424) 423583

Rocklands Holiday Park ★★★★
Holiday Park
Rocklands Lane, East Hill, Hastings TN35 5DY
t (01424) 423097

Stalkhurst Camping & Caravan Park ★★★
Holiday, Touring & Camping Park
Ivyhouse Lane, Hastings TN35 4NN
t (01424) 439015
e stalkhurstpark@btinternet.com

HAYLING ISLAND
Hampshire

Fishery Creek Caravan & Camping Park ★★★★
Touring & Camping Park
Fishery Lane, Hayling Island PO11 9NR
t (023) 9246 2164
e camping@fisherycreek.fsnet.co.uk
w keyparks.co.uk

Hayling Island Holiday Park ★★★★ ROSE AWARD
Holiday Park
Manor Road, Hayling Island PO11 0QS
t 0870 777 6754
e hayling@weststarholidays.co.uk
w weststarholidays.co.uk

HOLMSLEY
Hampshire

Holmsley Caravan & Camping Site ★★★
Touring & Camping Park
Forest Road, Holmsley BH23 7EQ
t (01425) 674502
e holmsley.site@forestholidays.co.uk
w forestholidays.co.uk

HORAM
East Sussex

Horam Manor Touring Park ★★★★
Touring & Camping Park
Horam, Heathfield TN21 0YD
t (01435) 813662
e camp@horam-manor.co.uk
w horam-manor.co.uk

HORSHAM
West Sussex

Honeybridge Park ★★★★
Holiday Park
Honeybridge Lane, Dial Post, Horsham RH13 8NX
t (01403) 710923
e enquiries@honeybridgepark.co.uk
w honeybridgepark.co.uk

HURLEY
Berkshire

Hurley Riverside Park ★★★★
Holiday Park
Hurley, Maidenhead SL6 5NE
t (01628) 824493
e info@hurleyriversidepark.co.uk
w hurleyriversidepark.co.uk

Hurleyford Farm ★★★★
Holiday Park
Mill Lane, Hurley, Maidenhead SL6 5ND
t (01628) 829009

KINGHAM
Oxfordshire

Bluewood Park ★★★★★ ROSE AWARD
Holiday Park
Kingham, Chipping Norton OX7 6UJ
t (01608) 659946
e rachel@bluewoodpark.com
w bluewoodpark.com

KINGSDOWN
Kent

Kingsdown Park Holiday Village ★★★★★
Holiday Park
Upper Street, Kingsdown, Deal CT14 8AU
t (01304) 361205
e info@kingsdownpark.net
w kingsdownpark.net

LEYSDOWN ON SEA
Kent

Harts Holiday Park
Rating Applied For
Holiday, Touring & Camping Park
Leysdown Road, Sheerness ME12 4RG
t (01795) 510225

LYMINSTER
West Sussex

Brookside Caravan Park ★★★
Holiday Park
Lyminster Road, Lyminster BN17 7QE
t (01903) 713292
e mark@brooksideuk.com
w brooksideuk.com

LYNDHURST
Hampshire

Denny & Matley Wood Caravan & Camping Site
Rating Applied For
Holiday, Touring & Camping Park
Beaulieu Road, Lyndhurst SO43 7FZ
t (023) 8029 3144
e dennywood@hotmail.co.uk
w forestholidays.co.uk

MAIDSTONE
Kent

Bearsted Caravan Club Site
Rating Applied For
Touring & Camping Park
Ashford Road, Hollingbourne, Maidstone ME17 1XH
t (01622) 730018
w caravanclub.co.uk

MARDEN
Kent

Tanner Farm Touring Caravan & Camping Park ★★★★★
Touring & Camping Park
Goudhurst Road, Tonbridge TN12 9ND
t (01622) 832399
e enquiries@tannerfarmpark.co.uk
w tannerfarmpark.co.uk

MILFORD ON SEA
Hampshire

Carrington Park ★★★★★
Holiday Park
New Lane, Milford on Sea SO41 0UQ
t (01590) 642654
e office@carringtonpark.co.uk
w ukparks.co.uk/carrington

Downton Holiday Park ★★★★ ROSE AWARD
Holiday Park
Shorefield Road, Milford on Sea SO41 0LH
t (01425) 476131 & (01590) 642515
e info@downtonholidaypark.co.uk
w downtonholidaypark.co.uk

Lytton Lawn Touring Park ★★★★
Touring & Camping Park
Lymore Lane, Milford on Sea, Lymington SO41 0TX
t (01590) 648331
e holidays@shorefield.co.uk
w shorefield.co.uk

Shorefield Country Park ★★★★★ ROSE AWARD
Holiday Park
Shorefield Road, Milford on Sea SO41 0LH
t (01590) 648331

MINSTER-IN-THANET
Kent

Wayside Caravan Park ★★★★★
Holiday Park
Way Hill, Minster, Ramsgate CT12 4HW
t (01843) 821272
e lydia@scott9330.freeserve.co.uk
w waysidecaravanpark.co.uk

MOLLINGTON
Oxfordshire

Anita's Touring Caravan Park ★★★★
Touring & Camping Park
Church Farm, Mollington, Banbury OX17 1AZ
t (01295) 750731
e anitagail@btopenworld.com
w caravancampingsites.co.uk

MONKTON
Kent

The Foxhunter Park ★★★★★ ROSE AWARD
Holiday Park
Monkton Street, Monkton, Ramsgate CT12 4JG
t (01843) 821311
e foxhunterpark@aol.com
w thefoxhunterpark.co.uk

NEW MILTON
Hampshire

Glen Orchard Holiday Park ★★★★
Holiday Park
Walkford Lane, New Milton BH25 5NH
t (01425) 616463
e enquiries@glenorchard.co.uk
w glenorchard.co.uk

Hoburne Bashley ★★★★
Holiday Park
Sway Road, New Milton
BH25 5QR
t (01425) 612340
e enquiries@hoburne.com
w hoburne.com

Hoburne Naish ★★★★★ ROSE AWARD
Holiday Park
Christchurch Road, New Milton
BH25 7RE
t (01425) 273586
e enquiries@hoburne.com
w hoburne.com

Setthorns Caravan & Camping Site
Rating Applied For
Holiday, Touring & Camping Park
Wotton, New Milton
BH25 5WA
t (01590) 681020
w forestholidays.co.uk

NEW ROMNEY
Kent

Marlie Farm Holiday Park
Rating Applied For
Holiday, Touring & Camping Park
Dymchurch Road, New Romney TN28 8UE
t (01797) 363060

Romney Sands Holiday Park ★★★★
Holiday Park
The Parade, Greatstone, New Romney TN28 8RN
t 0871 664 9760
e holidaysales.romneysands@park-resorts.com
w park-resorts.com

NEWCHURCH
Isle of Wight

Southland Camping Park ★★★★★
Touring & Camping Park
Winford Road, Sandown
PO36 0LZ
t (01983) 865385
e info@southland.co.uk
w southland.co.uk

NITON
Isle of Wight

Meadow View Caravan Site ★
Holiday Park
Newport Road, Ventnor
PO38 2NS
t (01983) 730015

OLNEY
Buckinghamshire

Emberton Country Park ★★
Touring & Camping Park
Emberton, Olney MK46 5FJ
t (01234) 711575
e embertonpark@milton-keynes.gov.uk
w mkweb.co.uk/embertonpark

OWER
Hampshire

Green Pastures Caravan Park ★★★
Touring Park
Green Pastures Farm, Whitemoor Lane, Romsey
SO51 6AJ
t (023) 8081 4444
e enquiries@greenpasturesfarm.com
w greenpasturesfarm.com

PAGHAM
West Sussex

Church Farm Holiday Village ★★★★ ROSE AWARD
Holiday Park
Church Lane, Bognor Regis
PO21 4NR
t 0870 405 0151
e churchfarm@bourne-leisure.co.uk
w churchfarm-park.co.uk

PEVENSEY
East Sussex

Camping & Caravanning Club Site – Normans Bay ★★★★
Touring & Camping Park
Normans Bay, Pevensey
BN24 6PR
t (01323) 761190
w campingandcaravanning club.co.uk

PEVENSEY BAY
East Sussex

Bay View Park Ltd ★★★
Holiday, Touring & Camping Park
Old Martello Road, Pevensey Bay BN24 6DX
t (01323) 768688
e holidays@bay-view.co.uk
w bay-view.co.uk

RAMSGATE
Kent

Manston Caravan & Camping Park ★★★★
Holiday, Touring & Camping Park
Manston Court Road, Manston, Ramsgate CT12 5AU
t (01843) 823442

Nethercourt Touring Park ★★★
Touring & Camping Park
Nethercourt Hill, Ramsgate
CT11 0RX
t (01843) 595485

READING
Berkshire

Wellington Country Park ★★★★
Touring & Camping Park
Odiham Road, Riseley, Reading
RG7 1SP
t (0118) 932 6444
e info@wellington-country-park.co.uk
w wellington-country-park.co.uk

REDHILL
Surrey

Alderstead Heath Caravan Club Site ★★★★
Touring Park
Dean Lane, Redhill RH1 3AH
t (01737) 644629
w caravanclub.co.uk

RINGWOOD
Hampshire

Shamba Holidays ★★★★
Touring & Camping Park
230 Ringwood Road, St Leonards, Ringwood BH24 2SB
t (01202) 873302
e enquiries@shambaholidays.co.uk
w shambaholidays.co.uk

ROCHESTER
Kent

Allhallows Leisure Park ★★★★
Holiday Park
Allhallows, Rochester
ME3 9QD
t 0870 405 0152
e trina.davis@bourneleisure.co.uk
w havenholidays.com/allhallows

ROMSEY
Hampshire

Hill Farm Caravan Park ★★★★
Holiday, Touring & Camping Park
Branches Lane, Sherfield English, Romsey SO51 6FH
t (01794) 340402
e gib@hillfarmpark.com
w hillfarmpark.com

ROOKLEY
Isle of Wight

Rookley Country Park ★★★★
Holiday, Touring & Camping Park
Main Road, Ventnor PO38 3LU
t (01983) 721606
e info@islandviewhols.co.uk
w islandviewhols.co.uk

RUNCTON
West Sussex

Chichester Lakeside Holiday Park
Rating Applied For
Holiday, Touring & Camping Park
Vinnetrow Road, Runcton, Chichester PO20 1QH
t (01243) 787715
e lakeside@parkholidaysuk.com
w parkholidaysuk.com/caravansales/parks/sussex/chichester_lakeside

RYDE
Isle of Wight

Beaper Farm ★★★
Touring & Camping Park
Brading Road, Ryde PO33 1QJ
t (01983) 615210
e beaper@btinternet.com
w beaperfarm.com

Isle of Wight Self Catering – Pondwell Bungalows ★★★
Holiday, Touring & Camping Park
Salterns Road, Seaview
PO34 5AQ
t (01983) 612330
e info@isleofwightselfcatering.co.uk
w isleofwightselfcatering.co.uk

Roebeck Camping and Caravan Park ★★
Touring & Camping Park
Gatehouse Road, Upton Cross
PO33 4BP
t (01983) 611475
e andrew.cross@roebeck-farm.co.uk
w roebeck-farm.co.uk

Whitefield Forest Touring Park ★★★★
Touring & Camping Park
Brading Road PO33 1QL
t (01983) 617069
e pat&louise@whitefieldforest.co.uk
w whitefieldforest.co.uk

RYE HARBOUR
East Sussex

Frenchman's Beach Holiday Park
Rating Applied For
Holiday, Touring & Camping Park
Rye Harbour Road, Rye
TN31 7TX
t (01797) 223011

ST HELENS
Isle of Wight

Carpenters Farm Campsite ★★★
Touring & Camping Park
Carpenters Road, St Helens, Ryde PO33 1YL
t (01983) 874557
e info@carpentersfarm.co.uk
w carpentersfarm.co.uk

Field Lane Holiday Park ★★★★★
Holiday Park
Field Lane, Ryde PO33 1UX
t (01983) 872779
w fieldlane.com

Nodes Point Holiday Park ★★★★
Holiday, Touring & Camping Park
Nodes Road, Ryde PO33 1YA
t 0871 664 9758
e holidaysales.nodespoint@park-resorts.com
w park-resorts.com

Old Mill Holiday Park ★★★★★ ROSE AWARD
Holiday Park
Mill Road, Ryde PO33 1UE
t (01983) 872507
e web@oldmill.co.uk
w oldmill.co.uk

ST LAWRENCE
Isle of Wight

The Undercliff Glen Caravan Park ★★★★★
Holiday Park
Undercliff Drive, Ventnor
PO38 1XY
t (01983) 730261
e info@undercliffglencaravanpark.co.uk
w undercliffglencaravanpark.co.uk

ST LEONARDS
East Sussex

Beauport Holiday Park ★★★
Holiday Park
The Ridge West, St Leonards-on-Sea TN37 7PP
t (01424) 851246

ST-MARGARETS-AT-CLIFFE
Kent

St Margarets Holiday Park ★★★★★
Holiday Park
Reach Road, St Margarets-at-Cliffe, Dover CT15 6AE
t 0871 664 9772
e holidaysales.stmargaretsbay@park-resorts.com
w park-resorts.com

ST NICHOLAS AT WADE
Kent

St Nicholas Camping Site ★★
Touring & Camping Park
Court Road, St Nicholas at Wade, Birchington CT7 0NH
t (01843) 847245

SANDOWN
Isle of Wight

Adgestone Camping & Caravanning Club ★★★★
Touring & Camping Park
Lower Adgestone Road, Adgestone PO36 0HL
t (01983) 403432
w campingandcaravanningclub.co.uk

Cheverton Copse Holiday Park ★★★★ ROSE AWARD
Holiday Park
Scotchells Brook Lane, Sandown PO36 0JP
t (01983) 403161
e holidays@chevertoncopse.com
w chevertoncopse.com

Fairway Holiday Park ★★★
Holiday Park
The Fairway, Sandown
PO36 9PS
t (01983) 403462
e enquiries@fairwayholidaypark.co.uk
w fairwayholidaypark.co.uk

Fort Holiday Park ★★★
Holiday Park
Avenue Road, Sandown
PO36 8BD
t (01983) 402858
e bookings@fortholidaypark.co.uk
w fortholidaypark.co.uk

SANDWICH
Kent

Sandwich Leisure Park ★★★★★
Holiday, Touring & Camping Park
Woodnesborough Road, Sandwich CT13 0AA
t (01304) 612681
e info@coastandcountryleisure.com
w coastandcountryleisure.com

SEAFORD
East Sussex

Sunnyside Caravan Park ★★★★
Holiday Park
Marine Parade, Seaford
BN25 2QW
t (01323) 892825
e managers@sunnyside-caravan-park.co.uk
w sunnyside-caravan-park.co.uk

SEAL
Kent

Camping & Caravanning Club Site – Oldbury Hill ★★★★
Touring & Camping Park
Styants Bottom, Seal, Sevenoaks TN15 0ET
t (01732) 762728
w campingandcaravanningclub.co.uk

SEASALTER
Kent

Alberta Holiday Park ★★★
Holiday, Touring & Camping Park
Faversham Road, Whitstable CT5 4BJ
t (01227) 274485

Homing Park ★★★★
Holiday, Touring & Camping Park
Church Lane, Seasalter, Whitstable CT5 4BU
t (01227) 771777
e info@homingpark.co.uk
w homingpark.co.uk

SEAVIEW
Isle of Wight

Isle of Wight Self Catering – Salterns ★★★
Holiday Park
Salterns Road, Seaview
PO34 5AQ
t (01983) 612330
e info@isleofwightselfcatering.co.uk
w isleofwightselfcatering.co.uk

Isle of Wight Self Catering – Tollgate ★★★
Holiday Park
Salterns Road, Seaview
PO34 5AQ
t (01983) 612330
e info@isleofwightselfcatering.co.uk
w isleofwightselfcatering.co.uk

SELSEY
West Sussex

Green Lawns Holiday Park ★★★★★ ROSE AWARD
Holiday Park
Paddock Lane, Selsey PO20 9EJ
t (01243) 606080
e holidays@bunnleisure.co.uk
w bunnleisure.co.uk

Warner Farm Touring Park ★★★★★
Touring Park
Warner Lane, Selsey, Chichester PO20 9EL
t (01243) 604499 & (01243) 606080
e touring@bunnleisure.co.uk
w warnerfarm.co.uk

West Sands Holiday Park ★★★★ ROSE AWARD
Holiday Park
Mill Lane, Selsey, Chichester
PO20 9BH
t (01243) 606080
e holidays@bunnleisure.co.uk
w bunnleisure.co.uk

White Horse Caravan Park ★★★★ ROSE AWARD
Holiday Park
Paddock Lane, Selsey, Chichester PO20 9EJ
t (01243) 606080
e holidays@bunnleisure.co.uk
w bunnleisure.co.uk

SHANKLIN
Isle of Wight

Landguard Holidays – Davidson Leisure Resorts ★★★★ ROSE AWARD
Holiday Park
Landguard Manor Road, Shanklin PO37 7PJ
t (01983) 863100
e enquiries@landguardholidays.co.uk
w landguardholidays.co.uk

Lower Hyde Holiday Park ★★★★ ROSE AWARD
Holiday, Touring & Camping Park
Landguard Road, Shanklin
PO37 7LL
t 0871 664 9752
e holidaysales.lowerhyde@park-resorts.com
w park-resorts.com

SHEERNESS
Kent

Sheerness Holiday Park
Rating Applied For
Holiday, Touring & Camping Park
Halfway Road, Milford-on-Sea, Sheerness ME12 3AA
t (01795) 662638
w cinqueportleisure.com

SLINDON
West Sussex

Camping & Caravanning Club Site – Slindon ★★
Touring Park
Slindon Park, Arundel
BN18 0RG
t (01243) 814387
w campingandcaravanningclub.co.uk

SMALL DOLE
West Sussex

Southdown Caravan Park ★★★
Holiday & Touring Park
Henfield Road, Small Dole, Henfield BN5 9XH
t (01903) 814323

SOUTHBOURNE
West Sussex

Chichester Camping & Caravan Club ★★★
Touring & Camping Park
Main Road, Southbourne, Chichester PO10 8JH
t 0845 130 7633
w campingandcaravanningclub.co.uk

STANDLAKE
Oxfordshire

Hardwick Parks ★★★
Holiday, Touring & Camping Park
The Downs, Standlake, Witney
OX29 7PZ
t (01865) 300501
e info@hardwickparks.co.uk
w hardwickparks.co.uk

Lincoln Farm Park ★★★★★
Touring & Camping Park
High Street, Standlake
OX29 7RH
t (01865) 300239
e info@lincolnfarm.co.uk
w lincolnfarmpark.co.uk

THORNESS BAY
Isle of Wight

Thorness Bay Holiday Park ★★★★ ROSE AWARD
Holiday, Touring & Camping Park
Thorness Lane, Cowes
PO31 8NJ
t 0871 664 9779
e holidaysales.thornessbay@park-resorts.com
w park-resorts.com

UCKFIELD
East Sussex

Honeys Green Touring Caravan Park ★★★
Holiday, Touring & Camping Park
Oak Lodge, Hartfield Road, Uckfield TN8 5NF
t (01732) 860205

WALTON-ON-THAMES
Surrey

Walton on Thames Camping & Caravanning Club Site ★★★
Camping Park
Fieldcommon Lane, Walton-on-Thames KT12 3QG
t (01932) 220392
w campingandcaravanningclub.co.uk

WARSASH
Hampshire

Dibles Park Company ★★★★
Touring Park
Dibles Park, Dibles Road, Warsash SO31 9SA
t (01489) 575232
e dibles.park@btconnect.com
w diblespark.co.uk

Solent Breezes Holiday Park ★★★
Holiday Park
Hook Lane, Southampton SO31 9HG
t (01489) 572084

WASHINGTON
West Sussex

Washington Caravan & Camping Park ★★★★
Touring & Camping Park
London Road, Washington RH20 4AJ
t (01903) 892869
e washcamp@amserve.com
w washcamp.com

WHITSTABLE
Kent

Seaview Holiday Park
Rating Applied For
Holiday, Touring & Camping Park
St Johns Road, Whitstable CT5 2RY
t (01227) 792246

WINCHELSEA BEACH
East Sussex

Winchelsea Sands Holiday Park
Rating Applied For
Holiday, Touring & Camping Park
Winchelsea TN36 4NB
t (01797) 226442

WINCHESTER
Hampshire

Morn Hill Caravan Club Site ★★★
Touring & Camping Park
Morn Hill, Winchester SO21 2PH
t (01962) 869877
w caravanclub.co.uk

WORTHING
West Sussex

Northbrook Farm Caravan Club Site ★★★★
Touring Park
Titnore Way, Worthing BN13 3RT
t (01903) 502962
e enquiries@caravanclub.co.uk
w caravanclub.co.uk

Onslow Caravan Park ★★★
Holiday Park
Onslow Drive, Worthing BN12 5RX
t (01903) 243170
e islandmeadow@fsmail-net.uk
w islandmeadow.co.uk

WROTHAM HEATH
Kent

Gate House Wood Touring Park ★★★★★
Touring Park
Ford Road, Wrotham Heath, Sevenoaks TN15 7SD
t (01732) 843062
e gatehousewood@btinternet.com

WROXALL
Isle of Wight

Appuldurcombe Gardens Holiday Park ★★★★ ROSE AWARD
Holiday, Touring & Camping Park
Appuldurcombe Road, Ventnor PO38 3EP
t (01983) 852597
e info@appuldurcombegardens.co.uk
w appuldurcombegardens.co.uk

YARMOUTH
Isle of Wight

The Orchards Holiday Caravan & Camping Park ★★★★★ ROSE AWARD
Holiday & Touring Park
Main Road PO41 0TS
t (01983) 531331
e info@orchards-holiday-park.co.uk
w orchards-holiday-park.co.uk

Silver Glades Caravan Park ★★★★
Holiday Park
Solent Road, Yarmouth PO41 0XZ
t (01983) 760172
e holiday@silvergladesiow.co.uk
w silvergladesiow.co.uk

LONDON

INNER LONDON
E4

Lee Valley Campsite ★★★★
Touring & Camping Park
Sewardstone Road, Chingford, Waltham Forest E4 7RA
t (020) 8529 5689
e scs@leevalleypark.org.uk
w leevalleypark.org.uk

SE2

Abbey Wood Caravan Club Site ★★★★★
Touring & Camping Park
Federation Road, Abbey Wood, London SE2 0LS
t (020) 8311 7708
w caravanclub.co.uk

SE19

Crystal Palace Caravan Club Site ★★★★★
Touring & Camping Park
Crystal Palace Parade, London SE19 1UF
t (020) 8778 7155
w caravanclub.co.uk

SOUTH WEST ENGLAND

ALDERHOLT
Dorset

Hill Cottage Farm Camping & Caravan Park ★★★★
Touring & Camping Park
Sandleheath Road, Alderholt, Fordingbridge SP6 3EG
t (01425) 650513
e hillcottagefarmcaravansite@supanet.com
w hillcottagefarmcampingandcaravanpark.co.uk

ASHBURTON
Devon

Parkers Farm Holiday Park ★★★★
Holiday, Touring & Camping Park
Higher Mead Farm, Alston Cross, Ashburton, Newton Abbot TQ13 7LJ
t (01364) 654869
e parkersfarm@btconnect.com
w parkersfarm.co.uk

River Dart Adventures ★★★★
Touring & Camping Park
Holne Park, Ashburton, Newton Abbot TQ13 7NP
t (01364) 652511
e enquiries@riverdart.co.uk
w riverdart.co.uk

AXMINSTER
Devon

Andrewshayes Caravan Park ★★★★
Holiday Park
Dalwood, Axminster EX13 7DY
t (01404) 831225
e enquiries@andrewshayes.co.uk
w andrewshayes.co.uk

Hunters Moon Country Estate ★★★★
Holiday, Touring & Camping Park
Hawkchurch, Axminster EX13 5UL
t (01297) 678402
w ukparks.co.uk/huntersmoon

BARNSTAPLE
Devon

Kentisbury Grange Country Park ★★★★
Holiday, Touring & Camping Park
Kentisbury, Barnstaple EX31 4NL
t (01271) 883454
e info@kentisburygrange.co.uk
w kentisburygrange.co.uk

 Look out for parks participating in the National Accessible Scheme

BATH
Somerset

Newton Mill Camping ★★★★
Touring & Camping Park
Twaebrook Ltd, Newton Mill Camping Park, Newton Road, Bath BA2 9JF
t (01225) 333909
e newtonmill@hotmail.com
w campinginbath.co.uk

BEETHAM
Somerset

Five Acres Caravan Club Site ★★★★
Touring Park
Giants Grave Road, Chard TA20 3QA
t (01460) 234519
e enquiries@caravanclub.co.uk
w caravanclub.co.uk

BERE REGIS
Dorset

Rowlands Wait Touring Park ★★★
Touring & Camping Park
Rye Hill, Bere Regis, Wareham BH20 7LP
t (01929) 472727
e enquiries@rowlandswait.co.uk
w rowlandswait.co.uk

BERRY HEAD
Devon

Landscove Holiday Village ★★★★
Holiday Park
Gillard Road, Brixham TQ5 9EP
t 0870 442 9750
e bookings@landscove.biz
w southdevonholidays.biz

BERRYNARBOR
Devon

Sandaway Beach Holiday Park ★★★★ ROSE AWARD
Holiday Park
Berrynarbor, Ilfracombe EX34 9ST
t (01271) 866766
e stay@johnfowlerholidays.com
w johnfowlerholidays.com

BIDEFORD
Devon

Bideford Bay Holiday Park ★★★★ ROSE AWARD
Holiday Park
Bucks Cross, Bideford EX39 5DU
t 0871 664 9707
e holidaysales.bidefordbay@park-resorts.com
w park-resorts.com

BISHOP SUTTON
Somerset

Bath Chew Valley Caravan Park ★★★★★
Touring Park
Ham Lane, Bishop Sutton, Bristol BS39 5TZ
t (01275) 332127
e enquiries@bathchewvalley.co.uk
w bathchewvalley.co.uk

BLACKWATER
Cornwall

Trevarth Holiday Park ★★★★ ROSE AWARD
Holiday, Touring & Camping Park
Blackwater, Truro TR4 8HR
t (01872) 560266
e trevarth@lineone.net
w trevarth.co.uk

BLANDFORD FORUM
Dorset

The Inside Park ★★★★
Touring & Camping Park
Down House Estate, Blandford St Mary, Blandford Forum DT11 9AD
t (01258) 453719
e inspark@aol.com
w members.aol.com/inspark/inspark

BLUE ANCHOR
Somerset

Hoburne Blue Anchor ★★★★ ROSE AWARD
Holiday & Touring Park
Carhampton Road, Minehead TA24 6JT
t (01643) 821360
e enquiries@hoburne.com
w hoburne.com

BODMIN
Cornwall

Camping & Caravanning Club Site – Bodmin ★★★★
Touring & Camping Park
Old Callywith Road, Bodmin PL31 2DZ
t (01872) 501658
w campingandcaravanningclub.co.uk

Ruthern Valley Holidays ★★★★
Holiday, Touring & Camping Park
Ruthern Bridge, Bodmin PL30 5LU
t (01208) 831395

BOURNEMOUTH
Dorset

Meadow Bank Holidays ★★★★★ ROSE AWARD
Holiday & Touring Park
Stour Way, Christchurch BH23 2PQ
t (01202) 483597
e enquiries@meadowbank-holidays.co.uk
w meadowbank-holiday.co.uk

BOVISAND
Devon

Bovisand Lodge Estate ★★★★ ROSE AWARD
Holiday Park
Bovisand Lodge, Bovisand, Plymouth PL9 0AA
t (01752) 403554
e stay@bovisand.com
w bovisand.com

BRATTON CLOVELLY
Devon

South Breazle Holidays ★★★★
Holiday, Touring & Camping Park
Okehampton EX20 4JS
t (01837) 871701
e louise@southbreazleholidays.co.uk
w southbreazleholidays.co.uk

BRATTON FLEMING
Devon

Greenacres Farm Touring Caravan Park ★★★★
Touring Park
Bratton Fleming, Barnstaple EX31 4SG
t (01598) 763334

BRAUNTON
Devon

Lobb Fields Caravan and Camping Park ★★★★
Touring & Camping Park
Saunton Road, Braunton EX33 1EB
t (01271) 812090
e info@lobbfields.com
w lobbfields.com

BREAN
Somerset

Diamond Farm ★★★
Touring & Camping Park
Weston Road, Burnham-on-Sea TA8 2RL
t (01278) 751263
e trevor@diamondfarm42.freeserve.co.uk
w diamondfarm.co.uk

Dolphin Caravan Park ★★★★★
Holiday Park
Coast Road, Burnham-on-Sea TA8 2QY
t (01278) 751258
w dolphincaravanpark.co.uk

Holiday Resort Unity ★★★
Holiday Village
Coast Road, Brean Sands TA8 2RB
t (01278) 751235
e admin@hru.co.uk
w hru.co.uk

Northam Farm Touring Park ★★★★
Holiday, Touring & Camping Park
Brean Sands, Burnham-on-Sea TA8 2SE
t (01278) 751244
e enquiries@northamfarm.co.uk
w northamfarm.co.uk

Warren Farm Holiday Centre ★★★★ ROSE AWARD
Holiday Park
Warren Road, Brean Sands, Burnham-on-Sea TA8 2RP
t (01278) 751227
e enquiries@warren-farm.co.uk
w warren-farm.co.uk

Warren Farm Holiday Centre ★★★★
Holiday, Touring & Camping Park
Warren Road, Brean Sands, Burnham-on-Sea TA8 2RP
t (01278) 751227
e enquiries@warren-farm.co.uk
w warren-farm.co.uk

BRIDESTOWE
Devon

Glebe Park ★★★
Holiday & Touring Park
Bridestowe, Okehampton EX20 4ER
t (01837) 861261

BRIDGWATER
Somerset

Fairways International Touring Caravan & Camping Park ★★★
Touring & Camping Park
Bath Road, Bridgwater TA7 8PP
t (01278) 685569
e holiday@fairwaysinternational.co.uk
w fairwaysinternational.co.uk

BRIDPORT
Dorset

Binghams Farm Touring Park ★★★★
Touring & Camping Park
Binghams Farm, Melplash DT6 3TT
t (01308) 488234
e enquiries@binghamsfarm.co.uk
w binghamsfarm.co.uk

Eype House Caravan Park ★★★
Holiday, Touring & Camping Park
Eype, Bridport DT6 6AL
t (01308) 424903
e enquiries@eypehouse.co.uk
w eypehouse.co.uk

Freshwater Beach Holiday Park ★★★★
Holiday, Touring & Camping Park
Burton Bradstock, Bridport DT6 4PT
t (01308) 897317
e office@freshwaterbeach.co.uk
w freshwaterbeach.co.uk

Golden Cap Holiday Park
★★★★★ ROSE AWARD
Holiday, Touring & Camping Park
Seatown, Chideock, Bridport DT6 6JX
t (01308) 422139
e holidays@wdlh.co.uk
w wdlh.co.uk

Highlands End Holiday Park
★★★★★ ROSE AWARD
Holiday, Touring & Camping Park
Eype, Bridport DT6 6AR
t (01308) 422139
e holidays@wdlh.co.uk
w wdlh.co.uk

BRISTOL
City of Bristol

Baltic Wharf Caravan Club Site ★★★★
Touring Park
Cumberland Road, Southville BS1 6XG
t (0117) 926 8030
e enquiries@caravanclub.co.uk
w caravanclub.co.uk

BRIXHAM
Devon

Brixham Holiday Park
★★★★ ROSE AWARD
Holiday Park
Fishcombe Road, Brixham TQ5 8RB
t (01803) 853324
e enquiries@brixhamholpk.fsnet.co.uk
w brixhamholidaypark.co.uk

Galmpton Touring Park
★★★★
Touring & Camping Park
Greenway Road, Galmpton, Brixham TQ5 0EP
t (01803) 842066
e galmptontouringpark@hotmail.com
w galmptontouringpark.co.uk

Hillhead Holiday Park Caravan Club Site ★★★★★
Touring & Camping Park
Hillhead, Brixham TQ5 0HH
t (01803) 853204
w caravanclub.co.uk

Riviera Bay Holiday Centre
★★★★
Holiday Park
Mudstone Lane, Brixham TQ5 9EJ
t (01803) 856335
e info@rivierabay.biz
w rivierabay.biz

BUDE
Cornwall

Bude Holiday Park (Cranstar Holidays) ★★★
Holiday, Touring & Camping Park
Maer Lane, Bude EX23 9EE
t (01288) 355955
e enquiries@budeholidaypark.co.uk
w budeholidaypark.co.uk

Budemeadows Touring Park
★★★★★
Touring Park
Budemeadows, Bude EX23 0NA
t (01288) 361646
e holiday@budemeadows.com
w budemeadows.com

Penhalt Farm Holiday Park
★★★
Touring & Camping Park
Poundstock, Bude EX23 0DG
t (01288) 361210
e denandjennie@penhaltfarm.fsnet.co.uk
w penhaltfarm.co.uk

Sandymouth Holiday Park
★★★★
Holiday & Touring Park
Sandymouth Bay, Bude EX23 9HW
t (01288) 352563
e reception@sandymouthbay.co.uk
w sandymouthbay.co.uk

Upper Lynstone Caravan and Camping Site ★★★★
Holiday, Touring & Camping Park
Upton, Bude EX23 0LP
t (01288) 352017
e reception@upperlynstone.co.uk
w upperlynstone.co.uk

Wooda Farm Park ★★★★★
Holiday & Touring Park
Poughill, Bude EX23 9HJ
t (01288) 352069
e enquiries@wooda.co.uk
w wooda.co.uk

BURNHAM-ON-SEA
Somerset

Burnham-on-Sea Holiday Village ★★★★
Holiday, Touring & Camping Park
Marine Drive, Burnham-on-Sea TA8 1LA
t (01278) 783391
e enquiries@british-holidays.co.uk
w british-holidays.co.uk

Home Farm Holiday Park
★★★★★
Holiday & Touring Park
Edithmead, Highbridge TA9 4HD
t (01278) 788888
e office@homefarmholidaypark.co.uk
w homefarmholidaypark.co.uk

Lakeside Holiday Park
★★★★
Holiday Park
Westfield Road, Burnham-on-Sea TA8 2AE
t (01278) 792222
e booking-enquiries@btconnect.com
w lakesideholidays.co.uk

The Retreat Caravan Park
★★★★★
Holiday Park
Berrow Road, Burnham-on-Sea TA8 2ES
t 07007 387328
e roger@retreat.uk.com
w retreatcaravanpark.co.uk

BURTON BRADSTOCK
Dorset

Coastal Caravan Park ★★★
Holiday, Touring & Camping Park
Annings Lane, Burton Bradstock, Bridport DT6 4QP
t (01308) 422139
e holidays@wdlh.co.uk
w wdlh.co.uk

CAMELFORD
Cornwall

Juliots Well Holiday Park
★★★
Holiday, Touring & Camping Park
Camelford PL32 9RF
t (01840) 213302
e juliotswell@breaksincornwall.com
w juliotswell.com

Lanteglos Hotel & Villas
★★★★
Holiday Village
Camelford, Camelford PL32 9RF
t (01840) 213551

CARDINHAM
Cornwall

Gwel-an-nans Farm ★★★
Touring & Camping Park
Little Downs, Cardinham, Bodmin PL30 4EF
t (01208) 821359
e info@gwelannans.co.uk

CARNON DOWNS
Cornwall

Carnon Downs Caravan & Camping Park ★★★★★
Touring & Camping Park
Carnon Downs, Truro TR3 6JJ
t (01872) 862283
e info@carnon-downs-caravanpark.co.uk
w carnon-downs-caravanpark.co.uk

CHACEWATER
Cornwall

Chacewater Park ★★★★
Touring & Camping Park
Cox Hill, Chacewater, Truro TR4 8LY
t (01209) 820762
e enquiries@chacewaterpark.co.uk
w chacewaterpark.co.uk

CHARD
Somerset

Alpine Grove Touring Park
★★★★
Touring Park
Chard TA20 4HD
t (01460) 63479
e stay@alpinegrovetouringpark.com
w alpinegrovetouringpark.com

CHARMOUTH
Dorset

Camping & Caravanning Club Site – Charmouth
★★★★★
Touring & Camping Park
Monkton Wyld, Bridport DT6 6DB
t (01297) 32965
w campingandcaravanningclub.co.uk

Dolphins River Park ★★★★
Holiday Park
Berne Lane, Charmouth DT6 6RD
t 0800 074 6375
e info@dolphinsriverpark.co.uk
w dolphinsriverpark.co.uk

Manor Farm Holiday Centre
★★★
Holiday, Touring & Camping Park
The Street, Charmouth, Bridport DT6 6QL
t (01297) 560226
e enq@manorfarmholidaycentre.co.uk
w manorfarmholidaycentre.co.uk

Newlands Holidays
★★★★★
Holiday, Touring & Camping Park
Newlands Holiday Park, Charmouth DT6 6RB
t (01297) 560259
e enq@newlandsholidays.co.uk
w newlandsholidays.co.uk

Seadown Holiday Park
★★★★★
Holiday, Touring & Camping Park
Bridge Road, Charmouth, Bridport DT6 6QS
t (01297) 560154
w seadowncaravanpark.co.uk

Wood Farm Caravan and Camping Park ★★★★★
Holiday, Touring & Camping Park
Charmouth, Bridport DT6 6BT
t (01297) 560697
e holidays@woodfarm.co.uk
w woodfarm.co.uk

CHEDDAR
Somerset

Broadway House Holiday Touring Caravan and Camping Park ★★★★ ROSE AWARD
Holiday, Touring & Camping Park
Axbridge Road, Cheddar BS27 3DB
t (01934) 742610
e info@broadwayhouse.uk.com
w broadwayhouse.uk.com

Cheddar Bridge Touring Park ★★★★
Holiday, Touring & Camping Park
Draycott Road, Cheddar BS27 3RJ
t (01934) 743048
e enquiries@cheddarbridge.co.uk
w cheddarbridge.co.uk

Cheddar, Mendip Heights Camping & Caravanning Club Site ★★★★
Touring & Camping Park
Townsend, Wells BA5 3BP
t (01749) 870241
e cheddar@campingandcaravanningclub.co.uk
w campingandcaravanningclub.co.uk

CHELTENHAM Gloucestershire

Cheltenham Racecourse Caravan Club Site ★★★
Touring & Camping Park
Prestbury Park, Evesham Road, Cheltenham GL50 4SH
t (01242) 523102
e enquiries@caravanclub.co.uk
w caravanclub.co.uk

CHICKERELL Dorset

Bagwell Farm Touring Park ★★★★
Touring & Camping Park
Knights in the Bottom, Chickerell, Weymouth DT3 4EA
t (01305) 782575
e enquiries@bagwellfarm.co.uk
w bagwellfarm.co.uk

CHRISTCHURCH Dorset

Harrow Wood Farm Caravan Park ★★★
Touring & Camping Park
Poplar Lane, Bransgore, Christchurch BH23 8JE
t (01425) 672487
e harrowwood@caravan-sites.co.uk
w caravan-sites.co.uk

Hoburne Park ★★★★★ ROSE AWARD
Holiday Park
Hoburne Caravan Park, Hoburne Lane, Christchurch BH23 4HU
t (01425) 273379
e enquiries@hoburne.com
w hoburne.com

Sandhills Holiday Park ★★★
Holiday Park
Mudeford, Christchurch BH23 4AL
t (01425) 274584

CHRISTCHURCH Gloucestershire

Woodland Caravan & Camping Site
Rating Applied For
Holiday, Touring & Camping Park
Bracelands Drive, Coleford GL16 7NN
t (01594) 837258
e fod.site@forestholidays.co.uk
w forestholidays.co.uk

CHUDLEIGH Devon

Holmans Wood Holiday Park ★★★★
Holiday, Touring & Camping Park
Harcombe Cross, Chudleigh TQ13 0DZ
t (01626) 853785
e enquiries@holmanswood.co.uk
w holmanswood.co.uk

COLEFORD Gloucestershire

Bracelands Campsite ★★★
Touring & Camping Park
Bracelands Drive, Christchurch, Coleford GL16 7NN
t (0131) 314 6100
w forestholidays.co.uk

Christchurch Campsite ★★★
Touring & Camping Park
Bracelands Drive, Christchurch, Coleford GL16 7NN
t (0131) 314 6100
w forestholidays.co.uk

Rushmere Farm ★★
Camping Park
Crossways, Coleford GL16 8QP
t (01594) 835319

COMBE MARTIN Devon

Newberry Valley Park ★★★★
Touring & Camping Park
Newberry Farm, Woodlands EX34 0AT
t (01271) 882334
e enq@newberrycampsite.co.uk
w newberrycampsite.co.uk

Stowford Farm Meadows ★★★★
Touring & Camping Park
Combe Martin, Ilfracombe EX34 0PW
t (01271) 882476
e enquiries@stowford.co.uk
w stowford.co.uk

CONNOR DOWNS Cornwall

Higher Trevaskis Park ★★★★
Touring & Camping Park
Gwinear Road, Connor Downs TR27 5JQ
t (01209) 831736

COOMBE BISSETT Wiltshire

Summerlands Caravan Park ★★★
Touring & Camping Park
College Farm, Rockbourne Road, Coombe Bissett SP5 4LP
t (01722) 718259
e summerlands-park@compaqnet.co.uk
w summerlands-park.com

CORFE CASTLE Dorset

Norden Farm Campsite ★★
Holiday, Touring & Camping Park
Norden Farm, Wareham BH20 5DS
t (01929) 480098
e nordenfarm@fsmail.net
w nordenfarm.com

Woodyhyde Camp Site ★
Camping Park
Valley Road, Corfe Castle, Wareham BH20 5HT
t (01929) 480274
e camp@woodyhyde.fsnet.co.uk
w woodyhyde.co.uk

CRACKINGTON HAVEN Cornwall

Hentervene (Caravan & Lodges) ★★★
Holiday, Touring & Camping Park
Crackington Haven, Boscastle, Bude EX23 0LF
t (01840) 230365
e contact@hentervene.co.uk
w hentervene.co.uk

CROWCOMBE Somerset

Quantock Orchard Caravan Park ★★★★★
Holiday, Touring & Camping Park
Taunton TA4 4AW
t (01984) 618618
e qocp@flaxpool.freeserve.co.uk
w quantockorchard.co.uk

CROYDE Devon

Croyde Bay Holiday Village (Unison) ★★★★
Holiday Village
Croyde, Braunton EX33 1QB
t (01271) 890890
w croydeunison.co.uk

CROYDE BAY Devon

Ruda Holiday Park ★★★★ ROSE AWARD
Holiday, Touring & Camping Park
Croyde Bay, Braunton EX33 1NY
t 0871 641 0410
e enquiries@parkdeanholidays.co.uk
w parkdeanholidays.co.uk

CUBERT Cornwall

Treworgans Holiday Park ★★★★★
Holiday Park
Cubert, Newquay TR8 5HH
t (01637) 830200
e contact-us@treworgansholidaypark.co.uk
w treworgansholidaypark.co.uk

DAWLISH Devon

Cofton Country Holidays ★★★★ ROSE AWARD
Holiday, Touring & Camping Park
Cofton, Starcross, Exeter EX6 8RP
t (01626) 890111
e info@coftonholidays.co.uk
w coftonholidays.co.uk

Dawlish Sands Holiday Park ★★★★
Holiday Park
Warren Road, Dawlish Warren, Dawlish EX7 0PG
t (01626) 862038

Lady's Mile Touring & Camping Park ★★★★ ROSE AWARD
Holiday Park
Exeter Road, Exeter EX7 0LX
t (01626) 863411
e info@ladysmile.co.uk
w ladysmile.co.uk

Leadstone Camping ★★★
Touring & Camping Park
Warren Road, Exeter EX7 0NG
t (01626) 864411
e post@leadstonecamping.co.uk
w leadstonecamping.co.uk

Oakcliff Holiday Park ★★★★ ROSE AWARD
Holiday Park
Mount Pleasant Road, Dawlish Warren EX7 0ND
t (01626) 863347
e info@oakcliff.co.uk
w oakcliff.co.uk

Welcome Family Holiday Park ★★★★ ROSE AWARD
Holiday Park
Warren Road, Dawlish Warren, Dawlish EX7 0PH
t (01626) 862070
e fun@welcomefamily.co.uk
w welcomefamily.co.uk

DAWLISH WARREN Devon

Hazelwood Park ★★★
Holiday Park
Warren Road, Hazelwood Park, Dawlish Warren EX7 0PF
t (01626) 862955
w hazelwood.co.uk

DOBWALLS
Cornwall

Hoburne Doublebois ★★★★
Holiday Park
Dobwalls, Liskeard PL14 6LD
t (01579) 320049
e enquiries@hoburne.com
w hoburne.com

DONIFORD
Somerset

Doniford Bay Holiday Park ★★★★
Holiday Park
Sea Lane, Watchet TA23 0TJ
t (01984) 632423
e doniford.bay@bourne-leisure.co.uk
w donifordbay-park.co.uk

DORCHESTER
Dorset

Giants Head Caravan & Camping Park ★★
Touring & Camping Park
Old Sherborne Road, Dorchester DT2 7TR
t (01300) 341242
e holidays@giantshead.co.uk
w giantshead.co.uk

Morn Gate Caravan Park ★★★★
Holiday Park
Bridport Road, Dorchester DT2 9DS
t (01305) 889284
e morngate@ukonline.co.uk
w morngate.co.uk

DOUBLEBOIS
Cornwall

Pine Green Caravan Park ★★★★
Touring & Camping Park
Doublebois, Dobwalls, Liskeard PL14 6LE
t (01579) 320183
e mary.ruhleman@btinternet.com
w pinegreenpark.co.uk

DREWSTEIGNTON
Devon

Woodland Springs Touring Park ★★★★
Touring & Camping Park
Venton, Drewsteignton EX6 6PG
t (01647) 231695
e enquiries@woodlandsprings.co.uk
w woodlandsprings.co.uk

DRYBROOK
Gloucestershire

Greenway Farm Caravan & Camping Park ★★★★
Holiday, Touring & Camping Park
Puddlebrook Road, Hawthorns, Drybrook GL17 9HW
t (01594) 543737
e greenwayfarm@aic.co.uk
w greenwayfarm.org

DULVERTON
Somerset

Exmoor House Caravan Club Site ★★★★
Touring Park
Dulverton TA22 9HL
t (01398) 323268
w caravanclub.co.uk

Lakeside Caravan Club Site ★★★★★
Touring Park
Higher Grants, Exebridge, Dulverton TA22 9BE
t (01398) 324068
w caravanclub.co.uk

EAST HUNTSPILL
Somerset

Cripps Farm Caravan Park ★★★★
Holiday & Touring Park
Merry Lane, Highbridge TA9 3PS
t (01278) 783762
e gharris@gotadsl.co.uk
w crippsfarm.co.uk

EAST WORLINGTON
Devon

Yeatheridge Farm Caravan Park ★★★★
Touring & Camping Park
East Worlington, Crediton EX17 4TN
t (01884) 860330

EXFORD
Somerset

Westermill Farm Camping ★★
Camping Park
Exford, Minehead TA24 7NJ
t (01643) 831238
e st@westermill.com
w westermill.com

EXMOUTH
Devon

Webbers Caravan & Camping Park ★★★★★
Holiday & Touring Park
Castle Lane, Woodbury, Exeter EX5 1EA
t (01395) 232276
e reception@webberspark.co.uk
w webberspark.co.uk

FALMOUTH
Cornwall

Pennance Mill Farm ★★★
Holiday, Touring & Camping Park
Maenporth, Falmouth TR11 5HJ
t (01326) 317431
e pennancemill@amserve.com
w pennancemill.co.uk

FOWEY
Cornwall

Penhale Caravan & Camping Park ★★★
Holiday, Touring & Camping Park
Fowey PL23 1JU
t (01726) 833425
e info@penhale-fowey.co.uk
w penhale-fowey.co.uk

Penmarlam Caravan & Camping Park ★★★★
Touring & Camping Park
Bodinnick by Fowey, Fowey PL23 1LZ
t (01726) 870088
e info@penmarlampark.co.uk
w penmarlampark.co.uk

GLASTONBURY
Somerset

The Old Oaks Touring Park ★★★★★
Touring & Camping Park
Wick, Glastonbury BA6 8JS
t (01458) 831437
e info@theoldoaks.co.uk
w theoldoaks.co.uk

GOONHAVERN
Cornwall

Perran Springs Holiday Park ★★★
Holiday, Touring & Camping Park
Goonhavern, Truro TR4 9QG
t (01872) 540568
e info@perransprings.co.uk
w perransprings.co.uk

GREAT TORRINGTON
Devon

Greenways Valley Holiday Park ★★★★
Holiday Park
Caddywell Lane, Great Torrington, Devon EX38 7EW
t (01805) 622153
e enquiries@greenwaysvalley.co.uk
w greenwaysvalley.co.uk

Smytham Manor Holiday Park ★★★★
Holiday & Touring Park
Little Torrington, Torrington EX38 8PU
t (01805) 622110
e info@smytham.co.uk
w smytham.co.uk

HAMWORTHY
Dorset

Rockley Park Holiday Park ★★★★★ ROSE AWARD
Holiday, Touring & Camping Park
Napier Road, Poole BH15 4LZ
t (01202) 679393
e enquiries@british-holidays.co.uk
w british-holidays.co.uk

HAYLE
Cornwall

Atlantic Coast Caravan Park ★★★★
Holiday & Touring Park
53 Upton Towans, Hayle TR27 5BL
t (01736) 752071
e enquiries@atlanticcoast-caravanpark.co.uk
w coastdaleparks.co.uk

Beachside Holiday Park ★★★★
Holiday, Touring & Camping Park
Lethlean Lane, Phillack, Hayle TR27 5AW
t (01736) 753080
e reception@beachside.demon.co.uk
w beachside.co.uk

Churchtown Farm Caravan & Camping ★★★
Touring & Camping Park
Gwithian, Hayle TR27 5BX
t (01736) 753219
e caravanning@churchtownfarmgwithian.fsnet.co.uk
w churchtownfarm.org.uk

Riviere Sands Holiday Park ★★★★
Holiday Park
Riviere Towans, Hayle TR27 5AX
t (01736) 752132
e carla.tarpey@bourne-leisure.co.uk
w havenholidays.com/rivieresands

St Ives Bay Holiday Park ★★★★
Holiday, Touring & Camping Park
73 Loggans Road, Upton Towans TR27 5BH
t (01736) 752274
e stivesbay@dial.pipex.com
w stivesbay.co.uk

HELSTON
Cornwall

Poldown Camping & Caravan Park ★★★★
Holiday, Touring & Camping Park
Carleen, Breage TR13 9NN
t (01326) 574560
e stay@poldown.co.uk
w poldown.co.uk

Sea Acres Holiday Park ★★★★ ROSE AWARD
Holiday Park
Kennack Sands, Ruan Minor, Helston TR12 7LT
t 0871 641 0191
e enquiries@parkdeanholidays.co.uk
w parkdeanholidays.co.uk

Seaview Holiday Park ★★★
Holiday & Touring Park
Gwendreath, Ruan Minor, Helston TR12 7LZ
t (01326) 290635
e reception@seaviewcaravanpark.com
w seaviewcaravanpark.com

HIGHBRIDGE
Somerset

Greenacre Place Touring Caravan Park & Holiday Cottage ★★★★
Touring Park
Bristol Road, Highbridge TA9 4HA
t (01278) 785227
e info@greenacreplace.com
w greenacreplace.com

Look out for parks participating in the National Accessible Scheme

HIGHCLIFFE
Dorset

Cobb's Holiday Park ★★★★ ROSE AWARD
Holiday Park
32 Gordon Road, Highcliffe-on-Sea BH23 5HN
t (01425) 273301
e enquiries@cobbsholidaypark.co.uk
w cobbsholidaypark.co.uk

HOLSWORTHY
Devon

Noteworthy Caravan & Camping Site ★★
Holiday, Touring & Camping Park
Bude Road, Holsworthy EX22 7JB
t (01409) 253731 & 07811 000071
e enquiries@noteworthy-devon.co.uk
w noteworthy-devon.co.uk

HOLTON HEATH
Dorset

Sandford Holiday Park ★★★★
Holiday, Touring & Camping Park
Organford Road, Holton Heath BH16 6JZ
t 0870 444 7774
e bookings@parkdean.com
w parkdean.co.uk

HOLYWELL BAY
Cornwall

The Meadow ★★★
Holiday, Touring & Camping Park
Newquay TR8 5PP
t (01872) 572752
w holywellbeachholidays.co.uk

HORN'S CROSS
Devon

Steart Farm Touring Park ★★★
Touring & Camping Park
Horn's Cross, Bideford EX39 5DW
t (01237) 431836
e steart@tiscali.co.uk

ILFRACOMBE
Devon

Hele Valley Holiday Park ★★★★ ROSE AWARD
Holiday, Touring & Camping Park
Hele Bay, Ilfracombe EX34 9RD
t (01271) 862460
e holidays@helevalley.co.uk
w helevalley.co.uk

Hidden Valley Touring & Camping Park ★★★★★
Touring & Camping Park
West Down, Ilfracombe EX34 8NU
t (01271) 813837
e relax@hiddenvalleypark.com
w hiddenvalleypark.com

Mullacott Park ★★★★ ROSE AWARD
Holiday Park
Mullacott Cross, Woolacombe EX34 8NB
t (01271) 862212
e info@mullacottpark.co.uk
w mullacottpark.co.uk

IPPLEPEN
Devon

Ross Park ★★★★★
Touring & Camping Park
Moor Road, Ipplepen TQ12 5TT
t (01803) 812983
e enquiries@rossparkcaravanpark.co.uk
w rossparkcaravanpark.co.uk

Woodville Touring Park ★★★★
Touring Park
Totnes Road, Ipplepen TQ12 5TN
t (01803) 812240
e woodvillepark@lineone.net
w caravan-sitefinder.co.uk/sthwest/devon/woodville.html

ISLES OF SCILLY
Isles of Scilly

St Martin's Campsite ★★★★
Camping Park
Middle Town, St Martin's TR25 0QN
t (01720) 422888
e chris@stmartinscampsite.freeserve.co.uk
w stmartinscampsite.co.uk

Troytown Farm Campsite ★★★
Camping Park
St Agnes TR22 0PL
t (01720) 422360
e troytown@talk21.com
w st-agnes-scilly.org

KENNFORD
Devon

Exeter Racecourse Caravan Club Site ★★★
Touring & Camping Park
Kennford, Exeter EX6 7XS
t (01392) 832107
e enquiries@caravanclub.co.uk
w caravanclub.co.uk

KENTISBEARE
Devon

Forest Glade Holiday Park ★★★★ ROSE AWARD
Holiday & Touring Park
Kentisbeare, Cullompton EX15 2DT
t (01404) 841381
e enquiries@forest-glade.co.uk
w forest-glade.co.uk

KEWSTOKE
Somerset

Ardnave Holiday Park ★★★
Holiday & Touring Park
Crookes Lane, Kewstoke BS22 9XJ
t (01934) 622319
e enquiries@ardnaveholidaypark.co.uk
w ardnaveholidaypark.co.uk

Kewside Caravans ★★
Holiday Park
Crookes Lane, Weston-super-Mare BS22 9XF
t (01934) 521486

KILKHAMPTON
Cornwall

Penstowe Park Holiday Village ★★★★
Holiday Village
Bude EX23 9QY
t (01288) 321354
e info@penstoweholidays.co.uk
w penstoweholidays.co.uk

KINGSBRIDGE
Devon

Challaborough Bay Holiday Park ★★★★ ROSE AWARD
Holiday Park
Challaborough Beach, Kingsbridge TQ7 4HU
t 0871 641 0191
e enquiries@parkdeanholidays.co.uk
w parkdeanholidays.co.uk

KINGTON LANGLEY
Wiltshire

Plough Lane Caravan Site ★★★★★
Touring Park
Plough Lane, Kington Langley SN15 5PS
t (01249) 750146
e ploughlane@lineone.net
w ploughlane.co.uk

LACOCK
Wiltshire

Piccadilly Caravan Park ★★★★★
Touring & Camping Park
Folly Lane (West), Lacock, Chippenham SN15 2LP
t (01249) 730260
e piccadillylacock@aol.com

LANDRAKE
Cornwall

Dolbeare Park, Caravan & Camping ★★★★
Touring & Camping Park
St Ive Road, Landrake, Saltash PL12 5AF
t (01752) 851332
e reception@dolbeare.co.uk
w dolbeare.co.uk

LAND'S END
Cornwall

Cardinney Caravan & Camping Park ★★★★
Touring & Camping Park
Penberth Valley, St Buryan, Penzance TR19 6HX
t (01736) 810880
e cardinney@btinternet.com
w cardinney-camping-park.co.uk

LANGPORT
Somerset

Bowdens Crest Caravan & Camping Park ★★★★
Holiday, Touring & Camping Park
Bowdens, Langport TA10 0DD
t (01458) 250553
e bowcrest@btconnect.com
w bowdenscrest.co.uk

LANIVET
Cornwall

Kernow Caravan Park ★★★
Holiday Park
Clann Lane, Lanivet, Bodmin PL30 5HD
t (01208) 831343

LONGLEAT
Wiltshire

Center Parcs Longleat Forest ★★★★★
Forest Holiday Village
Warminster BA12 7PU
t 0870 067 3030
w centerparcs.co.uk/villages/longleat/index.jsp

LOOE
Cornwall

Looe Bay Holiday Park ★★★★ ROSE AWARD
Holiday Park
St Martins, Looe PL13 1NX
t 0870 444 7774
e bookings@weststarholidays.co.uk
w weststarholidays.co.uk/ic

Seaview Holiday Village ★★★★
Holiday Park
Polperro, Looe PL13 2JE
t (01503) 272335
e reception@seaviewholidayvillage.co.uk
w seaviewholidayvillage.co.uk

Tencreek Caravan Park ★★★★
Holiday, Touring & Camping Park
Polperro Road, Looe PL13 2JR
t (01503) 262447
e reception@tencreek.co.uk
w dolphinholidays.co.uk

Tregoad Park Quality Family Touring Site ★★★★
Holiday, Touring & Camping Park
St Martins, Looe PL13 1PB
t (01503) 262718
e info@tregoadpark.co.uk
w tregoadpark.co.uk

LUXULYAN
Cornwall

Croft Farm Holiday Park ★★★★
Holiday, Touring & Camping Park
Luxulyan, Bodmin PL30 5EQ
t (01726) 850228
e lynpick@ukonline.co.uk
w croftfarm.co.uk

LYDFORD
Devon

Camping & Caravanning Club Site – Lydford ★★★★
Touring & Camping Park
Lydford, Okehampton
EX20 4BE
t (01822) 820275
w campingandcaravanningclub.co.uk

LYME REGIS
Dorset

Shrubbery Caravan Park ★★★★
Touring & Camping Park
Rousdon, Lyme Regis
DT7 3XW
t (01297) 442227
e enqshrubberypark@tiscali.co.uk
w ukparks.co.uk/shrubbery

LYNTON
Devon

Camping & Caravanning Club Site – Lynton ★★★
Touring & Camping Park
Caffyn's Cross, Lynton
EX35 6JS
t (01598) 752379
w campingandcaravanningclub.co.uk

Channel View Caravan & Camping Park ★★★★ ROSE AWARD
Holiday & Touring Park
Manor Farm, Lynton EX35 6LD
t (01598) 753349
e relax@channel-view.co.uk
w channel-view.co.uk

LYTCHETT MINSTER
Dorset

South Lytchett Manor Touring Caravan & Camping Park ★★★★
Holiday, Touring & Camping Park
Dorchester Road, Poole
BH16 6JB
t (01202) 622577
e info@southlytchettmanor.co.uk
w southlytchettmanor.co.uk

MALMESBURY
Wiltshire

Burton Hill Caravan & Camping Park ★★★
Touring & Camping Park
Arches Lane, Malmesbury
SN16 0EH
t (01666) 826880
e info@burtonhill.co.uk
w burtonhill.co.uk

MARAZION
Cornwall

Mounts Bay Caravan Park ★★★★★ ROSE AWARD
Holiday Park
Green Lane, Marazion
TR17 0HQ
t (01736) 710307
e reception@mountsbay-caravanpark.co.uk
w mountsbay-caravanpark.co.uk

Wayfarers Caravan Park ★★★★
Holiday, Touring & Camping Park
Relubbus Lane, St Hilary
TR20 9EF
t (01736) 763326
e elaine@wayfarerspark.co.uk
w wayfarerspark.co.uk

MARLBOROUGH
Wiltshire

Postern Hill Caravan & Camping Site ★★★
Touring & Camping Park
Postern Hill, Marlborough
SN8 4ND
t (01672) 515195
e posternhill.site@forestholidays.co.uk
w forestholidays.co.uk

MARLDON
Devon

Widend Touring Park ★★★★
Holiday, Touring & Camping Park
Totnes Road, Marldon
TQ3 1RT
t (01803) 550116

MARTOCK
Somerset

Southfork Caravan Park ★★★★★ ROSE AWARD
Holiday, Touring & Camping Park
Parrett Works, Martock
TA12 6AE
t (01935) 825661
e southforkcaravans@btconnect.com
w southforkcaravans.co.uk

MAWGAN PORTH
Cornwall

Marver Holiday Park ★★
Holiday, Touring & Camping Park
Marver Chalets, Mawgan Porth
TR8 4BB
t (01637) 860493
e familyholidays@aol.com
w marverholidaypark.co.uk

Sun Haven Valley Country Holiday Park ★★★★★ ROSE AWARD
Holiday, Touring & Camping Park
Mawgan Porth, Cornwall
TR8 4BQ
t (01637) 860373
e sunhaven@hotmail.co.uk
w sunhavenvalley.com

MEVAGISSEY
Cornwall

Sea View International ★★★★★ ROSE AWARD
Holiday, Touring & Camping Park
Boswinger, Gorran, St Austell
PL26 6LL
t (01726) 843425
e holidays@seaviewinternational.com
w seaviewinternational.com

MINEHEAD
Somerset

Beeches Holiday Park ★★★★ ROSE AWARD
Holiday Park
Blue Anchor Bay, Minehead
TA24 6JW
t (01984) 640391
e info@beeches-park.co.uk
w beeches-park.co.uk

Butlins Skyline Holiday Park Minehead ★★
Holiday, Touring & Camping Park
Warren Road, Minehead
TA24 5SH
t (01643) 703331
w butlins.com

Butlins Skyline ★★★★
Holiday Village
Warren Road, Minehead
TA24 5SH
t (01643) 703331
e minehead.hbs@bourne-leisure.co.uk
w butlins.com

Minehead Camping & Caravanning Club ★★★★
Camping Park
Hill Road, North Hill, Minehead
TA24 5LB
t (01643) 704138
w campingandcaravanningclub.co.uk

MODBURY
Devon

Broad Park Caravan Club Site ★★★★
Touring Park
Higher East Leigh, Modbury,
Ivybridge PL21 0SH
t (01548) 830714
w caravanclub.co.uk

Camping & Caravanning Club Site – California Cross ★★★★
Touring & Camping Park
Modbury, Ivybridge PL21 0SG
t (01548) 821297
w campingandcaravanningclub.co.uk

Moor View Touring Park ★★★★
Touring & Camping Park
Modbury, Ivybridge PL21 0SG
t (01548) 821485
e moorview@tinyworld.co.uk
w moorviewtouringpark.co.uk

Pennymoor Camping & Caravan Park ★★★★
Holiday, Touring & Camping Park
Modbury, Ivybridge PL21 0SB
t (01548) 830542
w pennymoor-camping.co.uk

MOORSHOP
Devon

Higher Longford Caravan & Camping Park ★★★★
Touring & Camping Park
Moorshop, Tavistock PL19 9LQ
t (01822) 613360
e stay@higherlongford.co.uk
w higherlongford.co.uk

MORETON
Dorset

Moreton Camping & Caravanning Club Site ★★★★
Touring & Camping Park
Station Road, Moreton
DT2 8BB
t (01305) 853801
w campingandcaravanningclub.co.uk

MORETON-IN-MARSH
Gloucestershire

Moreton-in-Marsh Caravan Club Site ★★★★★
Touring Park
Bourton Road, Moreton-in-Marsh GL56 0BT
t (01608) 650519
w caravanclub.co.uk

MORTEHOE
Devon

Easewell Farm Holiday Park & Golf Club ★★★
Holiday, Touring & Camping Park
Mortehoe, Woolacombe
EX34 7EH
t (01271) 870343
w woolacombe.com

North Morte Farm Caravan and Camping Park ★★★★
Holiday, Touring & Camping Park
North Morte Road, Mortehoe,
Woolacombe EX34 7EG
t (01271) 870381
e info@northmortefarm.co.uk
w northmortefarm.co.uk

Twitchen House Holiday Parc ★★★★
Holiday, Touring & Camping Park
Mortehoe Station Road,
Woolacombe EX34 7ES
t (01271) 870343
e goodtimes@woolacombe.com
w woolacombe.com

Look out for parks participating in the National Accessible Scheme

Warcombe Farm Camping Park ★★★★
Touring & Camping Park
Station Road, Woolacombe
EX34 7EJ
t (01271) 870690
e info@warcombefarm.co.uk
w warcombefarm.co.uk/devon-campsite.html

MUCHELNEY
Somerset

Thorney Lakes & Caravan Park ★★★
Touring & Camping Park
Thorney Lakes, Langport
TA10 0DW
t (01458) 250811
e enquiries@thorneylakes.co.uk
w thorneylakes.co.uk

MULLION
Cornwall

Mullion Holiday Park ★★★★
Holiday, Touring & Camping Park
Ruan Minor, Helston TR12 7LJ
t 0870 444 5344

NANCLEDRA
Cornwall

Higher Chellew Camp Site ★★★★
Touring & Camping Park
Nancledra, Penzance
TR20 8BD
t (01736) 364532
e camping@higherchellew.co.uk
w higherchellewcamping.co.uk

NEWQUAY
Cornwall

Crantock Beach Holiday Park ★★★★ ROSE AWARD
Holiday Park
Crantock, Newquay TR8 5RH
t 0871 641 0191
e enquiries@parkdeanholidays.co.uk
w parkdeanholidays.co.uk

Headland Cottages ★★★★★
Holiday Village
Headland Road, Fistral Beach, Newquay TR7 1EW
t (01637) 872211
e reception@headlandhotel.co.uk
w headlandhotel.co.uk

Hendra Holiday Park ★★★★★ ROSE AWARD
Holiday, Touring & Camping Park
Newquay TR8 4NY
t (01637) 875778
e enquiries@hendra-holidays.com
w hendra-holidays.com

Holywell Bay Holiday Park ★★★★ ROSE AWARD
Holiday, Touring & Camping Park
Holywell Bay, Newquay
TR8 5PR
t 0871 641 0191
e enquiries@parkdeanholidays.co.uk
w parkdeanholidays.co.uk

Mawgan Porth Holiday Park ★★★★★
Holiday Park
Mawgan Porth, Newquay
TR8 4BD
t (01637) 860322
e mawganporth@btconnect.com
w mawganporth.co.uk

Nancolleth Caravan Gardens ★★★★
Holiday Park
Summercourt, Newquay
TR8 4PN
t (01872) 510236
e nancolleth@summercourt.freeserve.co.uk
w nancolleth.co.uk

Newperran Holiday Park ★★★★★ ROSE AWARD
Holiday Park
Rejerrah, Newquay TR8 5QJ
t (01872) 572407
e holidays@newperran.co.uk
w newperran.co.uk

Newquay Holiday Park ★★★★ ROSE AWARD
Holiday Park
Newquay TR8 4HS
t 0871 641 0191
e enquiries@parkdeanholidays.co.uk
w parkdeanholidays.co.uk

Porth Beach Tourist Park ★★★★ ROSE AWARD
Holiday, Touring & Camping Park
Porth, Newquay TR7 3NH
t (01637) 876531
e info@porthbeach.co.uk
w porthbeach.co.uk

Riverside Holiday Park ★★★★
Holiday, Touring & Camping Park
Gwills Lane, Newquay TR8 4PE
t (01637) 873617
e info@riversideholidaypark.co.uk
w riversideholidaypark.co.uk

Trekenning Tourist Park ★★★
Holiday, Touring & Camping Park
Newquay TR8 4JF
t (01637) 880462
e holidays@trekenning.co.uk
w trekenning.co.uk

Treloy Touring Park ★★★★
Touring & Camping Park
Newquay TR8 4JN
t (01637) 872063 & (01637) 876279
e treloy.tp@btconnect.com
w treloy.co.uk

Trethiggey Touring Park ★★★★ ROSE AWARD
Holiday, Touring & Camping Park
Quintrell Downs, Newquay
TR8 4QR
t (01637) 877672
e enquiries@trethiggey.co.uk
w trethiggey.co.uk

Trevella Caravan & Camping Park ★★★★★ ROSE AWARD
Holiday, Touring & Camping Park
Crantock, Newquay TR8 5EW
t (01637) 830308
e holidays@trevella.co.uk
w trevella.co.uk

Trevornick Holiday Park ★★★★★
Holiday Park
Holywell Bay, Newquay
TR8 5PW
t (01637) 832906
e paul@trevornick.co.uk
w trevornick.co.uk

NEWTON ABBOT
Devon

Dornafield ★★★★★
Touring & Camping Park
Two Mile Oak, Newton Abbot
TQ12 6DD
t (01803) 812732
e enquiries@dornafield.com
w dornafield.com

NORTH MOLTON
Devon

Riverside Caravan Park ★★★★
Touring & Camping Park
Marsh Lane, North Molton Road, South Molton EX36 3HQ
t (01769) 579269
e relax@exmoorriverside.co.uk
w exmoorriverside.co.uk

OARE
Wiltshire

Hill-View Park ★★★
Touring & Camping Park
Sunnyhill Lane, Oare SN8 4JG
t (01672) 563151

ORCHESTON
Wiltshire

Stonehenge Touring Park ★★★
Touring & Camping Park
Stonehenge Park, Orcheston
SP3 4SH
t (01980) 620304
e stay@stonehengetouringpark.com
w stonehengetouringpark.com

OSMINGTON
Dorset

White Horse Holiday Park ★★★
Holiday Park
Osmington Hill, Osmington
DT3 6ED
t (01305) 832164
e hols@whitehorsepark.co.uk
w whitehorsepark.co.uk

OTTERTON
Devon

Ladram Bay Holiday Centre ★★★★ ROSE AWARD
Holiday, Touring & Camping Park
Otterton, Budleigh Salterton
EX9 7BX
t (01395) 568398
e welcome@ladrambay.co.uk
w ladrambay.co.uk

OWERMOIGNE
Dorset

Sandyholme Holiday Park ★★★★
Holiday, Touring & Camping Park
Moreton Road, Owermoigne, Dorchester DT2 8HZ
t (01305) 852677
e smeatons@sandyholme.co.uk
w sandyholme.co.uk

PADSTOW
Cornwall

Carnevas Farm Holiday Park (Camping) ★★★★ ROSE AWARD
Holiday, Touring & Camping Park
Carnevas Farm, St Merryn, Padstow PL28 8PN
t (01841) 520230
e carnevascampsite@aol.com
w carnevasholidaypark.co.uk

The Laurels Touring Park ★★★★
Touring & Camping Park
Padstow Road, Whitecross, Wadebridge PL27 7JQ
t (01209) 313474
e info@thelaurelsholidaypark.co.uk
w thelaurelsholidaypark.co.uk

Mother Iveys Bay Caravan Park ★★★★★ ROSE AWARD
Holiday, Touring & Camping Park
Trevose Head, Padstow
PL28 8SL
t (01841) 520990
e info@motheriveysbay.com
w motheriveysbay.com

Padstow Touring Park ★★★★
Touring & Camping Park
Padstow PL28 8LE
t (01841) 532061
e mail@padstowtouringpark.co.uk
w padstowtouringpark.co.uk

PAIGNTON
Devon

Ashvale Holiday Park ★★★★
Holiday Park
Goodrington Road, Paignton
TQ4 7JD
t (01803) 843887
e info@beverley-holidays.co.uk
w beverley-holidays.co.uk

Beverley Park ★★★★★ ROSE AWARD
Holiday, Touring & Camping Park
Goodrington Road, Paignton TQ4 7JE
t (01803) 843887
e info@beverley-holidays.co.uk
w beverley-holidays.co.uk

Byslades International Touring & Camping Park ★★★★
Touring & Camping Park
Totnes Road, Paignton TQ4 7PY
t (01803) 555072
e info@byslades.co.uk
w byslades.co.uk

Higher Well Farm Holiday Park ★★★★
Holiday, Touring & Camping Park
Waddeton Road, Stoke Gabriel, Totnes TQ9 6RN
t (01803) 782289
e higherwell@talk21.com
w higherwellfarmholidaypark.co.uk

Hoburne Torbay ★★★★ ROSE AWARD
Holiday & Touring Park
Grange Road, Paignton TQ4 7JP
t (01803) 558010
e enquiries@hoburne.com
w hoburne.com

Marine Park Holiday Centre ★★★★
Holiday & Touring Park
Grange Road, Paignton TQ4 7JR
t (01803) 843887
e info@beverley-holidays.co.uk
w beverley-holidays.co.uk

Waterside Holiday Park ★★★★
Holiday Park
Three Beaches, Dartmouth Road, Paignton TQ4 6NS
t (01803) 842400
w watersidepark.co.uk

Whitehill Country Park ★★★★
Holiday, Touring & Camping Park
Stoke Road, Paignton TQ4 7PF
t (01803) 782338
e info@whitehill-park.co.uk
w whitehill-park.co.uk

PAR Cornwall

Par Sands Holiday Park ★★★★ ROSE AWARD
Holiday, Touring & Camping Park
Par Beach, Par PL24 2AS
t (01726) 812868
e holiday@parsands.co.uk
w parsands.co.uk

PENTEWAN Cornwall

Pentewan Sands Holiday Park ★★★★ ROSE AWARD
Holiday, Touring & Camping Park
Mevagissey PL26 6BT
t (01726) 843485
e info@pentewan.co.uk
w pentewan.co.uk

PENZANCE Cornwall

Tower Park Caravans & Camping ★★★★
Holiday, Touring & Camping Park
St Buryan, Penzance TR19 6BZ
t (01736) 810286
e enquiries@towerparkcamping.co.uk
w towerparkcamping.co.uk

PERRANPORTH Cornwall

Haven Perran Sands Holiday Park ★★★★
Holiday, Touring & Camping Park
Perranporth TR6 0AQ
t 0870 405 0144
e lisa.spickett@bourne-leisure.co.uk
w perransands-park.co.uk

Perranporth Caravan Holidays ★★★
Holiday Park
1 Crow Hill, Bolingey, Perranporth TR6 0DG
t (01872) 572385
w caravanscornwall.co.uk

PERROTTS BROOK Gloucestershire

Mayfield Touring Park ★★★★
Touring Park
Cheltenham Road, Bagendon GL7 7BH
t (01285) 831301
e mayfield-park@cirencester.fsbusiness.co.uk
w mayfieldpark.co.uk

PLYMOUTH Devon

Plymouth Sound Caravan Club Site ★★★★
Holiday & Touring Park
Bovisand Lane, Down Thomas, Plymouth PL9 0AE
t (01752) 862325
w caravanclub.co.uk

POLGOOTH Cornwall

St Margarets Park ★★★★★
Holiday Park
Tregongeeves Lane, St Austell PL26 7AX
t (01726) 74283

POLRUAN-BY-FOWEY Cornwall

Polruan Holidays (Camping & Caravanning) ★★★★
Holiday, Touring & Camping Park
Townsend, Polruan PL23 1QH
t (01726) 870263
e polholiday@aol.com
w polruanholidays.co.uk

POLZEATH Cornwall

Polzeath Beach Holiday Park ★★★★
Holiday Park
Trenant Nook, Polzeath, Wadebridge PL27 6ST
t (01208) 863320
e info@polzeathbeachholidaypark.com
w polzeathbeachholidaypark.com

Valley Caravan Park ★★
Holiday, Touring & Camping Park
Polzeath, Wadebridge PL27 6SS
t (01208) 862391
e martin@valleycaravanpark.co.uk
w valleycaravanpark.co.uk

POOLE Somerset

Cadeside Caravan Club Site ★★★★
Touring Park
Nynehead Road, Wellington TA21 9HN
t (01823) 663103
e enquiries@caravanclub.co.uk
w caravanclub.co.uk

PORLOCK Somerset

Burrowhayes Farm Caravan and Camping Site and Riding Stables ★★★★
Holiday, Touring & Camping Park
West Luccombe, Porlock, Minehead TA24 8HT
t (01643) 862463
e info@burrowhayes.co.uk
w burrowhayes.co.uk

Porlock Caravan Park ★★★★ ROSE AWARD
Holiday, Touring & Camping Park
Highbank TA24 8ND
t (01643) 862269
e info@porlockcaravanpark.co.uk
w porlockcaravanpark.co.uk

PORTH Cornwall

Trevelgue Holiday Park ★★★
Holiday, Touring & Camping Park
Trevelgue Road, Porth, Newquay TR8 4AS
t (01637) 851850

PORTHTOWAN Cornwall

Porthtowan Tourist Park ★★★★
Touring & Camping Park
Mile Hill, Porthtowan, Truro TR4 8TY
t (01209) 890256
e admin@porthtowantouristpark.co.uk
w porthtowantouristpark.co.uk

PORTLAND Dorset

Cove Holiday Park ★★★★★
Holiday Park
Pennsylvania Road, Portland DT5 1HU
t (01305) 821286
e enquiries@coveholidaypark.co.uk
w coveholidaypark.co.uk

PORTREATH Cornwall

Cambrose Touring Park ★★★
Touring & Camping Park
Portreath Road, Cambrose, Redruth TR16 4HT
t (01209) 890747
e cambrosetouringpark@supanet.com
w cambrosetouringpark.co.uk

Gwel an Mor ★★★★★
Holiday Village
Tregea Hill, Portreath TR16 4PE
t (023) 8064 2610
e hannah@gwelanmor.com
w gwelanmor.co.uk

Tehidy Holiday Park ★★★★
Holiday, Touring & Camping Park
Harris Mill, Illogan, Redruth TR16 4JQ
t (01209) 216489
e holiday@tehidy.co.uk
w tehidy.co.uk

PRAA SANDS Cornwall

The Old Farm ★★★
Holiday, Touring & Camping Park
Lower Pentreath Caravan & Campsite, Lower Pentreath TR20 9TL
t (01736) 763221
e info@theoldfarmpraasands.co.uk
w theoldfarmpraasands.co.uk

PRESTON Dorset

Weymouth Bay Holiday Park ★★★★
Holiday Park
Preston Road, Preston DT3 6BQ
t (01305) 832271

REDHILL
Somerset

Brook Lodge Farm Touring Caravan & Tent Park ★★★
Touring & Camping Park
Brook Lodge Farm, Cowslip Green, Bristol BS40 5RB
t (01934) 862311
e brooklodgefarm@aol.com
w brooklodgefarm.com

REDRUTH
Cornwall

Lanyon Holiday Park ★★★★
Holiday, Touring & Camping Park
Loscombe Lane, Four Lanes, Redruth TR16 6LP
t (01209) 313474
e info@lanyonholidaypark.co.uk
w lanyonholidaypark.co.uk

RELUBBUS
Cornwall

River Valley Country Park ★★★★★ ROSE AWARD
Holiday Park
Relubbus, Penzance TR20 9ER
t (01736) 763398
e rivervalley@surfbay.dircon.co.uk
w surfbayholidays.co.uk

RODNEY STOKE
Somerset

Bucklegrove Caravan & Camping Park ★★★★
Holiday, Touring & Camping Park
Wells Road, Rodney Stoke BS27 3UZ
t (01749) 870261
w bucklegrove.co.uk

ROSUDGEON
Cornwall

Kenneggy Cove Holiday Park ★★★★ ROSE AWARD
Holiday, Touring & Camping Park
Higher Kenneggy, Rosudgeon, Penzance TR20 9AU
t (01736) 763453
e enquiries@kenneggycove.co.uk
w kenneggycove.co.uk

ROUSDON
Devon

Pinewood Holiday Homes ★★★★★
Holiday Park
Sidmouth Road, Rousdon DT7 3RD
t (01297) 22055
e info@pinewood.uk.net
w pinewood.uk.net

RUAN MINOR
Cornwall

Silver Sands Holiday Park ★★★★
Holiday, Touring & Camping Park
Gwendreath, Nr Kennack Sands, Ruan Minor, Helston TR12 7LZ
t (01326) 290631
e enquiries@silversandsholidaypark.co.uk
w silversandsholidaypark.co.uk

ST AGNES
Cornwall

Beacon Cottage Farm Touring Park ★★★★
Touring & Camping Park
Beacon Drive, St Agnes TR5 0NU
t (01872) 552347
e beaconcottagefarm@lineone.net
w beaconcottagefarmholidays.co.uk

ST AUSTELL
Cornwall

Carlyon Bay Caravan & Camping ★★★★★
Touring & Camping Park
Cypress Avenue, Carylon Bay, St Austell PL25 3RE
t (01726) 812735
e holidays@carlyonbay.net
w carlyonbay.net

River Valley Holiday Park ★★★★★
Holiday, Touring & Camping Park
Pentewan Road, London Apprentice, St Austell PL26 7AP
t (01726) 73533
w cornwall-holidays.co.uk

Sun Valley Holiday Park ★★★★★ ROSE AWARD
Holiday, Touring & Camping Park
Pentewan Road, St Austell PL26 6DJ
t (01726) 843266
e reception@sunvalleyholidays.co.uk
w sunvalleyholidays.co.uk

Trencreek Farm Country Holiday Park ★★★★
Holiday, Touring & Camping Park
Hewaswater, St Austell PL26 7JG
t (01726) 882540
e reception@trencreek.co.uk
w surfbayholidays.co.uk

ST BURYAN
Cornwall

Camping & Caravanning Club Site – Sennen Cove ★★★★
Touring & Camping Park
Higher Tregiffian Farm, St Buryan TR19 6JB
t (01736) 871588
w campingandcaravanningclub.co.uk

ST EWE
Cornwall

Heligan Woods Camping & Caravan Park ★★★★ ROSE AWARD
Holiday, Touring & Camping Park
Mevagissey PL26 6BT
t (01726) 843485
e info@pentewan.co.uk
w pentewan.co.uk

ST GENNYS
Cornwall

Camping & Caravanning Club Site – Bude ★★★★
Touring & Camping Park
Gillards Moor, St Gennys, Bude EX23 0BG
t (01840) 230650
w campingandcaravanningclub.co.uk

ST IVES
Cornwall

Ayr Holiday Park ★★★★ ROSE AWARD
Holiday, Touring & Camping Park
Higher Ayr, St Ives TR26 1EJ
t (01736) 795855
e andrew@ayrholidaypark.co.uk
w ayrholidaypark.co.uk

Little Trevarrack Holiday Park ★★★★
Touring & Camping Park
Laity Lane, Carbis Bay TR26 3HW
t (01736) 797580
e info@littletrevarrack.co.uk
w littletrevarrack.co.uk

Polmanter Touring Park ★★★★★
Touring & Camping Park
St Ives TR26 3LX
t (01736) 795640
e reception@polmanter.com
w polmanter.com

Trevalgan Touring Park ★★★★
Touring & Camping Park
St Ives TR26 3BJ
t (01736) 796433
e recept@trevalgantouringpark.co.uk
w trevalgantouringpark.co.uk

ST JUST-IN-PENWITH
Cornwall

Roselands Caravan Park ★★★★
Holiday, Touring & Camping Park
Dowran, St Just TR19 7RS
t (01736) 788571
e camping@roseland84.freeserve.co.uk
w roselands.co.uk

ST JUST IN ROSELAND
Cornwall

Trethem Mill Touring Park ★★★★★
Touring & Camping Park
Trethem, St Just in Roseland TR2 5JF
t (01872) 580504
e reception@trethem.com
w trethem.com

ST LEONARDS
Dorset

Back-of-Beyond Touring Park ★★★★
Touring & Camping Park
Ringwood Road, St Leonards BH24 2SB
t (01202) 876968
e melandsuepike@aol.com
w backofbeyondtouringpark.co.uk

Oakdene Forest Park ★★★★
Holiday Park
St Leonards BH24 2RZ
t (01590) 648331
e holidays@shorefield.co.uk
w shorefield.co.uk

ST MERRYN
Cornwall

Trethias Farm Caravan Park ★★★
Touring Park
Trethias, St Merryn, Padstow PL28 8PL
t (01841) 520323

Trevean Farm ★★★★
Holiday, Touring & Camping Park
St Merryn, Padstow PL28 8PR
t (01841) 520772
e trevean.info@virgin.net

ST MINVER
Cornwall

Dinham Farm Camping ★★★★
Holiday, Touring & Camping Park
St Minver, Wadebridge PL27 6RH
t (01208) 812878
e info@dinhamfarm.co.uk
w dinhamfarm.co.uk

Little Dinham Woodland Caravan Park ★★★★
Holiday Park
St Minver, Wadebridge PL27 6RH
t (01208) 812538
e littledinham@hotmail.com
w littledinham.co.uk

St Minver Holiday Park ★★★★ ROSE AWARD
Holiday, Touring & Camping Park
St Minver, Wadebridge PL27 6RR
t 0871 641 0191
e enquiries@parkdeanholidays.co.uk
w parkdeanholidays.co.uk

ST TUDY
Cornwall

Hengar Manor Country Park ★★★★★
Holiday Park
St Tudy, Bodmin PL30 3PL
t (01208) 850382
e holidays@hengarmanor.co.uk
w hengarmanor.co.uk

Michaelstow Manor Holiday Park ★★★★
Holiday Park
Michaelstow, St Tudy, Bodmin PL30 3PB
t (01208) 850244
e michaelstow@eclipse.co.uk
w michaelstow-holidays.co.uk

SALCOMBE
Devon

Bolberry House Farm Caravan & Camping Park ★★★
Holiday, Touring & Camping Park
Bolberry, Malborough
TQ7 3DY
t (01548) 561251
e bolberry.house@virgin.net
w bolberryparks.co.uk

Higher Rew Touring Caravan & Camping Park ★★★★
Touring & Camping Park
Higher Rew, Malborough
TQ7 3DW
t (01548) 842681
e enquiries@higherrew.co.uk
w higherrew.co.uk

SALCOMBE REGIS
Devon

Kings Down Tail Caravan & Camping Park ★★★★
Touring & Camping Park
Salcombe Regis, Sidmouth
EX10 0PD
t (01297) 680313
e info@kingsdowntail.co.uk
w kingsdowntail.co.uk

SALISBURY
Wiltshire

Camping & Caravanning Club Site – Salisbury ★★★★
Touring & Camping Park
Hudson's Field, Castle Road, Salisbury SP1 3RR
t (01722) 320713
w campingandcaravanningclub.co.uk

SANDY BAY
Devon

Devon Cliffs Holiday Park ★★★★★
Holiday Park
Sandy Bay, Exmouth EX8 5BT
t (01395) 226226
e john.ball@bourne-leisure.co.uk
w devoncliffs-park.co.uk

SEATON
Devon

Axe Vale Caravan Park ★★★★
Holiday Park
Colyford Road, Seaton
EX12 2DF
t 0800 068816
e info@axevale.co.uk
w axevale.co.uk

SEEND
Wiltshire

Camping & Caravanning Club Site – Devizes ★★★★
Touring & Camping Park
Spout Lane, Seend, Melksham
SN12 6RN
t (01380) 828839
w campingandcaravanningclub.co.uk

SHALDON
Devon

Coast View Holiday Park ★★★
Holiday, Touring & Camping Park
Torquay Road, Shaldon
TQ14 0BG
t (01626) 872392
e info@coast-view.co.uk
w coast-view.co.uk

Devon Valley Holiday Village ★★★★ **ROSE AWARD**
Holiday Park
Coombe Road, Ringmore, Teignmouth TQ14 0EY
t 0870 442 9750
e info@devonvalley.biz
w southdevonholidays.biz

SHIRWELL
Devon

Brightly Cott Barton ★★★
Touring Park
Shirwell, Barnstaple EX31 4JJ
t (01271) 850330
e friend.brightlycott@virgin.net

SIDBURY
Devon

Putts Corner Caravan Club Site ★★★★★
Touring Park
Sidbury, Sidmouth EX10 0QQ
t (01404) 42875
w caravanclub.co.uk

SIDMOUTH
Devon

Salcombe Regis Camping & Caravan Park ★★★★★ **ROSE AWARD**
Holiday, Touring & Camping Park
Salcombe Regis, Sidmouth
EX10 0JH
t (01395) 514303
e info@salcombe-regis.co.uk
w salcombe-regis.co.uk

SIXPENNY HANDLEY
Dorset

Church Farm Caravan & Camping Park ★★★
Touring & Camping Park
High Street, Sixpenny Handley, Salisbury SP5 5ND
t (01725) 552563
e churchfarmcandcpark@yahoo.co.uk
w churchfarmcandcpark.co.uk

SLAPTON
Devon

Camping & Caravanning Club Site – Slapton Sands ★★★★
Touring & Camping Park
Middle Grounds, Slapton, Kingsbridge TQ7 2QW
t (01548) 580538
w campingandcaravanningclub.co.uk

SOUTH CERNEY
Gloucestershire

Hoburne Cotswold ★★★★
Holiday Park
Broadway Lane, South Cerney
GL7 5UQ
t (01285) 860216
e cotswold@hoburne.com
w hoburne.com

STOKE FLEMING
Devon

Dartmouth Camping & Caravanning Club Site ★★★★
Touring & Camping Park
Dartmouth Road, Dartmouth
TQ6 0RF
t (01803) 770253
w campingandcaravanningclub.co.uk

SWANAGE
Dorset

Haycraft Caravan Club Site ★★★★★
Touring Park
Haycrafts Lane, Swanage
BH19 3EB
t (01929) 480572
e enquiries@caravanclub.co.uk
w caravanclub.co.uk

Swanage Caravan Park ★★★
Holiday Park
Panorama Road, Swanage
BH19 2QS
t (01929) 422130

Ulwell Cottage Caravan Park ★★★★
Holiday, Touring & Camping Park
Ulwell BH19 3DG
t (01929) 422823
e enq@ulwellcottagepark.co.uk
w ulwellcottagepark.co.uk

Ulwell Farm Caravan Park ★★★
Holiday Park
Ulwell, Swanage BH19 3DG
t (01929) 422825
e ulwell.farm@virgin.net
w ukparks.co.uk/ulwellfarm

TAUNTON
Somerset

Ashe Farm Caravan and Campsite ★★★
Touring & Camping Park
Thornfalcon, Taunton
TA3 5NW
t (01823) 443764
e camping@ashe-farm.fsnet.co.uk

Holly Bush Park ★★★★
Touring & Camping Park
Culmhead, Taunton TA3 7EA
t (01823) 421515
e info@hollybushpark.com
w hollybushpark.com

TAVISTOCK
Devon

Harford Bridge Holiday Park ★★★★ **ROSE AWARD**
Holiday, Touring & Camping Park
Peter Tavy, Tavistock PL19 9LS
t (01822) 810349
e enquiry@harfordbridge.co.uk
w harfordbridge.co.uk

Langstone Manor Caravan and Camping Park ★★★★ **ROSE AWARD**
Holiday, Touring & Camping Park
Moortown, Tavistock PL19 9JZ
t (01822) 613371
e jane@langstone-manor.co.uk
w langstone-manor.co.uk

Woodovis Park ★★★★★ **ROSE AWARD**
Holiday, Touring & Camping Park
Gulworthy, Tavistock PL19 8NY
t (01822) 832968
e info@woodovis.com
w woodovis.com

TEIGNGRACE
Devon

Twelve Oaks Farm Caravan Park ★★★★
Touring & Camping Park
Teigngrace, Newton Abbot
TQ12 6QT
t (01626) 352769
e info@twelveoaksfarm.co.uk
w twelveoaksfarm.co.uk

TEWKESBURY
Gloucestershire

Croft Farm Waterpark ★★★
Holiday & Touring Park
Croft Farm, Bredons Hardwick, Tewkesbury GL20 7EE
t (01684) 772321
e enquiries@croftfarmleisure.co.uk

Look out for parks participating in the National Accessible Scheme

Tewkesbury Abbey Caravan Club Site ★★★★
Touring & Camping Park
Gander Lane, Tewkesbury GL20 5PG
t (01684) 294035
w caravanclub.co.uk

TINTAGEL Cornwall

Trewethett Farm Caravan Club Site ★★★★★
Touring & Camping Park
Trethevy, Tintagel PL34 0BQ
t (01840) 770222
w caravanclub.co.uk

TORQUAY Devon

TLH Leisure Resort ★★★★
Holiday Village
Derwent Hotel, 22-28 Belgrave Road, Torquay TQ2 5HT
t (01803) 400500
e rooms@tlh.co.uk
w tlh.co.uk

Torquay Holiday Park ★★★★ ROSE AWARD
Holiday Park
Kingskerswell Road, Torquay TQ2 8JU
t 0871 641 0410
e enquiries@parkdeanholidays.co.uk
w parkdeanholidays.co.uk

Widdicombe Farm Touring Park ★★★★
Holiday, Touring & Camping Park
Marldon, Paignton TQ3 1ST
t (01803) 558325
e info@widdicombefarm.co.uk
w widdicombefarm.co.uk

TOTNES Devon

Broadleigh Farm Park ★★★★
Touring & Camping Park
Coombe House Lane, Aish, Stoke Gabriel, Totnes TQ9 6PU
t (01803) 782309
e enquiries@broadleighfarm.co.uk
w gotorbay.com/accommodation

Steamer Quay Caravan Club Site ★★★
Touring Park
Steamer Quay Road, Totnes TQ9 5AL
t (01803) 862738
e enquiries@caravanclub.co.uk
w caravanclub.co.uk

TREGURRIAN Cornwall

Camping & Caravanning Club Site – Tregurrian ★★★★
Touring & Camping Park
Tregurrian, Newquay TR8 4AE
t 0845 130 7633
w campingandcaravanningclub.co.uk

TRURO Cornwall

Summer Valley Touring Park ★★★★
Touring Park
Shortlanesend, Truro TR4 9DW
t (01872) 277878
e res@summervalley.co.uk
w summervalley.co.uk

UMBERLEIGH Devon

Camping & Caravanning Club Site – Umberleigh ★★★★
Touring & Camping Park
Over Weir, Umberleigh EX37 9DU
t (01769) 560009
w campingandcaravanningclub.co.uk

UPTON Somerset

Lowtrow Cross Caravan & Camping Site ★★★★
Holiday, Touring & Camping Park
Lowtrow Cross, Taunton TA4 2DB
t (01398) 371199
e info@lowtrowcross.co.uk
w lowtrowcross.co.uk

VERYAN Cornwall

Camping & Caravanning Club Site – Veryan ★★★★
Touring & Camping Park
Tretheake Manor, Veryan, Truro TR2 5PP
t (01872) 501658
w campingandcaravanningclub.co.uk

WADEBRIDGE Cornwall

Little Bodieve Holiday Park (Camping) ★★★★
Holiday, Touring & Camping Park
Bodieve Road, Wadebridge PL27 6EG
t (01208) 812323
e berry@littlebodieveholidaypark.fsnet.co.uk
w littlebodieve.co.uk

WAREHAM Dorset

Birchwood Tourist Park ★★★★
Touring & Camping Park
Bere Road, Coldharbour, Wareham BH20 7PA
t (01929) 554763
e birchwoodtouristpark@hotmail.com

The Lookout Holiday Park ★★★★ ROSE AWARD
Holiday, Touring & Camping Park
Corfe Road, Stoborough, Wareham BH20 5AZ
t (01929) 552546
e enquiries@caravan-sites.co.uk
w caravan-sites.co.uk

Luckford Wood Farm Caravan & Camping Park ★
Holiday, Touring & Camping Park
Luckford Wood House, East Stoke, Wareham BH20 6AW
t (01929) 463098 & 07888 719002
e luckfordleisure@hotmail.co.uk
w luckfordleisure.co.uk

Wareham Forest Tourist Park ★★★★★
Touring & Camping Park
Bere Road, North Trigon, Wareham BH20 7NZ
t (01929) 551393
e holiday@wareham-forest.co.uk
w wareham-forest.co.uk

WARMINSTER Wiltshire

Longleat Caravan Club Site ★★★★★
Touring Park
Longleat, Warminster BA12 7NL
t (01985) 844663
w caravanclub.co.uk

WARMWELL Dorset

Warmwell Caravan Park ★★★★
Holiday, Touring & Camping Park
Warmwell, Dorchester DT2 8JD
t (01305) 852313
e stay@warmwellcaravanpark.co.uk
w warmwellcaravanpark.co.uk

Warmwell Leisure Resort ★★★★ ROSE AWARD
Holiday Park
Warmwell, Dorchester DT2 8JE
t 0871 641 0191
e enquiries@parkdeanholidays.co.uk
w parkdeanholidays.co.uk

WATERGATE BAY Cornwall

Watergate Bay Touring Park ★★★★
Holiday, Touring & Camping Park
Watergate Bay TR8 4AD
t (01637) 860387
e email@watergatebaytouringpark.co.uk
w watergatebaytouringpark.co.uk

WATERROW Somerset

Waterrow Touring Park ★★★★★
Touring & Camping Park
Waterrow, Taunton TA4 2AZ
t (01984) 623464
e taylor@waterrowpark.u-net.com
w waterrowpark.co.uk

WEMBURY Devon

Churchwood Valley Holiday Cabins ★★★★
Holiday Park
Churchwood Valley, Wembury Bay, Plymouth PL9 0DZ
t (01752) 862382
e churchwoodvalley@btconnect.com
w churchwoodvalley.com

WEST BAY Dorset

West Bay Holiday Park ★★★★ ROSE AWARD
Holiday, Touring & Camping Park
West Bay, Bridport DT6 4HB
t 0871 641 0191
e enquiries@parkdeanholidays.co.uk
w parkdeanholidays.co.uk

WEST BEXINGTON Dorset

Gorselands Caravan Park ★★★★
Holiday Park
West Bexington Road, West Bexington DT2 9DJ
t (01308) 897232
e info@gorselands.co.uk
w gorselands.co.uk

WEST DOWN Devon

Brook Lea ★★★★
Touring Park
Brooklea Caravan Club Site, Woolacombe EX34 8NE
t (01271) 862848
e enquiries@caravanclub.co.uk
w caravanclub.co.uk

WEST LULWORTH Dorset

Durdle Door Holiday Park ★★★
Holiday, Touring & Camping Park
West Lulworth, Wareham BH20 5PU
t (01929) 400200
e durdle.door@lulworth.com
w lulworth.com

WEST QUANTOXHEAD Somerset

St Audries Bay ★★★★
Holiday & Touring Park
West Quantoxhead, Taunton TA4 4DY
t (01984) 632515
e info@staudriesbay.co.uk
w staudriesbay.co.uk

WESTON Devon

Oakdown Touring & Holiday Caravan Park ★★★★★ ROSE AWARD
Holiday & Touring Park
Gatedown Lane, Weston EX10 0PH
t (01297) 680387
e enquiries@oakdown.co.uk
w oakdown.co.uk

WESTON-SUPER-MARE
Somerset

Carefree Holiday Park ★★★★★
Holiday Park
12 Beach Road, Kewstoke
BS22 9UZ
t (01934) 624541
e crichardson@hotmail.co.uk

Country View Holiday Park ★★★★
Holiday, Touring & Camping Park
29 Sand Road, Sand Bay, Weston-super-Mare BS22 9UJ
t (01934) 627595
e giles@cvhp.co.uk
w cvhp.co.uk

Dulhorn Farm Camping Site ★★★
Touring & Camping Park
Weston Road, Lympsham, Weston-super-Mare BS24 0JQ
t (01934) 750298

Sand Bay Holiday Village ★★★
Holiday Village
67 Beach Road, Kewstoke
BS22 9UR
t (01934) 428200
e cro@hollybushhotels.co.uk
w sandbayholidayvillage.co.uk

Weston-super-Mare Camping & Caravanning Club Site ★★★
Touring Park
West End Farm, Locking
BS24 8RH
t (01934) 822548
w campingandcaravanningclub.co.uk

WESTWARD HO!
Devon

Beachside Holiday Park ★★★★ ROSE AWARD
Holiday Park
Merley Road, Westward Ho!, Bideford EX39 1JX
t 0845 601 2541 & 0845 601 2541
e beachside@surfbay.dircon.co.uk
w beachsideholidays.co.uk

Surf Bay Holiday Park ★★★★ ROSE AWARD
Holiday Park
Golf Links Road, Westward Ho!, Bideford EX39 1HD
t 0845 601132 & 0845 601 1132
e surfbayholidaypark@surfbay.dircon.co.uk
w surfbay.co.uk

WEYMOUTH
Dorset

Chesil Beach Holiday Park ★★★★★ ROSE AWARD
Holiday Park
Chesil Beach, Portland Road, Weymouth DT4 9AG
t (01305) 773233
e info@chesilholidays.co.uk
w chesilholidays.co.uk

Crossways Caravan Club Site ★★★★
Touring Park
Crossways, Dorchester
DT2 8BE
t (01305) 852032
w caravanclub.co.uk

East Fleet Farm Touring Park ★★★★
Touring & Camping Park
Chickerell, Weymouth
DT3 4DW
t (01305) 785768
e enquiries@eastfleet.co.uk
w eastfleet.co.uk

Littlesea Holiday Park ★★★★★
Holiday, Touring & Camping Park
Lynch Lane, Weymouth
DT4 9DT
t (01305) 774414
e david.bennett@bourne-leisure.co.uk
w littlesea-park.co.uk

Pebble Bank Caravan Park ★★★
Holiday, Touring & Camping Park
90 Camp Road, Wyke Regis, Weymouth DT4 9HF
t (01305) 774844
e info@pebblebank.co.uk
w pebblebank.co.uk

Seaview Holiday Park ★★★
Holiday, Touring & Camping Park
Preston, Weymouth DT3 6DZ
t (01305) 833037
w haven.com/seaview

Waterside Holiday Park ★★★★★ ROSE AWARD
Holiday & Touring Park
Bowleaze Coveway, Weymouth DT3 6PP
t (01305) 833103
e info@watersideholidays.co.uk
w watersideholidays.co.uk

WHITE CROSS
Cornwall

White Acres Country Park ★★★★★ ROSE AWARD
Holiday Park
Whitecross, Newquay
TR8 4LW
t 0871 641 0191
e enquiries@parkdeanholidays.co.uk
w parkdeanholidays.co.uk

WIMBORNE MINSTER
Dorset

Merley Court Touring Park ★★★★★
Touring Park
Merley Court, Merley, Wimborne BH21 3AA
t (01590) 648331
e holidays@shorefield.co.uk
w shorefield.co.uk

Wilksworth Farm Caravan Park ★★★★★
Touring & Camping Park
Cranborne Road, Furzehill, Wimborne BH21 4HW
t (01202) 885467
e rayandwendy@wilksworthfarmcaravanpark.co.uk
w wilksworthfarmcaravanpark.co.uk

WINCANTON
Somerset

Wincanton Racecourse Campsite ★★★
Touring & Camping Park
Old Hill, Wincanton BA9 8BJ
t (01963) 34276
e enquiries@caravanclub.co.uk
w caravanclub.co.uk

WINCHCOMBE
Gloucestershire

Camping & Caravanning Club Site – Winchcombe ★★★★
Touring & Camping Park
Brooklands Farm, Alderton, Tewkesbury GL20 8NX
t (01242) 620259
w campingandcaravanningclub.co.uk

WINSFORD
Somerset

Halse Farm Caravan & Tent Park ★★★★
Touring & Camping Park
Winsford, Minehead TA24 7JL
t (01643) 851259
e brit@halsefarm.co.uk
w halsefarm.co.uk

WOODBURY
Devon

Castle Brake Holiday Park ★★★★ ROSE AWARD
Holiday & Touring Park
Castle Lane, Woodbury
EX5 1HA
t (01395) 232431
e reception@castlebrake.co.uk
w castlebrake.co.uk

WOODLANDS
Dorset

Camping & Caravanning Club Site – Verwood, New Forest ★★★
Touring & Camping Park
Sutton Hill, Woodlands
BH21 8NQ
t (01202) 822763
w campingandcaravanningclub.co.uk

WOOL
Dorset

Whitemead Caravan Park ★★★★
Touring & Camping Park
East Burton Road, Wool, Wareham BH20 6HG
t (01929) 462241
e whitemeadcp@aol.com
w whitemeadcaravanpark.co.uk

WOOLACOMBE
Devon

Golden Coast Holiday Village ★★★★
Holiday Park
Golden Coast Sporting Villas, Woolacombe EX34 7HW
t (01271) 870343
e goodtimes@woolacombe.com
w woolacombe.com

Woolacombe Bay Holiday Parcs (Cleavewood House) ★★★★
Holiday, Touring & Camping Park
Woolacombe EX34 7HW
t (01271) 870343

Woolacombe Bay Holiday Village ★★★★
Holiday, Touring & Camping Park
Seymour, Sandy Lane, Woolacombe EX34 7AH
t (01271) 870343
e goodtimes@woolacombe.com
w woolacombe.com

Woolacombe Sands Holiday Park ★★★★
Holiday, Touring & Camping Park
Beach Road, Woolacombe
EX34 7AF
t (01271) 870569
e lifesabeach@woolacombe-sands.co.uk
w woolacombe-sands.co.uk

YEOVIL
Somerset

Long Hazel Park ★★★★
Holiday, Touring & Camping Park
High Street, Sparkford, Yeovil
BA22 7JH
t (01963) 440002
e longhazelpark@hotmail.com
w sparkford.f9.co.uk/lhi.htm

Look out for parks participating in the National Accessible Scheme

Further information

Clockwise: Botany Bay, Kent; Whinstone Lee Tor, Peak District, Derbyshire; Sherwood Pines Forest Park, Nottinghamshire

The British Graded Holiday Parks Scheme

When you're looking for a place to stay, you need a rating system you can trust. The British Graded Holiday Parks Scheme, operated jointly by the national tourist boards for England, Scotland, Wales and Northern Ireland, was devised in association with the British Holiday and Home Parks Association and the National Caravan Council. It gives you a clear guide of what to expect in an easy-to-understand form.

The process to arrive at a star rating is very thorough to ensure that when you make a booking you can be confident it will meet your expectations. Professional assessors visit parks annually and take into account over 50 separate aspects, from landscaping and layout to maintenance, customer care and, most importantly, cleanliness.

Strict guidelines are in place to ensure that every park is assessed to the same criteria. A random check is made of a sample of accommodation provided for hire (caravans, chalets etc) **but the quality of the accommodation itself is not included in the grading assessment**.

In addition to The British Graded Holiday Parks Scheme, VisitBritain operates a rating scheme for Holiday Villages. The assessor stays on the site overnight and grades the overall quality of the visitor experience, including accommodation, facilities, cleanliness, service and food.

Holiday, touring and camping parks

Parks are required to meet progressively higher standards of quality as they move up the scale from one to five stars:

ONE STAR Acceptable
To achieve this grade, the park must be clean with good standards of maintenance and customer care.

TWO STAR Good
All the above points plus an improved level of landscaping, lighting, refuse disposal and maintenance. May be less expensive than more highly rated parks.

THREE STAR Very good
Most parks fall within this category; three stars represent the industry standard. The range of facilities provided may vary from park to park, but they will be of a very good standard and will be well maintained.

FOUR STAR Excellent
You can expect careful attention to detail in the provision of all services and facilities. Four star parks rank among the industry's best.

FIVE STAR Exceptional
Highest levels of customer care will be provided. All facilities will be maintained in pristine condition in attractive surroundings.

Holiday villages

Holiday Villages are assessed under a separate rating scheme and are awarded one to five stars based on both the quality of facilities and the range of services provided. The option to include breakfast and dinner is normally available. A variety of accommodation is offered, mostly in chalets.

★ Simple, practical, no frills
★★ Well presented and well run
★★★ Good level of quality and comfort
★★★★ Very good standard throughout
★★★★★ Excellent facilities and services

Advice and information

Making a booking

When enquiring about a place to stay, make sure you check prices, the quality rating, and other important details. You will also need to state your requirements clearly and precisely.

Booking by letter or email

Misunderstandings can easily happen over the telephone, so do request a written confirmation together with details of any terms and conditions.

Deposits and advance payments

In the case of caravan, camping and touring parks, and holiday villages the full charge often has to be paid in advance. This may be in two instalments – a deposit at the time of booking and the balance by, say, two weeks before the start of the booked period.

Cancellations

Legal contract

When you accept a booking that is offered to you, by telephone or in writing, you enter a legally binding contract with the proprietor. This means that if you cancel or fail to take up your booking or leave early, the proprietor may be entitled to compensation if he or she cannot re-let for all or a good part of the booked period. You will probably forfeit any deposit you have paid and may well be asked for an additional payment.

At the time of booking you should be advised of what charges would be made in the event of cancelling the accommodation or leaving early. If this is not mentioned you should ask so that future disputes can be avoided. The proprietor cannot make a claim until after the booked period, and during that time he or she should make every effort to re-let the accommodation. If there is a dispute it is sensible for both sides to seek legal advice on the matter. If you do have to change your travel plans, it is in your own interests to let the proprietor know in writing as soon as possible, to give them a chance to re-let your accommodation.

And remember, if you book by telephone and are asked for your credit card number, you should check whether the proprietor intends charging your credit card account should you later cancel your booking. A proprietor should not be able to charge your credit card account with a cancellation fee unless he or she has made this clear at the time of your booking and you have agreed. However, to avoid later disputes, we suggest you check whether this is the intention.

Insurance

A travel or holiday insurance policy will safeguard you if you have to cancel or change your holiday plans. You can arrange a policy quite cheaply through your insurance company or travel agent.

Finding a park

Tourist signs similar to the one shown here are designed to help visitors find their park. They clearly show whether the park is for tents or caravans or both.

Tourist information centres throughout Britain are able to give campers and caravanners information about parks in their areas. Some tourist information centres have camping and caravanning advisory services that provide details of park availability and often assist with park booking.

Electric hook-up points

Most parks now have electric hook-up points for caravans and tents. Voltage is generally 240v AC, 50 cycles. Parks may charge extra for this facility, and it is advisable to check rates when making a booking.

Avoiding peak season

In the summer months of June to September, parks in popular areas such as North Wales, Cumbria, the West Country or the New Forest in Hampshire may become full. Campers should aim to arrive at parks early in the day or, where possible, should book in advance. Some parks have overnight holding areas for visitors who arrive late. This helps to prevent disturbing other campers and caravanners late at night and means that fewer visitors are turned away. Caravans or tents are directed to a pitch the following morning.

Other caravan and camping places

If you enjoy making your own route through Britain's countryside, it may interest you to know that the Forestry Commission operates campsites in Britain's Forest Parks as well as in the New Forest. Some offer reduced charges for youth organisations on organised camping trips, and all enquiries about them should be made, well in advance of your intended stay, to the Forestry Commission.

Bringing pets to Britain

Dogs, cats, ferrets and some other pet mammals can be brought into the UK from certain countries without having to undertake six months' quarantine on arrival provided they meet all the rules of the Pet Travel Scheme (PETS).

For full details, visit the PETS website at
w defra.gov.uk/animalh/quarantine/index.htm
or contact the PETS Helpline
t +44 (0)870 241 1710
e quarantine@animalhealth.gsi.gov.uk
Ask for fact sheets which cover dogs and cats, ferrets or domestic rabbits and rodents.

What to expect at holiday, touring and camping parks

In addition to fulfilling its statutory obligations, including having applied for a certificate under the Fire Precautions Act 1971 (if applicable) and holding public liability insurance, and ensuring that all caravan holiday homes/chalets for hire and the park and all buildings and facilities thereon, the fixtures, furnishings, fittings and decor are maintained in sound and clean condition and are fit for the purposes intended, the management is required to undertake the following:

- To ensure high standards of courtesy, cleanliness, catering and service appropriate to the type of park;
- To describe to all visitors and prospective visitors the amenities, facilities and services provided by the park and/or caravan holiday homes/chalets whether by advertisement, brochure, word of mouth or other means;
- To allow visitors to see the park or caravan holiday homes/chalets for hire, if requested, before booking;
- To present grading awards and/or any other national tourist board awards unambiguously;
- To make clear to visitors exactly what is included in prices quoted for the park or caravan holiday homes/chalets, meals and refreshments, including service charge, taxes and other surcharges. Details of charges, if any, for heating or for additional services or facilities available should also be made clear;
- To adhere to, and not to exceed, prices current at time of occupation for caravan holiday homes/chalets or other services;
- To advise visitors at the time of booking, and subsequently if any change, if the caravan holiday home/chalet or pitch offered is in a different location or on another park, and to indicate the location of this and any difference in comfort and amenities;
- To give each visitor, on request, details of payments due and a receipt if required;
- To advise visitors at the time of booking of the charges that might be incurred if the booking is subsequently cancelled;
- To register all guests on arrival;
- To deal promptly and courteously with all visitors and prospective visitors, including enquiries, requests, reservations, correspondence and complaints;
- To allow a national tourist board representative reasonable access to the park and/or caravan holiday homes/chalet whether by prior appointment or on an unannounced assessment, to confirm that the VisitBritain Code of Conduct is being observed and that the appropriate quality standard is being maintained;
- The operator must comply with the provision of the caravan industry Codes of Practice.

What to expect at holiday villages

The operator/manager is required to undertake the following:

- To maintain standards of guest care, cleanliness, and service appropriate to the type of establishment;
- To describe accurately in any advertisement, brochure, or other printed or electronic media, the facilities and services provided;
- To make clear to visitors exactly what is included in all prices quoted for accommodation, including taxes, and any other surcharges. Details of charges for additional services/facilities should also be made clear;
- To give a clear statement of the policy on cancellations to guests at the time of booking ie by telephone, fax, email as well as information given in a printed format;
- To adhere to, and not to exceed prices quoted at the time of booking for accommodation and other services;
- To advise visitors at the time of booking, and subsequently of any change, if the accommodation offered is in an unconnected annexe or similar, and to indicate the location of such accommodation and any difference in comfort and/or amenities from accommodation in the establishment;
- To give each visitor, on request, details of payments due and a receipt, if required;
- To register all guests on arrival;
- To deal promptly and courteously with all enquiries, requests, bookings and correspondence from visitors;
- To ensure complaint handling procedures are in place and that complaints received are investigated promptly and courteously and that the outcome is communicated to the visitor;
- To give due consideration to the requirements of visitors with special needs, and to make suitable provision where applicable;
- To provide public liability insurance or comparable arrangement and to comply with applicable planning, safety and other statutory requirements;
- To allow a national tourist board representative reasonable access to the establishment, on request, to confirm the Code of Conduct is being observed.

Comments and complaints

Information

The proprietors themselves supply the descriptions of their establishments and other information for the entries (except ratings). They have all signed a declaration that their information conforms to the Trade Description Acts 1968 and 1972. VisitBritain cannot guarantee the accuracy of information in this guide, and accepts no responsibility for any error or misrepresentation.

All liability for loss, disappointment, negligence or other damage caused by reliance on the information contained in this guide, or in the event of bankruptcy or liquidation or cessation of trade of any company, individual or firm mentioned, is hereby excluded. We strongly recommend that you carefully check prices and other details when you book your accommodation.

Problems

Of course, we hope you will not have cause for complaint, but problems do occur from time to time.

If you are dissatisfied with anything, make your complaint to the management immediately. Then the management can take action at once to investigate the matter and put things right. The longer you leave a complaint, the harder it is to deal with it effectively.

In certain circumstances, VisitBritain may look into complaints. However, VisitBritain has no statutory control over establishments or their methods of operating. VisitBritain cannot become involved in legal or contractual matters or in seeking financial compensation.

If you do have problems that have not been resolved by the proprietor and which you would like to bring to our attention, please write to:

England
Quality in Tourism, Farncombe House, Broadway, Worcestershire WR12 7LJ

Scotland
Customer Feedback Department, VisitScotland, Cowan House, Inverness Retail and Business Park, Inverness IV2 7GF

Wales
VisitWales, Ty Glyndwr, Treowain Enterprise Park, Machynlleth, Powys SY20 8WW

Useful contacts

British Holiday & Home Parks Association

Chichester House, 6 Pullman Court,
Great Western Road, Gloucester GL1 3ND
t (01452) 526911 (enquiries and brochure requests)
w parkholidayengland.org.uk

Professional UK park owners are represented by the British Holiday and Home Parks Association. Over 3,000 parks are in membership, and each year welcome millions of visitors seeking quality surroundings in which to enjoy a good value stay.

Parks provide caravan holiday homes and lodges for hire, and pitches for your own touring caravan, motor home or tent. On many, you can opt to buy your own holiday home.

A major strength of the UK's park industry is its diversity. Whatever your idea of holiday pleasure, there's sure to be a park which can provide it. If your preference is for a quiet, peaceful holiday in tranquil rural surroundings, you'll find many idyllic locations.

Alternatively, many parks are to be found at our most popular resorts – and reflect the holiday atmosphere with plenty of entertainment and leisure facilities. And for more adventurous families, parks often provide excellent bases from which to enjoy outdoor activities.

Literature available from BH&HPA includes a guide to over 600 parks which have this year achieved the David Bellamy Conservation Award for environmental excellence.

The Camping and Caravanning Club

Greenfields House, Westwood Way,
Coventry CV4 8JH
t 0845 130 7631
t 0845 130 7633 (advance bookings)
w campingandcaravanningclub.co.uk

Discover the peace and quiet of over 100 award-winning Club Sites. Experience a different backdrop to your holiday every time you go away, with sites in the lakes and mountains, coastal and woodland glades or cultural and heritage locations.

The Club is proud of its prestigious pedigree and regularly achieves awards for spotless campsites, friendly service and caring for the environment – a guarantee that you will enjoy your holiday.

Non-members are welcome at the majority of our sites and we offer special deals for families, backpackers, overseas visitors and members aged 55 and over. Recoup your membership fee in just six nights and gain access to over 1,300 Certificated Sites around the country.

For more details please refer to our entries listed at the back of this publication or if you require any more information on what The Friendly Club can offer you then telephone 0845 130 7632. Or call to request your free guide to The Club.

The Caravan Club

East Grinstead House,
East Grinstead,
West Sussex RH19 1UA
t (01342) 326944
w caravanclub.co.uk

The Caravan Club offers 200 sites in the UK and Ireland. These include city locations such as London, Edinburgh, York and Chester, plus sites near leading heritage attractions such as Longleat, Sandringham, Chatsworth and Blenheim Palace. A further 30 sites are in National Parks.

Virtually all pitches have an electric hook-up point. The toilet blocks and play areas are of the highest quality. Friendly, knowledgeable site wardens are on hand too.

Most Caravan Club Sites are graded four or five stars according to The British Graded Holiday Parks Scheme, run by VisitBritain, so that you can be assured of quality at all times. Over 130 sites are open to non-members, but why not become a member and gain access to all sites, plus a further 2,500 Certificated Locations – rural sites for no more than five vans. Tent campers are welcome at over 60 sites.

Join The Club and you can save the cost of your subscription fee in just five nights with member discounts on site fees!

Forest Holidays

Heart of the National Forest, Bath Yard, Moira, Derbyshire DE12 6BA
t 0845 130 8223 (cabins)
t 0845 130 8224 (campsites)
w forestholidays.co.uk

Forest Holidays, a new partnership between the Forestry Commission and the Camping and Caravanning Club, have over 20 camping and caravan sites in stunning forest locations throughout Great Britain in addition to three cabin sites. Choose from locations such as the Scottish Highlands, the New Forest, Snowdonia National Park, the Forest of Dean, or the banks of Loch Lomond. Some sites are open all year and dogs are welcome at most. Advance bookings are accepted for many sites.

For a unique forest experience, call Forest Holidays for a brochure on 0845 130 8224 or visit our website.

The Motor Caravanners' Club Ltd

FREEPOST (TK 1292), Twickenham TW2 5BR
t (020) 8893 3883
f (020) 8893 8324
e info@motorcaravanners.eu
w motorcaravanners.eu

The Motor Caravanners' Club is authorised to issue the Camping Card International (CCI). It also produces a monthly magazine, Motor Caravanner, for all members. Member of The Federation Internationale de Camping et de Caravanning (FICC).

The National Caravan Council

The National Caravan Council, Catherine House, Victoria Road, Aldershot, Hampshire GU11 1SS
t (01252) 318251
w thecaravan.net

The National Caravan Council (NCC) is the trade body for the British caravan industry – not just touring caravans and motorhomes but also caravan holiday homes. It has in its membership parks, manufacturers, dealers and suppliers to the industry – all NCC member companies are committed continually to raise standards of technical and commercial excellence.

So, if you want to know where to buy a caravan, where to find a caravan holiday park or simply need advice on caravans and caravanning, see the website thecaravan.net where there is lots of helpful advice including:

- How to check whether the caravan, motorhome or caravan holiday home you are buying complies with European Standards and essential UK health and safety regulations (through the Certification scheme that the NCC operates).
- Where to find quality parks to visit on holiday.
- Where to find approved caravan and motorhome workshops for servicing and repair.

Caravan holidays are one of the most popular choices for holidaymakers in Britain – the NCC works closely with VisitBritain to promote caravan holidays in all their forms and parks that are part of the British Graded Quality Parks Scheme.

Bank holiday dates

holiday	2009	2010
New Year's Day	1 January	1 January
January Bank Holiday (Scotland)	2 January	4 January
Good Friday	10 April	2 April
Easter Monday (England & Wales)	13 April	5 April
Early May Bank Holiday	4 May	3 May
Spring Bank Holiday	25 May	31 May
Summer Bank Holiday (Scotland)	3 August	2 August
Summer Bank Holiday (England & Wales)	31 August	30 August
St Andrews Day* (Scotland)	30 November	30 November
Christmas Day Holiday	25 December	27 December
Boxing Day Holiday	28 December	28 December

***(a voluntary public holiday)**

About the accommodation entries

Entries

All the sites featured in this guide have been assessed or have applied for assessment under The British Graded Holiday Parks Scheme. Assessment automatically entitles sites to a listing in this guide. Start your search for a place to stay by looking in the regional sections of this guide where proprietors have paid to have their site featured in either a standard entry (includes description, facilities and prices) or an enhanced entry (photograph and extended details). If you can't find what you're looking for, turn to the listing section on the yellow pages for an even wider choice of sites in England.

Locations

Places to stay are listed under the town, city or village where they are located. If a place is in the countryside, you may find it listed under a nearby village or town (providing it is within a seven-mile radius). Place names are listed alphabetically within each regional section of the guide, along with the name of the ceremonial county they are in and their map reference.

Map references

These refer to the colour location maps at the front of the guide. The first figure shown is the map number, the following letter and figure indicate the grid reference on the map. Only place names under which standard or enhanced entries (see above) feature appear on the maps. Some entries were included just before the guide went to press, so they do not appear on the maps.

Addresses

County names, which appear in the place headings, are not repeated in the entries. When you are writing, you should of course make sure you use the full address and postcode.

Telephone numbers

Booking telephone numbers are listed below the contact address for each entry. Area codes are shown in brackets.

Prices

The prices shown are only a general guide and include VAT where applicable; they were supplied to us by proprietors in summer 2008. Remember, changes may occur after the guide goes to press, so we strongly advise you to check prices when you book your accommodation.

Touring pitch prices are based on the minimum and maximum charges for one night for two persons, car and either caravan or tent. (Some parks may charge separately for car, caravan or tent, and for each person and there may be an extra charge for caravan awnings.) Minimum and maximum prices for caravan holiday homes are given per week.

Prices often vary through the year, and may be significantly lower outside peak holiday weeks. You can get details of other bargain packages that may be available from the sites themselves, regional tourism organisations or your local tourist information centre (TIC). Your local travel agent may also have information, and can help you make bookings.

Opening period

If an entry does not indicate an opening period, please check directly with the site.

Symbols

The at-a-glance symbols included at the end of each entry show many of the services and facilities available at each site. You will find the key to these symbols on page 7.

Pets

Many places accept visitors with dogs, but we do advise that you check this when you book, and ask if there are any extra charges or rules about exactly where your pet is allowed. The acceptance of dogs is not always extended to cats, and it is strongly advised that cat owners contact the site well in advance. Some sites do not accept pets at all. Pets are welcome where you see this symbol 🐕.

The quarantine laws have changed in England, and dogs, cats and ferrets are able to come into Britain from over 50 countries. For details of the Pet Travel Scheme (PETS) please turn to page 298.

Payment accepted

The types of payment accepted by a site are listed in the payment accepted section. If you plan to pay by card, check that your particular card is acceptable before you book. Some proprietors will charge you a higher rate if you pay by credit card rather than cash or cheque. The difference is to cover the percentage paid by the proprietor to the credit card company. When you book by telephone, you may be asked for your credit card number as confirmation. But remember, the proprietor may then charge your credit card account if you cancel your booking. See under Cancellations on page 297.

Awaiting confirmation of rating

At the time of going to press some parks featured in this guide had not yet been assessed for their rating for the year 2009 and so their new rating could not be included. Rating Applied For indicates this.

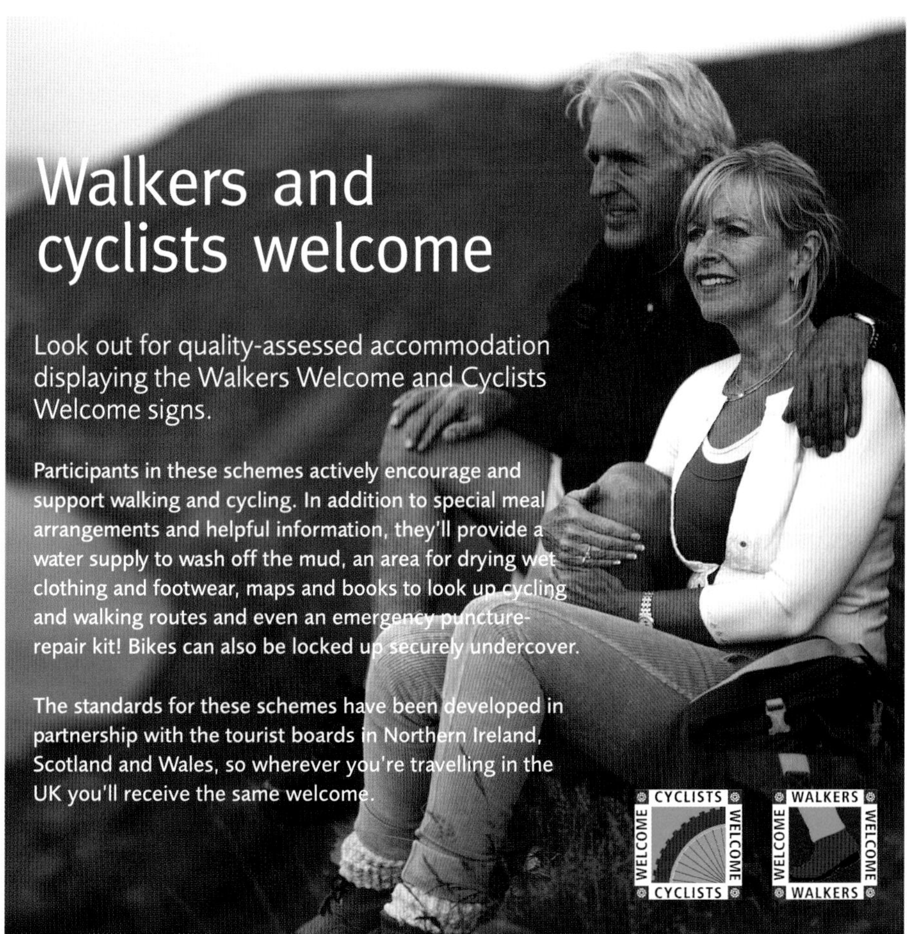

Walkers and cyclists welcome
Look out for quality-assessed accommodation displaying the Walkers Welcome and Cyclists Welcome signs.
Participants in these schemes actively encourage and support walking and cycling. In addition to special meal arrangements and helpful information, they'll provide a water supply to wash off the mud, an area for drying wet clothing and footwear, maps and books to look up cycling and walking routes and even an emergency puncture-repair kit! Bikes can also be locked up securely undercover.
The standards for these schemes have been developed in partnership with the tourist boards in Northern Ireland, Scotland and Wales, so wherever you're travelling in the UK you'll receive the same welcome.
CYCLISTS WELCOME
WALKERS WELCOME

Getting around Britain

Travelling in London

London transport

London Underground has 12 lines, each with its own unique colour, so you can easily follow them on the Underground map. Most lines run through central London, and many serve parts of Greater London.

Buses are a quick, convenient way to travel around London, providing plenty of sightseeing opportunities on the way. There are over 6,500 buses in London operating 700 routes every day. You will need to buy a ticket before you board the bus – available from machines at the bus stop – or have a valid Oyster card (see below).

London's National Rail system stretches all over London. Many lines start at the main London railway stations (Paddington, Victoria, Waterloo, Kings Cross) with links to the tube. Trains mainly serve areas outside central London, and travel over ground.

Children usually travel free, or at reduced fare, on all public transport in London.

Oyster cards

Oyster cards can be used to pay fares on all London Underground, buses, Docklands Light Railway and trams; they are generally not valid for National Rail services in London.

Oyster cards are very easy to use – you just touch the card on sensors at stations or on buses and it always charges you the lowest fare available for your journey. You buy credit for your journey and when it runs out you simply top up with more.

Oyster is available to adults only. Children below the age of 11 can accompany adults free of charge. Children between the ages of 11 and 15 should use the standard child travel card. You can get an Oyster card at any underground station, at one of 3,000 Oyster points around London displaying the London Underground sign (usually shops), or from visitbritaindirect.com.

London congestion charge

The congestion charge is an £8 daily charge to drive in central London at certain times. Check whether the congestion charge is included in the cost of your car when you book. If your car's pick up point is in the congestion-charging zone, the company may pay the charge for the first day of your hire.

Low Emission Zone

The Low Emission Zone is an area covering most of Greater London, within which the most polluting diesel-engine vehicles are required to meet specific emissions standards. If your vehicle does not, you will need to pay a daily charge.

Vehicles affected by the Low Emission Zone are older diesel-engine lorries, buses, coaches, large vans, minibuses and other heavy vehicles such as motor caravans and motorised horse boxes. This includes vehicles registered outside of Great Britain. Cars and motorcycles are not affected by the scheme.

For more information visit tfl.gov.uk/roadusers/lez.

Rail and train travel

Britain's rail network covers all main cities and smaller regional towns. Trains on the network are operated by a few large companies running routes from London to stations all over Britain, and smaller companies running routes in regional areas. You can find up-to-the-minute information about routes, fares and train times on National Rail Enquiries (nationalrail.co.uk). For detailed information about routes and services, refer to the train operators' websites (see page 310).

Railway passes

BritRail offers a wide selection of passes and tickets giving you freedom to travel on all National Rail services. Passes can also include sleeper services, city and attraction passes and boat tours. Passes can normally be bought from travel agents outside Britain or by visiting the Britrail website (britrail.com).

Bus and coach travel

Public buses

Every city and town in Britain has a local bus service. These services are privatised and run by separate companies. The largest bus companies in Britain are First (firstgroup.com/bustravel.php), Stagecoach (stagecoachbus.com), and Arriva (arrivabus.co.uk), which run buses in most UK towns. Outside London, buses usually travel to and from the town centre or busiest part of town. Most towns have a bus station, where you'll be able to find maps and information about routes. Bus route information may also be posted at bus stops.

Tickets and fares

The cost of a bus ticket normally depends on how far you're travelling. Return fares may be available on some buses, but you usually need to buy a 'single' ticket for each individual journey.

You can buy your ticket when you board a bus, by telling the driver where you are going. One-day and weekly travel cards are available in some towns, and these can be bought from the driver or from an information centre at the bus station. Tickets are valid for each separate journey rather than for a period of time, so if you get off the bus you'll need to buy a new ticket when getting on another bus.

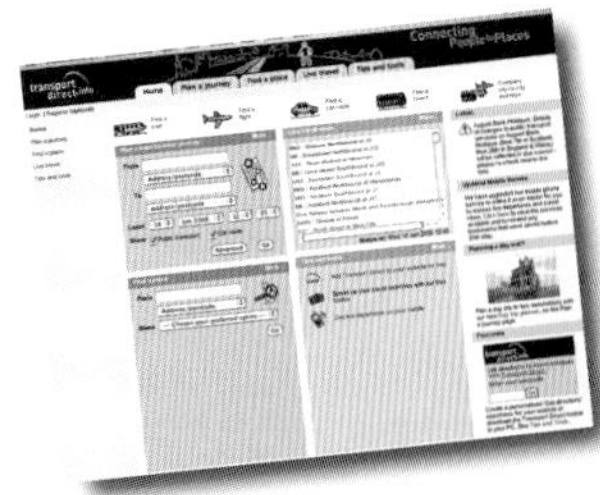

Domestic flights

Flying is a time-saving alternative to road or rail when it comes to travelling around Britain. Domestic flights are fast and frequent and there are 33 airports across Britain operating domestic routes. You will find airports marked on the maps at the front of this guide.

Domestic flight advice

Photo ID is required to travel on domestic flights. It is advisable to bring your passport, as not all airlines will accept other forms of photo identification.

There are very high security measures at all airports in Britain. These include restrictions on items that may be carried in hand luggage. It is important that you check with your airline prior to travel, as these restrictions may vary over time. Make sure you allow adequate time for check-in and boarding.

Cycling

Cycling is a good way to see some of Britain's best scenery and there are many networks of cycling routes. The National Cycle Network offers over 10,000 miles of walking and cycling routes connecting towns and villages, countryside and coast across the UK. For more information and routes see page 313 or visit Sustrans at sustrans.co.uk.

Think green

If you'd rather leave your car behind and travel by 'green transport' when visiting some of the attractions highlighted in this guide you'll be helping to reduce congestion and pollution as well as supporting conservation charities in their commitment to green travel.

The National Trust encourages visits made by non-car travellers. It offers admission discounts or a voucher for the tea room at a selection of its properties if you arrive on foot, cycle or public transport. (You'll need to produce a valid bus or train ticket if travelling by public transport.)

More information about The National Trust's work to encourage car-free days out can be found at nationaltrust.org.uk. Refer to the section entitled Information for Visitors.

To help you on your way you'll find a list of useful contacts at the end of this section.

Britain at a glance

SCOTLAND

CENTRAL ENGLAND
Bedfordshire, Cambridgeshire, Derbyshire, Essex, Herefordshire, Hertfordshire, Leicestershire, Lincolnshire, Norfolk, Northamptonshire, Nottinghamshire, Rutland, Shropshire, Staffordshire, Suffolk, Warwickshire, West Midlands, Worcestershire

NORTHERN ENGLAND
Cheshire, Cumbria, Durham, East Yorkshire, Greater Manchester, Lancashire, Merseyside, North Yorkshire, Northumberland, South Yorkshire, Tees Valley, Tyne and Wear, West Yorkshire

WALES

LONDON

SOUTH WEST ENGLAND
Bristol, Cornwall, Devon, Dorset, Gloucestershire, Isles of Scilly, Somerset, Wiltshire

SOUTH EAST ENGLAND
Berkshire, Buckinghamshire, East Sussex, Hampshire, Isle of Wight, Kent, London, Oxfordshire, Surrey, West Sussex

A guide to English counties

If you know what English county you wish to visit you'll find it in the regional section shown below.

County	Region
Bedfordshire	Central England
Berkshire	South East England
Bristol	South West England
Buckinghamshire	South East England
Cambridgeshire	Central England
Cheshire	Northern England
Cornwall	South West England
Cumbria	Northern England
Derbyshire	Central England
Devon	South West England
Dorset	South West England
Durham	Northern England
East Yorkshire	Northern England
East Sussex	South East England
Essex	Central England
Gloucestershire	South West England
Greater Manchester	Northern England
Hampshire	South East England
Herefordshire	Central England
Hertfordshire	Central England
Isle of Wight	South East England
Isles of Scilly	South West England
Kent	South East England
Lancashire	Northern England

County	Region
Leicestershire	Central England
Lincolnshire	Central England
Merseyside	Northern England
Norfolk	Central England
North Yorkshire	Northern England
Northamptonshire	Central England
Northumberland	Northern England
Nottinghamshire	Central England
Oxfordshire	South East England
Rutland	Central England
Shropshire	Central England
Somerset	South West England
South Yorkshire	Northern England
Staffordshire	Central England
Suffolk	Central England
Surrey	South East England
Tees Valley	Northern England
Tyne and Wear	Northern England
Warwickshire	Central England
West Midlands	Central England
West Sussex	South East England
West Yorkshire	Northern England
Wiltshire	South West England
Worcestershire	Central England

To help readers we do not refer to unitary authorities in this guide.

By car and by train

Distance chart

The distances between towns on the chart below are given to the nearest mile, and are measured along routes based on the quickest travelling time, making maximum use of motorways or dual-carriageway roads. The chart is based upon information supplied by the Automobile Association.

To calculate the distance in kilometres multiply the mileage by 1.6

For example: Brighton to Dover
82 miles x 1.6 =131.2 kilometres

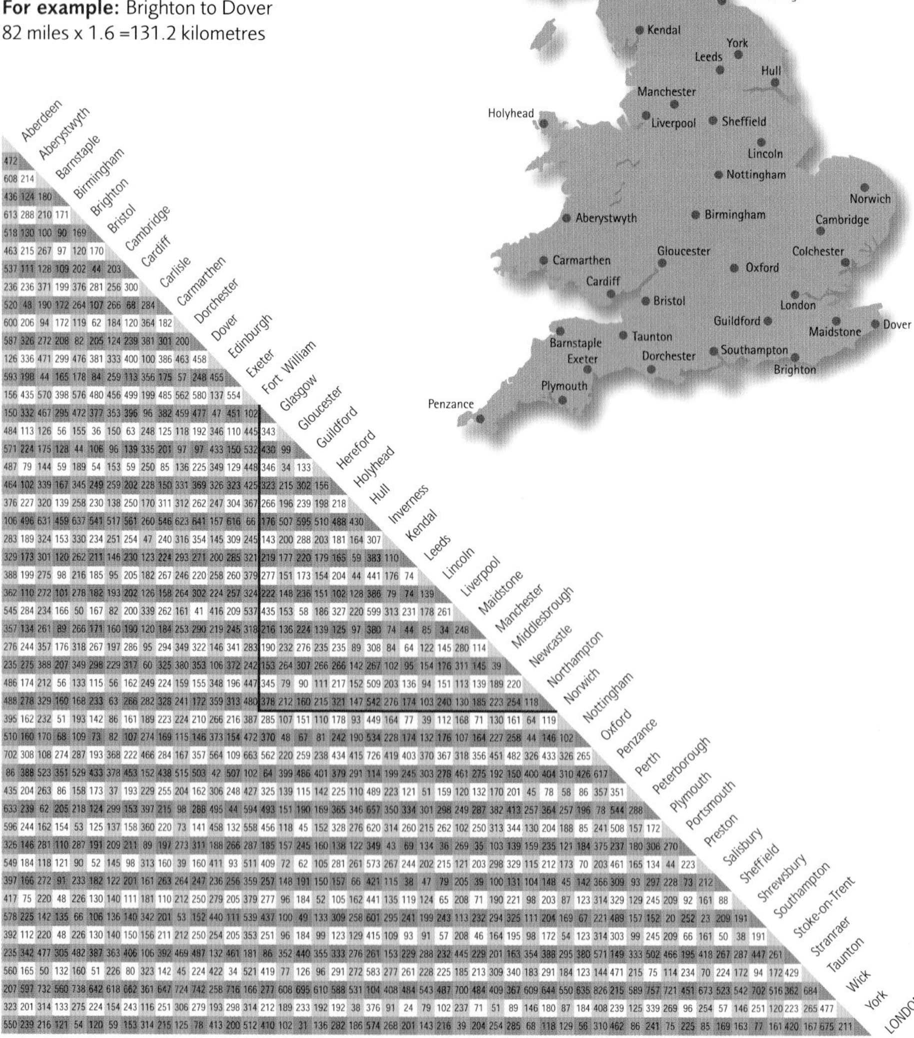

	Aberdeen	Aberystwyth	Barnstaple	Birmingham	Brighton	Bristol	Cambridge	Cardiff	Carlisle	Carmarthen	Dorchester	Dover	Edinburgh	Exeter	Fort William	Glasgow	Gloucester	Guildford	Hereford	Holyhead	Hull	Inverness	Kendal	Leeds	Lincoln	Liverpool	Maidstone	Manchester	Middlesbrough	Newcastle	Northampton	Norwich	Nottingham	Oxford	Penzance	Perth	Peterborough	Plymouth	Portsmouth	Preston	Salisbury	Sheffield	Shrewsbury	Southampton	Stoke-on-Trent	Stranraer	Taunton	Wick	York
Aberystwyth	472																																																
Barnstaple	608	214																																															
Birmingham	436	124	180																																														
Brighton	613	288	210	171																																													
Bristol	518	130	100	90	169																																												
Cambridge	463	215	267	97	120	170																																											
Cardiff	537	111	128	109	202	44	203																																										
Carlisle	236	236	371	199	376	281	256	300																																									
Carmarthen	520	48	190	172	264	107	266	68	284																																								
Dorchester	600	206	94	172	119	62	184	120	364	182																																							
Dover	587	326	272	208	82	205	124	239	381	301	200																																						
Edinburgh	126	336	471	299	476	381	333	400	100	386	463	458																																					
Exeter	593	198	44	165	178	84	259	113	356	175	57	248	455																																				
Fort William	156	435	570	398	576	480	456	499	199	485	562	580	137	554																																			
Glasgow	150	332	467	295	472	377	353	396	96	382	459	477	47	451	102																																		
Gloucester	484	113	126	56	155	36	150	63	248	125	118	192	346	110	445	343																																	
Guildford	571	224	175	128	44	106	96	139	335	201	97	97	433	150	532	430	99																																
Hereford	487	79	144	59	189	54	153	59	250	85	136	225	349	129	448	346	34	133																															
Holyhead	464	102	339	167	345	249	259	202	228	150	331	369	326	323	425	323	215	302	156																														
Hull	376	227	320	139	258	230	138	250	170	311	312	262	247	304	367	266	196	239	198	218																													
Inverness	106	496	631	459	637	541	517	561	260	546	623	641	157	616	66	176	507	595	510	488	430																												
Kendal	283	189	324	153	330	234	251	254	47	240	316	354	145	309	245	143	200	288	203	181	164	307																											
Leeds	329	173	301	120	262	211	146	230	123	224	293	271	200	285	321	219	177	220	179	165	59	383	110																										
Lincoln	388	199	275	98	216	185	95	205	182	267	246	220	258	260	379	277	151	173	154	204	44	441	176	74																									
Liverpool	362	110	272	101	278	182	193	202	126	158	264	302	224	257	324	222	148	236	151	102	128	386	79	74	139																								
Maidstone	545	284	234	166	50	167	82	200	339	262	161	41	416	209	537	435	153	58	186	327	220	599	313	231	178	261																							
Manchester	357	134	261	89	266	171	160	190	120	184	253	290	219	245	318	216	136	224	139	125	97	380	74	44	85	34	248																						
Middlesbrough	276	244	357	176	318	267	197	286	95	294	349	322	146	341	283	190	232	276	235	235	89	308	84	64	122	145	280	114																					
Newcastle	235	275	388	207	349	298	229	317	60	325	380	353	106	372	242	153	264	307	266	266	142	267	102	95	154	176	311	145	39																				
Northampton	486	174	212	56	133	115	56	162	249	224	159	155	348	196	447	345	79	90	111	217	152	509	203	136	94	151	113	139	189	220																			
Norwich	488	278	329	160	168	233	63	266	282	328	241	172	359	313	480	378	212	160	215	321	147	542	276	174	103	240	130	185	223	254	118																		
Nottingham	395	162	232	51	193	142	86	161	189	223	224	210	266	216	387	285	107	151	110	178	93	449	164	77	39	112	168	71	130	161	64	119																	
Oxford	510	160	170	68	109	73	82	107	274	169	115	146	373	154	472	370	48	67	81	242	190	534	228	174	132	176	107	164	227	258	44	146	102																
Penzance	702	308	108	274	287	193	368	222	466	284	167	357	564	109	663	562	220	259	238	434	415	726	419	403	370	367	318	356	451	482	326	433	326	265															
Perth	86	388	523	351	529	433	378	453	152	438	515	503	42	507	102	64	399	486	401	379	291	114	199	245	303	278	461	275	192	150	400	404	310	426	617														
Peterborough	435	204	263	86	158	173	37	193	229	255	204	162	306	248	427	325	139	115	142	225	110	489	223	121	51	159	120	132	170	201	45	78	58	86	357	351													
Plymouth	633	239	62	205	218	124	299	153	397	215	98	288	495	44	594	493	151	190	169	365	346	657	350	334	301	298	249	287	382	413	257	364	257	196	78	544	288												
Portsmouth	596	244	162	154	53	125	137	158	360	220	73	141	458	132	558	456	118	45	152	328	276	620	314	260	215	262	102	250	313	344	130	204	188	85	241	508	157	172											
Preston	326	146	281	110	287	191	209	211	89	197	273	311	188	266	287	185	157	245	160	138	122	349	43	69	134	36	269	35	103	139	159	235	121	184	375	237	180	306	270										
Salisbury	549	184	118	121	90	52	145	98	313	160	39	160	411	93	511	409	72	62	105	281	261	573	267	244	202	215	121	203	298	329	115	212	173	70	203	461	165	134	44	223									
Sheffield	397	166	272	91	233	182	122	201	161	263	264	247	236	256	359	257	148	191	150	157	66	421	115	38	47	79	205	39	100	131	104	148	45	142	366	309	93	297	228	73	212								
Shrewsbury	417	75	220	48	226	130	140	111	181	110	212	250	279	205	379	277	96	184	52	105	162	441	135	119	124	65	208	71	190	221	98	203	87	123	314	329	129	245	209	92	161	88							
Southampton	578	225	142	135	66	106	136	140	342	201	53	152	440	111	539	437	100	49	133	309	258	601	295	241	199	243	113	232	294	325	111	204	169	67	221	489	157	152	20	252	23	209	191						
Stoke-on-Trent	392	112	220	48	226	130	140	150	156	211	212	250	254	205	353	251	96	184	99	123	129	415	109	93	91	57	208	46	164	195	98	172	54	123	314	303	99	245	209	66	161	50	38	191					
Stranraer	235	342	477	305	482	387	363	406	106	392	469	487	132	461	181	86	352	440	355	333	276	261	153	229	288	232	445	229	201	163	354	388	295	380	571	149	333	502	466	195	418	267	287	447	261				
Taunton	560	165	50	132	160	51	226	80	323	142	45	224	422	34	521	419	77	126	96	291	272	583	277	261	228	225	185	213	309	340	183	291	184	123	144	471	215	75	114	234	70	224	172	94	172	429			
Wick	207	597	732	560	738	642	618	662	361	647	724	742	258	716	166	277	608	695	610	588	531	104	408	484	543	487	700	484	409	367	609	644	550	635	826	215	589	757	721	451	673	523	542	702	516	362	684		
York	323	201	314	133	275	224	154	243	116	251	306	279	193	298	314	212	189	233	192	192	38	376	91	24	79	102	237	71	51	89	146	180	87	184	408	239	125	339	269	96	254	57	146	251	120	223	265	477	
LONDON	550	239	216	121	54	120	59	153	314	215	125	78	413	200	512	410	102	31	136	282	186	574	268	201	143	216	39	204	254	285	68	118	129	56	310	462	86	241	75	225	85	169	163	77	161	420	167	675	211

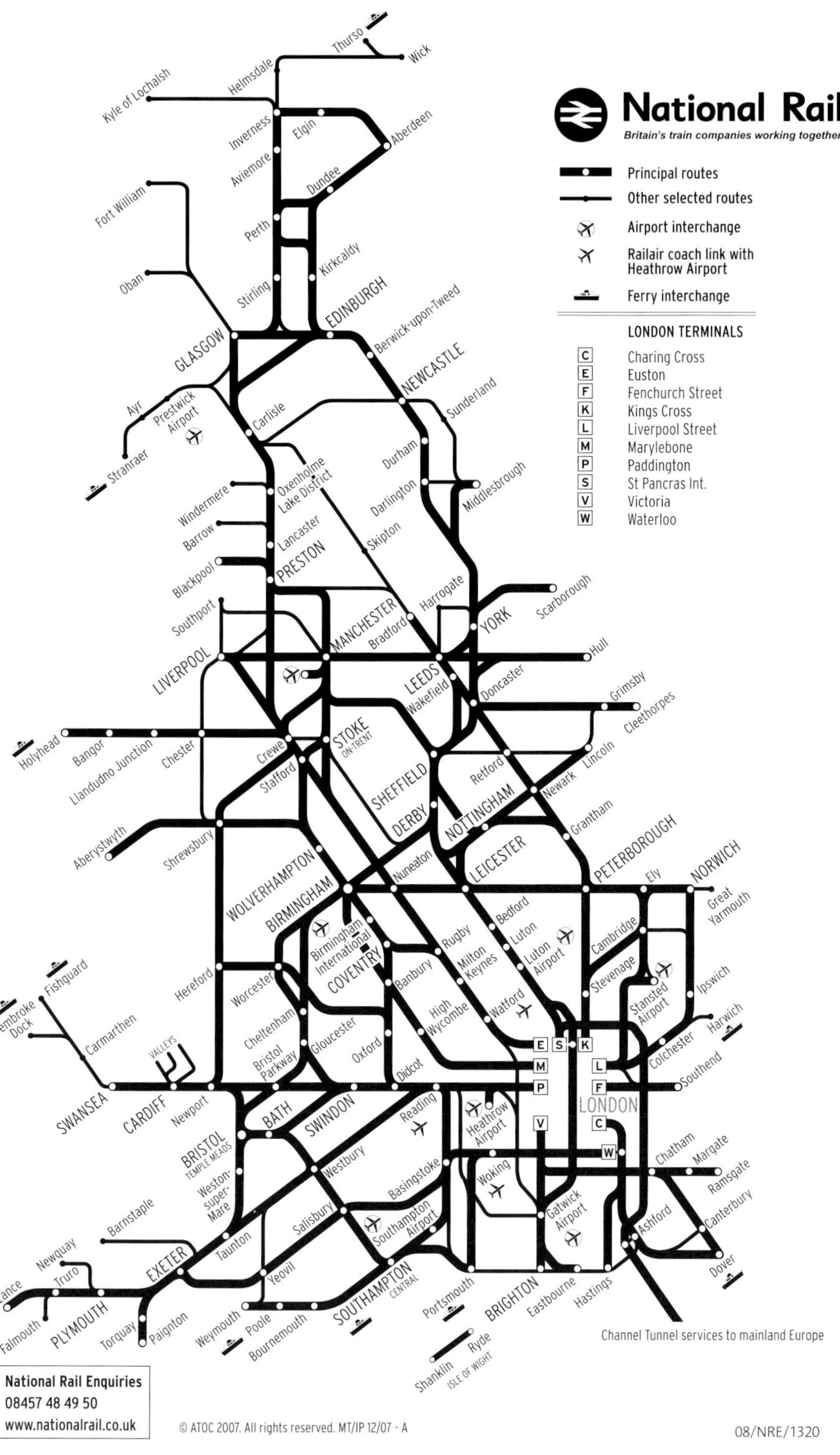
National Rail
Britain's train companies working together
Principal routes
Other selected routes
Airport interchange
Railair coach link with Heathrow Airport
Ferry interchange
LONDON TERMINALS
C Charing Cross
E Euston
F Fenchurch Street
K Kings Cross
L Liverpool Street
M Marylebone
P Paddington
S St Pancras Int.
V Victoria
W Waterloo
Thurso
Wick
Helmsdale
Kyle of Lochalsh
Inverness
Elgin
Aberdeen
Aviemore
Dundee
Fort William
Perth
Kirkcaldy
Oban
Stirling
EDINBURGH
Berwick-upon-Tweed
GLASGOW
NEWCASTLE
Sunderland
Ayr
Prestwick Airport
Carlisle
Stranraer
Durham
Oxenholme Lake District
Middlesbrough
Windermere
Darlington
Barrow
Lancaster
Skipton
Blackpool
PRESTON
Harrogate
Scarborough
Southport
MANCHESTER
Bradford
YORK
LIVERPOOL
LEEDS
Wakefield
Hull
Doncaster
Grimsby
Holyhead
Bangor
Llandudno Junction
Chester
Crewe
Stafford
STOKE ON-TRENT
Cleethorpes
SHEFFIELD
Retford
Lincoln
DERBY
NOTTINGHAM
Newark
Aberystwyth
Shrewsbury
Grantham
WOLVERHAMPTON
Nuneaton
LEICESTER
PETERBOROUGH
NORWICH
BIRMINGHAM
Ely
Great Yarmouth
Birmingham International
Bedford
Rugby
Luton
Cambridge
COVENTRY
Milton Keynes
Luton Airport
Stevenage
Ipswich
Banbury
Stansted Airport
Fishguard
Hereford
Worcester
High Wycombe
Watford
Pembroke Dock
Harwich
Carmarthen
Cheltenham
Gloucester
Bristol Parkway
Oxford
Colchester
VALLEYS
Didcot
Southend
SWANSEA
CARDIFF
Newport
BATH
SWINDON
Reading
Heathrow Airport
LONDON
BRISTOL TEMPLE MEADS
Chatham
Margate
Ramsgate
Westbury
Basingstoke
Woking
Weston-super-Mare
Gatwick Airport
Canterbury
Barnstaple
Salisbury
Southampton Airport
Ashford
Taunton
Newquay
EXETER
Dover
Truro
Yeovil
Penzance
SOUTHAMPTON CENTRAL
Portsmouth
BRIGHTON
Eastbourne
Hastings
Falmouth
PLYMOUTH
Torquay
Paignton
Weymouth
Poole
Bournemouth
Ryde
Shanklin
ISLE OF WIGHT
Channel Tunnel services to mainland Europe
National Rail Enquiries
08457 48 49 50
www.nationalrail.co.uk
© ATOC 2007. All rights reserved. MT/IP 12/07 - A
08/NRE/1320

Travel information

General travel information

Streetmap	streetmap.co.uk	
Transport Direct (a journey planner)	transportdirect.info	
Transport for London	tfl.gov.uk	(020) 7222 1234
Travel Services	departures-arrivals.com	
Traveline (public transport information)	traveline.org.uk	0870 200 2233

Bus & coach

Megabus	megabus.com	0901 331 0031
National Express	nationalexpress.com	0870 580 8080
WA Shearings	washearings.com	(01942) 823371

Car & car hire

AA	theaa.com	0870 600 0371
Green Flag	greenflag.co.uk	0845 246 1557
RAC	rac.co.uk	0870 572 2722
Alamo	alamo.co.uk	0870 400 4562*
Avis	avis.co.uk	0844 581 0147
Budget	budget.co.uk	0844 581 2231
Easycar	easycar.com	0906 333 3333
Enterprise	enterprise.com	0870 350 3000*
Hertz	hertz.co.uk	0870 844 8844*
Holiday Autos	holidayautos.co.uk	0870 400 4461
National	nationalcar.co.uk	0870 400 4581
Thrifty	thrifty.co.uk	(01494) 751500

Air

Air Southwest	airsouthwest.com	0870 043 4553
Blue Islands (Channel Islands)	blueislands.com	0845 620 2122
BMI	flybmi.com	0870 607 0555
BMI Baby	bmibaby.com	0871 224 0224
British Airways	ba.com	0844 493 0787
British International (Isles of Scilly to Penzance)	islesofscillyhelicopter.com	(01736) 363871*
Eastern Airways	easternairways.com	0870 366 9989
Easyjet	easyjet.com	0871 244 2366
Flybe	flybe.com	0871 700 2000*
Flyglobespan	flyglobespan.com	0871 271 0415*
Jet2.com	jet2.com	0871 226 1737*
Manx2	manx2.com	0871 200 0440*
Ryanair	ryanair.com	0871 246 0000
Skybus (Isles of Scilly)	islesofscilly-travel.co.uk	0845 710 5555
Thomsonfly	tomsonfly.com	0871 231 4869
VLM	flyvlm.com	0871 666 5050

Train

National Rail Enquiries	nationalrail.co.uk	0845 748 4950
Consult National Rail Enquiries for up-to-the-minute advice on journey planning, train times and service updates.		
The Trainline (online booking)	trainline.co.uk	
UK train operating companies	rail.co.uk	
Arriva Trains	arriva.co.uk	0845 748 4950
c2c	c2c-online.co.uk	0845 601 4873
Chiltern Railways	chilternrailways.co.uk	0845 600 5165
CrossCountry	crosscountrytrains.co.uk	0870 010 0084
East Midlands Trains	eastmidlandstrains.co.uk	0845 712 5678
Eurostar	eurostar.com	0870 518 6186*
First Capital Connect	firstcapitalconnect.co.uk	0845 026 4700
First Great Western	firstgreatwestern.co.uk	0845 700 0125
Gatwick Express	gatwickexpress.com	0845 850 1530
Heathrow Connect	heathrowconnect.com	0845 678 6975
Heathrow Express	heathrowexpress.com	0845 600 1515
Hull Trains	hulltrains.co.uk	0845 071 0222
Island Line	island-line.co.uk	0845 748 4950
London Midland	londonmidland.com	0844 811 0133
Merseyrail	merseyrail.org	(0151) 702 2071
National Express East Anglia	nationalexpresseastanglia.com	0845 600 7245
National Express East Coast	nationalexpresseastcoast.com	0845 722 5333
Northern Rail	northernrail.org	0845 000 0125
ScotRail	firstgroup.com/scotrail	0845 601 5929
South Eastern Trains	southeasternrailway.co.uk	0845 000 2222
South West Trains	southwesttrains.co.uk	0845 600 0650
Southern	southernrailway.com	0845 127 2920
Stansted Express	stanstedexpress.com	0845 600 7245
Translink	nirailways.co.uk	(028) 9066 6630
Transpennine Express	tpexpress.co.uk	0845 600 1671
Virgin Trains	virgintrains.co.uk	0845 722 2333*

Ferry

Ferry information	sailanddrive.com	
Condor Ferries (Channel Islands)	condorferries.co.uk	0845 609 1024*
Steam Packet Company (Isle of Man)	steam-packet.com	0871 222 1333
Isles of Scilly Travel	islesofscilly-travel.co.uk	0845 710 5555
Red Funnel (Isle of Wight)	redfunnel.co.uk	0870 444 8898
Wight Link (Isle of Wight)	wightlink.co.uk	0871 376 4342

Phone numbers listed are for general enquiries unless otherwise stated.

* Booking line only

Help before you go

When it comes to your next break, the first stage of your journey could be closer than you think.

You've probably got a Tourist Information Centre nearby which is there to serve the local community – as well as visitors. Knowledgeable staff will be happy to help you, wherever you're heading.

Many Tourist Information Centres can provide you with maps and guides, and it's often possible to book accommodation and travel tickets too.

You'll find the address of your nearest centre in your local phone book, or look in the regional sections in this guide for a list of Tourist Information Centres.

National cycle network

Sections of the National Cycle Network are shown on the maps in this guide. The numbers on the maps will appear on the signs along your route 3 . Here are some tips about finding and using a route.

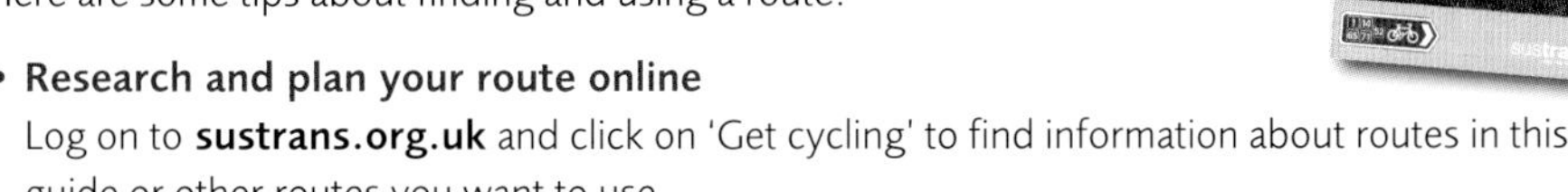

- **Research and plan your route online**
  Log on to **sustrans.org.uk** and click on 'Get cycling' to find information about routes in this guide or other routes you want to use.

- **Order a route map**
  Useful, easy-to-use maps of many of the most popular routes of the National Cycle Network are available from Sustrans, the charity behind the Network. These can be purchased online or by mail order – visit **sustransshop.co.uk** or call **0845 113 0065.**

- **Order Cycling in the UK**
  The official guide to the National Cycle Network gives details of rides all over the UK, detailing 148 routes and profiles of 43 days rides on traffic-free paths and quiet roads.

ROUTE NUMBER	ROUTE/MAP NAME	START/END OF ROUTE
South West		
3 & 32	The Cornish Way	Land's End – Bude
South East		
4 & 5	Thames Valley	London – Oxford via Reading
4	Kennet & Avon	Reading – Bristol
Northern England		
1	Coast & Castles South	Newcastle – Berwick-upon-Tweed – Edinburgh
7, 14 & 71	Sea to Sea (C2C)	Whitehaven/Workington – Sunderland/Newcastle upon Tyne
14	Three Rivers	Middlesbrough – Durham – South Shields
65 & Regional 52 (W2W)	Yorkshire Moors & Coast	Middlesbrough – Easingwold & Barnard Castle – Whitby
65 & 66	Yorkshire Wolds, York & Hull	Easingwold – York – Hull
68	Pennine Cycleway (South Pennines & the Dales)	Holmfirth – Appleby-in-Westmorland/Kendal
72	Hadrian's Cycleway	Ravenglass – South Shields
Wales		
4 & 47	Celtic Trail East	Chepstow – Cardiff – Swansea
4 & 47	Celtic Trail West	Swansea – Fishguard
81 & 82	Lôn Cambria & Lôn Teifi	Fishguard – Aberystwyth – Shrewsbury
Scotland		
7	Lochs & Glens South	Carlisle – Ayr – Glasgow
7	Lochs & Glens North	Glasgow – Inverness
76	Round the Forth	Edinburgh – Stirling
77	The Salmon Run	Dundee – Perth – Pitlochry
78	Oban to Campbeltown	Oban – Campbeltown

David Bellamy Conservation Award

"These well-deserved awards are a signpost to parks which are making real achievements in protecting our environment. Go there and experience wrap-around nature....you could be amazed at what you find!" says Professor David Bellamy.

Many of Britain's holiday parks have become 'green champions' of conservation in the countryside, according to leading conservationist David Bellamy. More than 600 gold, silver and bronze parks were this year named in the David Bellamy Conservation Awards, organised in conjunction with the British Holiday and Home Parks Association. These parks are recognised for their commitment to conservation and the environment through their management of landscaping, recycling policies, waste management, the cultivation of flora and fauna and the creation of habitats designed to encourage a variety of wildlife onto the park. Links with the local community and the use of local materials are also important considerations.

Parks wishing to enter for a David Bellamy Conservation Award must complete a detailed questionnaire covering different aspects of their environmental policies, and describe what positive conservation steps they have taken. The park must also undergo an independent audit from a local wildlife or conservation body which is familiar with the area. Final assessments and the appropriate level of any award are then made personally by Professor Bellamy.

Parks with Bellamy Awards offer a variety of accommodation from pitches for touring caravans, motor homes and tents, to caravan holiday homes, holiday lodges and cottages for rent or to buy. Holiday parks with these awards are not just those in quiet corners of the countryside. Amongst the winners are much larger centres in popular holiday areas that offer a wide range of entertainments and attractions.

The parks listed on the following pages all have a detailed entry in this guide and have received a Gold, Silver or Bronze David Bellamy Conservation Award. Use the park index to find the page number.

For a free brochure featuring a full list of award-winning parks please contact:
BH&HPA,
6 Pullman Court,
Great Western Road,
Gloucester GL1 3ND
t (01452) 526911
e enquiries@bhhpa.org.uk
w davidbellamyconservation.org.uk

Park	Award	Location	Region
Allerton Park Caravan Park	GOLD	York	Northern England
Castlerigg Hall Caravan & Camping Park	GOLD	Keswick	Northern England
Cayton Village Caravan Park	GOLD	Scarborough	Northern England
Fallbarrow Park	GOLD	Windermere	Northern England
Finchale Abbey Caravan Park	SILVER	Durham	Northern England
Flusco Wood Caravan Park	GOLD	Penrith	Northern England
Gelder Wood Country Park	GOLD	Rochdale	Northern England
Hill of Oaks and Blakeholme Caravans	GOLD	Windermere	Northern England
Holme Valley Camping and Caravan Park	GOLD	Holmfirth	Northern England
Ladycross Plantation Caravan Park	GOLD	Whitby	Northern England
Lebberston Touring Park	GOLD	Scarborough	Northern England
Manor Wood Country Caravan Park	SILVER	Chester	Northern England
Middlewood Farm Holiday Park	GOLD	Whitby	Northern England
Rudding Holiday Park	GOLD	Harrogate	Northern England
Sleningford Watermill Caravan & Camping Park	GOLD	Ripon	Northern England
Three Rivers Woodland Park	GOLD	West Bradford	Northern England
Wild Rose Park	GOLD	Appleby-in-Westmorland	Northern England
Woodclose Caravan Park	GOLD	Kirkby Lonsdale	Northern England
Ashby Park	GOLD	Horncastle	Central England
Cable Gap Holiday Park	SILVER	Bacton-on-Sea	Central England
Deer's Glade Caravan & Camping Park	GOLD	Hanworth	Central England
Fernwood Caravan Park	GOLD	Ellesmere	Central England
Golden Valley Caravan & Camping	GOLD	Ripley	Central England
Grasmere Caravan Park	BRONZE	Great Yarmouth	Central England
Island Meadow Caravan Park	GOLD	Aston Cantlow	Central England
Rivendale Caravan and Leisure Park	GOLD	Alsop-en-le-Dale	Central England
Sandy Gulls Cliff Top Touring Park	GOLD	Mundesley	Central England
Searles Leisure	GOLD	Hunstanton	Central England
Star Caravan & Camping Park	SILVER	Stoke-on-Trent	Central England
Waldegraves Holiday Park	GOLD	Mersea Island	Central England
Wyton Lakes Holiday Park	SILVER	Wyton	Central England
Cobbs Hill Farm Caravan & Camping Park	SILVER	Bexhill-on-Sea	South East England
Riverside Holidays	BRONZE	Hamble	South East England
Sandy Balls Holiday Centre	GOLD	Fordingbridge	South East England
Shamba Holidays	SILVER	Ringwood	South East England
Tanner Farm Touring Caravan & Camping Park	GOLD	Marden	South East England
Beverley Park	GOLD	Paignton	South West England
Broadway House Holiday Touring Caravan and Camping Park	GOLD	Cheddar	South West England
Churchwood Valley Holiday Cabins	GOLD	Wembury	South West England
Cofton Country Holidays	GOLD	Dawlish	South West England
Dornafield	GOLD	Newton Abbot	South West England
Forest Glade Holiday Park	GOLD	Kentisbeare	South West England
Freshwater Beach Holiday Park	BRONZE	Bridport	South West England
Golden Cap Holiday Park	GOLD	Bridport	South West England
Greenways Valley Holiday Park	SILVER	Great Torrington	South West England
Halse Farm Caravan & Tent Park	GOLD	Winsford	South West England
Harford Bridge Holiday Park	GOLD	Tavistock	South West England

Higher Longford Caravan & Camping Park	GOLD	Moorshop	South West England
Highlands End Holiday Park	GOLD	Bridport	South West England
Newton Mill Camping	GOLD	Bath	South West England
Padstow Touring Park	SILVER	Padstow	South West England
Porlock Caravan Park	GOLD	Porlock	South West England
Porthtowan Tourist Park	SILVER	Porthtowan	South West England
Silver Sands Holiday Park	GOLD	Ruan Minor	South West England
Summer Valley Touring Park	SILVER	Truro	South West England
Tehidy Holiday Park	SILVER	Portreath	South West England
Treloy Touring Park	SILVER	Newquay	South West England
Ulwell Cottage Caravan Park	GOLD	Swanage	South West England
Warmwell Caravan Park	SILVER	Warmwell	South West England
Whitehill Country Park	GOLD	Paignton	South West England
Wooda Farm Park	GOLD	Bude	South West England
Barnsoul Farm	GOLD	Dumfries	Scotland
Dovecot Caravan Park	GOLD	Laurencekirk	Scotland
Glen Nevis Caravan & Camping Park	GOLD	Fort William	Scotland
Linnhe Lochside Holidays	GOLD	Fort William	Scotland
Loch Ken Holiday Park	GOLD	Parton	Scotland
Lomond Woods Holiday Park	GOLD	Balloch	Scotland
Mortonhall Caravan Park	GOLD	Edinburgh	Scotland
Kingsbridge Touring and Camping	GOLD	Beaumaris	Wales
Lakeside Caravan Park	GOLD	Llangorse	Wales

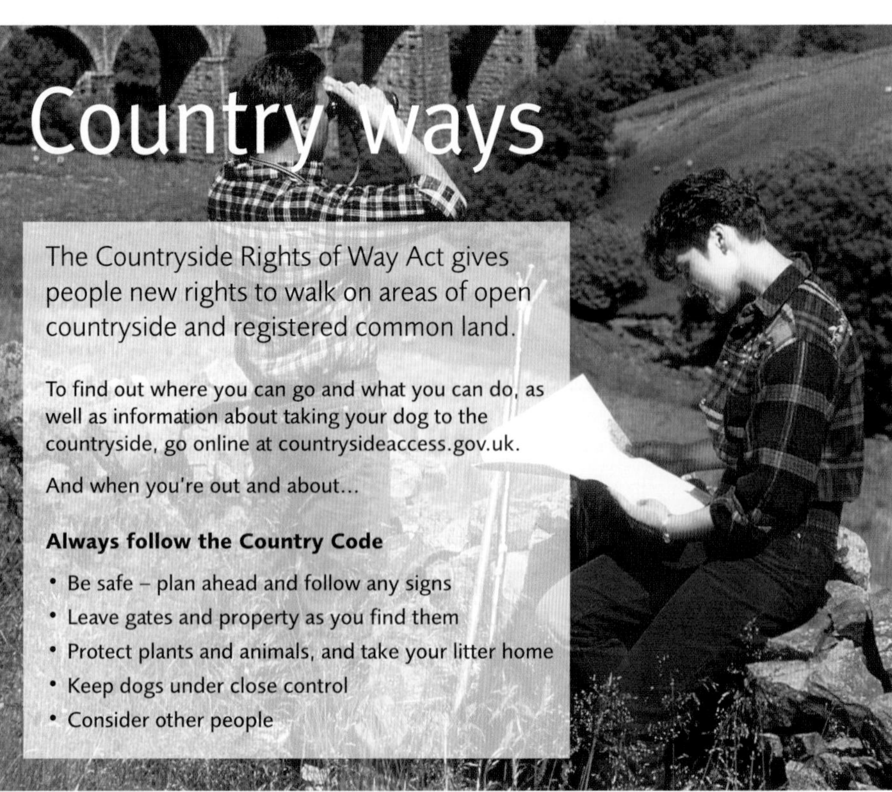

Country ways
The Countryside Rights of Way Act gives people new rights to walk on areas of open countryside and registered common land.
To find out where you can go and what you can do, as well as information about taking your dog to the countryside, go online at countrysideaccess.gov.uk.
And when you're out and about...
Always follow the Country Code
• Be safe – plan ahead and follow any signs
• Leave gates and property as you find them
• Protect plants and animals, and take your litter home
• Keep dogs under close control
• Consider other people

National Accessible Scheme index

Parks participating in the National Accessible Scheme are listed below. At the front of the guide you can find information about the scheme. Parks in colour have a detailed entry in this guide. Place names are listed alphabetically within each region.

Mobility level 1

Mobility level 1 continued

Mobility level 2

Quick reference index

If you're looking for a specific facility use this index to see at-a-glance parks that match your requirement. Establishments are listed alphabetically by place name within each region.

Indoor pool

Indoor pool continued

Outdoor pool

Outdoor pool continued

Walkers Welcome and Cyclists Welcome

Walkers Welcome

Families and Pets Welcome

Families Welcome

Pets Welcome

Holiday villages

Establishments in colour have a detailed entry in this guide.

Holiday Villages

Index by park name

All parks with a detailed entry in this guide are listed below.

a

b

c

d

e

f

f continued page

g page

h page

i page

j page

k page

l page

m page

n page

o page

Parks listed here have a detailed entry in this guide.

Index by place name

The following places all have detailed park entries in this guide. If the place where you wish to stay is not shown, the location maps (starting on page 32) will help you to find somewhere to stay in the area.

Index to display advertisers

Published by: Heritage House Group (Ketteringham Hall, Wymondham, Norfolk NR18 9RS; t (01603) 819420; f (01603) 814325; hhgroup.co.uk) on behalf of VisitBritain, Thames Road, Blacks Road, London W6 9EL
Publishing Manager: Tess Lugos
Production Manager: Iris Buckley
Compilation, design, copywriting, production and advertisement sales: Jackson Lowe Marketing, 3 St Andrews Place, Southover Road, Lewes, East Sussex BN7 1UP t (01273) 487487 jacksonlowe.com
Cover design: Jamieson Eley, Nick McCann
Typesetting: Marlinzo Services, Somerset and Jackson Lowe Marketing
Accommodation maps: Based on digital map data © ESR Cartography, 2008
Touring maps: © VisitBritain 2005. National Parks, Areas of Outstanding Natural Beauty, National Trails and Heritage Coast based on information supplied by Natural England, the Countryside Council for Wales and Scottish Natural Heritage. Cycle Networks provided by Sustrans
Printing and binding: 1010 Printing International Ltd, China

Front cover: Trewethett Farm Caravan Club Site, Tintagel, Cornwall (britainonview/Andy Stothert)
Back cover (from top)**:** Sandy Balls, Fordingbridge, Hampshire; Oban Camping & Caravan Park, Oban, Argyll and Bute

Photography credits:© Crown copyright (2008) Visit Wales; britainonview/David Angel/ANPA/Daniel Bosworth/Martin Brent/brightononview/Caravan Club/Alan Chandler/East Midlands Tourism/East of England Tourism/Eden Project/Rod Edwards/Damir Fabijanic/FCO/Klaus Hagmeier/Joanna Henderson/Adrian Houston/Kent Tourism Alliance/Simon Kreitem/Lee Valley Regional Park/Pawel Libera/James McCormick/McCormick-McAdam/Eric Nathan/David Noton/NWDA/Tony Pleavin/Grant Pritchard/Olivier Roques-Ro/David Sellman/Andy Sewell/Jon Spaull/Thanet District Council/Troika/Visit Chester & Cheshire/Wales Tourist Board Photo Library/Michael Walter/Juliet White/Worcestershire County Council; Iris Buckley; Caravan Club; cumbriaphoto.co.uk/Ben Barden/Cumbria Tourism; The Deep; Imperial War Museum North; Michael Jackson; Allan McPhail; NTPL/Rob Judges; One NorthEast Tourism; Mark Passmore; South West News Service; Thermae Bath Spa/Matt Cardy; P Tomkins/VisitScotland/Scottishviewpoint; Visit Bristol; Visit Wales; visitlondonimages/ britainonview; VisitScotland/Scottishviewpoint

ISBN 978-0-7095-8445-2

A VisitBritain Publishing guide